CRITICAL DEBATES ON
COUNTER-TERRORISM JUDICIAL REVIEW

Is judicial review an effective and appropriate way to regulate counter-terrorism measures? Some argue that the judiciary is ill-equipped to examine such measures, for instance because they lack the expertise of the institutions which bring them about under exigent conditions. Others claim that subjecting counter-terrorism measures to judicial review is crucial for maintaining a jurisdiction's principles of constitutionalism. This volume brings together voices from all sides of the debate from a broad range of jurisdictions, from North America, Europe and Australasia. It does not attempt to 'resolve' the argument but rather to explore it in all its dimensions. The debates are essentially concerned with fundamental questions of organising and making accountable the exercise of power in a particularly challenging environment. The book is necessary reading for all those concerned with counter-terrorism, but also with broader public law, constitutional law and administrative law principles.

FERGAL F. DAVIS is a Senior Lecturer in the School of Law at the University of New South Wales, Sydney.

FIONA DE LONDRAS is a Professor of Law at Durham University where she is also Co-Director of Durham Human Rights Centre.

CRITICAL DEBATES ON COUNTER-TERRORISM JUDICIAL REVIEW

Edited by

FERGAL F. DAVIS

and

FIONA DE LONDRAS

CAMBRIDGE
UNIVERSITY PRESS

CAMBRIDGE
UNIVERSITY PRESS

University Printing House, Cambridge CB2 8BS, United Kingdom

Cambridge University Press is part of the University of Cambridge.

It furthers the University's mission by disseminating knowledge in the pursuit of education, learning and research at the highest international levels of excellence.

www.cambridge.org
Information on this title: www.cambridge.org/9781107662964

© Cambridge University Press 2014

First published 2014
First paperback edition 2016

A catalogue record for this publication is available from the British Library

Library of Congress Cataloguing in Publication data
Critical debates on counter-terrorist judicial review / edited by Fergal F. Davis, Fiona de Londras.
pages   cm
"This collection emerged from a workshop held in Durham Human Rights Centre in June 2013, which was supported by a small grant from the British Academy and Leverhulme and by the Laureate Fellowship: Anti-Terror Laws and the Democratic Challenge Project in the Gilbert + Tobin Centre of Public Law, UNSW. There was a follow up symposium hosted by the NSW Bar Association in Sydney in November 2013" – CIP galley.
ISBN 978-1-107-05361-8 (Hardback)
1. Terrorism–Prevention–Law and legislation–Congresses.   2. Judicial review–Congresses.
3. Political questions and judicial power–Congresses.   I. Davis, Fergal Francis, editor of compilation.   II. De Londras, Fiona, editor of compilation.
K5256.C75 2014
344.05'325–dc23   2014007627

ISBN 978-1-107-05361-8 Hardback
ISBN 978-1-107-66296-4 Paperback

CONTENTS

CONTRIBUTORS

JESSIE BLACKBOURN is a Postdoctoral Research Fellow on the Australian Research Council Laureate Fellowship 'Anti-Terror Laws and the Democratic Challenge' Project in the Gilbert and Tobin Centre of Public Law at the University of New South Wales.

CORA CHAN is an Assistant Professor at the Faculty of Law of the University of Hong Kong.

FERGAL F. DAVIS is a Senior Lecturer and member of the Australian Research Council Laureate Fellowship 'Anti-Terror Laws and the Democratic Challenge' Project in the Gilbert and Tobin Centre of Public Law in the University of New South Wales.

FIONA DE LONDRAS is a Professor of Law and Co-Director of the Human Rights Centre at Durham Law School.

HELEN DUFFY runs an international human rights law practice (Human Rights in Practice) in The Hague. Previously she was a Legal Officer at the International Criminal Tribunal for the former Yugoslavia, Counsel to Human Rights Watch, Legal Director of the Centre for Human Rights Legal Action in Guatemala and Legal Adviser to the UK 'Arms for Iraq' Inquiry and the UK government legal service.

HELEN FENWICK is Professor of Law at Durham University and a Human Rights Consultant to Doughty Street Chambers in London.

DAVID JENKINS is an Associate Professor at the University of Copenhagen School of Law.

JULES LOBEL is the Bessie McKee Wathour Endowed Chair at the University of Pittsburgh School of Law and President of the Center for Constitutional Rights.

ROGER MASTERMAN is Professor of Law and Head of Durham Law School.

CIAN C. MURPHY is a Lecturer in Law at King's College London. He was previously a Fulbright-Schumann Research Scholar at Georgetown University Center on National Security and the Law.

GAVIN PHILLIPSON is a Professor of Law at Durham Law School.

KENT ROACH is Professor of Law and Prichard-Wilson Chair of Law and Public Policy at the University of Toronto, Faculty of Law.

JENS ELO RYTTER is Professor of Constitutional Law at the Centre for Comparative and European Constitutional Studies, University of Copenhagen.

MARK TUSHNET is William Nelson Cromwell Professor of Law at Harvard Law School and a fellow of the American Academy of Arts and Sciences.

ACKNOWLEDGEMENTS

This collection emerged from a workshop held in Durham Human Rights Centre in June 2013, which was supported by a small grant from the British Academy and Leverhulme and by the Laureate Fellowship 'Anti-Terror Laws and the Democratic Challenge' Project in the Gilbert + Tobin Centre of Public Law, University of New South Wales. There was a follow up symposium hosted by the NSW Bar Association in Sydney in November 2013, also funded from the British Academy/Leverhulme small grant. These events provided opportunities for ideas in the collection to be explored and challenged and ultimately resulted in a stronger final product. We are grateful to all of our sponsors for their support of the workshop and to the speakers and commentators who attended. We are also grateful to Elizabeth Spicer and her team at Cambridge University Press and Rumyana Grozdanova in Durham who provided excellent research assistance and workshop support. We are also, of course, thankful to the authors for their responsiveness and willingness to engage in person and in writing with the competing ideas and arguments we aimed to bring together in this collection.

Fergal F. Davis and Fiona de Londras

~

Introduction

Counter-terrorism judicial review: beyond dichotomies

FERGAL F. DAVIS AND FIONA DE LONDRAS

The contemporary context of terrorism and counter-terrorism is one in which the impossible has become possible. For most people the conversion of a passenger jet into a weapon that would be purpose-fully flown into civilian buildings at the cost of thousands of lives was unimaginable before 11 September 2001; today those era-defining images have seeped into the collective consciousness. It had been assumed that debates about the morality of torture had long since been resolved; not so it seems. An actual or perceived threat of terrorism has the capacity to greatly rupture our politics. It creates an atmosphere in which the 'normal' commitment of liberal democra-cies to constitutionalism and human rights is challenged, with illiberal measures being introduced and potentially embedded. The possible impact of such measures, and the febrile politico-legal counter-terrorism atmosphere, hold such significant possibilities that it is not surprising that understanding and responding to terrorism and counter-terrorism has become such an active field of legal, political, operational and scholarly endeavour. One approach to understanding and responding to (counter-)terrorism is to sometimes reduce the debate to simple dichotomies: terrorist v. freedom fighter; terrorism v. counter-terrorism; vengeance v. protection; fundamentalism v. necessity; security v. liberty. However, such an approach is unhelpful; it masks the murkiness of the subject. After all this is an area in which we cannot even agree on a definition of the core subject matter; as Walter Laqueur declared 'disputes about a detailed, comprehensive definition of terrorism will continue for a long time and will make no noticeable contribution towards the understanding of terrorism'.[1] The depth of this 'murkiness' is further reflected in debates as to the

---

[1] W. Laqueur, *The Age of Terrorism* (Boston, NJ: Little Brown and Co., 1987), p. 72.

1

proportionality of responses to attacks or perceived threats, in disputes about the legality of new counter-terrorist mechanisms, and in political and other debates about how far a state ought to go to defend itself and its people against a seemingly uncontrollable risk of terrorist attack. In practice, this 'murkiness' has contributed to some extent to the design, appropriation, implementation and exercise of extensive powers of counter-terrorism, often without even a legislative basis. Even where legislation *is* used, it tends (at least relatively close to the attack in question) to be proposed by the executive and passed by a fairly compliant legislature.[2] All of this means that, generally speaking, counter-terrorism tends to be characterised by (at the very least, an attempt at) executive supremacy and unilateralism in introducing extremely repressive counter-terrorist measures that sit uncomfortably with constitutionalist principles of proportionality, limited power, respect for individual rights, and equal application of the law.[3]

This is of clear concern to many scholars, including us. In 2010 we wrote that

> Within a system of separated powers, there are three potential responses to the limitation of individual liberties resulting from Executive actions during the times of violent, terrorism-related emergency: (i) trust the Executive to behave responsibly and lawfully; (ii) rely on the Legislature and the popular democratic processes to force the Executive to behave responsibly and lawfully and minimize judicial intervention; or (iii) call on the Judiciary to intervene and restrict unlawful behaviour produced by the Executive, the parliament or both acting together.[4]

We both accepted that executive supremacy was inappropriate, agreeing that some restraint on executive power was desirable. The ongoing use of closed material and a general air of secrecy in counter-terrorism give rise to an opaque environment causing us to be even more suspicious of

---

[2] F. de Londras, *Detention in the 'War on Terror': Can Human Rights Fight Back?* (Cambridge University Press, 2011), ch. 1.

[3] Although supranational bodies involved in counter-terrorism do not generally have a clearly identifiable executive branch per se, Murphy outlines how an executive type power can be observed in these contexts. See Chapter 12 in this volume, C. C. Murphy, 'Counter-terrorism law and judicial review: the challenge for the Court of Justice of the European Union'.

[4] F. de Londras and F. Davis, 'Controlling the Executive in Times of Terrorism: Competing Perspectives on Effective Oversight Mechanisms' (2010) 30 *Oxford Journal of Legal Studies* 19.

simply trusting the executive. However, we disagreed on which of the remaining two responses would provide the most effective means of controlling executive power. Since then there has been some convergence of opinion; in some respects we are less absolute in our positions.[5] However, while the common ground has expanded, the end result remains the same: de Londras favours enhanced judicial review while Davis sees judicial review as both ineffective and undermining of parliamentary scrutiny. Our debate – and our disagreements – form only part of a broader set of concerns about judicial review generally, and about judicial review in the context of counter-terrorism (or, indeed, other violent emergency) more particularly. This broader debate, which takes place across legal systems and continents, has a number of branches that are reflected in this collection: institutional appropriateness, quality, sufficiency and internationalisation.

All of these elements of the debate about counter-terrorism judicial review speak to a core concern that we address later in this Introduction: what is the purpose of judicial review? Once we can ascertain that in normative terms, the secondary concern (how can that purpose best be achieved within and outside of judicial review structures?) becomes germane. The purpose of this volume is to deal in an open, although discursive, manner with that second concern. To that end, the collection brings together some of the key contributors to this debate in both scholarship and practice to engage in a dialogue, not with a view to resolving our differences but rather to exploring them.

I   What is at stake?

Debates about counter-terrorism judicial review are important and wide-ranging, reflecting the fact that when it comes to counter-terrorism the stakes are high. As Lord Chief Justice Coke stated in *Calvin's Case* the

---

[5] For example, de Londras has recently called for a more 'virtuous' politics to improve counter-terrorist law and policies both before and in response to judicial intervention: "Guantánamo Bay, the Rise of Courts and the Revenge of Politics" in D. Jenkins, A. Henriksen and A. Jacobsen (eds.), *The Long Decade: How 9/11 Has Changed the Law* (Oxford University Press, 2014), pp. 155–67. Davis has attributed a greater role to courts in the process of dialogue. Where he previously saw them simply as raising an alarm through a simple declaration of incompatibility he now acknowledges a role for judgments to engage popular and parliamentary debate: 'Parliamentary Supremacy and the Re-invigoration of Institutional Dialogue in the UK' (2013) *Parliamentary Affairs* forthcoming.

sovereign is bound 'to govern and protect his subjects'.[6] A successful act of terrorism demonstrates a failure on the part of a sovereign state to fulfil that most basic of duties. This can undermine public confidence and inspire moral panic. Indeed:

> [T]errorism is an anxiety-inspiring method of repeated violent action, employed by (semi-) clandestine individual, group or state actors, for idiosyncratic, criminal or political reasons, whereby – in contrast to assassination – the direct targets of violence are not the main targets. The immediate human victims of violence are generally chosen randomly (targets of opportunity) or selectively (representative or symbolic targets) from a target population, and serve as message generators. Threat- and violence-based communication processes between terrorist (organiza-tion), (imperilled) victims, and main targets are used to manipulate the main target (audience(s)), turning it into a target of terror, a target of demands, or a target of attention, depending on whether intimidation, coercion, or propaganda is primarily sought.[7]

If we accept this definition, for the moment at least, it becomes appar-ent that manipulation of the target is central to terrorism. Given that the target is often the public, this manipulation is likely to impact upon the quality of democratic debate. It is therefore unsurprising that the state of exception arising from an act of terrorism often has a distorting effect on democracy. For example, in the United States post 11 September 2001:

> instead of the rowdy, rhetorical deliberations appropriate to agnostic politics in a healthy pluralistic polity, the nation experienced a wave of patriotic fervor and political conformity in which the expression of dissenting opinions and the defence of civil liberties were equated with anti-Americanism.[8]

This distortion of democracy has an impact on the quality of political debate and meaningful engagement with political society. Where these negative impacts on democracy coincide with a general 'security bias' the resulting impact on liberty can be extreme. Internment without trial, extraordinary rendition, control orders, and special trial procedures such as those employed at Guantánamo Bay, have all been utilised by

---

[6] 7 Coke Report 4 b, 77 ER 382.
[7] A. P. Schmid and A. J. Jongman, *Political Terrorism: a New Guide to Actors, Authors, Concepts, Data Bases, Theories, and Literature* (Piscataway, NJ: Transaction Publishers, 2005), p. 28.
[8] R. L. Ivie, 'Rhetorical Deliberation and Democratic Politics in the Here and Now' (2002) 5 (2) *Rhetoric and Public Affairs* 277, 281.

otherwise liberal democratic states on the basis that a terror threat needed to be faced down. The illiberal nature of these provisions is, in and of itself, problematic but it also has the potential to impact on the wider legal system through normalisation, (perceived or actual) illegitimacy of state action, and the mounting of a serious challenge to the core elements of constitutionalism.

The designation of counter-terrorist law and policy as an 'exceptional' phenomenon, introduced in exceptional situations, is contingent upon what is known as the emergency-normalcy dichotomy.[9] This postulates that there are discrete and quantifiable situations of emergency that exist as aberrations from the (general) normalcy in which the state operates. This dichotomy is reflected throughout law at both domestic and international levels,[10] and it is designed – as Greene has written – to allow for the concept of emergency to act as both a shield and a sword.[11] As a shield it is intended to protect the populace from generally repressive laws by holding the state to strict limits in the normal course of events; as a sword it is intended to give states the latitude they are thought to require to take firm and (we are to hope) decisive action against terrorist threats.[12] However, as is so often the case, law and life are mismatched. The emergency in which exceptional laws and policies are tolerated has tended to extend far beyond the aberrational; it has tended to become entrenched (either generally or in particular regards) domestically and now risks doing so internationally. The risk of entrenchment is the normalisation of emergency measures; their continued application, their widening scope, their recalibrating potential. A core concern in any debate about limiting counter-terrorist activity by judicial review or otherwise has to be the maintenance of a division between the exceptional and the normal and, moreover, the quarantining of repressive powers in terms of time and scope.

A belief in the likelihood of a return to normalcy at the end of a period of exception is dependent on a number of factors. First, it seems likely that the capacity of the various arms of government to 'reclaim their status and functions once the danger has passed' will be dependent on

---

[9] See generally O. Gross and F. Ni Aolain, *Law in Times of Crisis: Emergency Powers in Theory and Practice* (Cambridge University Press, 2006), ch. 4.

[10] *Ibid.* chs. 5 and 6.

[11] A. Greene, 'Shielding the State of Emergency: Organised Crime in Ireland and the State's Response' (2011) 62(3) *Northern Ireland Legal Quarterly* 15.

[12] *Ibid.*

the strength of democratic culture in the state.[13] More fundamentally a
return to normalcy rests on the ability to define the end of the state of
exception. The decade since 11 September 2001 has caused many to
question whether the response to terrorism can genuinely be seen as
'exceptional' in the sense of it being temporary.[14] As a result any measures adopted are likely to have an ongoing effect. Furthermore, it can be
demonstrated that repealing and unpicking complex counter-terrorism
measures is often problematic. For example, although the UK Conserva-
tive/Liberal Democrat Coalition government expressed a desire to repeal
the worst excesses of the Labour Government's counter-terrorism measures, their Terrorism Prevention and Investigation Measures Act 2011
and Freedom Bill had only limited success if measured against civil
liberties yardsticks that would be applied in a period of 'normalcy'. So
too is such unpicking dependent on the maintenance of our understandings of the content of rights during the crisis itself. As the contributions
from Chan, Jenkins and Fenwick in this collection make clear,[15] that
which is exceptional must be named as exceptional; its particularity must
be clearly identified *even if* it is to be accepted as necessary and justifiable
given the circumstances in which it occurs. To do otherwise is both to
potentially apply the emergency power to *everyone* (not just 'the threat')
and to ratchet down the starting point of civil liberties and empty out to
some degree our understanding of constitutionalism, creating a diminished rights culture after the present crisis (and at the commencement of
the next one).[16]

---

[13] A. Lynch, 'Legislating Anti-terrorism: Observations on Form and Process' in V. V.
Ramraj, M. Hor, K. Roach and G. Williams (eds.), *Global Anti-Terrorism Law and Policy*
(2nd edn, Cambridge University Press, 2012), p. 151.

[14] *Ibid.*; but cf. the decision of the European Court of Human Rights in *A* v. *United Kingdom*
[2009] ECHR 301 (19 February 2009) holding that temporariness is not a requirement of
emergency for the purposes of Article 15 ECHR.

[15] See Chapters 3, 10 and 13 in this volume, D. Jenkins, 'When good cases go bad:
unintended consequences of rights-friendly judgments'; C. Chan, 'Business as usual:
deference in counter-terrorism rights review'; and H. Fenwick, 'Post 9/11 UK counter-
terrorism cases in the European Court of Human Rights: a "dialogic" approach to rights
protection or appeasement of national authorities?'.

[16] An important contribution to the debate on control mechanisms has been the extra-legal
measures model proposed by Oren Gross, which is fundamentally concerned with
attempting to prevent this kind of ratcheting down. Under this model, state actors would
make an assessment about whether something was necessary whether or not it was lawful,
undertake the action if they considered it necessary, and make a full *ex post facto*
disclosure allowing for the risk of censure or of endorsement. In this model, crucially,
laws allowing for the previously disallowed are not introduced; rather the positive law

If one thought that emergencies were really containable, and that politics were not opportunistic when it comes to making the most out of a 'good crisis',[17] one might argue that none of this matters *too much* for the short period of time that the emergency or crisis persists. However, history and experience tell us that this is not so, and that counter-terrorism without the counterweight of constitutionalism has significant repercussions for civil liberties. In this respect, counter-terrorism is an iterative and cumulative process. This is well illustrated by the journey from detention without trial to control order 'lite' in the United Kingdom. The Anti-Terrorism, Crime and Security Act 2001 provided for indefinite detention of foreign nationals suspected of terrorism.[18] The control order regime replaced this with a system of virtual house arrest that was repeatedly criticised by the courts[19] and the Joint Committee on Human Rights,[20] and that in turn was replaced by the restrictive Terrorism Prevention and Investigation Measures (TPIMs), now operating, that still allow for extensive restrictions on personal liberty.[21] Although this represents a movement towards less repressive measures, it has also resulted in a shift in judicial and political approaches to accept that being

---

retains its integrity. The model is critiqued, particularly in its apparent distinction of the positive law from the politico-legal culture in which it operates. The model does not feature prominently in this collection. See O. Gross, 'Chaos and Rules: Should Responses to Violent Crises Always be Constitutional?' (2003) 112 *Yale Law Journal* 1011; D. Dyzenhaus, 'The Compulsion of Legality' in V. V. Ramraj (ed.), *Emergencies and the Limits of Legality* (Cambridge University Press, 2008), p. 33; O. Gross, 'Extra-legality and the Ethic of Political Responsibility' in V. V. Ramraj (ed.), *Emergencies and the Limits of Legality* (Cambridge University Press, 2008), p. 60.

[17] White House Chief of Staff, Rahm Emmanuel, famously said 'You never want a serious crisis to go to waste. And what I mean by that is an opportunity to do things you think you could not do before'. The video clip of him making this statement is available at www.youtube.com/watch?v=1yeA_kHHLow.

[18] Anti-Terrorism, Crime and Security Act 2001, s. 23.

[19] *Secretary of State for the Home Department* v. *JJ* [2006] EWHC 1623 (Admin); *Secretary of State for the Home Department* v. *E* [2008] 1 AC 499; *Secretary of State for the Home Department* v. *MB and AF* [2008] 1 AC 440; *Secretary of State for the Home Department* v. *AF (No. 3)* [2010] 2 AC 269.

[20] See e.g., Joint Committee on Human Rights, *Counter-Terrorism Policy and Human Rights (Sixteenth Report): Annual Renewal of Control Orders Legislation 2010* (calling for the control orders scheme to be discontinued).

[21] F. Davis, 'The Human Rights Act and Juridification: Saving Democracy from Law' (2010) 30(2) *Politics* 91, 93; K. Ewing and J. Tham, 'The Continuing Futility of the Human Rights Act' (2008) *Public Law* 668; H. Fenwick and G. Phillipson, 'Covert Derogations and Judicial Deference: Redefining Liberty and Due Process Rights in Counterterrorism' (2011) 56(4) *McGill Law Journal* 863, 865–918.

confined to one's home for up to fourteen hours a day and then limited in activity and interaction outside of that time does not qualify as detention and therefore is not attached with all of the safeguards that the law provides for detainees.[22] The imminent introduction of 'Enhanced' TPIMs also calls into some question how substantive that shift has truly been.[23]

Furthermore, even the most entrenched and normatively accepted constitutionalist standards have been honoured more in the breach than the observance over the past ten years, calling into question their capacity to retain their absolute nature. The prohibition on torture is the clearest example of this.[24] States have used the cover of 'counter-terrorism' to justify the torture of suspected terrorists (themselves, by 'partners', through the collusion of third states and by the involvement of private entities).[25] Indeed, torture has undergone a quasi-rehabilitation following the assassination of Osama Bin Laden, located, it seems, at least partly as a result of information gleaned from Khalid Sheikh Mohammed under 'coercive interrogation' while held incommunicado in a secret prison. The Kafkaesque nature of this kind of scenario can hardly go unnoticed, but there now exists a culture, politics and even a scholarship around torture that was almost unimaginable a decade ago. Such a situation not only has implications for the immediate period of the emergency or crisis but also for the future shape of criminal justice, which can be affected by the 'creeping consequentialism'[26] of counter-terrorist measures.

In addition, the adoption of exceptional counter-terrorism regimes can undermine the perception of the legal system's legitimacy. Legitimacy is,

---

[22] See especially, L. Zedner, 'Preventive Justice or Pre-Punishment? The Case of Control Orders' (2007) 60 *Current Legal Problems* 174.

[23] See H. Fenwick, 'Designing ETPIMS around ECHR Review or Normalisation of "Preventive" Non-Trial-Based Executive Measures?' (2013) 76(5) *Modern Law Review* 877.

[24] The use of torture and coercive interrogation in the 'War on Terrorism' has attracted substantial amounts of literature. For an excellent collection of essays reflecting on torture in the 'War on Terrorism' see S. Levinson (ed.), *Torture: A Collection* (Oxford University Press, 2004).

[25] F. de Londras, 'Privatised Sovereign Performance: Regulating in the "Gap" between Security and Rights?' (2011) 38 *Journal of Law and Society* 96.

[26] A. Ashworth, 'Crime, Community and Creeping Consequentialism' (1996) *Criminal Law Review* 220; see also L. Donohue, *The Cost of Counter Terrorism: Power, Politics and Liberty* (Cambridge University Press, 2008), ch. 1 and p. 71. The use of control orders against Australia's 'Bikie Gangs', for example, demonstrates a seepage of repressive counter-terrorism measures into the ordinary criminal law: A. Loughnan, 'The Legislation We Had to Have?: the Crimes (Criminal Organisations Control) Act 2009 (NSW)' (2009) 20(3) *Current Issues in Criminal Justice* 457.

of course, a contested concept in law but in constitutional democracies it contains at the very least adherence to democratic principles of deliberation, equality before the law, and inter-institutional respect within separated powers.[27] The past decade of counter-terrorism has called into serious question the legitimacy of a system of law that can allow for what seems to be the outright rejection of these core principles. The detention centre at Guantánamo Bay and the protracted attempts at prosecuting Khalid Sheik Mohammed illustrate this point. Detainees were sent to Guantánamo Bay so that they could be interrogated – not with a view to building a case for criminal prosecution but rather as an intelligence-gathering exercise.[28] The existence of an extra-legal regime at Guantánamo makes it difficult to bring those detainees back within the 'ordinary' legal order. Roach has argued that Guantánamo Bay became a 'symbolic rejection of criminal justice norms'.[29] The reality of that rejection becomes all the more stark when we consider the successful record of the US federal courts in prosecuting hundreds of terrorist suspects since 11 September 2001.[30] It is difficult to maintain a perception of legitimacy around the prosecution of Khalid Sheik Mohammed and his co-accused when they are being tried by a tribunal whose legitimacy they reject on the basis of information that would be excluded for illegality in an ordinary trial, where their previous attempts at pleading guilty were ignored, and when the ordinary courts have provided a sound basis for conducting other terror trials.[31]

The use of counter-terrorist regimes in a manner that (at least seems) discriminatory further undermines the legitimacy of the legal system. Muslim communities have become 'suspect communities'[32] and elements

---

[27] F. de Londras, 'Can Counter-Terrorist Detention ever be Legitimate?' (2011) 33(3) *Human Rights Quarterly* 592, 597–604.

[28] M. Davis, 'Historical Perspectives on Guantánamo Bay: the Arrival of the High Value Detainees' (2009) 42 *Case Western Reserve Journal of International Law* 115.

[29] K. Roach, 'The Criminal Law and its Less Restrained Alternatives' in V. V. Ramraj, M. Hor, K. Roach and G. Williams (eds.), *Global Anti-Terrorism Law and Policy* (2nd edn, Cambridge University Press, 2012), pp. 91, 108.

[30] E. Holder, 'Statement of the Attorney General on the Prosecution of the 9/11 Conspirators' (4 April 2011), available at www.justice.gov/iso/opa/ag/speeches/2011/ag-speech-110404.html.

[31] K. Roach, *The 9/11 Effect: Comparative Counter-Terrorism* (Cambridge University Press, 2011), p. 213; E. Pilkington, '9/11 families angered over behaviour of alleged plotters at Guantánamo Bay', *Guardian*, 6 May 2012, available at www.guardian.co.uk/world/2012/may/06/9-11-families-angered-guantanamo-trial?INTCMP=SRCH.

[32] On the concept of the suspect community see P. Hillyard, *Suspect Community: People's Experience of the Prevention of Terrorism Acts in Britain* (London: Pluto Press, 1993); for

of religious practice important to many (although not all) Muslims have come under what to many seems like Islamaphobic attack; laws have been crafted in expressly discriminatory terms (such as the section 23 power of detention under the Anti-Terrorism, Crime and Security Act 2001 in the United Kingdom) or applied in what seems like a discriminatory manner even when neutrally worded.[33] Suspected terrorists detained in Guantánamo Bay and accused of inchoate offences have their capacity even to see a lawyer severely curtailed before being tried (if at all) in military commissions without full capacity to build a defence, while people who perpetrate vicious gun attacks in mainland United States, killing dozens of people, get full and fair trials. It is not difficult to see why at least some people at the sharp end of these measures lose their faith in the law, the state and the international community with potentially devastating effects in the future.

II   Counter-terrorist judicial review

All of this shows clearly that when it comes to counter-terrorism the stakes are high, not just from a security perspective but also for law, the legal system and the normative integrity of the state. The question with which this collection is fundamentally concerned is whether what we term 'counter-terrorism judicial review' can help to protect the state from the corrosive impact of counter-terrorism and 'the people' from its more invidious effects. In this respect, and for the purposes of placing parameters on the debate undertaken and engaged with in this book, we can define counter-terrorism judicial review as the use of judicialised processes to challenge state behaviours that fall into the broad category of 'counter-terrorism'.[34] Thus, 'traditional' or administrative judicial review can be counter-terrorism judicial review, but so too can other judicialised

---

the Muslim community's experience see e.g., T. Choudhury and H. Fenwick, *The Impact of Counter-Terrorism Measures on Muslim Communities*, Equality and Human Rights Commission Research Report 72 (2011).

[33] See e.g., the operation of Schedule 7 to the Terrorism Act 2000 in the United Kingdom (the port search provision), which is perceived as having a disproportionate impact on Muslim communities. (See Choudhury and Fenwick, *The Impact of Counter-Terrorism Measures on Muslim Communities*, n. 32 above.)

[34] Although we refer to 'state' here, this can also encompass judicialised challenges to counter-terrorism measures undertaken by supranational bodies such as the EU. This is discussed in Chapter 12 in this volume, C. C. Murphy, 'Counter-terrorism law and judicial review: the challenge for the Court of Justice of the European Union'.

processes, such as challenges to the constitutionality or human rights compliance of counter-terrorist measures either in unique proceedings (usually constitutional challenge) or as part of broader proceedings (such as *habeas corpus* petitions or defences to criminal charges).

At a conceptual level, judicial review is traditionally understood somewhat differently in different constitutional systems. As a result, at least a short meditation on the phenomenon is appropriate at this juncture. In systems of constitutional supremacy, judicial review has tended to have two different guises: judicial review *per se* as part of administrative law, and *constitutional* judicial review as part of constitutional law. The former is and was concerned with the fairly straightforward question of whether or not a particular action taken by the state (or some public body amenable to judicial review) was within the authority of the body concerned and taken in accordance with appropriate processes. The question, here, has tended to be one of process rather than outcome. Constitutional judicial review generally addresses the fundamental question of whether a particular law, measure, action or decision was in compliance with a constitution, the violation of which will normally invalidate the impugned law, measure or action. It would be overly simplistic to categorise administrative and constitutional judicial review as entirely separate phenomena; an administrative judicial review proceeding can (and frequently does) involve a question of constitutional compliance. However, administrative judicial review is possible without a constitutional question arising. Constitutional judicial review, of course, is fundamentally concerned with constitutionality.

In a system of parliamentary supremacy, on the other hand, judicial review has traditionally been administrative and organised around the core concept of *ultra vires*.[35] Under such judicial review, questions about executive measures concerned with a prerogative power (in which space many questions relating to security and counter-terrorism would reside) were generally considered to be beyond the reach of judicial review.[36]

---

[35] M. Elliott, *The Constitutional Foundations of Judicial Review* (Portland, OR: Hart Publishing, 2001).

[36] Whether or not something falls within the prerogative power has long been subject to judicial review in the United Kingdom, but the exercise of that power traditionally was not. The conventional position was summarised by Fraser LJ in *Council of Civil Service Unions* v. *Minister for the Civil Service* [1985] AC 374, 398, as 'the courts will inquire into whether a particular prerogative power exists or not, and, if it does exist, into its extent. But once the existence and extent of a power are established ... the courts cannot ... inquire into the propriety of its exercise'. The courts have, however, gradually moved

The growth of a human rights culture, and – in states such as the United Kingdom in particular – the creation of written Bills of Rights by means of statute (such as the Human Rights Act 1998) has led to an expansion in judicial review to include something that looks far more like constitutional judicial review (albeit without the strike down powers associated with a system of constitutional supremacy).[37] Mark Elliott has noted that this expansion has never been satisfactorily explained as a matter of doctrine, but is clearly connected with a normative belief that as much as possible the exercise of public power ought to be capable of being subjected to judicial scrutiny.[38]

That core normative proposition is key to any debate about counter-terrorism judicial review and reflects the inherently constitutionalist nature of the questions it raises. If, at its heart, the debate is (as we think is almost always the case) about *how* rather than *whether* to ensure that counter-terrorist powers and measures do not constitute excessive exercises of power, then two important questions arise. The first relates to how those limits might be identified; the second to how we will assess whether counter-terrorist measures have exceeded those limits or not.

The matter of identifying limits is not a simple one. It brings into the equation a number of complex questions: should limits be sourced only in domestic law, or does international law have a role here? How do relatively nebulous but normatively important concepts such as 'the rule of law', natural justice and the principle of limited power get taken into account? Might it be that extra-legal concepts such as necessity or expertise ought to dictate where the limits lie or should they, at least, play some role in limit-identification? Certainly, constitutions are relevant sources, but the content of a constitution is not necessarily uncontested. Neither is the question of whether any particular constitution might leave the design, implementation and governance of counter-terrorism and other security measures to the executive with little or no application of 'normal' constitutional principles. In some constitutions, such as the Irish Constitution, one can find a clear and unambiguous

---

away from this position to subject prerogative power to some judicial review; see Elliott, *The Constitutional Foundations of Judicial Review*, n. 35 above, pp. 178–82 and Chapter 9 in this volume, R. Masterman, 'Rebalancing the unbalanced constitution: juridification and national security in the United Kingdom'.

[37] Under the Human Rights Act 1998 the UK courts can declare a measure to be incompatible with the Human Rights Act but this does not impact on the operation, validity or continuation in force of that measure: Human Rights Act 1998, s. 4.

[38] Elliott, *The Constitutional Foundations of Judicial Review*, n. 35 above, pp. 5–10.

statement of emergency power that is, on its face at least, expressly unlimited by the remainder of the constitution.[39] In others, such as the US Constitution, 'war powers' management is institutionally allocated to the executive with some congressional involvement by means, especially, of the power of the purse but without much clarity as to whether the judiciary has a role or what other elements of the Constitution might apply to limit (especially) extra-territorial counter-terrorist activities or the activities of covert agencies. Thus, to say that 'the constitution' acts as a source of limits is to slightly obscure the complexity of that proposition. Furthermore, in at least some constitutional systems, legislation that has a constitutionalist nature can play a constitution-type role in terms of identifying limits, but raises questions as to whether a parliamentary instrument can be (or should be) used to restrain parliament and the executive by means of judicial intervention.

Similarly, questions of scope, limit and applicability arise with international law. Depending on the intensity of the measures deployed an armed conflict of sufficient intensity to engage (at least some) of international humanitarian law might exist. If international humanitarian law is engaged, international human rights law continues to apply *but* through the prism of international humanitarian law.[40] Furthermore, the exact requirements of international humanitarian law are contested, especially in relation to non-state actors. So too are there disputes as to what role international law *per se* plays in extra-territorial activity, what account (if any) can (or should) be taken of it in domestic judicial review, and sometimes whether it even governs contemporary terrorism at all. The relationship between different international legal regimes is also a source of complexity here, particularly given the internationalised nature of some counter-terrorism measures that might originate through a UN Security Council Resolution, be applied in a unified way by the European Union (EU) through Directives and Regulations, and then implemented nationally though primary or secondary legislation.[41] How do general

---

[39] Bunreacht na hÉireann, art. 28.3.3. For analysis see A. Greene, 'The Historical Evolution of Article 28.3.3 of the Irish Constitution' (2012) *Irish Jurist* 117.

[40] *Advisory Opinion on the Legality of the Threat or Use of Nuclear Weapons* [1996] ICJ Rep. 226; *Advisory Opinion on the Legal Consequences of the Construction of a Wall in the Occupied Territory* (2004) 43 ILM 1009; *Case concerning Armed Activities on the Territory of the Congo (DRC v. Uganda)* [2005] ICJ Rep. 116 (19 December 2005).

[41] The prime example is the freezing of suspected terrorists' assets in the EU based on EU measures introduced to give effect to Security Council resolutions, and black-listing decisions of the (Security Council) Counter-Terrorist Committee. For an overview of

international law (such as UN Security Council resolutions), EU law, European Convention of Human Rights (ECHR) law and general international human rights law (all of which apply to the states in question) interact, first with one another and then with the domestic legal system? Furthermore, to what extent might international institutions (such as the Court of Justice of the European Communities (CJEU) and the European Court of Human Rights (ECtHR)) be able to understand that interaction and identify applicable limits by means of such understanding?[42]

Once limits have been identified, we confront the question of how to ensure that they are adhered to. We ought to make it clear that in the ideal situation self-regulation would operate to ensure compliance. Thus, government departments, the public service, coalition partners (where applicable), the public, and parliament together with the executive itself would create a regulatory mass that would ensure compliance, and laws, measures, plans, regimes and activities that overstepped the agreed-upon limits would simply not make it to the implementation phase. History, however, tells us that – by any standard – this does not happen. Any account of historical, or indeed contemporary, counter-terrorist measures by states and regional and international institutions will include an analysis of measures that were variously found to be unconstitutional, incompatible with constitutionalist legislation such as statutory Bills of Rights, in contravention of international human rights law, non-compliant with international humanitarian law, ineffective from an operational perspective, unnecessary from a risk-assessment perspective and fundamentally counter-productive. All of this makes it difficult to accept the proposition (still made)[43] that extreme deference should be shown to the executive in the context of counter-terrorism based on the fact that they know what they are doing and respect the realistic limits inherent in the exercise of public power. It is on this second question that substantial clashes in opinion tend to arise.

how this works see e.g., C. Murphy, *EU Counter-Terrorism Law: Pre-Emption and the Rule of Law* (Portland, OR: Hart Publishing, 2012), ch. 5.

[42] See Chapter 12 in this volume, C. C. Murphy, 'Counter-terrorism law and judicial review: the challenge for the Court of Justice of the European Union'.

[43] E. A. Posner and A. Vermeule, *Terror in the Balance: Security, Liberty and the Courts* (Oxford University Press, 2007).

III   Competing Perspectives

Broadly speaking there are four topics across which opinion is divided in relation to counter-terrorism judicial review, all of which are addressed throughout this volume, but in relation to which an initial reflection is appropriate. These are institutional appropriateness; extra-constitutionalism and institutional dialogue; judicial muscularity; and internationalism.

(a)   Institutional appropriateness

Questions of institutional appropriateness ask not only whether the judiciary is best (or even 'well') placed to determine whether a particular element of counter-terrorism has overstepped the line, but also whether international institutions have any appropriate or legitimate role in asking similar questions. In the main, scholars contrast the capacity of the judiciary and the legislature to play a limiting role, bringing into the debate the inherent tensions between constitutionalism, on the one hand, and representative democracy, on the other.[44] A pure system of representative democracy would suggest that it is 'the People' who should ultimately decide the principles and policies to be pursued by means of their elected representatives. In this model there are no limits *beyond* the will of the People. However, constitutionalism gives us just such an exogenous limitation. As Tushnet puts it:

> Today, constitutionalism requires that a nation be committed to the proposition that a nation's people should determine the policies under which they will live, by some form of democratic governance. Yet, constitutionalism also requires that there be some limits on the policy choices the people can make democratically.[45]

The question then becomes whether such constitutionalist limitations are desirable in a situation of exigency such as a terrorist threat and, if so, who ought to determine where those limitations lie. That controversy goes to the heart of this collection and is the core issue when viewed from the institutional appropriateness perspective.

---

[44] See Chapter 11 in this volume, G. Phillipson, 'Deference and dialogue in the real-world counter-terrorism context'.

[45] M. Tushnet, *Weak Courts, Strong Rights: Judicial Review and Social Welfare Rights in Comparative Constitutional Law* (Princeton University Press, 2008), p. 19.

Political theorist Carl Schmitt directly addressed the tension within constitutionalism between people setting limits and there being limits on that process itself. In *Constitutional Theory*, he articulated the difference between the constitution (*verfassung*) as a substantive and integral source of legitimacy for the state and *verfassungsgesetze*, the individual positive constitutional laws, which set out procedures and subsidiary norms for state action. The *verfassung* are derived from an original act of constituent power; that is, from a 'conscious decision' of a historically unified nation concerning its fundamental political form.[46] The substantive constitution should be considered the innermost existential expression of the constituent body (the People). He thus concluded that the constitution, standing above all secondary laws, needed to be viewed as an original source of supra-legality.[47] Implicit in this theory is a hierarchical concept of legitimacy: the constitution as an expression of constituent power has the highest legitimacy, and in order to protect this substantive constitution other laws might be suspended or temporarily set aside. This would be particularly true in a state of exception where, he claimed, constitutional laws could legitimately be 'suspended', whereas the constitution itself could not be subject to suspension and had to be considered 'inviolable'.[48] It is apparent that within his scheme the only restraint upon the executive is the potential power of the people to exercise their constituent power. The legitimacy of this relatively unfettered executive is dependent on temporal limitation, although Roman history demonstrates the difficulty in ensuring Commissarial rather than Sovereign Dictatorship.[49]

While rejecting the executive supremacy of Schmitt, many advocates of popular sovereignty still derive the legitimacy of constitutional norms from the constituent power of the people.[50] This brings us back to the original contradiction: a commitment to constitutionalism limits the

---

[46] C. Schmitt, *Verfassungslehre* (Berlin: Duncker und Humblot, 1928), p. 21.

[47] *Ibid.* p. 22. For excellent comment in agreement with this reading see A. Kalyvas, *Democracy and the Politics of the Extraordinary: Max Weber, Carl Schmitt, and Hannah Arendt* (Cambridge University Press, 2008), p. 131.

[48] Schmitt, *Verfassungslehre*, n. 46 above, p. 26.

[49] C. Nicolet, 'Dictatorship in Rome' in P. Baehr and M. Richter (eds.), *Dictatorship in History and Theory: Bonapartism, Caesarism, and Totalitarianism* (Cambridge University Press, 2004), p. 263.

[50] See e.g., F. Davis, 'Extra-Constitutionalism, the Human Rights Act and the "Labour Rebels": Applying Prof. Tushnet's Theories in the UK' (2006) 4 *Web Journal of Current Legal Issues*, http://webjcli.ncl.ac.uk/2006/issue4/davis4.html, citing correspondence with M. Tushnet.

choices available to the People. Parliamentary supremacists argue that the legislature – possessing as it does a democratic mandate – is best placed to represent the general will of the People. Thus the representative organ of the state ought to act as a check on executive power in the state of exception. This check may be deferential but it should also be robust. In other words, parliament may choose to accommodate the executive in light of some perceived threat to national security but it must be willing to interrogate whether an emergency exists and whether the measures proposed or actions taken are proportionate. This approach treats rights-enforcement as inherently a matter for politics. The role of parliament is to engage in the debate; if the people dislike the actions of the executive and feel that parliament is failing in its duty to restrain the executive they ought to exercise their power as a constitutional actor (most clearly by protesting and using their electoral power). Such an outlook can spawn many alternative responses, ranging from a belief in institutional dialogue perhaps permitting a weak form judicial review, through to a Diceyean commitment to the unfettered supremacy of parliament.

Of course, there are those who argue that the constituent power of the People is neither capable nor willing to restrain the executive in the context of counter-terrorism.[51] But, for some, an apparent process of social learning observable in US counter-terrorism illustrates just such a potential. Writing elsewhere, Mark Tushnet has claimed that the United States has in fact ratcheted down its response to each successive emergency, going from a wholesale suspension of *habeas corpus* during the civil war, to the internment of citizens and non-citizens (primarily of Japanese descent) in the Second World War, to the detention of non-citizens in Guantánamo Bay.[52] While hardly a commendable record it might be argued that this at least demonstrates movement in the right direction, although seen in the round (beyond merely the detention context) the counter-terrorist regime operated by the United States since 2001 may speak against such an optimistic reading.[53] Even if such a historicist analysis is accurate it can be argued that it fails to provide any protection against an atavistic response reversing this slow but progressive trend. Furthermore, it does nothing to alleviate the situation for

---

[51] De Londras, *Detention in the 'War on Terror'*, n. 2 above, ch. 1.

[52] M. Tushnet, 'Civil Liberties in a Time of Terror: Defending *Korematsu*?: Reflections on Civil Liberties in Wartime' (2003) *Wisconsin Law Review* 273, 283–94.

[53] See Chapter 3 in this volume, D. Jenkins, 'When good cases go bad: unintended consequences of rights-friendly judgments'.

current victims of rights abuse; the inmates in Guantánamo Bay will hardly rejoice at playing an unwilling part in an ongoing process of social improvement, nor have they experienced the 'Hope' promised by President Obama.

Others argue that in fact the conduct of global counter-terrorism since the attacks of 11 September 2001 ('9/11') shows that the impulse towards excessive repression has not waned.[54] It may be the case that the most intrusive and repressive measures have been taken against non-citizens and undertaken primarily abroad, but there are two important points to be borne in mind here. The first is that the particular targeting of non-citizens does not necessarily mitigate the measures taken in the eyes of anyone *apart from* the (seemingly) untargeted citizen. For the targeted non-citizen, extreme measures have been applied including detention without trial for up to ten years (to date), irregular trial processes in military commissions, extraordinary rendition and torture. By any measure these are grave intrusions on personal liberties and the fact that they are limited to non-citizens does not make them less concerning. The second point to bear in mind here is that in fact counter-terrorism measures are being imposed on both citizens and non-citizens, sometimes openly and sometimes more covertly. These measures might not be as extreme as those imposed exclusively on non-citizens, but they are nevertheless significant. Surveillance, both overt and covert, is a hugely significant trend in the past ten years,[55] as is the use of technology to both survey and govern our behaviours. The unimagined extent of such covert surveillance was laid bare by the Snowden leaks regarding the US National Security Agency PRISM surveillance programme.[56] However, many of these mechanisms of 'universal counter-terrorism' are either considered to be 'worth it' for the purposes of 'security' or are so pervasive and overt as to be more or less unnoticed. Thus, the use by state apparatus of private corporations that we engage with on a daily basis (transaction tracking mechanisms, Internet search engines and airlines, for example) may simply be unknown to 'the People'. Even if these kinds of mechanisms seem initially to be relatively harmless, or at least to be proportionate infringements, we ought to remember that the

---

[54] Roach, *The 9/11 Effect*, n. 31 above.

[55] See generally, F. Davis, N. McGarity and G. Williams (eds.), *Surveillance, Counter-Terrorism and Comparative Constitutionalism* (London: Routledge, 2014).

[56] M. Gidda, 'Edward Snowden and the NSA files: timeline', *Guardian*, 26 July 2013, available at www.theguardian.com/world/2013/jun/23/edward-snowden-nsa-files-timeline.

information and profiles built through this kind of everyday counter-
terrorist governance can be used to identify individuals who then find
themselves subjected to more extreme kinds of counter-terrorism, such
as asset freezing, inclusion on no fly lists, and maybe even extraordinary
rendition.

A further concern is that there is a real possibility (if not a probability)
that 'the People' may simply be unmoved by the plight of those who find
themselves at the sharp end of the counter-terrorist apparatus of the
state. There are a number of reasons for this. The first is the real and
genuinely felt fear and panic (described by de Londras as 'popular
panic')[57] that a massive attack brings about in the populace. There is a
danger that 'we' (analysts, academics, specialists – people divided from
the reality of the risk) might become detached or even jaded, forgetting
that terrorism and the risk of terrorism are experienced as real and
frightening phenomena. For some theorists it is difficult to accept that
we might realistically ask 'the People' to fight against these understand-
able and genuinely felt emotions to demand that their representatives
would respect some kind of nebulous conceptualisation of constitutionalism and resist the introduction of measures that are unlikely to be
imposed in their most extreme forms on them or people with whom
they associate.[58] The second concern about relying on representative
democracy is that it might simply fail; supporting extreme measures
might well be the politically astute thing to do, not only because of
popular demands for repressive counter-terrorist measures, but also in
some systems because the structures and dynamics of parliamentary
systems reward compliance and punish opposition.[59] Taking these kinds
of views into account, some kind of 'weak judicial review' might be
welcome, but absolute deference to 'the political branches' would be
considered unwise.

Thus, one of the core arguments in the debate about counter-
terrorism judicial review relates not only to whether or not representative democracy is capable of ensuring that constitutionalist limits are
imposed to prevent these kinds of excesses, but also to whether it is
institutionally appropriate for any other organ of the state to undertake
this function.

---

[57] De Londras, *Detention in the 'War on Terror'*, n. 2 above, ch. 1.
[58] *Ibid.*; D. Dyzenhaus, 'The Compulsion of Legality' in V. V. Ramraj (ed.), *Emergencies and the Limits of Legality* (Cambridge University Press, 2008), p. 33.
[59] De Londras and Davis, 'Controlling the Executive in Times of Terrorism', n. 4 above.

Another element of the debate around counter-terrorism judicial review is the need to explore whether there really are only two alternatives to executive dominance: parliamentary oversight and judicial review. Increasingly, alternative mechanisms of accountability are being designed and implemented. Thus, Blackbourn examines the potential for independent reviewers to undertake significant roles in keeping counter-terrorist measures under a rolling review and, in particular, in challenging the underlying claims of necessity that the executive tends to make to justify the introduction or maintenance of certain repressive counter-terrorist regimes.[60] On a less systematic, more ad hoc basis, commissions of inquiry have the capacity to at least expose executive excesses and create – or create momentum towards – some kind of accountability for them. The role of such ad hoc reviews is set out by Roach, using the examples of the Commission of Inquiry into the case of Maher Arar and the Gibson Inquiry in the United Kingdom.[61] In his contribution, Davis questions the utility in disaggregating our conception of parliament and judiciary to some extent, arguing that specialised parliamentary oversight committees or judicial enquiries might bring to bear the particular attributes of the different institutions (majoritarian democracy and independence, respectively) without their perceived institutional disadvantages (majoritarian populism and democratic illegitimacy).[62] In his contribution, Phillipson argues for a collaborative approach to oversight between courts and parliament in the context of counter-terrorism and rejects the general absolutism of judicial review scepticism and enthusiasm. Rather, he argues, 'the legislature can only protect the individual through inserting judicial safeguards; and the judiciary must then police those safeguards rigorously, realising that to do otherwise is not to pay respect to the elected branches, but simply to betray the trust of the legislature and frustrate the joint enterprise of providing a serious, interlocking constitutional check upon the national security executive'.[63] Thus, simply constructing the debate about counter-terrorism judicial review as one between parliamentary and judicial control *simpliciter*

---

[60] See Chapter 7 in this volume, J. Blackbourn, 'Independent reviewers as alternative: an empirical study from Australia and the United Kingdom'.

[61] See Chapter 8 in this volume, K. Roach, 'Public inquiries as an attempt to fill accountability gaps left by judicial and legislative review'.

[62] See Chapter 6 in this volume, F. F. Davis, 'The politics of counter-terrorism judicial review: creating effective parliamentary scrutiny'.

[63] See Chapter 11 in this volume, G. Phillipson, 'Deference and dialogue in the real-world counter-terrorism context'.

arguably excludes consideration of alternatives and ought to be avoided where possible. Indeed, Tushnet suggests in his contribution that any such debate can be avoided and an arguably more effective oversight regime introduced by treating counter-terrorism as, to all intents and purposes, another regulatory regime within the state and subjecting it to the normal rigours of administrative law.[64] Whether this would, however, resolve some of the tensions that currently manifest in these contexts is questioned by Chan. In her chapter she argues that claims for deference (which would inevitably arise within an administrative law framework) tend to be accompanied by an implicit or explicit demand for substantial amounts of deference where the context is security so that merely folding this into general administrative law may not be unproblematic.[65]

(b) Extra-constitutionalism and institutional dialogue

As already noted, considerations of institutional appropriateness do not necessarily require us to decide definitively between one option and the other: between judicial or parliamentary supremacy.[66] Although legislative supremacy, in the traditional Diceyean sense, is somewhat rare, the Australian Human Rights (Parliamentary Scrutiny) Act (Cth) 2011 exemplifies the model. Australia does not possess a federal Bill of Rights, but legislation has established a Joint Committee on Human Rights that is tasked with assessing the compliance of all legislation with certain human rights norms. As under the UK Human Rights Act 1998, the proposer of a Bill must make a statement of human rights compliance, but unlike the UK model there is no mechanism for judicial or any other oversight. The only oversight mechanism is parliamentary. This is dealt with in greater detail in the chapter by Fergal Davis. Notwithstanding this example, the general political and constitutional reality is such that in fact the supremacy of one institution over the other is unlikely to arise in any situation, not to mention in a situation of extreme tension and political disruption. Taking this into account, scholars attempting to resolve the contradiction between constitutionalism and representative

---

[64] See Chapter 5 in this volume, M. Tushnet, 'Emergency law as administrative law'.

[65] See Chapter 10 in this volume, C. Chan, 'Business as usual: deference in counter-terrorism rights review'.

[66] See Chapter 11 in this volume, G. Phillipson, 'Deference and dialogue in the real-world counter-terrorism context'.

democracy have identified a new commonwealth, or dialogic, model of review.[67] Examples of new commonwealth review include the 'notwith-standing clause' contained in section 33 of the Canadian Charter of Rights and Freedoms 1982,[68] the UK Human Rights Act 1998 and the Australian State of Victoria's Charter of Human Rights and Responsi-bilities Act 2006 (Vic.). The approaches are operationally different but at their core each new commonwealth model acknowledges that there can be 'competing reasonable interpretations of constitutional provisions';[69] they enable the judiciary to express their interpretation but ensure that, in the end, only the legislature's interpretation is legally effective. The attractiveness of such an approach is that it seeks to emphasise the strengths and weaknesses of each institution. Directly elected legislatures are thought to be 'less likely than courts to be attentive to the limits constitutionalism places on democratic self-governance'[70] but unelected courts are accused of lacking democratic legitimacy. By allowing courts to declare that acts of parliament are inconsistent (or incompatible) with human rights norms we empower the judiciary to sound the alarm.[71] Once the issue has been brought to the legislature's attention, we can then advance the value of democratic self-governance by leaving the final decision to the legislature.[72] Theoretically, this dialogic approach permits courts to robustly defend rights while deferring to 'legislative sequels that evidence clear and considered disagreement with their rulings'.[73] Such a dialogic approach, however, does require courts to engage in a meaning-ful review of measures and to approach with some caution claims made by the executive. In their contributions to this volume, Roger Masterman and Helen Fenwick emphasise not only that this is necessary, but also

[67] S. Gardbaum, *The New Commonwealth Model of Constitutionalism: Theory and Practice* (Cambridge University Press, 2012); S. Gardbaum, 'Reassessing the New Commonwealth Model of Constitutionalism' (2010) 8 *I.CON* 167.

[68] Section 33 of the Canadian Charter permits the federal parliament and provincial legislatures of Canada to pass legislation 'notwithstanding the possibility (or certainty) that the legislation might be understood by some, including the courts, as inconsistent with one of a significant number of rights contained in the charter'. Thus the legislatures can anticipate a judicial objection to the legislation and determine that the legislation should remain valid notwithstanding that judicial objection (M. Tushnet, 'The Hartman Hotz Lecture: Dialogic Judicial Review' (2008) 61 *Arkansas Law Review* 205, 205–6); see also www.efc.ca/pages/law/charter/charter.text.html.

[69] Tushnet, 'The Hartman Hotz Lecture', n. 68 above, 209.   [70] *Ibid.* 212.

[71] De Londras and Davis, 'Controlling the Executive in Times of Terrorism', n. 4 above, 25.

[72] Tushnet, 'The Hartman Hotz Lecture', n. 68 above, 212.

[73] R. Dixon, 'Creating Dialogue about Socioeconomic Rights: Strong-form versus Weak-form Judicial Review Revisited' (2007) 5(3) *I.CON* 391, 393.

that it is sometimes lacking even in contexts where courts generally engage in stricter review. Considering counter-terrorism judicial review in the United Kingdom, Masterman compellingly traces the residual caution of courts to scrutinise claims as to security and counter-terrorism in judicial review even while the scope and nature of judicial review in that jurisdiction has been expanding.[74] Considering the European Court of Human Rights (ECtHR) since 9/11, Fenwick argues that rather than dialogue with the UK government there has been appeasement influenced, to at least some extent, by the broader tensions between the United Kingdom and the ECtHR.[75] These two contributions emphasise that claims of dialogue are sustainable only inasmuch as the court takes a robust approach to scrutiny in the first place.

Extra-constitutionalism can be seen as a subset of dialogic review, which has been proposed in the US context. Rather than declaring an executive act or piece of legislation to be constitutional or unconstitutional the courts can declare it to be extra-constitutional, that is, beyond the scope of responses anticipated by the constitution. The mechanism would operate as follows:

> [T]he government introduces legislation that is inherently suspect from the prospective of the rule of law, but avoids ... provisions that seem in flagrant violation of rule of law principles. The dirty work is done by those charged with implementing the law and the government expects that judges who hear challenges to the validity of particular acts will put aside their role as guardians of the rule of law because in issue is the security of the state.[76]

Extra-constitutionalism enables the courts to acknowledge the exceptional nature of the proposed acts and leaves it to the other constitutional actors to determine if such exceptional measures are justified. In that respect extra-constitutionalism is similar to other forms of institutional dialogue. Crucially, such approaches avoid the need for courts to justify abhorrent acts as somehow constitutional or to boldly strike down

---

[74] See Chapter 9 in this volume, R. Masterman, 'Rebalancing the unbalanced constitution: juridification and national security in the United Kingdom'.

[75] See Chapter 13 in this volume, H. Fenwick, 'Post 9/11 UK counter-terrorism cases in the European Court of Human Rights: a "dialogic" approach to rights protection or appeasement of national authorities?'.

[76] Tushnet, 'Civil Liberties in a Time of Terror', n. 52 above, n. 118, quoting David Dyzenhaus.

executive measures in the face of genuine concerns that such measures might actually be necessary. As Justice Jackson noted in *Korematsu*:

> [O]nce a judicial opinion rationalizes such an order to show that it conforms to the Constitution, or rather rationalizes the Constitution to show that the Constitution sanctions such an order, the Court for all time has validated ... [a] principle [that] lies about like a loaded weapon ready for the hand of any authority that bring forward a plausible claim of urgent need.[77]

As a result, extra-constitutionalists argue that 'it is better to have emergency powers exercised in an extra-constitutional way, so that everyone understands that the actions are extraordinary, than to have the actions rationalised away as consistent with the constitution and thereby normalised'.[78] Extra-constitutionalism forms part of an institutional dialogue because the courts are placing the other actors on alert that the actions complained of are not within the category of actions that can be deemed constitutional. That places the responsibility on those other actors to determine if they are satisfied that such exceptional actions are justified.

A structure of dialogue is not confined to Commonwealth states, of course. Even in states with constitutional supremacy a dialogic approach to counter-terrorism judicial review is possible, with courts using judicial review to try to 'nudge' the political branches towards a more limited and rights-compliant approach to counter-terrorism even in the absence of striking an impugned measure down. In the United States, for example, numerous commentators have categorised the 'to and fro' between the US Supreme Court and the political branches in relation to Guantánamo Bay as a form of dialogue by which the Supreme Court slowly moved the detention centre there from a place where detainees had no effective review mechanism to one in which those detained there have recognised constitutional *habeas corpus* rights.[79] In spite of that progression (which seems to remove at least part of the legal rationale for detaining people in Guantánamo Bay)[80] the detention centre remains open and all attempts to close it have been blocked by Congress, either as an act of political

---

[77] 323 US 244, 247 (1944).
[78] Tushnet, 'Civil Liberties in a Time of Terror', n. 52 above, 306.
[79] F. de Londras, 'Guantánamo Bay: Towards Legality?' (2008) 71 *Modern Law Review* 36.
[80] D. Jenkins, 'The Closure of Guantánamo Bay: What Next for the Detainees?' (2010) *Public Law* 46; F. de Londras, 'Closing Guantánamo Bay: the Triumph of Politics over Law?' (2012) *Public Law* 18.

constitutionalism (as claimed by Tushnet)[81] or as a result of pure quotidian politics (as claimed by de Londras).[82] The example of Guantánamo
Bay litigation in the United States suggests that muscular judicial review
is not incapable of having a dialogic impact but also highlights that it
does not necessarily over judicialise politics. Although in some jurisdictions, such as the United Kingdom, there is now an established record of
changing counter-terrorist measures so that they become more rights
compliant than they previously were in response to judicial findings of
incompatibility, this is not the inevitable outcome of such cases. Concerns about the judicialisation of politics, then, which Masterman
addresses in his chapter,[83] must take the broader constitutional and
political climate into account.

(c) Judicial muscularity

In the ordinary course of events (or what we might call 'normalcy'), we
tend to rely on the judiciary to identify where the limits of allowable
government action lie. This is so even in systems of parliamentary
supremacy where, as considered above, the doctrine of *ultra vires* provides the key underlying principle justifying judicial review. *Ultra vires*,
by means of reminder, requires that institutions of the state do not
exercise power to any greater extent than expressly permitted and in this
way constitutes a clear manifestation of the constitutionalist principle of
limited power. In jurisdictions defined by constitutional supremacy, the
power to decide on limits of allowable governmental action lies clearly
within the jurisdiction of the courts. However, even in these jurisdictions
there is an unedifying history of what we would call counter-terrorism
judicial review. The same goes for the European Court of Human Rights,
whose record in relation to trying to restrain repressive state practices
done in the name of 'national security' has rarely been described as
impressive.[84]

---

[81] M. Tushnet, 'Legal and Political Constitutionalism, and the Response to Terrorism' in
D. Jenkins, A. Jacobsen and A. Henriksen (eds.), *The 'Long Decade': How 9/11 Changed
the Law* (Oxford University Press, 2014).

[82] De Londras, 'Guantánamo Bay, the Rise of Courts and the Revenge of Politics', n. 5 above.

[83] See Chapter 9 in this volume, R. Masterman, 'Rebalancing the unbalanced constitution:
juridification and national security in the United Kingdom'.

[84] F. Ní Aoláin and O. Gross, 'From Discretion to Scrutiny: Revisiting the Application of the
Margin of Appreciation Doctrine in the Context of Article 15 of the European Convention on Human Rights' (2001) 23 *Human Rights Quarterly* 625; A. Greene, 'Separating

Historically, domestic and some international courts have been faced with two questions when it comes to counter-terrorist or other national security measures: (i) do the extant circumstances justify the imposition of *some kind* of extraordinary security measures with impacts on individual rights beyond what we would normally consider acceptable? And (ii) if so, are the measures under direct challenge in the case at bar within the limits of acceptability, even taking these extraordinary circumstances into account? The first of these questions – what we might call the threshold question – is one in relation to which courts have traditionally shown, and continue to show, substantial deference to the executive's determination of levels of risk.[85] This is one area in which, it is often argued, judicial deference is appropriate if not advisable because it is essentially an assessment of knowledge and factors that require a particular kind of expertise to understand, compute and assess. There are some scholars who argue that this threshold question should receive a closer degree of scrutiny by the courts,[86] but in the main the concentration in the scholarship has been on the second, substantive, question relating to the impugned counter-terrorist measures.

Here too the historical record of courts shows that a high degree of deference has been shown. The classical examples are the US Supreme Court's decision in *Korematsu*[87] and the UK House of Lords' decision in *Liversidge*,[88] in both of which a substantial degree of privilege was assigned to the judgement of political and military actors as to whether or not certain (in both cases internment) measures were necessary, with necessity being used as a quasi-equivalent to appropriateness or acceptability. These cases are not particularly exceptional, it has to be said; other superior domestic courts have made similar decisions,[89] as has the ECtHR.[90] This record often feeds into arguments about institutional appropriateness inasmuch as it is taken as evidence of poor quality

---

Normalcy from Emergency: the Jurisprudence of Article 15 of the European Convention on Human Rights' (2011) 12 *German Law Journal* 1764.

[85] Ní Aoláin and Gross, 'From Discretion to Scrutiny, n. 84 above; but cf. the strident objection of Hoffman LJ to the emergency classification post-9/11 in the United Kingdom in *A and others* v. *Secretary of State for the Home Department* [2004] UKHL 56 (paras. 86–97).

[86] Greene, 'Separating Normalcy from Emergency', n. 84 above.

[87] *Korematsu* v. *United States*, 323 US 214 (1944).

[88] *Liversidge* v. *Anderson* [1942] AC 206.

[89] *The State (Hughes)* v. *Lennon and others* [1935] IR 128, 148.

[90] *Ireland* v. *United Kingdom* [1978] ECHR 1 (18 January 1978).

decision-making by courts, with the resultant argument being that if courts are going to make such poor decisions perhaps they ought to make no decisions at all and simply leave it to the political branches to deal with national security measures.[91] In making decisions of this kind, it is argued, courts are simultaneously leaving the political branches' judgement undisturbed without any particular scrutiny *and* removing incentives for rigorous deliberation at the political level. Indeed, this is the core of the extra-constitutionalism thesis itself.[92]

However, at least some scholars have argued that the judicial record in the ten or so years since the attacks of 9/11 has been rather different to the historical one and that in fact there has been a lesser degree of judicial deference – or a greater degree of judicial muscularity – than was previously the case.[93] Again, there are a number of *causes célèbres* that are frequently cited to support this position: the *Belmarsh* decision in the United Kingdom,[94] *Hamdan*[95] and *Boumediene*[96] in the United States, *Saadi*[97] and *Othman (Abu Qatada)*[98] in the ECtHR. These decisions, however, also have their critics. On the one hand are those who argue (as alluded to above) that judicial adjudication of counter-terrorist measures is simply institutionally inappropriate.[99] So too are there those who argue that, even if courts appear to be being less deferential than was previously the case, the quality of decision-making remains questionable, either because there is a misapplication of law[100] or because courts are giving the impression of muscularity while actually acceding too easily to executive claims and, in so doing, recalibrating downwards our previous

---

[91] M. Tushnet, 'Controlling Executive Power in the War on Terrorism' (2005) 118 *Harvard Law Review* 2673, 2680; F. Davis, 'The Human Rights Act and Juridification: Saving Democracy from Law' (2010) 30(2) *Politics* 91.

[92] De Londras and Davis, 'Controlling the Executive in Times of Terrorism', n. 4 above, pp. 24–34.

[93] De Londras, *Detention in the 'War on Terror'*, n. 2 above; J. Ip, 'The Supreme Court and the House of Lords in the War on Terror: Inter Arma Silent Leges?' (2010) 19 *Michigan State Journal of International Law* 1.

[94] *A and others* v. *Secretary of State for the Home Department* [2004] UKHL 56.

[95] *Hamdan* v. *Rumsfeld*, 548 US 557 (2006).

[96] *Boumediene* v. *Bush*, 553 US 723 (2008).

[97] *Saadi* v. *Italy* (Application no. 37201/06), ECtHR Grand Chamber, Judgment of 28 February 2008.

[98] *Othman (Abu Qatada)* v. *United Kingdom* [2012] ECHR 56.

[99] Posner and Vermeule, *Terror in the Balance*, n. 43 above.

[100] For example, Ní Aoláin identifies doctrinal difficulties in the celebrated *Hamdan* case in spite of the constitutionalist desirability of the outcome: 'Hamdan and Common Article 3: Did the Supreme Court Get it Right?' (2007) 91 *Minnesota Law Review* 1525.

understandings of some core concepts (such as detention and due process).[101] Further criticisms accuse 'muscular' courts of in fact engaging in a futile exercise designed to maintain the relevance of the judiciary in spite of courts' frequent incapacity (or unwillingness) to actually secure an adequate and appropriate remedy for litigants.[102]

The debate on judicial muscularity, then, cuts across a number of themes: institutional appropriateness, quality and capacity in particular. Contributors to this collection address all of these. In his chapter David Jenkins critiques superior courts for abandoning a distinction between the citizen and non-citizen, claiming that such a distinction in fact maintained a higher *general* level of rights protection because, without it, *all* are subjected to more repressive laws.[103] For Jenkins, then, muscularity from a rights-based perspective is a double-edged sword. However, even when appearing to be muscular superior courts can sometimes be too vague in laying down principles or overly selective in what they will review. In his chapter Jules Lobel identifies these trends in the United States where, he says, the Supreme Court's lack of clarity as to what detainees in Guantánamo Bay are actually entitled to has enabled a hollowing out of celebrated judgments such as *Boumediene*[104] in reality while, at the same time, the Supreme Court refuses to consider cases relating to detention in Bagram, for example, thus further narrowing its capacity to meaningfully improve rights protection.[105] What Jenkins and Lobel suggest when read together is that what appears to be muscularity in particular cases must actually be seen in its round before any qualitative conclusions are reached. In her contribution de Londras argues, somewhat in contrast to this, that there may be an implicit muscularity in some cases that appear, at least at first, to have been futile or unsatisfactory because courts have felt constrained in their findings as a result of concerns as to inter-state comity and foreign affairs.[106] Rather than see these cases as simply unsatisfactory, de Londras argues that, understanding them in the context of a reflexive state built on constitutionalist

---

[101] Fenwick and Phillipson, 'Covert Derogations and Judicial Deference', n. 21 above.

[102] See the dissent of Justice Scalia in *Boumediene* v. *Bush*, 553 US 723 (2008), for example.

[103] See Chapter 3 in this volume, D. Jenkins, 'When good cases go bad: unintended consequences of rights-friendly judgments'.

[104] *Boumediene* v. *Bush*, 553 US 723 (2008).

[105] See Chapter 4 in this volume, J. Lobel, 'The rhetoric and reality of judicial review of counter-terrorism actions: the United States experience'.

[106] See Chapter 1 in this volume, F. de Londras, 'Counter-terrorism judicial review as regulatory constitutionalism'.

principles, one can see within them the potential for what she calls regulatory constitutionalism.

(d)   Internationalism

In the current climate it is practically impossible to adequately discuss counter-terrorism and counter-terrorism judicial review without addressing internationalism to at least some extent. This is so not only because of the internationalised nature of what is perceived to be the main contemporary terrorist threat and, indeed, the internationalism of many of the responses, but also because of the now clearly enmeshed nature of the national and the international and the challenge that counter-terrorism potentially poses to that.

This enmeshing is a result of various factors that have been widely considered elsewhere and need no more than a mention here: globalisation; international cooperation; the proliferation and governance capacities of international institutions; the emergence and growing importance of internationalised technologies of governance; the development of global and regional human rights regimes including enforcement mechanisms; and the creation of close regional unions sometimes with autonomous constitutional power. All of these elements are important in counter-terrorism. Globalisation both colours the risk that terrorism poses and at least to some extent dictates the response; traditions and links of international cooperation extend into (and are sometimes challenged by) counter-terrorist activity; international institutions create autonomous counter-terrorist policies and powers and (at least in the case of the European Union) give effect to international obligations relating to counter-terrorism, and so on. When it comes to counter-terrorism judicial review, internationalism plays a number of roles that are significant here.

The first role relates, as already noted, to the identification of limits to which we intend to hold the state in the context of counter-terrorism. Even where domestic law and politics may become saturated in fear, panic and zealous counter-terrorism, international legal standards arguably have *some* resilience against panic that can identify them as more stable standards upon which to rely than domestic ones.[107] This can then act as a mechanism for courts in assessing whether or not any impugned

---

[107] De Londras, *Detention in the 'War on Terror'*, n. 2 above, ch. 5.

activity was within the bounds permissible. This role extends most obviously, perhaps, to the standards found in international human rights law but can also be played by international humanitarian law. It is likely, at least in dualist states, that the extent to which what we might here describe as a rule of international law plays such a role will be determined by its domestic status (with incorporated provisions being more likely to be invoked and imposed by courts than unincorporated provisions), but incorporation has not shown itself to be definitive in this respect.[108] Counter-terrorism judicial review at the domestic level, then, has a potentially complex relationship with international law. On the one hand, it can involve the use (or rejection) of international standards to shape judicial response; on the other hand, it can either reinforce or call into question the relevance of international law and international principles in situations of risk when sovereignty arguably finds its fullest voice. In her chapter Helen Duffy outlines the ways in which international standards are being used in litigation and criminal prosecutions in the attempt to achieve accountability for repressive counter-terrorist measures.[109] In contrast, perhaps, to the somewhat critical approach adopted by Fenwick in this volume in the context of the ECtHR, Duffy exhibits a faith in international law's capacity to aid in laying down clear limitations that emanates from her use of these standards in practice. Her chapter also, however, makes clear that a core challenge to successful counter-terrorism judicial review has little to do with the identification of standards or institutional concerns but rather with access to information and the capacity to effectively represent one's client in an atmosphere that is saturated with secrecy. In his chapter, Rytter identifies the critical role that the standards laid down by the ECtHR have played in emboldening Danish courts – traditionally extremely deferential to executive claims of security need – to enforce constitutionalist limits in the counter-terrorism context, reiterating the role that internationalisation can play in counter-terrorism judicial review.[110]

---

[108] In *Hamdan*, for example, the US Supreme Court applied unincorporated elements of the Geneva Conventions in domestic law; *Hamdan* v. *Rumsfeld*, 548 US 557 (2006).

[109] See Chapter 14 in this volume, H. Duffy, 'Accountability for counter-terrorism: challenges and potential in the role of the courts'.

[110] See Chapter 2 in this volume, J. E. Rytter, 'Counter-terrorism judicial review by a traditionally weak judiciary'.

Internationalism and counter-terrorism judicial review are also related inasmuch as international courts and other adjudicative mechanisms can be used to play a judicial review role when a litigant does not achieve satisfaction domestically *or* when the impugned measure originates from an international institution that has a judicial review body within it. Regional human rights courts, which generally enjoy subsidiary jurisdiction and are therefore used where domestic legal remedies have been exhausted, clearly play an important role in counter-terrorism judicial review. This is not only because they themselves can carry out judicial review against applicable standards, but also because their approach to this role has the potential to influence how domestic courts from member states are likely to handle difficult questions of, for example, deference and the content of rights in a situation of emergency in subsequent proceedings.[111] Where international institutions with judicial review mechanisms have themselves undertaken counter-terrorism and introduced repressive measures, their own judicial review procedures come into play. The EU is the obvious example in this context and Murphy considers the potential for the judgments of its CJEU and the ECtHR to have significant impacts for the rule of law in a counter-terrorism context both within and beyond its Member States, while also challenging the widely held view that, after the *Kadi* jurisprudence, the CJEU is ideally placed to protect the rule of law in the counter-terrorism context.[112]

Conclusion

At its very heart, what is at stake when we debate whether and how counter-terrorism can be limited and especially the possible role of judicial review in such limiting exercises is a commitment to constitutionalism even in a situation of crisis, whether that be of a terrorist or a counter-terrorist nature. The contributors to this book share a commitment to the concept of constitutionalism, containing as it does a nebulous notion of justice inasmuch as it commits to power being openly

---

[111] See Chapter 13 in this volume, H. Fenwick, 'Post 9/11 UK counter-terrorism cases in the European Court of Human Rights: a "dialogic" approach to rights protection or appeasement of national authorities?'; and Chapter 14, H. Duffy, 'Accountability for counter-terrorism: challenges and potential in the role of the courts'.

[112] See Chapter 12 in this volume, C. C. Murphy, 'Counter-terrorism law and judicial review: the challenge for the Court of Justice of the European Union'.

exercised, limited and accountable. What is at stake when we debate the appropriateness, effectiveness, quality and practice of counter-terrorism judicial review – and what is at the core of this collection, notwith-standing its internal debates and disagreements – is the maintenance of this basic constitutionalist commitment in the difficult, fractious and precarious state of counter-terrorist crisis.

PART I

Judging counter-terrorism judicial review

Counter-terrorism judicial review as regulatory constitutionalism

FIONA DE LONDRAS

As the other contributions in this volume attest, since 9/11 courts, inquiries,[1] politics[2] and independent reviewers[3] have been working to try to maintain and enforce constitutionalist principles in the face of counter-terrorist powers. Experience has shown that politics has struggled to resolve the challenges these powers pose to constitutionalism[4] – broadly understood here as a rule of law based commitment to limited, accountable and transparent power – so that courts have become central to resolving these tensions. In large part, courts have been asked to deal with counter-terrorist policies and laws directly imposed on litigants by respondent states, in relation to which some commentators have claimed courts are being less deferential than might have been expected.[5] Adjacent to these kinds of cases, however, is the complex situation of the suspected terrorist with some kind of relational connection to one state who is either detained abroad by another state or by his own state, which intends to transfer him into the custody of another. These cases are truly acute; they bring into question not only the fine

---

[1] See Chapter 8 in this volume, K. Roach, 'Public inquiries as an attempt to fill accountability gaps left by judicial and legislative review'.

[2] See Chapter 6 in this volume, F. Davis, 'The politics of counter-terrorism judicial review: creating effective parliamentary scrutiny'.

[3] See Chapter 7 in this volume, J. Blackbourn, 'Independent reviewers as alternative: an empirical study from Australia and the United Kingdom'.

[4] See Chapter 6 in this volume, F. F. Davis, 'The politics of counter-terrorism judicial review: creating effective parliamentary scrutiny' and Chapter 11, G. Phillipson, 'Deference and dialogue in the real-world counter-terrorism context'.

[5] F. de Londras, *Detention in the 'War on Terror': Can Human Rights Fight Back?* (Cambridge University Press, 2011), ch. 6; F. de Londras and F. Davis, 'Controlling the Executive in Times of Terrorism: Competing Perspectives on Effective Oversight Mechanisms' (2010) 30 *Oxford Journal of Legal Studies* 19; J. Ip, 'The Supreme Court and the House of Lords in the War on Terror: Inter Armes Silent Leges?' (2010) 19 *Michigan State Journal of International Law* 1.

lines of rights protection and security activity, but also complex and vital
questions of institutional competence heightened by the 'foreign affairs'
context. Their acute nature allows for them to be an especially stern test
for any claims that courts are in fact engaging in muscular counter-
terrorism judicial review. Thus, in this chapter, I explore such cases
across three jurisdictions in an attempt to explore what it is that courts
are doing.

Through an analysis of three cases from Canada, the United States and
the United Kingdom, I argue that courts are quite carefully carving these
kinds of cases into conceptual pieces (which I classify as internal and
external questions) to engage in what I term 'regulatory constitutionalism'. Here internal questions speak to the relationship between the
suspected terrorist and the respondent state, whereas external questions
concern the relationship between the respondent and third party states as
it relates to the suspected terrorist. When dealing with internal questions,
I argue courts are muscular notwithstanding the broader 'external' context in which they are considered, but when it comes to external questions a substantial amount of deference is apparent. This begs the
question of whether such internal muscularity is worthwhile if external
deference remains, however I argue that understanding counter-
terrorism judicial review as a mechanism of regulatory constitutionalism
provides at least some reassurance to constitutionalists.

This argument rests to a large extent on a starting position that
considers judicial review (construed broadly) to be an important manifestation of regulatory constitutionalism. I define regulatory constitutionalism as a process through which information about governmental
behaviour can be gathered, standards outlining the appropriate parameters of governmental authority outlined by reference to constitutionalist
principles of limited and accountable power, and governmental behaviour ultimately modified to align more clearly with the constitutionalist
ideal outlined in these standards. This builds on an understanding of
regulation as involving information gathering, standard setting and
behaviour modification,[6] as well as David Feldman's characterisation of
judicial review as having directing, limiting and structuring effects on
government,[7] to which, following the Human Rights Act 1998, Harlow

---

[6] C. Hood, H. Rothstein and R. Baldwin, *The Government of Risk: Understanding Risk
Regulation Regimes* (Oxford University Press, 2001), p. 23.
[7] D. Feldman, 'Judicial Review: A Way of Controlling Government?' (1988) 66 *Public
Administration* 21.

and Rawlings have added 'vindicating'.[8] This view of the role of judicial review is not by any means universally held, and certainly not in the United Kingdom where the superior courts have not traditionally had an 'apex' review role of this nature in spite of the increasingly constitutionalist approach to judicial review that has been developing over the past few decades in that jurisdiction.[9] If we understand the constitution as more than *merely* political and in fact as an *autonomously* limiting instrument, such a development is relatively undisturbing (if not, perhaps, welcome) and a comparison along these lines with the traditionally 'apex' US Supreme Court and increasingly 'apex' Canadian Supreme Court can be usefully constructed. Although not a universally held view of the function and legitimacy of judicial review, this is my starting point in this chapter.

I   The cases

The three cases that are considered here, from Canada, the United States and the United Kingdom, raise difficult questions for courts, which are asked to make orders protecting the rights of suspected terrorists held abroad; orders which, if granted, would have implications not only for claims of security imperatives but also for comity between states.

(a)   Khadr

Omar Khadr was fifteen when he was detained by the United States in Afghanistan after allegedly throwing a grenade that resulted in the death of a US soldier. Having been moved to Guantánamo Bay, Khadr was charged with war crimes in 2004. He was interrogated by agents of the Canadian Security Intelligence Service (in 2003) and the Foreign Intelligence Division of the Department of Foreign Affairs and International Trade (in 2003 and 2004). The transcripts of these interviews were shared with the United States, and the 2004 interview proceeded in spite of the fact that the Canadian personnel knew that Khadr had been subjected to sleep deprivation techniques for three weeks.

---

[8] C. Harlow and R. Rawlings, *Law and Administration* (3rd edn, Cambridge University Press, 2009), p. 728.

[9] M. Elliot, *The Constitutional Foundations of Judicial Review* (Portland, OR: Hart Publishing, 2001). See also Chapter 9 in this volume, R. Masterman, 'Rebalancing the unbalanced constitution: juridification and national security in the United Kingdom'.

Before this case, Khadr had already obtained orders from the Canadian courts prohibiting any further interviews by Canadian agents[10] and compelling the disclosure of interview transcripts to him,[11] in both of which cases a violation of section 7 of the Canadian Charter of Rights and Freedoms was found. In contrast, *Canada (Prime Minister)* v. *Khadr*[12] was decidedly 'external', with Khadr seeking an order compelling the government to make representations to the United States seeking his repatriation. This forced the Supreme Court of Canada to reconcile its own already established position that Khadr's Charter rights had been violated, with strong executive-based arguments for non-interference with the conduct of foreign affairs.

The Court reiterated its earlier view that Canadian agents' involvement in Khadr's detention breached Canada's international legal obligations and fundamental rights norms and, thus, this case fell into the exceptional situations when the Charter could be applied to extra-territorial activity.[13] The Court held that Canada's involvement contributed to the continuing deprivation of Khadr's liberty because of the use of information elicited through an interview by Canadian agents. Thus, an internal question was established and constructed: was there a breach of section 7 of the Charter? The Court found that there was a 'sufficient causal connection'[14] between Canada's activity and Khadr's detention to apply the Charter and find a breach of section 7.

Once a breach of section 7 was established as regards the internal question, the Court had to decide what remedy would be appropriate. Khadr sought a mandatory order requiring the Canadian government to make diplomatic representations to the United States for repatriation. Within Canadian constitutional jurisprudence it is well established that breaches of Charter rights must be answered with an appropriate and just order 'that meaningfully vindicates the rights and freedoms of the claimant'.[15] Furthermore, the remedy must 'employ means that are legitimate within the framework of our constitutional democracy'[16] and 'invoke[e] the functions and powers of a court'.[17] Although the exercise of foreign affairs powers in the context of making representations to another government was within the prerogative power of the executive, the Court

---

[10] *Khadr* v. *Canada* [2006] 2 FCR 505.   [11] *Canada (Justice)* v. Khadr [2008] 2 SCR 125.
[12] [2010] 1 SCR 44.   [13] Drawing on *R* v. *Hape* [2007] 2 SCR 292.
[14] *Suresh* v. *Canada (Minister for Citizenship and Immigration)* [2002] 1 SCR 3, para. 54.
[15] *Doucet-Boudreau* v. *Nova Scotia (Minister for Education)* [2003] 3 SCR 3, para. 55.
[16] *Ibid.* para. 56.   [17] *Ibid.* para. 57.

held that this did not exempt such exercise from constitutional scrutiny.[18] However, the strictness of that scrutiny and, in particular, the forcefulness of any remedy ordered in relation to the same, would (it quickly became clear) be limited by pragmatic concerns of institutional competence and comity. Thus, while the *possibility* of remedy was an internal question, the *nature* of the remedy was clearly impacted by the external question. Paragraph 37 of the judgment reads:

> The limited power of the courts to review exercises of the prerogative power for constitutionality reflects the fact that in a constitutional democracy, all government power must be exercised in accordance with the Constitution. This said, judicial review of the exercise of the prerogative power for constitutionality remains sensitive to the fact that the executive branch of government is responsible for decisions under this power, and that the executive is better placed to make such decisions within a range of constitutional options ... it is for the courts to determine the legal and constitutional limits within which such decisions are to be taken. It follows that in the case of refusal by a government to abide by constitutional constraints, courts are empowered to make orders ensuring that the government's foreign affairs prerogative is exercised in accordance with the constitution.

The Court went on to hold that where the applicant detainee is under the control of another state, sufficient weight must be given to the executive's foreign affairs role and the complex and ever-changing needs of the national interest. Taking all of this into account, and considering the fact that Khadr was detained by the United States, that a governmental representation requesting repatriation would not necessarily succeed, and that the Court was not fully appraised of the nature of the diplomatic exchanges between the two governments in this case, no such mandatory order would be granted. Instead, the Court found that declaratory relief (by means of declaring the breach of Khadr's Charter rights) was the appropriate remedy.[19]

(b) Munaf

Munaf concerned the detention of two American citizens by the Multinational Force-Iraq (MNF-I) in Iraq. Shaqi Omar was a US/Jordanian citizen detained in 2004 and suspected of granting aid to Abu al-Zarqawi while he was the head of Al-Qaeda in Iraq. Omar was given a military

---

[18] [2010] 1 SCR 44, para. 36.   [19] [2010] 1 SCR 44, para. 47.

tribunal, deemed a 'security internee' and 'enemy combatant' and referred to the Central Criminal Court for Iraq for investigation. He remained in the custody of the MNF-I at Camp Cropper (a camp under the full operational control of the US military) as at an earlier stage he had succeeded in securing an order prohibiting his transfer to Iraqi custody, his handover to Iraq for investigation or prosecution, and the sharing of any information relating to his release with the Iraqi government. Mohammed Munaf was a US/Iraqi citizen who had gone to Iraq as a translator for some Romanian journalists. Those journalists were subsequently kidnapped by Al-Qaeda, as was Munaf, and upon their release Munaf was arrested by the MNF-I on suspicion of having orchestrated the kidnap. As with Omar, Munaf was given a military tribunal and deemed a 'security internee'. His case was also referred to the Central Criminal Court for Iraq where he was prosecuted and convicted for kidnapping. During his trial Munaf confessed in writing and on camera to having orchestrated the kidnap but this confession was recanted while the trial was still in process. Munaf was convicted of kidnapping, but his conviction was vacated by the Iraqi Court of Cassation, which remanded him in custody for further investigation. Munaf was also detained by the MNF-I in Camp Cropper and had failed in his attempt to secure an injunction against transfer or release on the basis of a lack of jurisdiction.

The US Supreme Court consolidated the two cases, both of which raised two significant issues: (1) whether the Court had jurisdiction to hear *habeas* petitions from the detainees; and (2) whether the Court could order the United States not to transfer the petitioners into Iraqi custody or allow them to be tried by Iraqi courts by means of the preliminary (or interlocutory) injunction sought.[20] These questions are clearly capable of being broken down into internal and external matters, the internal question being as to jurisdiction and the external question being as to the order sought.

As to jurisdiction, the Supreme Court held that it was an American unit (Task Force 134) that oversaw all detention operations and facilities in question, including Camp Cropper, and that in fact the unit was under the command of the United States and answered *only* to a US chain of command. That was sufficient to satisfy the statutory jurisdiction requirement of being detained 'under or by colour of the authority of the United States'[21] but even if this was not compelling on its own,

---

[20] *Munaf* v. *Geren*, 553 US 674 (2008).   [21] 28 USC s. 2241.

citizenship was sufficient to establish the jurisdictional link.[22] This reasoning suggests that the Supreme Court considered the jurisdictional question to be an internal one: a question about the relationship between the United States and a US detainee (who happened to be a citizen).

In contrast, Roberts CJ writing for a unanimous Court, placed the question of relief clearly within the realm of the 'external'. It was, he held, a question of 'whether United States district courts may exercise their *habeas* jurisdiction to enjoin our Armed Forces from transferring individuals detained within another sovereign territory to that sovereign's government for criminal prosecution'. With that sentence defining the issue at hand, the Court essentially stepped away from its internal construction of the jurisdiction question and reconstructed the case in an external manner, holding that when it came to remedy it must take into account the fact that this was 'inevitably entangled in the conduct of our international relations'.[23]

The petitioners had sought orders prohibiting both transfer *to* Iraq and release *in* Iraq itself, reliefs that the Court held 'would interfere with Iraq's sovereign right to punish offenses against its laws committed within its borders'. Given the equitable nature of *habeas* relief, the Court would proceed along what it considered to be the prudent course and, taking into account what was considered to be the extraordinary nature of the relief sought, prudence dictated that no relief be granted. Roberts CJ correctly held that 'At the end of the day, what petitioners are really after is a court order requiring the United States to shelter them from the sovereign government seeking to have them answer for alleged crimes committed within that sovereign's borders'.[24] The Court held that any order that would, in essence, 'compel ... the United States to harbour fugitives from the criminal justice system of a sovereign with undoubted authority to prosecute them'[25] could not be granted. The Court simply would not countenance any such order, especially since 'Omar and Munaf are being held by the United States Armed Forces at the behest of the Iraqi Government pending their prosecution in Iraqi courts'.

The petitioners were, thus, simultaneously held 'under the color' of the United States (to establish jurisdiction, the internal construction of the case) *and* by proxy for the Iraqi government (to refuse relief, the external construction of the case). Indeed, so strongly did the Court construct the

---

[22] *Johnson* v. *Eisentrager*, 339 US 763 (1950); *Rasul* v. *Bush*, 542 US 466 (2004).
[23] Citing *Romero* v. *International Terminal Operating Company*, 358 US 354, 383 (1959).
[24] *Munaf* v. *Geren*, 553 US 674 (2008), at 16.   [25] *Ibid.* 19.

external element of the case as one in which the Iraqi government was
implicated that it concluded that 'Any requirement that the MNF-I
release a detainee would, in effect, impose a release order on the Iraqi
government'.[26] Concerns about comity, foreign relations and the need
not to interfere with executive conduct of the same were equally clear in
the Court's response to the petitioners' claim that their risk of being
subjected to torture in Iraqi custody trumped any considerations already
expressed in relation to granting the order sought. Questions about the
likelihood or otherwise of torture were, the Court held, 'a matter of
serious concern' but 'to be addressed by the political branches, not the
judiciary'.[27] This is once again because of the Court's concern with
treading on executive toes in relation to foreign and diplomatic relations.
For courts to make such determinations would 'require federal courts to
pass judgements on foreign justice systems and undermine the Government's ability to speak with one voice in this area'.[28]

(c)   Rahmatullah

Although *Rahmatullah*[29] concerns a British subject, rather than a UK
citizen,[30] the case raises interesting and analogous issues to those arising
in *Khadr* and *Munaf* and is a further example of the internal/external
approach outlined above. In this case issues that were external at first
blush were reconstructed as internal, by means of which reconstruction a

---

[26] *Ibid*. 21.   [27] *Ibid*. 23.

[28] *Ibid*. 25. Contrast this with the approach of the ECtHR in *Othman*, for example, [2012]
ECHR 56. See also Chapter 13 in this volume, H. Fenwick, 'Post 9/11 UK counter-
terrorism cases in the European Court of Human Rights: a "dialogic" approach to rights
protection or appeasement of national authorities?'.

[29] *Rahmatullah* v. *Secretary of State for Foreign and Commonwealth Affairs and another*
[2011] EWCA Civ 1540; *Rahmatullah* v. *Secretary of State for Foreign and Commonwealth Affairs and others* [2012] EWCA Civ 182.

[30] Colin Murray has argued that subjects have extensive diplomatic rights under the
doctrine of allegiance that are in at least some ways analogous to those of citizens:
C. Murray, 'In the Shadow of Lord Haw Haw: Guantánamo Bay, Diplomatic Protection
and Allegiance' (2011) *Public Law* 115. While Christopher Trans accepts that British
residents abroad may have a duty of allegiance to the Crown, he questions the extent to
which this can be distilled into a duty of protection towards said residents when abroad:
C. Trans, 'Revisiting Allegiance and Diplomatic Protection' (2012) *Public Law* 197. For
present purposes, however, it is enough to say that there is sufficient agreement to place
Rahmatullah within the taxonomy being used in this chapter in order to illustrate the
way in which domestic courts might deal with the difficult questions arising in such
situations.

relatively muscular approach was taken by the Court of Appeal. Rahmatullah was a Pakistani citizen who was captured by UK forces in Iraq in 2004 and subsequently handed over to US forces, which detained him in Bagram near Kabul, Afghanistan. He has remained there since June 2004, notwithstanding a Detainee Review Board[31] finding in June 2010 that his continued detention was unnecessary and that he should be released to Pakistan.

At the time that Rahmatullah was handed over to the United States, a Memorandum of Understanding (MOU) between the two countries and Australia was in effect. This MOU[32] provided, *inter alia*, that it would be implemented in compliance with the Geneva Conventions and customary international law (clause 1); that any detainees would be returned to the original transferring power 'without delay upon request' (clause 4); that release or transfer of a detainee outside of Iraq would take place only pursuant to mutual agreement between the relevant powers (clause 5); that the transferring power had full right of access to detainees while they are in the custody of another of the signing parties (clause 6); and that all detainees would be treated as prisoners of war in advance of a determination under Articles 4 and 5 of the Third Geneva Convention (clause 9). A second MOU was agreed in October 2008 (and signed by the United Kingdom in March 2009), which provided that all detainees transferred by one power to another would be treated 'in accordance with applicable principles of international law, including humanitarian law' while in the custody of the United States (paragraph 4).[33] Although not legally binding, these memoranda were clearly intended to govern the treatment of detainees captured in Iraq and to commit the parties to compliance with relevant international legal standards. Rahmatullah claimed that his continued detention was a violation of the Geneva Conventions and that the United Kingdom either enjoyed a sufficient level of control over him to secure his release or that there was at least a doubt about whether such

---

[31] As it stands, those detained in Bagram Airbase are said not to have any right (constitutional or otherwise) to *habeas corpus* review. Instead, the appropriateness of continued detention is now determined by Detainee Review Boards made up primarily of military personnel. For more on the operation of DRBs in Bagram at the material time, see J. A. Bovarnick, 'Detainee Review Boards in Afghanistan: From Strategic Liability to Legitimacy' (2010) *Army Lawyer* 9.

[32] An Arrangement for the Transfer of Prisoners of War, Civilian Internees, and Civilian Detainees between the Forces of the United States, the United Kingdom and Australia, 23 March 2003; see discussion in *Rahmatullah* v. *Secretary of State for Foreign and Commonwealth Affairs and another* [2011] EWCA Civ 1540, paras. 3–6.

[33] See discussion *ibid.* paras. 7–8.

control lay with the United Kingdom.[34] As a result, *habeas corpus* was sought either in the normal way *or* in order to allow for the question of control to be determined. In response, it was argued that the United Kingdom did not exercise sufficient control for the writ to issue and that, furthermore, issuance of the writ would require the UK government to make a request of the United States which would involve the court in foreign relations.

This case was a complex one, concerning as it did three areas of real sensitivity: the conduct of hostilities, the interpretation and legal effect of MOUs, and bilateral foreign relations. The net question in legal terms was one of control: was the applicant under the control of the United Kingdom to allow the writ to issue or was there sufficient doubt as to that question to justify the issuance of the writ? Although this appears to be an essentially internal question, its handling of this case required the Court of Appeal to pay significant attention to whether or not the United States was in breach of its international legal obligations, a consideration with more than a hint of externality about it. The Court's treatment of this question ultimately fed into the decision as to whether or not a writ of *habeas corpus* ought to issue; it also centrally concerned Article 45 of the Fourth Geneva Convention, which includes the following provision:

> If protected persons are transferred under such circumstances, responsibility for the application of the present Convention rests on the Power accepting them, while they are in its custody. Nevertheless, if that Power fails to carry out the provisions of the present Convention in any important respect, the Power by which the protected persons were transferred shall, upon being so notified by the Protecting Power, take effective measures to correct the situation or shall request the return of the protected persons. Such request must be complied with.

Based on Article 45, together with the MOUs and the fact that Rahmatullah's continued detention had been deemed unnecessary by the Detainee Review Board, the Court of Appeal held that 'the UK Government is, again at least strongly arguably . . . entitled either to demand his release or to demand his return to UK custody under Article 45'.[35] If the

---

[34] The writ can issue where there is some doubt about whether a person is under the control of the respondent and the issuance of the writ would allow for the situation to be clarified: *Barnardo v. Ford* [1892] AC 326; *R v. Secretary of State for Home Affairs, ex parte O'Brien* [1923] 2 KB 361.

[35] *Rahmatullah v. Secretary of State for Foreign and Commonwealth Affairs and another* [2011] EWCA Civ 1540, para. 34.

failure to release Rahmatullah was a breach of the Geneva Conventions, the nexus between him and the United Kingdom would be reactivated and failure to act under Article 45 potentially engaged section 1 of the Geneva Conventions Act 1957. According to the Court of Appeal, this possibility resulted in sufficient uncertainty as to the United Kingdom's control over the applicant to justify issuing a writ of *habeas corpus*.

Here, the internal question was a complex one that involved matters of international law and may have required an oblique finding of a violation of international obligations by another state (making it quasi-external), but the Court of Appeal ensured that it remained a fundamentally internal question in relation to which at least some muscularity could be displayed. Once this question had been dealt with, there was still the possibility that the writ would not issue, especially as the argument against issuance was essentially that any request to the United States would be futile and that an order of *habeas corpus* would involve the court in the 'forbidden' area of foreign relations. The Court held that it was by no means certain that the United States would refuse to hand the applicant over and this, combined with the nature of *habeas corpus* within the British Constitution, pointed strongly in the direction of issuing the writ. The Court held that the argument as to foreign relations did not hold water, primarily because the argument was not made out in any real detail by the Secretaries of State. However, the Master of the Rolls also noted (albeit *obiter*) that the writ of *habeas corpus* can issue even where it might impede diplomatic relations,[36] and Kay LJ reiterated that the forbidden area continues to exist.[37] Accordingly, the writ of *habeas corpus* issued.

Rahmatullah, which could so easily have been unsuccessful if construed solely as an external case, was instead constructed as an internal case, concerned with the United Kingdom's control and capacity based on the MOUs and the Geneva Conventions. The Court of Appeal studiously maintained the notion that muscularity would not be appropriate in truly external cases, but neatly ensured that this case simply did not fall into that limited field. If it had done, then it seems clear to me that the applicant would not have succeeded.[38]

---

[36] *Ibid.* paras. 47–50.   [37] *Ibid.* para. 56.

[38] Here lies the apparent distinction from *R (on the application of Abbasi)* v. *Secretary of State for Foreign and Commonwealth Affairs* [2002] All ER (D) 70 and *R (on the application of Al-Rawi)* v. *Secretary of State for Foreign and Commonwealth Affairs* [2008] QB 289.

Rahmatullah also, however, serves as a cautionary tale, for the after-math of the original decision demonstrates how limited domestic courts can be in handing down remedies in these cases, even where an internal question *is* constructed. The US government refused to hand Rahmatullah over in pursuance of the *habeas corpus* order[39] and there were no means, within the handover protocols between the United Kingdom and the United States, through which the UK government could compel the United States to do so. Following up on the issuance of the writ in February 2012, the Court of Appeal acknowledged that their writ could not secure Mr Rahmatullah's appearance before the Court but nevertheless rejected any suggestion that it had been futile to issue it in the first place.[40] Addressing this point, Neuberger MR (as he then was) held:

> That does not mean that the issue of the writ of *habeas corpus* was a pointless exercise in this case: it performed its minimum function of requiring the UK Government to account for its responsibility for the applicant's detention, and to attempt to get him released.[41]

On appeal in the UK Supreme Court, the decision to issue the writ was upheld and the implications that the United States was acting in violation of the Geneva Conventions reiterated.[42] In the Supreme Court the government placed somewhat more weight on the claims that the issuance of the writ was inappropriate on foreign affairs grounds, and in addressing this argument Kerr LJ resolutely reiterated the prior characterisation of the *habeas* question as an internal one. He absolutely rejected any contention that issuing the writ constituted an impermissible interference with foreign affairs, holding:

> [T]he Court of Appeal's decision does not amount to an 'instruction' to the Government to demand Mr Rahmatullah's return. Its judgment merely reflects the court's conclusion that there were sufficient grounds for believing that the UK Government had the means of obtaining control over the custody of Mr Rahmatullah ... It might well prove that the only means of establishing whether in fact it could obtain control was for the Government to ask for his return but that remained a matter for the ministers concerned.[43]

---

[39] *Rahmatullah v. Secretary of State for Foreign and Commonwealth Affairs and others* [2012] EWCA Civ 182.

[40] *Ibid.*   [41] *Ibid.* para. 17.

[42] *Secretary of State for Foreign and Commonwealth Affairs v. Rahmatullah* [2012] UKSC 48.

[43] *Ibid.* para. 60.

The decision in *Rahmatullah*, and particularly Neuberger LJ's comments recalled above, lead us neatly to the core question that arises in all three of these cases: what is the point in a court taking an internally muscular and externally deferential approach in these cases? If, in the end, no (effective) order mandating a particular activity or course of action can be handed down, is this internal muscularity not simply a futile exercise leaving an unregulated and unlimited power in the context of foreign affairs, even where fundamental matters of individual liberty are at issue? The answer, I contend, depends on how one reads these cases.

II Judicial Technique of Internal/External Construction

Cases of this kind raise distinct and problematic issues as the applicants involved seem to ask courts to tread into the 'forbidden area' of foreign affairs[44] to issue orders that, while directly addressed to their own governments, could be interpreted as being effectively addressed to the governments of a third state and have clear implications for foreign and diplomatic relations. At the same time, there is a legitimate concern with ensuring that 'citizens' (a term I use very broadly here in a sociological rather than a legal sense) are not left at the mercy of foreign powers, particularly when there is good reason to believe that they are or will be treated in a manner that would not be considered acceptable should the treatment in question be meted out by the respondent state. Courts, then, find themselves in something of a quandary, which *Khadr, Munaf* and *Rahmatullah* suggest they can resolve by constructing the case as being divisible into internal and external questions.

On the one hand, the conventional division of competence between the judicial and executive branch militates against intervention, while on the other the concern with citizen welfare suggests that something ought to be done. The weight of the first concern should not be underestimated. Indeed, it is so weighty as to be capable of overriding legal bonds of citizenship as a basis for intervention; the cases above show that *mere* citizenship was not enough to justify judicial supervision. Something more was required, such as the involvement of Canadian agents in *Khadr*. Once such a nexus can be established, the 'internal question' presents itself for consideration and courts adjudicate on it in the normal

---

[44] *R (on the application of Abbasi)* v. *Secretary of State for Foreign and Commonwealth Affairs* [2002] All ER (D) 70, para. 106(iii); *R (on the application of Al-Rawi)* v. *Secretary of State for Foreign and Commonwealth Affairs* [2008] QB 289, paras. 131, 134.

way, notwithstanding the 'emergency', 'war' or 'crisis' setting in which the question has arisen.

Once a sufficient link between the detainee and the respondent state has been identified, a second difficulty may arise. While these cases suggest that courts are willing to be relatively non-deferential towards the executive in terms of 'internal' questions,[45] 'external' questions belong to a greater degree to the 'pure' executive realm of foreign affairs into which courts are understandably reluctant to wander. In this context, the questions of comity and executive competence that arise are exacerbated by the counter-terrorism context. The 'external' question concerns the relationship between the state and the detainee as it relates to the state's relationship with another state and tends to implicate considerations as to remedy and, in particular, the extent to which courts can (or, perhaps more accurately, *will*) hand down orders that prescribe a certain kind of inter-state engagement. Here, the cases above suggest that there is what seems to be a self-imposed limitation on judicial muscularity whereby courts are unwilling to grant such orders or, at least, to acknowledge that the orders they might grant (which are ostensibly relevant to the 'internal' question only) have implications for foreign relations.

In some respects at least, this self-imposed limitation is linked to considerations of judicial competence, implications for comity, and an appreciation of the nature of inter-state diplomacy as a cautious and sensitive enterprise and one in which mandatory orders may do more harm than good. That said, for those who consider the judicial role to be one of maintaining constitutionalist principles, apparent self-imposed limitations are worrying; if there really is a 'forbidden area' into which the courts will not tread by means of judicial review, can judicial review truly be said to be a constitutionalist exercise? In my view, the cases of *Khadr*, *Munaf* and *Rahmatullah* suggest that it can be, because the forbidden area is not left entirely unregulated by domestic courts. Rather, the construction of the case as having both an internal and an external element means that legitimate judicial intervention can take place in relation to the internal question that has implications for the external question, even while the optical illusion that the court has not wandered into foreign affairs persists. In this way, domestic courts seem to maintain an appropriate degree of institutional respect for genuine concerns

---

[45] Of course, even in these cases some deference may be shown, as Chan illustrates in her Chapter 10, C. Chan, 'Business as usual: deference in counter-terrorism rights review'.

of comity and competence when it comes to foreign affairs, while simultaneously creating conditions where interactions with third countries may be influenced by constitutionalist concerns and principles enforced by the courts, i.e., engaging in regulatory constitutionalism.

III   Regulatory constitutionalism and the apparent self-imposed limitation on judicial muscularity

There are two – not necessarily conflicting – ways of interpreting the pattern identified in these three cases. The first is to read them as a 'constitutionalist optimist', seeing within them considerable muscularity and a resistance to the suggestion that context (i.e., terrorism and conflict) or actor (i.e., executive) ought necessarily to usher in deference by the courts, especially when core constitutionalist principles are at issue. On the other hand, a 'constitutionalist pessimist' might see them as perpetuating an essentially unreviewable area of executive power. The latter reading raises important questions of legitimacy. For those, like me, who consider counter-terrorism judicial review to be (ideally) an exercise in regulatory constitutionalism, such an approach raises the question of whether it is legitimate for the courts to be muscular, on the one hand, but to cultivate a fertile ground of potential abuse, on the other. It causes one to ask whether the maintenance of the 'forbidden area' severely undermines the existence of the reviewed area, and makes rights protection essentially contingent on circumstances beyond the control of the individual whose rights are jeopardised. These questions are important ones. They give rise to the possibility that in appearing to be 'muscular', courts are in fact flexing just enough muscle to appear relevant or maintain their own role, while leaving sufficient space for governments to do as they wish *provided* they do it in the right conceptual or geographical space.[46] If, indeed, that were the case it would undermine the constitutionalist nature of the muscularity witnessed in the 'internal' questions. I argue, however, that in fact the maintenance and acknowledgement of the forbidden area in respect of external questions *together with* the identification and muscular adjudication of internal questions may be mutually reconcilable and appropriate judicial approaches demonstrating a commitment to regulatory constitutionalism.

---

[46] This echoes concerns raised by Lobel in Chapter 4 in this volume, J. Lobel, 'The rhetoric and reality of judicial review of counter-terrorism actions: the United States experience'.

This requires us to acknowledge that even while not adjudicating on the external question, courts can and do make 'soft findings' that have an important regulatory impact on government action.[47] In *Khadr*,[48] the Canadian Supreme Court found that the conditions of Khadr's detention and interrogation were such as to violate the Charter, thus making a clear (and pejorative) finding with political, even if not legal, consequences, about the United States. Similarly, in *Rahmatullah*[49] the superior courts effectively found that the United States was acting in violation of the Geneva Conventions by holding Rahmatullah in Bagram after his eligibility for release had been determined. Although no such conclusion can be clearly drawn from *Munaf* (apart from a suggestion that the conditions of trial in Iraq might not be equal to the due process guarantees under the US Constitution),[50] both *Khadr* and *Rahmatullah* suggest the potential for some obtuse conclusions to be reached about the external actors or actions under consideration, even when no order can be made in relation to the same. This can in turn have an important impact on government action in relation to the litigant and the particular case in question *provided* it receives political attention.[51] Through publicisation, the non-binding nature of these elements of the decision may be mitigated by infusion with regulatory capacity. In other words, it is conceivable that even though these findings may not have been 'hardened' into remedies or court orders, they might acquire sufficient political and popular currency to direct government action, thus obliquely regulating government behaviour.

The possibility that this would happen is outside of courts' control, but is not precluded by doctrinal respect for the notion of a forbidden area. The importance of this kind of impact is clearest when one analyses judicial effectiveness through the prism of regulatory constitutionalism proposed above. Seen thus, judicial review is one part of a broader cultural commitment to the rule of law and accountability that includes legal, political, popular, external and internal elements. In this context,

---

[47] See C. Murray, 'The Ripple Effect: Guantánamo Bay in the United Kingdom's Courts' (2010) *Pace International Law Review (OC)* 15.

[48] *Canada (Prime Minister) v. Khadr* [2010] 1 SCR 44.

[49] *Rahmatullah v. Secretary of State for Foreign and Commonwealth Affairs and another* [2011] EWCA Civ 1540.

[50] *Munaf v. Geren*, 553 US 674 (2008).

[51] On the importance of popular pressure to follow through on judicial decisions see Chapter 4 in this volume, J. Lobel, 'The rhetoric and reality of judicial review of counter-terrorism actions: the United States experience'.

judicial decisions that appear to carry inappropriate or inadequate remedies (or, indeed, no traditional remedy at all) might still play an important role by catalysing a broader constitutionalist demand for accountability with the potential to make clear the standards expected of government from a normative perspective and to bring about changes in behaviour accordingly. Viewed thus, they seem less disappointing to the constitutionalist.

The second factor suggesting that maintaining the 'forbidden area' in respect of external questions while identifying and displaying muscularity in relation to internal questions are mutually reconcilable and appropriate judicial approaches is that the principles laid down and enforced through the muscular handling of the internal question may 'leak' into external affairs and have knock-on constitutionalist effects in a typically regulatory fashion. Such effects might, of course, be either negative or positive; both formal and informal responses to judicial review are possible and, indeed, negative reactions (such as ouster clauses or the effective limitation of the availability of judicial review)[52] are a distinct possibility that I do not mean here to discount. It is important to recall that in handing down a decision in any case of judicial review, courts can be sure only of what they themselves will do; the reaction of the other branches of government is beyond their direct control, however, where there is a clear culture of respect for decisions of the courts we can be relatively sure that even decisions unfavourable to the government will not simply be ignored. Negative reactions to judicial review may not be the ideal reaction when seen from the perspective of the 'outcome' narrowly construed, but they too reflect the nature of judicial review as regulatory constitutionalism bringing about changed behaviours. The most worrying outcome from a constitutionalist perspective would be for the state to simply ignore a decision of a court, undermining the delicate arrangement whereby political branches give effect to the decisions of the 'weakest' branch of government.

Taking that into account, we can explore further some of the positive reactions that decisions such as *Munaf*, *Khadr* and *Rahmatullah* might help to bring about. The first is that the respondent government might modify its interactions with other states using the finding as a basis. One can easily imagine that in a subsequent interaction relating to the

---

[52] Arguably the reaction to Guantánamo Bay litigation, where Congress attempted to expressly strip jurisdiction from the courts, reflects such a negative reaction. See F. de Londras, 'Guantánamo Bay: Towards Legality?' (2008) 71 *Modern Law Review* 36.

handing of a British subject over to the United States in Iraq or Afghanistan, for example, the UK authorities might stress to the US authorities the importance of ensuring compliance with the Geneva Conventions and having in place an *effective* mechanism of recovering the individual if required based on wanting to avoid a repeat of the criticism levied in *Rahmatullah*. Indeed, the United Kingdom might even become more reluctant to hand detainees over in such circumstances at all. In this way the fact that the findings relating to the external question did not 'harden' into mandatory orders does not necessarily mean that there is no impact on the external actor (the detaining state) in this and similar cases. Of course, there is no guarantee that this actually will happen; political considerations such as relative geopolitical power positions, desirability of outcome, government priorities and perceived necessity are likely to impact on the extent to which such a direct 'leak' into external relations would take place. However, the possibility of such leakage reminds us that even if an area is formally 'forbidden' to the courts in terms of adjudication, their findings can impact on it in terms of action.

Furthermore, findings as to the external question might impact on external relations as a result of their reflexive capacity. Reflexivity here represents a middle-way between detailed, 'command and control' regulation and absolute deregulation (at least in public regulatory terms).[53] Reflexive regulation (sometimes also termed 'reflexive law' or 'reflexive governance') is concerned with stimulating self-regulation in a manner that ensures that social policies are fulfilled.[54] While usually applied to industry sectors,[55] the concept of reflexive regulation also has potential in an area such as foreign affairs (especially in wartime) when too strong a judicial hand is considered institutionally inappropriate. Reflexive governance is essentially governance by design, whereby certain institutions

---

[53] For a meditation on regulation generally, including reflexive regulation's place within the field, see e.g., S. Picciotto, 'Introduction: Reconceptualizing Regulation in the Era of Globalization' (2002) 29 *Journal of Law and Society* 1.

[54] See generally, M. Aalders and T. Wilthagen, 'Moving Beyond Command-and-Control: Reflexivity in the Regulation of Occupational Safety and Health and the Environment' (1997) 19 *Law and Policy* 415, and E. Brousseau, T. Dedeurwaerdere and B. Siebenhuner (eds.), *Reflexive Governance for Public Goods* (Boston: MIT Press, 2012).

[55] See e.g., E. W. Orts, 'A Reflexive Model of Environmental Regulation' (1995) 5 *Business Ethics Quarterly* 779; R. Rogowski and T. Wilthagen, *Reflexive Labour Law: Studies in Industrial Relations and Employment Regulation* (Vienna: Springer, 1994); C. Scott, 'Reflexive Governance, Meta-Regulation and Corporate Social Responsibility: the "Heineken Effect"' in N. Boeger, R. Murray and C. Villiers, *Perspectives on Corporate Social Responsibility* (Cheltenham: Edward Elgar, 2008).

allow for the marrying of legal principles with the structural contexts in which they are to be applied. In the context of external relations, we might say that the bridging institution here would be the public service within the relevant government department (most likely departments or ministries of defence and foreign relations), possibly including the diplomatic service and the military.

The impact of judicial review on public servants and institutions has been well studied. Sunkin, Calvo and Platt have found that judicial review has significant impact in the local authority context, not least because of the bedded down public service ethos to be found there. In this respect they found that a mere challenge (whether successful or not) can have some (limited) impact on the quality of local authority services. Furthermore, if a challenge reaches the level of a judgment of a court there is a clear impact on the respondent particularly, but not exclusively, where the court finds against the local authority. Thirdly, a decision against local authority A can have an impact on the behaviour of local authority B which can now be clear on what is required of it and modify its behaviour to act accordingly partly to avoid being subjected to judicial review itself, and partly because of an ethos that compliance with the law is simply what public authorities ought to do.[56] Even taking into account the differences between local and national authorities, an understanding of judicial review as an exercise of regulatory constitutionalism shows that it at least has the potential for similar impacts at national level. Added to this we ought to take into account the growth of 'accountability culture' in public authorities and its capacity to influence the extent to which challenges, whether successful in remedies terms or not, may impact on individual public servant behaviour and contribute to broader behavioural change when understood in a reflexive manner.[57] Furthermore, the statutory obligation now placed on public authorities in some jurisdictions, including the United Kingdom,[58] to undertake their activities in a manner compliant with the state's obligations under the European Convention on Human Rights, may further catalyse reflexive responsiveness even to 'soft' and oblique findings relating to the treatment

---

[56] See, L. Platt, M. Sunkin and K. Calvo, 'Judicial Review Litigation as an Incentive to Change in Local Authority Public Services in England and Wales' (2010) 20 *Journal of Public Administration Research and Theory* 243.

[57] B. Romzek, 'Dynamics of Public Sector Accountability in an Era of Reform' (2000) 66 *International Review of Administrative Sciences* 21.

[58] Human Rights Act 1998, s. 6. An analogous responsibility lies on 'organs of the state' in Ireland as a result of European Convention on Human Rights Act 2003, s. 3.

of citizens or subjects held by another state but with sufficient nexus to the respondent state. If we assume (and it may, to be fair, be an assumption too far in some cases of extremity) that compliance with international law, respect for human rights and the maintenance of good diplomatic relations are all social policies to which the state is committed, and that the relevant elements of the public service are already acculturated to taking judicial pronouncements on board and cognisant of the potential fall-out from further 'external' findings that obliquely criticise strategic partners, as well as identifying possible complicity in violations of international law, it is not unreasonable to expect that such pronouncements may have a reflexive impact in the design and implementation (at departmental and government level) of approaches to particular, 'high-risk' inter-state engagement concerning citizens (or subjects) detained abroad.

Conclusion

It is no doubt frustrating for litigants, their families, scholars and commentators when courts hand down decisions that appear to find wrongdoing while 'doing nothing' about it. There are plentiful examples of scholars arguing that courts being relatively non-deferential while the litigants continue to linger in detention is a sheer exposition of the futility of the language and principles of human rights as a matter of law, or illustrates something akin to duplicity or connivance.[59] These critiques of course have their merits, especially when applied to the cases of individuals whose names and stories have become synonymous with great constitutionalist 'victories' but who remain in deplorable conditions of liberty deprivation. However, when it comes to citizens (or subjects) detained abroad real questions of legitimate limitations on judicial muscularity arise that exacerbate the usual challenges of judicial review in situations of emergency or crisis. Not only does a court have to think about whether it is appropriate to intervene in what the government is directly engaged in, but it must also take into consideration a wide range of broader considerations about comity, institutional capacities and diplomatic relations. Doing this does not undermine judicial review when it is seen as an exercise of regulatory constitutionalism in

---

[59] The strongest critique perhaps comes from Keith Ewing. K. Ewing, 'The Futility of the Human Rights Act' (2004) *Public Law* 829; K. Ewing, *Bonfire of the Liberties: New Labour, Human Rights and the Rule of Law* (Oxford University Press, 2010).

a context where judicial pronouncements have both an autonomous and a contextual force.

A court could quite conceivably apply the kinds of weighty considerations that arise in cases of this kind in order to avoid meaningful adjudication. Less likely, but nevertheless conceivable, is a court disregarding these considerations in order to take a stringent approach to assessing the foreign affairs elements of such cases. Realistically speaking, neither of these approaches would be particularly wise. In both cases, the individual in question would most likely find himself precisely where he always was and some fundamental relationship (either between the judiciary and the executive, or between the respondent and the detaining state) would be seriously wounded. The three cases considered here suggest that courts are, in fact, finding a middle ground between these two extreme situations. By carving the issues up into 'internal' and 'external' questions the courts have identified a space of muscularity and a space of self-restraint, but the self-restraint need not equate to abandonment by the courts when the regulatory capacity of the external findings is taken into account. This may not be ideal, and it may not secure the liberty or the welfare of the detainee, but it at least reinforces core constitutional principles and holds some potential to influence states' behaviour in such cases. Whether one is a judicial review sceptic or enthusiast, it is difficult to imagine what more a domestic court could do.

2

Counter-terrorism judicial review by a traditionally weak judiciary

JENS ELO RYTTER

Introduction

According to Danish constitutional tradition,[1] courts can only exercise judicial review with extensive self-restraint.[2] Could a judiciary informed by such a tradition be expected to perform any effective judicial review at all in a field as high-staked and politically sensitive as counter-terrorism? This question has practical relevance. Post the 11 September 2001 ('9/11') attacks, apart from taking active part in international efforts to combat terrorism, including by engaging in military operations in Afghanistan since 2001, Denmark has adopted a vast body of legislation designed to prevent and counter acts of terrorism, a large part of which was adopted to fulfil United Nations (UN) and European Union (EU) obligations. The new legislation increases the powers of the state *vis-à-vis* the individual. Among others, it criminalises acts of terrorism and acts in support of terrorism, including the financing of terrorism; strengthens the powers of the police and the intelligence service to prevent and combat terrorism, notably in the field of surveillance and investigation; increases the access to expel or control aliens – and to extradite individuals – believed to be engaged in terrorism; and obliges private operators to register information relating to telecommunication and airplane passengers.[3] This chapter highlights important instances of counter-terrorism judicial review in recent Danish case law. The material, although inconclusive,

---

[1] See for a general overview in English, L. A. Rehof, 'The Danes, their Constitution and the International Community' in B. Dahl, T. Melchior, L. A. Rehof and D. Tamm (eds.), *Danish Law in a European Perspective* (2nd edn, Copenhagen: Forlaget Thomson, 2002), pp. 61–97.

[2] See for further reference, J. E. Rytter and M. Wind, 'In Need of Juristocracy? The Silence of Demark in the Development of European Legal Norms' (2011) 9(2) *International Journal of Constitutional Law* 470, 475.

[3] Notably by two major 'counter-terrorism packages' adopted in 2002 (Act no. 378 of 6 June 2002) and 2006 (Act no. 542 of 8 June 2006), respectively.

suggests that the review by Danish courts is tailored to take into account the strong political interest in preserving the secrecy of counter-terrorism intelligence work and ensuring the efficiency of counter-terrorism efforts, yet sufficiently firm to protect fundamental human rights and rule of law principles. It is argued that recent counter-terrorism judicial review confirms the general picture of a Danish tradition of judicial deference that has in recent decades been modified by a more activist European trend. This is not a strictly Danish phenomenon; taking part in what gradually developed into a powerful pan-European machinery for the protection of human rights has had a similar effect on other national legal systems that were by constitutional tradition sceptical towards judicial review, leading to a transformation of constitutional principles in those states which Frowein terms 'revolutionary'.[4] It is also noted that the legal basis for the more active approach of the Danish courts in recent years has predominantly been the European Convention for Human Rights (ECHR), rather than 'homegrown' constitutional rights and principles, the Danish Constitution being old and in many respects outdated as regards human rights.

I   Background: role of the judiciary in Danish constitutional tradition

In Denmark, the tradition of judicial self-restraint has been strong. The Danish Constitution from 1849 does not explicitly provide for judicial review of legislation, as a result of strong disagreement among the founding fathers on the subject.[5] Thus, as in the United States,[6] a right of judicial review has been established by the case law of the Danish Supreme Court. The Supreme Court first asserted the power of judicial review under Danish constitutional law in a string of decisions from 1920 and 1921, all concerning the compatibility with the constitutional right to private property of legislation enacted to reform the feudal ownership

---

[4] See J. A. Frowein, 'The Transformation of Constitutional Law through the European Convention on Human Rights' (2008) 41(3) *Israel Law Review* 489, 491. See also, D. J. Harris, M. O'Boyle, E. P. Bates and C. M. Buckley, *Harris, O'Boyle and Warbrick: Law of the European Convention on Human Rights* (2nd edn, Oxford University Press, 2009), p. 31.

[5] For a detailed account see P. Andersen, 'Rigsdagen og domstolene' in *Den Danske Rigsdag 1849–1949* (Copenhagen: J. H. Schultz Forlag, 1953), vol. V, p. 477 *et seq.*

[6] Cf. Chief Justice Marshall's famous opinion in *Marbury* v. *Madison*, 5 US 1 Cranch 137 (1803).

structures.[7] The tradition of self-restraint can be traced back to one of those decisions: upholding by a narrow majority an Act of Parliament concerning land-ownership reform, the Supreme Court stated that the citizen's claim that the Act had not provided full compensation for his loss of property could not be affirmed with 'the *certainty* which is required for the courts to set aside an act of Parliament as unconstitutional'.[8]

The apparent requirement of 'certainty' here before the Court would strike a piece of legislation down indicates a restrained approach to constitutional judicial review in the Danish legal system. This very cautious standard of review defined by the Supreme Court in 1921 has traditionally been regarded as the general standard of judicial review in Danish constitutional law.[9] When the Danish Supreme Court applied such a strong version of judicial self-restraint it recognised a constitutional need for the courts to defer to the assessment of the legislator, and thus the Supreme Court itself implicitly provided legal authority for the view that in a democracy the political organs must, within broad constitutional limits, prevail over the judiciary which has no similar democratic mandate.[10] This Danish constitutional tradition may be regarded as a modified version of the British constitutional principle of the sovereignty of Parliament.

This constitutional tradition has been philosophically backed by Scandinavian Legal Realism, which flourished in the Nordic countries in most of the twentieth century.[11] Scandinavian Legal Realism, like

---

[7] The five decisions are published in (1921) *Ugeskrift for Retsvæsen* 148, 153, 168, 169 and 644, respectively.

[8] Published in (1921) *Ugeskrift for Retsvæsen* 644 (my translation and emphasis).

[9] Cf. e.g. E. Andersen, *Forfatning og Sædvane* (Copenhagen: Gads Forlag, 1947), pp. 71–2; B. Christensen, 'Rettens forhold til regeringen efter 1849' in *Højesteret 1661–1961* (Copenhagen: Gads Forlag, 1961), pp. 401–7; A. Ross, *Dansk Statsforfatningsret* (3rd edn, Copenhagen: Nyt Nordisk Forlag, 1980), p. 184.

[10] See also H. Koch, 'Dansk forfatningsret i transnational belysning' (1999) 6 *Juristen* 213, 217.

[11] The founder of Scandinavian Legal Realism is considered to be A. Hägerström, *Till frågan om den objectiva rättens begrepp* (Uppsala: Akademiska Bokhandlen, 1917). He inspired scholars in Sweden such as A. V. Lundstedt, *Superstition or Rationality in Action for Peace* (London: Longmans, Green and Co., 1925); K. Olivecrona, *Law as Fact* (Copenhagen: Munksgaard, 1939); in Denmark, V. Bentzon, *Retskilderne* (Copenhagen: G.E.C. Gad, 1907); A. Ross, *Virkelighed og Gyldighed i Retslæren* (Copenhagen University, 1934); in Norway, G. A. Hoel, *Den moderne retsmetode* (Copenhagen: Gyldendal, 1925); V. Aubert, 'Om rettsvitenskapens logiske grunnlag' (1943) 56 *Tidsskrift for Rettsvitenskap* 174.

American Legal Realism,[12] regards law as fact, thus rejecting the idealism of other legal theoretical traditions. Scandinavian Realism, consequently, is sceptical of the idealistic concept of human rights; rather, it asks the legal interpreter to take reality into account by interpreting legal norms in their political and societal context. Scandinavian Realism will thus allow for constitutional rights to be restricted by political needs, by accepting a restrictive political practice as relevant to the legal interpretation of rights.[13]

No doubt, this strong tradition of self-restraint and intellectual tradition of Scandinavian Realism contributed to the fact that, until 1999, no Act of Parliament was ever set aside as unconstitutional by a Danish court. That fact makes the following remarks by a Danish Supreme Court judge writing extra-judicially quite revealing:

> As is known, the Danish Supreme Court has not to this date set aside an act of [P]arliament as unconstitutional, although it seems at times there was occasion to do so. The access of the courts to set aside acts of parliament may be compared to an emergency brake: only if the machine runs wild, leaving the population and its general sense of justice behind, may one expect the use of the emergency brake.[14]

This quote is indicative of a Danish Supreme Court traditionally regarding itself a bureaucratic organ – civil servants of justice – rather than a guardian of the Constitution and civil liberties.[15]

Another explanatory factor behind the modest role of judicial review in Danish law has been the strong positivist tradition of legal interpretation in Danish law. The positivist tradition of interpretation is based on the need for objective sources of law and a corresponding predictability in legal adjudication. According to this tradition, the legal text, as represented for instance in statutes and other legislative documents, is the binding framework of interpretation. Where the meaning of a statutory text is unclear, interpretative guidance should be sought, above all, in the preparatory works. Accordingly, any (expansive) deviation from the

---

[12] See the landmark work of O. W. Holmes, 'The Path of the Law' (1897) 10 *Harvard Law Review* 457.

[13] See H. Zahle, 'Grundlovens Menneskerettigheder. Sammenstødet mellem legalistiske og dynamiske retstraditioner' in M. Kjærum *et al.* (eds.), *Grundloven og menneskerettigheder* (Copenhagen: DJØFs Forlag, 1997), pp. 361–80.

[14] M. Munch, 'Grænser for domstolenes retsskabende virksomhed i civile sager' (1989) 2 *Juristen* 43, 45 (my translation from Danish).

[15] The historical roots of this culture are traced by D. Tamm, 'Domstolene som Statsmagt' (1997) B *Ugeskrift for Retsvæsen* 87.

text based on considerations of the objective and spirit of the legal provision has been regarded with suspicion as a political exercise, from which judges ought to abstain as far as possible.[16]

The result of these constitutional and legal traditions of judicial self-restraint, Scandinavian Legal Realism and legal positivism has been a weak judicial review in which legal interpretation would never go beyond textual limits of constitutional provisions, but would rather occasionally accept restrictions of the textual protection with reference to political practice.[17]

While there has been sporadic criticism of this tradition on purely constitutional grounds,[18] it was the challenge from European law that provided the decisive impulse for rethinking the Danish constitutional and legal tradition, most notably in the sphere of human rights.[19] From the early 1990s and onwards, legal scholars and judges increasingly voiced the need to reconsider Danish constitutional and legal tradition in light of the case law from the European Court of Human Rights (ECtHR) and the Court of Justice of the European Communities (CJEU) – a call to accept a stronger constitutional role for Danish courts[20] as well as a more autonomous and dynamic style of constitutional interpretation.[21] Thus, the president of the Danish Supreme Court, Niels Pontoppidan, in a 1996 interview concerning the impact on the Danish judiciary of European developments, stated that 'in the

---

[16] See e.g., B. Gomard, 'Et retspolitisk program for dommerskabt ret' in T. Jensen et al. (eds.), Højesteret 1661–1986 (Copenhagen: Gads Forlag, 1986), pp. 45, 59; Munch, 'Grænser for domstolenes retsskabende virksomhed i civile sager', n. 14 above, 44; T. Jensen, 'Domstolenes retsskabende, retsudfyldende og responderende virksomhed' (1990) B Ugeskrift for Retsvæsen 441, 444.

[17] Cf. with numerous illustrations Zahle, 'Grundlovens Menneskerettigheder', n. 13 above; J. E. Rytter, Grundrettigheder (Copenhagen: Thomson, 2000), pp. 138–47.

[18] See e.g., P. Germer, Ytringsfrihedens væsen (Copenhagen: Juristforbundets Forlag, 1973), p. 93; Gomard, 'Et retspolitisk program for dommerskabt ret', n. 16 above, 60; J. P. Christensen, Forfatningsretten og det levende liv (Copenhagen: DJØFs Forlag, 1990), p. 213.

[19] See e.g., Rytter, Grundrettigheder, n. 17 above, pp. 61–9.

[20] Cf. T. Melchior (then a Supreme Court judge), 'The Danish Judiciary' in B. Dahl, T. Melchior, L. A. Rehof and D. Tamm (eds.), Danish Law in a European Perspective (Copenhagen: GadJura, 1996), p. 102; Zahle, 'Grundlovens Menneskerettigheder', n. 13 above, 376 with n. 39; T. Jensen (former Supreme Court judge), Højesteret og Retsplejen (Copenhagen: Gyldendal, 1999), p. 258.

[21] B. Gomard, 'Juraen under forandring og udvikling' (1993) B Ugeskrift for Retsvæsen 385, 392; H. Zahle, Dansk forfatningsret. Menneskerettigheder (2nd edn, Copenhagen: Christian Ejlers Forlag, 1997), p. 38.

future, Danish courts will come to play a more active role, and Danish judges will adopt a law-making function going beyond what we have been used to'.[22] Some even argued that a more active constitutional role for Danish courts was not only necessary to implement European (human rights) obligations in national law but had also become more legitimate in light of the way Europe's supranational courts developed and enforced European constitutional law. Thus, the prominent constitutional scholar, Henrik Zahle, referring to the bold approach of the Strasbourg and Luxembourg courts, wrote in 1997 that 'the legitimacy of the judiciary taking a critical stand against the political and administrative power has been strengthened'.[23] As well as the increased scholarly calls for a stronger judicial review, important jurisprudential developments took place in the 1990s, so much so that they were interpreted by many as a turning point for constitutional law: for the first time ever we had a Danish court setting aside an Act of Parliament. In 1999, the Supreme Court struck down an Act providing for the withdrawal of grants from seven individual free schools, holding the Act to be in contravention of the provision on the separation of powers in article 3 of the Danish Constitution.[24] In the same period, the Supreme Court in 1996 agreed for the first time ever to review the compatibility of Danish participation in the EU with the Danish Constitution,[25] and in 1998 it handed down its elaborate judgment on the merits of the case, finding the Danish accession to the Maastricht Treaty to be compatible with constitutional requirements, while defining, however, certain constitutional reservations for the future interaction between Danish law and EU law.[26]

The fact that these landmark constitutional judgments were delivered in the same period when a need to strengthen the courts' role in light of European developments was increasingly argued (see above) may or may not be a mere coincidence. It remains, however, that the perceived need to reinvent Danish legal and constitutional tradition in the face of European legal developments was very real, and even found expression in an official governmental report on the judiciary from 1996. The 1996

---

[22] N. Pontoppidan, Interview in the Danish newspaper *Weekendavisen*, 28 June 1996 (my translation from Danish).

[23] Zahle, 'Grundlovens Menneskerettigheder', n. 13 above, 376 (my translation from Danish).

[24] Published in (1999) *Ugeskrift for Retsvæsen* 841.

[25] Published in (1996) *Ugeskrift for Retsvæsen* 1300.

[26] Published in (1998) *Ugeskrift for Retsvæsen* 800.

report on the judiciary mentions the constitutional role of Danish courts as being connected with European developments. Referring to the impact of European legal developments, notably the increasing influence of human rights and case law from the Strasbourg and Luxembourg courts, it states that:

> [T]his development contributes to a changed role of the courts – a role where the courts must exercise to a higher degree than before an autonomous law-making function. Thus, it is to be expected that the judges will have to apply a broader style of interpretation and a doctrine of the sources of law, which goes beyond, and thereby partly differs, from the existing one. The development underlines the importance of the judiciary as an independent Third Power of the State.[27]

Accordingly, influenced by European developments in general and the case law of the ECtHR in particular, Danish courts (the Supreme Court standing out as the front-runner) seem in recent years to claim for themselves and be assigned a somewhat more prominent position in the constitutional scheme.[28] This is particularly so with regard to the enforcement of civil rights and political freedoms and fundamental rule of law principles, as opposed to rights in the economic and social field.[29] Certainly, the traditional wisdom that Danish courts ought to keep their hands off cases involving questions of substantial political interest or even political controversy no longer holds sway in its categorical form.[30] However, we are not witnessing a shift of paradigm. Rather, Danish courts are slowly adapting to new requirements, and a changed constitutional landscape.

---

[27] *Report on the Judiciary*, Governmental Report No. 1319 (Copenhagen, 1996), p. 175 (my translation from Danish).

[28] Rytter, *Grundrettigheder*, n. 17 above, pp. 66–8; H. Zahle, *Dansk forfatningsret. Menneskerettigheder* (3rd edn, Copenhagen: Christian Ejlers' Forlag, 2003), pp. 50–1; T. Melchior, 'Maastricht, Tvind – og hvad så?' (2003) *Hyldestskrift til Jørgen Nørgaard* 201, 212; J. P. Christensen, *Domstolene – den tredje statsmagt*, Magtudredningen (Aarhus University, 2003), p. 27; J. P. Christensen, 'Højesteret og statsmagten' in P. Magid *et al.* (eds.), *Højesteret – 350 år* (Copenhagen: Gyldendal, 2011), p. 211, 259; H. P. Olsen, *Magtfordeling* (Copenhagen: DJØFs Forlag, 2005), p. 582; J. E. Rytter, *Individets Grundlæggende rettigheder* (1st edn, Copenhagen, Karnov Group, 2013), pp. 88–9.

[29] Rytter, *Grundrettigheder*, n. 17 above, pp. 347–73; T. Melchior, 'Maastricht, Tvind – og hvad så?', n. 28 above, 203.

[30] Cf. J. E. Rytter, 'Dansk-europæisk menneskerettighedsbeskyttelse' (2010) *Juristen* 187, 194.

II   When the stakes get high: judicial review
in counter-terrorism cases

Despite recent developments, the deferential tradition of Danish courts still carries (great) weight. So how do Danish courts informed by such a tradition handle judicial review in the field of counter-terrorism? In Danish legal theory, one looks in vain for specific comments on counter-terrorism judicial review, presumably because until recently this field had only minor practical relevance in Denmark. However, the field of counter-terrorism generally has such characteristics that one would expect judicial review by Danish courts to be highly deferential. First of all, as many contributors to this collection have noted,[31] in terrorism cases the stakes are high, and so the cost of failure may be serious, perhaps even disastrous.[32] Secondly, protecting the state and the security of its people is arguably the very first responsibility of government, and an original *raison d'être* of state power and legitimacy.[33] While this may provide the political organs with a special responsibility for balancing security and liberty, this point becomes more contentious whenever the balancing encroaches upon constitutional and/or international rights and liberties, since courts are constitutionally entrusted with interpreting and enforcing those rights[34] – indeed that very contention goes to the heart of this collection. Thirdly, the executive with its expertise[35] is generally better equipped than courts to assess terrorist threats and decide what steps are necessary to counter it.[36] Fourthly, effective counter-terrorism efforts often involve secret intelligence; and so, to ensure the effectiveness

---

[31] For example, see Introduction to this volume, F. F. Davis and F. de Londras, 'Counter-terrorism judicial review: beyond dichotomies'.

[32] See E. A. Posner and A. Vermeule, *Terror in the Balance: Security, Liberty, and the Courts* (Oxford University Press, 2007), p. 119. See also House of Lords in *Secretary of State for the Home Department* v. *Rehman* [2001] UKHL 47, para. 62 (Hoffmann) and in *A and others* v. *Secretary of State for the Home Department* [2004] UKHL 56, para. 29 (Bingham), paras. 79–80 (Nicholls), paras. 112 and 116 (Hope), para. 154 (Scott), para. 226 (Hale).

[33] Cf. ECtHR in *Ireland* v. *United Kingdom* (Application no. 5310/71), Judgment of 18 January 1978, para. 207.

[34] This point was strongly emphasised by Lord Bingham in *A and others* v. *Secretary of State for the Home Department* [2004] UKHL 56, para. 42.

[35] Cf. on the general relevance of administrative expertise for the standard of judicial review in Danish law, among others, S. Bønsing, *Almindelig forvaltningsret* (2nd edn, Copenhagen: DJØFs Forlag, 2012), p. 392.

[36] See e.g., House of Lords in *Secretary of State for the Home Department* v. *Rehman* [2001] UKHL 47, para. 26 (Slynn), paras. 57 and 62 (Hoffmann).

of intelligence work, the confidentiality of intelligence methods and sources must be protected, also in the process of judicial review.[37]

III   Recent Danish counter-terrorism case law: measured not deferential review

Bearing this background in mind, we can now turn to recent Danish case law concerning counter-terrorism measures. The following survey is a selective but, I believe, representative picture of the current approach of Danish courts. It addresses counter-terrorism themes that have been high on the Danish political and legal agenda in recent years, and the cases have been selected on the basis of their relevance in showing the extent to which Danish courts engage in judicial review of counter-terrorism measures, including in cases where political pressure is high.

(a)   Lawfulness of detention of alien terrorist suspects subject to expulsion orders

The ECtHR recognises that in terrorist cases some restrictions of ordinary due process may be necessary to protect the secrecy of information relating to national security; however, it does insist that the essence of due process must be respected.[38] In a similar vein, the Danish Supreme Court has upheld ECHR requirements of due process in terrorism cases, despite legislative attempts following 9/11 to cut off judicial review in order to protect the secrecy of counter-terrorism intelligence.

After the 9/11 terrorist attacks in the United States, Danish legislation was enacted in 2002 empowering the executive to detain and deport aliens whom the intelligence service considered a danger to national security.[39] For security reasons, the grounds underlying the intelligence service's individual assessment were to be kept secret from the alien in question. Furthermore, the Act did not provide access for the courts to investigate the factual basis for this danger assessment.

---

[37] See Chapter 10 in this volume, C. Chan, 'Business as usual: deference in counter-terrorism rights review'.

[38] See e.g., *Chahal* v. *United Kingdom* (Application no. 22414/93), Judgment of 15 November 1996, para. 131; *Al-Nashif* v. *Bulgaria* (Application no. 50963/99), Judgment of 20 June 2002, paras. 136–7.

[39] Act no. 608 of 17 July 2002 on Amendment of the Aliens Act, notably ss. 45b and 25.

The Danish Supreme Court in the so-called 'Tunisian Case'[40] in 2008 reviewed the authorities' decision under the new 2002 legislation to detain a Tunisian terrorist suspect with a view to deporting him on the grounds that he posed a danger to national security. Based on secret surveillance and other such undisclosed information, the intelligence service suspected the alien, who was a Muslim, of having taken part in planning terrorist attacks against targets in Denmark. Both the Danish City Court and High Court approved the detention as a necessary measure to implement the decision to expel.[41] This was in conformity with the wording of the Danish Aliens Act 2002, according to which all that had to be ascertained by the courts was whether or not detention had a legal basis and could be considered necessary for the implementation of the decision to expel the alien. Under the legislation, the basis for the decision to expel, i.e., the assessment that the alien was a danger to national security, was in principle irrelevant in the proceedings concerning detention; the court was not entitled to review this assessment.

This formal interpretation of the Danish Aliens Act sat somewhat uncomfortably with Article 5(1)(f) and (4) ECHR as interpreted by the ECtHR. In *Chahal*, the ECtHR held that the lawfulness of detention under Article 5(1)(f) ECHR 'with a view to deportation' of an alien believed to pose a threat to national security does not depend upon whether or not the underlying decision to deport the alien is itself justified under national law and the ECHR; rather, to protect against arbitrariness there must at least be *prima facie* grounds for believing that the alien is a threat to national security. Consequently, as regards judicial review of the detention, Article 5(4) ECHR does not require review of the lawfulness of the underlying decision to deport, but only review to ensure against arbitrariness, i.e., ascertaining whether it has been established that there are *prima facie* grounds for believing that the alien is a threat to national security.[42]

The alien was allowed an appeal to the Danish Supreme Court. Before the Supreme Court, the Danish government, represented by the National Head of Police, argued that the decision of the inferior courts was correct under Danish law, which could not be considered incompatible with

---

[40] Danish Supreme Court, Judgment of 2 July 2008, (2008) *Ugeskrift for Retsvæsen* 2394.

[41] Copenhagen City Court, Judgment of 14 February 2008; Eastern High Court, 17 Dep., Judgment of 27 February 2008.

[42] *Chahal v. United Kingdom* (Application no. 22414/93), ECtHR, Judgment of 15 November 1996, paras. 112–13, 118, 122 and 128–9.

Article 5(4) ECHR. Furthermore, the National Head of Police reminded the Court that the 2002 legislation under which the alien had been detained was enacted to implement UN Security Council Resolution 1373 (28 September 2001) on national measures to be taken in the fight against terrorism – a higher ranking international obligation. As if to bring the maximum pressure to bear upon the Court, the National Head of Police added to these legal considerations a warning that:

> Denmark must not, in order to comply with Article 5(4) ECHR, bring herself in a situation, in which the effective fight against international terrorism and assaults against national security is rendered ineffective or impossible.

The Supreme Court (composed of nine judges for this important case, the usual number being five) was not subdued by these warnings. With Article 5(4) ECHR in mind, the Supreme Court took a less formalistic approach than the inferior courts, enabling the Court to require some substantial justification for the detention. The Supreme Court unanimously held that in order to ensure due process with regard to the detention, regardless of the wording of the Danish Aliens Act, the authorities were required to provide some substantiation for the claim that the assessment of the alien's danger to national security had a factual basis:

> Even if the decision to detain the alien has the purpose of securing the implementation of the decision to expel the alien, which in turn is based on the decision that the alien is a danger to national security, and even if the validity of the latter decisions cannot be reviewed in this case concerning the lawfulness of detention, the Supreme Court finds that judicial review of the lawfulness of detention must entail some review of the factual basis for the decision that the alien is a danger to national security. What is required is to show a reasonable probability that there is such a factual basis for the danger assessment that detention cannot be regarded as unlawful or groundless, cf. also Article 5(4) ECHR. The substantiation of the danger must happen by the authorities' presenting the Court with the necessary information and with appropriate access to adversarial proceedings.

The standard of substantiation required by the Supreme Court – reasonable probability – was one that the Court developed for the occasion. In so doing, the Supreme Court was clearly drawing inspiration from the statements by the ECtHR in *Chahal* requiring that '*prima facie* grounds' for believing that the alien poses a threat to national security must be established as a condition of lawful pre-expulsion detention (see above).

Although the Supreme Court itself did not explicitly say so, in accordance with a long-standing Danish judicial tradition of concise, to-the-point reasoning,[43] it seems clear that the standard of 'reasonable probability' was carefully designed to take into account the individual interest of due process as well as the public interest in dealing effectively with threats to national security while preserving as far as possible the secrecy of national intelligence investigation methods and sources. The standard was a compromise, requiring some substantiation to preclude outright arbitrariness, while accommodating national security interests by stopping far short of requiring proof of the allegations.

Applying this standard, the Supreme Court unanimously held that the authorities had not fulfilled the standard of substantiation in the case at hand and remanded the case to the inferior courts, giving the authorities an opportunity to present more specific information. In a subsequent proceeding, the intelligence agencies did reveal more information, but not enough to satisfy the Supreme Court which, therefore, held the detention to be unlawful.[44] In another Supreme Court case involving a co-suspect, the standard was fulfilled as the intelligence service had provided material evidence from searches and specific surveillance information and the alien had been fully able to counter the allegations in adversarial proceedings.[45]

The Danish government and legislature have taken note of the Supreme Court's decisions without (official) misgivings. Not only did the authorities abide by the decision, but the decisions were also crucial in moving the government to speed up ongoing considerations regarding the possible introduction of a new judicial process in cases concerning the expulsion of aliens suspected of terrorist activities, to which I now turn.

The above-mentioned Supreme Court decisions show a court that is willing, despite political pressure, to set aside Danish legislation in a counter-terrorism case in order to uphold basic due process requirements as defined by the ECHR and Strasbourg case law. It also shows a government respecting the court's position without hesitation.

---

[43] See further Rytter, *Grundrettigheder*, n. 17 above, p. 276.
[44] Danish Supreme Court, Judgment of 19 November 2008, (2009) *Ugeskrift for Retsvæsen* 426.
[45] *Ibid.* 420.

(b)   Due process and the expulsion of alien terrorist suspects

In light of the above-mentioned 2008 Supreme Court decision and taking into account the guidelines for due process in cases concerning national security developed by the ECtHR in *A and others*,[46] the Danish legislature in 2009 introduced a special judicial process with (partially) closed proceedings and special advocates with the aim of ensuring due process while at the same time protecting the confidentiality of secret intelligence information.[47] The role model for this new Danish process was the British Special Immigration Appeals Commission (SIAC). SIAC was established in 1997 as a response to the ECtHR's *Chahal* judgment. SIAC is a special court competent to review administrative decisions certifying an alien as a terrorist or other threat to national security (a certification implying possible detention and deportation). SIAC is designed to be able to investigate sensitive intelligence material, without compromising national security. SIAC is a fully independent court of law, competent to examine all relevant evidence, both closed and open, and to make a binding decision. What is special about SIAC is that the closed material is not revealed to the alien in question and his legal advisors; instead the Solicitor General appoints a special advocate to act on the alien's behalf with regard to the closed material. From the moment when closed material has been revealed to the special advocate, he/she may have no further contact with the alien and his legal advisors, save with the permission of SIAC.

The Danish Supreme Court has accepted the SIAC model in principle, while reserving its position with regard to specific cases.[48] In terrorism cases reviewed in accordance with the new model, the Supreme Court has both upheld and turned down specific expulsion decisions, depending on whether or not it believed that ECHR due process requirements had been met. A few examples are appropriate to illustrate this.

In a case concerning an Iraqi national suspected of being a leading figure in an international network organising the employment of terrorists in Iraq, the Supreme Court, after careful review of the evidence

---

[46] *A and others* v. *United Kingdom* (Application no. 3455/05), Judgment of 19 February 2009, notably paras. 205 and 218–20.

[47] Act no. 487 of 12 June 2009 on Amendment of the Aliens Act, introducing a new Chapter 7b. The Act is based on *Betænkning om administrative udvisning af udlændinge, der må anses for en fare for statens sikkerhed*, Governmental Report no. 1505 (2009).

[48] Danish Supreme Court, Judgment of 18 August 2012, (2010) *Ugeskrift for Retsvæsen* 2910.

presented, was satisfied that the open material in the case was sufficiently specific to justify the decision by the authorities that the person in question posed a danger to national security and should therefore be expelled. In the estimation of the Court, he had had sufficient opportunity to challenge the factual basis of the decision, and his due process rights had thus been respected.[49] In another case decided on the same day, the Supreme Court reviewed the decision to expel a Tunisian national suspected of having planned acts of terrorism in Denmark. The Court unanimously invalidated the decision on due process grounds, holding that the suspect had not been able to effectively challenge, through the special advocate, the allegations against him, since the open material in the case did not specify the factual basis for the allegations (time, place and circumstances), but contained merely general allegations.[50]

Once more, the Danish government and legislature have taken note of the Supreme Court's decisions without (official) misgivings.

These cases show that while the Supreme Court is prepared to apply the flexible SIAC model to protect national security, it does not take due process requirements lightly and will turn down applications for expulsions in those terrorism cases in which it is not satisfied that the individual suspect has been given a fair opportunity of adversarial proceedings. Again, it also shows a government respecting the court's position without hesitation.

(c)   Non-refoulement and the extradition of terrorist suspects

The 'Niels Holck Case' concerned the extradition of a Danish citizen for prosecution in India for acts of terrorism. In 1995, Niels Holck took an active and leading part in the dropping of weapons over the Indian state of West Bengal. The weapons were intended for use by private groups in the fight against the local government in West Bengal (allegedly in self-defence based on claims of the government's assaults on these groups). Holck had been notified by the Danish government in 2001 that he would not be extradited to India. However, in 2002 India formally requested his extradition on charges of complicity in the preparation of acts of terrorism and conspiracy to wage war against legitimate Indian state organs. The case was important to India, which used diplomatic and

---

[49] Danish Supreme Court, Judgment of 24 June 2011, (2011) *Ugeskrift for Retsvæsen* 2673.
[50] Danish Supreme Court, Judgment of 24 June 2011, (2011) *Ugeskrift for Retsvæsen* 2695.

political pressure on the highest levels of government to ensure Danish extradition of Niels Holck. The Danish government (Ministry of Justice) decided that he should be extradited despite India's record of systematic torture by the police, since Denmark had obtained assurances from the Indian government that he would be treated humanely by Indian authorities.

However, the Danish courts, in proceedings attended by representatives of the Indian government, set aside the decision to extradite. Both the City Court and, on appeal from the government (public prosecutor), the High Court held that there was a real risk a high profile terrorist suspect and enemy of the Indian government such as Niels Holck would be subjected to torture or inhuman treatment by the Indian authorities, the diplomatic assurances notwithstanding.[51] This would seem to be in line with ECtHR case law under Article 3 ECHR, according to which very strong diplomatic guarantees are required before an individual may be extradited or deported to a country where torture of detainees is known to be widespread and systematic.[52]

It may thus be said that in this case the Danish courts stood firm against considerable political pressure to extradite, not only from India, but also from the Danish government, which did not wish to harm Danish-Indian relations. The refusal by Danish courts to extradite Niels Holck has, indeed, led to a crisis in Danish-Indian relations. The Indian government has replied politically by cooling down bilateral cooperation with Denmark, diplomatically by tightening visa requirements for Danish visitors, and economically by cutting down on joint ventures and trade with Danish firms.

Even so, the Danish authorities have taken note of the court's decision without any objection (at least not officially). The High Court decision shows a court ignoring political pressure in order to implement a firm interpretation of the principle of non-refoulement under Article 3 ECHR. Again, it also shows a government respecting the court's position without (official) misgivings.

---

[51] Danish Eastern High Court, Judgment of 30 June 2011, (2011) *Ugeskrift for Retsvæsen* 2904.

[52] See among others *Saadi* v. *Italy* (Application no. 37201/06), Judgment of 28 February 2008; *Ismoilov and others* v. *Russia* (Application no. 2947/06) Judgment of 24 April 2008; *Ben Khemais* v. *Italy* (Application no. 246/07), Judgment of 24 February 2009. However, sufficient guarantees were held to be in place in *Othman (Abu Qatada)* v. *United Kingdom* (Application no. 8139/09), Judgment of 17 January 2012.

(d) Nulla poena *and the definition of terrorism in controversial circumstances*

In the 'Man who Attempted to Kill the Muhammad Cartoonist Case', the question was whether one individual's attempt to kill another private individual might be considered an act of terrorism, due to the symbolic importance of this individual and the motivation of the perpetrator. This was a significant question because the Danish Penal Code had been supplemented in 2002 by a new provision, section 114, concerning acts of terrorism, including killing with the intent of 'scaring the public' or 'destroying the basic political, constitutional or societal structures of the state'. The new section 114 was part of a whole package of new counter-terrorism legislation adopted to implement UN and EU decisions following the terrorist attacks of 9/11.

The crime was met with immediate political condemnation, labelling the act as terrorism. On the eve of the attempted murder the Danish Prime Minister, Lars Løkke Rasmussen, made a statement on public television, characterising the crime as 'not only an attack on [the cartoonist] but also an attack on our open society and our democracy'.[53] Similarly, the opposition leader, Helle Thorning Schmidt, condemned the crime as an 'act of terrorism'.[54]

While there is, as yet, no official, universally agreed definition of 'terrorism', the fact that the term relates in some way to the purpose of the actions is fairly well accepted.[55] For example, in 2004, the UN High Level Panel on Threats, Challenges and Change referred to any action carried out with the intention to: 'cause death or serious bodily harm to civilians or non-combatants, when the purpose of such action, by its nature or context, is to intimidate a population, or to compel a Government or an international organization to do or to abstain from doing any act' when considering the meaning of terrorism.[56]

In the Danish case, the public prosecutor sought to apply section 114 of the Danish Penal Code to a Somalian national who, in 2010, had attempted to kill a Danish cartoonist, because the cartoonist had drawn

---

[53] Statement of 2 January 2010 on Danmarks Radio, available at www.dr.dk/Nyheder/Politik/2010/01/02/160110.htm.

[54] See http://varde.lokalavisen.dk/apps/pbcs.dll/article?AID=/20100102/artikler/100109961.

[55] J. Blackbourn, F. Davis and N. Taylor, 'Academic Consensus and Legislative Definitions of Terrorism: Applying Schmid and Jongman' (2013) 34(3) *Statute Law Review* 239.

[56] UN High-Level Panel on Threats, Challenges and Change, *A More Secure World: Our Shared Responsibility* (New York: United Nations, 2004), para. 164.

one of the most notorious of the so-called 'Muhammad cartoons', published in 2005 in a Danish newspaper. This publication sparked the so-called 'cartoon crisis', in which Muslims in Denmark and all over the world, enraged by what they considered a blasphemous and insulting act against their prophet and their religion, protested against Denmark as well as against the people responsible for the drawings and their publication. The case at hand was controversial and the first of its kind.[57] The general scope of the new section 114 was itself subject to debate centring on the question of the definition of terrorism. But above all, it was unclear whether or not an attempt at killing a private individual like the cartoonist in question could be characterised as terrorism within the meaning of this provision.

The Danish courts answered this question in the affirmative. As regards the categorisation of the murder attempt as an act of terrorism the Danish courts referred to the fact that the 'Muhammad cartoons' had sparked violent reactions across the world, including attacks on Danish embassies abroad, and had put fundamental democratic principles, such as the freedom of speech and public debate, under pressure. In addition, the cartoonist who was the victim of the murder attempt had come to be seen in the public eye as the personification of the Muhammad cartoons and the values by which these drawings had been defended. Against this background the attempt to kill him should be regarded as an attempt to restrict free speech and public debate in Denmark. As such, the murder attempt could rightly be categorised under section 114 as an act of terrorism with the aim of seriously scaring the public and destroying fundamental political, constitutional and societal structures in Denmark. Accordingly, the Somali perpetrator was convicted of terrorism and sentenced to ten years' imprisonment and subsequent expulsion from Denmark.[58]

Applying section 114 to an attempt by one private individual, acting alone to kill another private individual (the cartoonist) was not uncontroversial. By categorising the crime as terrorism, the Danish courts took into account the political context and reality surrounding an act which, viewed in objective isolation, did not look like terrorism at all, but which in that context could reasonably be regarded as an act of terrorism. In so doing the Danish courts (also) accommodated a political interest in naming and shaming this act as terrorism.

---

[57] See commentary by J. Røn, 'Terror mod én person' (2012) *Juristen* 274.
[58] Danish Supreme Court, Judgment of 2 May 2012, (2012) *Ugeskrift for Retsvæsen* 2562.

This Supreme Court judgment arguably shows that the courts will lend an ear to political context in counter-terrorism cases, when the relevant law is subject to interpretation and when no human rights concerns preclude them from doing so.

Conclusion

It is crucial that judicial review be effective, even when it must be cautious. Too much judicial restraint might be as problematic and illegitimate as too much judicial activism, because excessive restraint might reduce the function of courts into that of constitutionally 'rubber stamping' political action, providing the latter with a legal legitimacy it may not deserve.[59]

The Danish judiciary, which is by constitutional tradition deferential to the political organs and extremely cautious in reviewing matters of significant political interest such as national security, has in recent years asserted a more autonomous position under the influence, among others, of European developments providing for powerful judicial review by supranational bodies like the Strasbourg and Luxembourg courts. In particular, this holds true for the Danish Supreme Court.

This is also visible with regard to judicial review of counter-terrorism legislation and measures. Recent counter-terrorism case law paints a picture of a Danish judiciary seeking a middle ground between undue deference and unsustainable activism in this field. While Danish courts seek to accommodate legitimate national security concerns and interests and are willing to compromise on certain aspects of ordinary legal protection when called upon to do so by the legislature, they will not decline to protect basic rule of law principles and fundamental human rights, even when such protection is alleged to be to the detriment of the fight against terrorism. If, however, in counter-terrorism cases the political push for action does not collide with human rights concerns, Danish courts seem willing to lend an ear to the political context.

It must be noted that the legal basis for such measured judicial review by Danish courts has been the European Convention on Human Rights as interpreted in ECtHR case law, rather than Danish constitutional

---

[59] Cf. D. Dyzenhaus, 'Deference, Security and Human Rights' in B. J. Goold and L. Lazarus (eds.), *Security and Human Rights* (Oxford: Hart Publishing, 2007), pp. 125–39. See also, Rytter, *Grundrettigheder*, n. 17 above, pp. 295 and 298.

norms.[60] The Danish Constitution was adopted in 1849, and the fundamental rights protection has been only sparsely amended since then.
Consequently, by modern standards the existing Danish constitutional
protection of fundamental rights appears to a large extent fragmented
and outdated. To some extent, the human rights situation in Denmark is
thus comparable to the situation in United Kingdom where no written
constitution exists. Were it not for the ECHR and ECtHR case law to
complement it, Danish courts, regardless of the trend towards a more
prominent constitutional role, would often be left without any legal basis
for challenging recent counter-terrorism measures. This also means, of
course, that any deference or appeasement on the part of the ECtHR in
counter-terrorism cases will have an immediate negative impact on the
level of human rights protection provided by Danish courts in such cases.
The more so, as Danish courts have by and large refrained from developing an autonomous ECHR jurisprudence, restricting themselves to
implementing ECtHR case law and its clear implications.[61]

Finally, it is worth reiterating that when Danish courts have thus
restricted or even invalidated counter-terrorism measures there has been
no (official) objection or criticism from the Danish government or
legislature. The strong legitimacy of the Danish judiciary may well help
to explain this fact. A century-old tradition of judicial restraint seems to
have earned the Danish judiciary a 'judicial capital of goodwill', a position of confidence and respect among politicians and the public, which
have come to view the judiciary as a state organ seated above, and
removed from, politics. In recent terrorism cases Danish courts have
been able to rely on this 'judicial capital', even though they are now
engaging in a more searching judicial review than used to be the case.

---

[60] For more on the operation of the ECtHR in the counter-terrorism context see Chapter 13 in this volume, H. Fenwick, 'Post 9/11 UK counter-terrorism cases in the European Court of Human Rights: a "dialogic" approach to rights protection or appeasement of national authorities?'.

[61] See J. E. Rytter and M. Wind, 'In Need of Juristocracy? The Silence of Demark in the Development of European Legal Norms' (2011) 9(2) *International Journal of Constitutional Law* 470, 479–84.

3

When good cases go bad: unintended consequences of rights-friendly judgments

DAVID JENKINS

Introduction

Debates about the judicial review of counter-terrorism legislation (including the debates in this volume) or executive decisions usually centre around two opposing positions: the desirability of muscular review to protect individual rights or more deferential review to promote effective government national security powers. Indeed, in their introduction to this volume, Fergal Davis and Fiona de Londras recognise the dichotomous (and hence problematic) nature of these and other debates surrounding the review of counter-terrorism measures in the courts.[1] Not surprisingly, then, proponents of these two opposing positions on judicial review often fall into the assumption that either more review (and more rights) or more deference (and more security) is, in every case, a desirable thing; that is, more of one is always constitutionally good, while more of the other is bad. For advocates of judicial deference, this can mean arguing for extreme expansions of state powers up to or beyond known constitutional boundaries, even at the expense of fundamental rights. Civil libertarians, in turn, are often eager to challenge government counter-terrorism powers in the courts, but with little concern for the impact of a winning decision beyond the result of a particular case. Either way, such a case-centred, simplified view of the desirability of either more deference or more judicial review underestimates the complex interrelationship between both individual rights and government national security powers throughout a legal system. As Davis and de Londras point out, there is far more 'murkiness' to this complex subject than dichotomous debates suggest, requiring more critical, nuanced views.[2] Moreover, as a

---

[1] See Introduction to this volume, F. F. Davis and F. de Londras, 'Counter-terrorism judicial review: beyond dichotomies'.
[2] *Ibid.*

pragmatic matter, it is civil libertarians who risk the most by giving insufficient attention to the broader constitutional context and possible political consequences of such polarised rights-argumentation: not only are civil-libertarian causes often politically unpopular in the hearts and minds of the general public, but even courtroom victories can sometimes result in an unforeseen, negative impact over a period of time. In this way, 'good cases' can 'go bad'.

This chapter gives several examples of pro-rights, counter-terrorism cases 'gone bad' over the past decade and suggests why this has happened, arguing that civil liberties advocates, lawyers and judges must all pay greater attention to these concerns when future rights claims conflict with state national security powers. Section I looks at two groups of such cases that have adversely affected overall rights, either by unexpectedly contributing to unwanted expansions of government national security powers over time or provoking political reactions hostile to civil liberties. The first group, the 'Belmarsh' case[3] in the United Kingdom and *Hamdi* v. *Rumsfeld*[4] in the United States, sacrificed rights to liberty or procedural fairness for the overall population, by weakening personal status distinctions that limited the application of government national security powers to a limited group of non-citizens. The second group, consisting of *Charkaoui* v. *Canada (Minister of Citizenship and Immigration)*[5] and the US Guantánamo cases,[6] highlights how pro-rights decisions can provoke latent or overt political 'blowback' against the judiciary and a constitutional rights culture that values civil liberties as an integral component of national security policy. Taking an overview of these cases, section II then suggests three risk factors that can cause pro-rights decisions to 'go bad'. These are the judiciary's removal of personal status distinctions that actually prevent the application of government national security powers to the wider population; its failure to set out clear and robust procedural rules for depriving any individual of his or her personal liberty for national security reasons; and its engagement in a dysfunctional institutional dialogue with security-obsessed political branches perhaps lacking full commitment to a constitutional rights culture. Civil libertarians, lawyers and judges, therefore, would all do well to consider the wider constitutional context and potential long-term

---

[3] *A and others* v. *Secretary of State* [2004] UKHL 56.   [4] 542 US 507 (2004).
[5] [2007] 1 SCR 350.
[6] *Rasul* v. *Bush*, 542 US 466 (2004); *Hamdan* v. *Rumsfeld*, 548 US 557 (2006); *Boumediene* v. *Bush*, 552 US 723 (2008).

implications of their arguments and carefully avoid these risks in future counter-terrorism cases.

I   Cases gone bad

Since 11 September 2001 ('9/11'), legal challenges to counter-terrorism measures in the United Kingdom, United States and Canada have resulted in several courtroom defeats for all three national governments. These decisions – 'Belmarsh', *Charkaoui*, *Hamdi* and the Guantánamo cases – departed from past patterns of judicial deference in national security matters and, for that reason alone, were welcome developments. Nevertheless, now seen with several years of hindsight, these cases have not been the complete civil liberties victories they were first thought to be. Instead, they have actually resulted in some important, negative consequences for individual rights that have offset whatever gains they seemed to have achieved at the time of their announcement. They have unfortunately enabled an expansion of state power to restrict personal liberty and provoked political actions hostile to civil liberties. Because these cases have been exhaustively discussed by legal academics over the years, they need little further description or analysis here. However, a brief, revisionist account of their long-term legal and political impact shows their constitutional legacies to be more ambivalent than often thought.

(a)   Group I: rights trade-offs

'Belmarsh'

Just a few weeks after the attacks of 9/11, the UK Parliament, at the behest of the then Labour government, passed the Anti-terrorism, Crime and Security Act 2001 (ATCSA), which, pursuant to section 23, allowed the indefinite detention of aliens suspected of involvement in terrorism, but who could not be deported because they faced a risk of torture upon return to their home countries. This detention decision was reviewed (administratively and by a High Court) by a special procedure, which permitted the government to refuse an opposing party access to relevant, security-sensitive evidence at the hearing. Courts had limited power to second-guess this executive determination. Once the ministerial determination was made, the information in question could only be heard in a closed hearing, from which the individual and his legal counsel were

excluded: only a court-appointed special advocate could see the closed
file and was forbidden from communicating with the person concerned.
Furthermore, in tandem with the government's accompanying derogation from the right to personal liberty under the European Convention
on Human Rights (ECHR), on the basis that the threat of terrorism
constituted a national emergency, the ATCSA exempted the government
from the existing legal requirement that aliens could only be detained
for a reasonable period of time necessary for their removal from the
country.[7] In the 'Belmarsh' case in December 2004, the House of Lords
found that the indefinite detention of non-deportable aliens for essentially preventive purposes was unjustifiably discriminatory under the
ECHR on the basis of national origin, because it did not apply to British
citizens who posed the same security risk as those non-deportable aliens
detained.

Civil liberties advocates, understandably, heralded 'Belmarsh' as a
victory for human rights. In so far as the House of Lords had bucked
the historical trend of deference in national security matters (seen only a
short time before in *Rehman*),[8] it was. Nevertheless, there was a catch to
the Law Lords' reasoning; they had only dealt with the discriminatory
nature of the ATCSA, rather than directly address the prospect of indefinite detention without trial or the controversial procedures used in its
imposition. By (mis)casting the central issue in the case in this way, the
House of Lords implied that the ATCSA could be rendered ECHR
compatible by removing the discriminatory element alone, thereby giving
a green light to the government to detain citizens preventively, indefinitely and on suspicion alone, outside of the criminal justice system.
Accordingly, what was a rights victory for those very few, non-deportable
aliens eligible for detention under the ATCSA was a rights setback for the
whole of the British population. While civil liberties campaigners celebrated 'Belmarsh', it sent a different message to a government determined to have its way; that is, all Parliament had to do was fashion a new
preventive detention regime that applied to everyone, citizens and aliens
alike. With the sole exception of Lord Hoffmann,[9] none of the Law Lords
in 'Belmarsh' acknowledged or addressed the possibility of just such a
government response. It is unclear on the official record whether this
silence reflected the traditional reticence of the Law Lords to speculate on

---

[7] *Ex parte Singh* [1984] 1 All ER 983 (QB).
[8] *Secretary of State for the Home Department* v. *Rehman* [2001] UKHL 47.
[9] See *A and others* v. *Secretary of State* [2004] UKHL 56, para. 86 (per Lord Hoffmann).

issues not put before them by counsel; their acceptance of (or at least lack of instinctive outrage at) the preventive detention of British citizens; or an unfortunate failure to canvass fully the constitutional consequences and likely political outcome of their decision – or some combination of all of the above.

Whatever the private expectations of the Law Lords, the Labour government was quick to exploit the limitations in the 'Belmarsh' reasoning, coming up with a novel solution that would be ECHR compatible, while neither releasing alien detainees nor going as far as authorising the outright imprisonment of citizen terrorist suspects. In spite of considerable parliamentary opposition, the government quickly forced through the Prevention of Terrorism Act in early 2005, replacing the detention provisions of the ATCSA with a controversial system of control orders, but using essentially the same procedures for section 23 detention: with limited judicial review, restricted rights to a hearing, and based only on a subjective risk assessment, the Home Secretary could now impose severe limitations on the movement, associations or other types of behaviour of any individual suspected of involvement in terrorism, whether an alien or a British citizen. The control order scheme became the subject of much litigation in subsequent years, particularly in regard to the special advocate system carried over from the ATCSA, seriously limiting an individual's rights to know the case, consult with legal counsel and have a fair, public hearing.[10] Although the later Conservative/Liberal-Democrat government replaced these control orders with a 'light-touch' version of Terrorism Prevention and Investigation Measures (TPIMs) intended to be more rights-friendly, there was never any serious question of abolishing a preventive control scheme entirely.[11] The preventive deprivation of (citizens' and aliens') liberty, in some shape or form, had entered British law to stay and it was 'Belmarsh' that had opened the door to it.

Unfortunately, 'Belmarsh' did not just lead to control orders and TPIMs; the case has also turned out to be a main catalyst for a wider-ranging government assault on both the individual's right to procedural fairness, as well as the constitutional principle of government accountability before the courts. The Justice and Security Act, introduced in 2012

---

[10] See e.g., *Secretary of State for the Home Department* v. *MB* [2007] UKHL 46; *Secretary of State for the Home Department* v. *JJ* [2007] UKHL 45; *Secretary of State* v. *AF* [2009] UKHL 28.

[11] See Terrorism Prevention and Investigation Measures Act 2011.

by the Conservative/Liberal-Democrat government and receiving Royal
Assent in April 2013, now expands the controversial procedures used in
control order/TPIM hearings (and earlier in detention hearings under
section 23 of the ATCSA) into the regular civil justice system, enabling
the government to trigger secret hearings whenever it wishes to prevent
the introduction of security-sensitive evidence into legal proceedings,
even outside of terrorism-related cases. As the House of Lords itself
pointed out in another context,[12] the introduction of these procedures
into civil trials represents a significant intrusion upon both the common
law and ECHR rights to a fair trial, thereby having serious constitutional
implications. The Justice and Security Act 2012's expansion of the special
advocate system would not have been possible without 'Belmarsh': with
that decision, as well-intentioned as it was, the House of Lords gave a
legal green light to the government to expand exceptional counter-
terrorism preventive measures against the whole of the British
population, further threatening individual rights to personal liberty and
procedural fairness far beyond the very narrow category of unremovable
aliens targeted by section 23 of the ATCSA.

Hamdi

It was not only British citizens, however, who lost something in litigation
challenging a preventive detention scheme. About six months before the
decision in 'Belmarsh', the US Supreme Court had already dealt with the
detention of American citizens in an altogether different military context.
As is well known, soon after 9/11 the Bush administration began
interning hundreds of foreign 'enemy combatants' in make-shift prisons
at Guantánamo Bay Naval Base. What is not so well known, however, is
that the administration also militarily detained two American citizens,
José Padilla and Yaser Esam Hamdi,[13] without criminal prosecution,
access to legal counsel or a hearing of any sort. There was some legal
authority for the proposition that the President could detain (and try by
military commission) a citizen who was a member of enemy armed forces
during time of war or a civilian belligerent captured in a war-zone.[14]
However, Padilla and Hamdi sought release on a writ of *habeas corpus*

---

[12] *Al Rawi and others* v. *Security Service* [2011] UKSC 34.

[13] The US government also militarily detained a third individual as an enemy combatant,
Ali Saleh Kahlah al-Marri, a Qatari living legally in Illinois.

[14] *Ex parte Milligan*, 71 US (4 Wall.) 2 (1866); *Ex parte Quirin*, 317 US 1 (1942); *In re
Territo*, 156 F.2d 142 (9th Cir. 1946); *Colepaugh* v. *Looney*, 235 F.2d 429 (10th Cir. 1956).

on the grounds that they were civilians captured outside the course of combat operations, who could only be detained pursuant to criminal process. While Padilla's case became entangled in a procedural quagmire, where it would remain for many years until his eventual transfer to civilian custody and criminal prosecution, Hamdi's eventually made it to the Supreme Court. Writing for a plurality, Justice O'Connor explained that, pursuant to Congress' Authorization of the Use of Military Force (AUMF), the President did have military authority to detain a narrow class of citizens captured while fighting against the United States in the course of an armed conflict, even if not a member of a foreign state's military or captured by US forces in battle. Under the Supreme Court's subtle but important expansion in the definition of an 'enemy combatant', government allegations (if true) that Hamdi had fought for the Taliban against the United States in Afghanistan, where he was captured and later turned over to the United States by Northern Alliance forces, would therefore justify his detention. However, where a citizen, like Hamdi, disputed such allegations, constitutional due process first required that he 'be given a meaningful opportunity to contest the factual basis for that detention before a neutral decision maker'.[15]

Because of this due process requirement, *Hamdi* v. *Rumsfeld* was, on its surface, a defeat for the Bush administration and a victory for civil liberties. Justice O'Connor made it clear that a citizen 'enemy combatant' was entitled to know the factual allegations made against him, to have legal counsel and to contest government allegations in a fair hearing.[16] That, however, was as far as *Hamdi* went. Seen from a different perspective – which Justice Scalia acerbically pointed out in his dissent[17] – the Supreme Court had actually delivered a judgment that, for the first time, expressly recognised an executive war power to detain citizens, who were not members of a foreign military, without criminal due process. Furthermore, Justice O'Connor made clear that due process, in this military context, did not require the same procedural protections of a criminal trial, a hearing before a civilian tribunal, or even the prohibition of hearsay evidence. Instead, the precise contours of due process would in this and future cases have to be determined between the government and the federal courts on an ad hoc basis, depending on the circumstances. While detention could only last so long as the related armed conflict (in this case, that in Afghanistan, a conflict that would continue for another

---

[15] *Hamdi* v. *Rumsfeld*, 542 US 507, 509 (2004).   [16] *Ibid.* 533.   [17] *Ibid.* 554.

eight years), the Court refused to address the obvious problem of exceptionally long-term or potentially indefinite detention during the unconventional military and counter-terrorism operations. So, despite its due process pronouncement, *Hamdi* nevertheless raised the worrisome prospect that, in a future dominated by the frontless, never-ending 'War on Terror', the President could order the military arrest of any US citizen suspected of terrorism anywhere, thereby bypassing the Constitution's usual requirements for criminal indictment and trial.

Soon after the decision, the administration agreed to release Hamdi on the condition he renounce his citizenship and leave for Saudi Arabia. Rather than risk another adverse decision, the administration also transferred Padilla from military to civilian custody, prosecuting him in federal court for various criminal offences. The effects of *Hamdi* were even felt in Guantánamo, where the administration introduced Combatant Status Review Tribunals to give some due process to the foreign detainees, even though they were not covered by the *Hamdi* ruling. However, although the immediate consequences of *Hamdi* suggested that the Supreme Court had somewhat cowed the Bush administration, in the longer term the decision has come to support an expansion, not a rollback, of exceptional executive powers. As such, *Hamdi* did not represent a significant moment of 'social learning', described by Mark Tushnet as a process whereby the government tempers its intrusions into civil liberties during national security crises in recognition of past overreactions, whether identified through historical retrospection, political controversies or legal setbacks.[18] Instead, it was the later administration of President Obama, who had promised in his 2008 elections campaign to close the Guantánamo Bay prisons and end military detentions, that actually exploited to the fullest *Hamdi*'s recognition of an executive detention power. With the support of that administration, Congress passed the National Defense Authorization Act (NDAA) in 2012, giving the military broad authority to detain individuals associated with Al-Qaeda, the Taliban, or otherwise suspected of involvement in terrorist attacks against the United States or other countries.[19] This controversial statute did not specifically include or exclude citizens from such detention, but the decision in *Hamdi* fills in the blanks: subject to some minimal due process requirement, the President can now claim authority

---

[18] See generally M. Tushnet, 'Defending *Korematsu*?: Reflections on Civil Liberties in Wartime' (2003) *Wisconsin Law Review* 273.

[19] Pub. L No. 112–81, 125 Stat. 1298, ss. 1021–1034.

under the NDAA (as well as the AUMF) to detain US citizens in military custody, without trial, solely on suspicion of terrorism. *Hamdi*, no doubt, will stand at the top of this or another administration's list of legal authorities in any future challenge to the NDAA by a citizen detainee.

Hamdi's recognition of an executive war-power to detain citizens has since taken an even more bizarre turn probably never imagined by either the justices of the plurality or those civil libertarians who condoned the decision (prematurely, as it now seems): the Obama administration has expressly relied on *Hamdi* to claim an executive war-power to *kill* – without any due process whatsoever – US citizens suspected of plotting terrorist acts. On 30 September 2011, for example, the President ordered an automated drone strike against two Al-Qaeda propagandists in Yemen, Anwar al-Awlaki and Samir Khan, both US citizens. Not surprisingly, this has been highly controversial and constitutionally problematic, with civil liberties advocates criticizing the administration strongly, and the families of the deceased filing civil suit against the government in federal court.[20] In February 2013, NBC News obtained a leaked legal memorandum circulating within the Obama administration,[21] setting out legal justifications for the executively ordered killing of al-Awlaki and Khan, or any other citizen terrorist suspects targeted in the future. In that memo, *Hamdi* or the flexible due process analysis it prescribes (adopted from the case of *Mathews* v. *Eldridge*)[22] are together

---

[20] See C. Savage, 'Relatives sue officials over U.S. citizens killed by drone strikes in Yemen', *New York Times*, 18 July 2012. A third US citizen, al-Awlaki's grandson, was later accidentally killed in another drone strike.

[21] US Department of Justice, White Paper, *Lawfulness of a Lethal Operation Directed Against a U.S. Citizen Who is a Senior Operational Leader of Al-Qa'ida or an Associated Force* (undated), available at http://msnbcmedia.msn.com/i/msnbc/sections/news/020413_DOJ_White_Paper.pdf.

[22] *Mathews* v. *Eldridge*, 424 US 319 (1976); it is worth noting here that *Mathews* is a landmark case in *administrative* law for determining the process due before the government may deprive an individual of a right in the pursuit of a public policy interest. As such, its introduction as a due process test for military detentions was entirely novel and not without controversy. In his dissent in *Hamdi* v. *Rumsfeld*, 542 US 507, 575 (2004), Justice Scalia strongly criticised the plurality in that case for claiming 'authority to engage in this sort of "judicious balancing" from ... a case involving ... *the withdrawal of disability benefits!*' (emphasis original). As such, he found its administrative due process analysis wholly inappropriate for determining the extent of any presidential military power to deprive a citizen of personal liberty. Nevertheless, *Hamdi*'s invocation of *Mathews*, and the Obama administration's use of it in its White Paper, may nevertheless be indicative of a jurisprudential shift towards assessing national security powers and rights under ordinary administrative law concepts, rather than under other long-standing analytical frameworks that demarcate constitutional areas of 'exception', such as national

cited sixteen times in support of a unilateral executive war-power to target US citizens with lethal force.[23] It is troubling, to say the least, that a decision intended to limit the President's military power to deprive citizens of their liberty is now the main precedent for another executive claim to an extra-judicial war-power to kill Americans. As with the 'Belmarsh' case, then, *Hamdi* has turned out to have a significantly deleterious, rather than wholly positive, effect on civil liberties by opening a door to the expansion of national security powers in other, unexpected ways.

(b)   Group II: political blowback
Charkaoui

Both 'Belmarsh' and *Hamdi* were Phyrric civil liberties victories that, in their own ways, weakened the general population's rights to personal liberty and procedural fairness over the long run. Despite suffering embarrassment and temporary setbacks with these decisions, the British and US governments were nevertheless able and willing to exploit them to claim new national security powers. Such responses formally complied with these cases' legal requirements, but they violated rights to liberty and procedural fairness in other imaginative and novel ways. However, some cases 'go bad' not just by enabling an expansion of national security powers, but by provoking political 'blowback' by which the legislature or executive (or both) resist the courts and a wider constitutional rights culture in responding to the decision. As the 2007 *Charkaoui* case from Canada illustrates, even well meaning judicial invitations to the political branches for a positive 'rights dialogue' can sometimes only serve to mask a latent legislative hostility to an unwelcome judgment.

In *Charkaoui* v. *Canada (Minister of Citizenship and Immigration)*, the Supreme Court of Canada heard challenges to an alien detention scheme under the Immigration and Refugee Protection Act (IRPA),[24] which were very similar to the issues raised in 'Belmarsh'. The IRPA allowed ministers to issue certificates that an alien was inadmissible to Canada for national security reasons, triggering special procedures that limited the

---

security or war. The doctrinal characteristics and constitutional ramifications of any such shift, however, are unpredictable, as Mark Tushnet explores in Chapter 5 in this volume, M. Tushnet, 'Emergency law as administrative law'.

[23] US Department of Justice, White Paper, n. 21 above, pp. 2, 3, 5, 6, 7, 15.

[24] SC 2001, c. 27.

alien's rights to an open, adversarial hearing and representation by legal counsel. As under the UK's ATCSA, those aliens who could not be deported due to a risk of torture upon return to their home countries were subject to detention for an indeterminate period. Unlike the House of Lords in 'Belmarsh', however, the Supreme Court of Canada found that such detention was not unlawfully discriminatory *per se*; nevertheless, the IRPA's exceptional procedural requirement of *ex parte, in camera* hearings – in which the detainee had no right to appear, to hear the government's case or to have legal representation – were violations of the right to a fair hearing guaranteed under section 7 of the Charter of Rights and Freedoms. In one sense, by refusing the discrimination claim and focusing on the procedural deficiencies, *Charkaoui* was the judgment that 'Belmarsh' ought to have been: it did not do away with the citizen/ alien distinction, thereby opening up the possibility that the government could detain Canadian citizens who posed the same suspected terrorist threat as aliens. By conservatively retaining this distinction, *Charkaoui* continued to protect the vast majority of the Canadian population from a preventive detention scheme of some sort, while raising the procedural protections due to that relatively tiny class of non-deportable aliens subject to the security certificate scheme. Nevertheless, while setting out some general principles, like *Hamdi*, the Supreme Court of Canada failed to establish clear procedural requirements in such cases. It instead deferred back to Parliament, giving it one year to propose a new procedural regime compatible with *Charkaoui*'s guidelines.

The Supreme Court of Canada did, however, offer *dicta* on more proportionate alternatives to the existing IRPA process, pointing to the United Kingdom's special advocate system as an example. In this dialogical context, the Court's *dicta* on British special advocates was illustrative, not prescriptive; it was intended only as an example of more proportionate options available to Parliament, and was not a judicially-pronounced, constitutional mandate. These *dicta*, however, sent a different message to the political branches. The government quickly seized upon the Supreme Court's apparent approval of the British special advocate system and copied it almost wholesale into new legislation to amend the IRPA, which Parliament adopted with little debate.[25] While this new system was certainly an improvement over the one-sided, secret

---

[25] D. Jenkins, 'There and Back Again: the Strange Journey of Special Advocates and Comparative Law Methodology' (2011) 42 *Columbia Human Rights Law Review* 279, 346–8.

hearings that *Charkaoui* had denounced, neither Parliament nor the government gave much serious consideration to other possible, more robust procedures. The Supreme Court's invitation for institutional dialogue had quietly backfired, as both the government and Parliament relied upon *Charkaoui's dicta* merely to justify adoption of the lowest procedural standards they thought most likely to withstand another constitutional challenge.

With hindsight, the Supreme Court might have done better to lay down clear, robust and constitutionally mandated procedures for security certificate cases, leaving it to Parliament either to justify a legislative departure from those standards in future legislation (pursuant to section 1 of the Charter) or expressly enact non-compliant procedures notwithstanding Charter requirements (as section 33 of the Charter itself permits) – both politically difficult for Parliament to achieve. Instead, in a well-intentioned but mistaken effort at dialogue, the Court in *Charkaoui* deferred to the political branches, which remained more committed to their national security agenda than to an institutional conversation about rights. The result was a disappointing, copy-cat adoption of the controversial and procedurally flawed British special advocate system into Canadian law, cloaked in the veil of dialogue, rather than a sincere attempt to strike an optimal balance between procedural fairness and national security needs.

Rasul, Hamdan and *Boumediene*

If, instead of openly inviting dialogue, a court does strictly and clearly limit government counter-terrorism measures, as the US Supreme Court did by extending *habeas corpus* to alien detainees at Guantánamo Bay, it still risks provoking direct, open political blowback. In the three cases of *Rasul, Hamdan* and *Boumediene*, the US Supreme Court rebuffed attempts by the Bush administration to deny the Guantánamo detainees any form of judicial review in the federal courts. The administration's arguments in all of these cases were based on the *Eisentrager* precedent,[26] denying the federal courts an extra-territorial *habeas* jurisdiction over aliens held outside of *de jure* US territory. Without fundamentally altering this jurisdictional rule, the Court carved out, case by case, a narrow jurisdictional exception for Guantánamo Bay, due to the fact that it was uniquely under the complete *de facto* control of the US government.

---

[26] *Johnson v. Eisentrager*, 339 US 763 (1950).

The political responses to each of the three decisions, in turn, were striking in their open confrontation with the Supreme Court, an institutional conflict that de Londras has elsewhere characterised as a 'counter-constitutionalist turn', whereby an intransigent (even antagonistic) Congress was more interested in *quotidian* political opportunism and the pursuit of party advantage, rather than in abiding by the constitutional spirit of the Supreme Court's judgments.[27] *Rasul* was the first case to extend judicial review to Guantánamo Bay, interpreting the federal *habeas* statute to apply to the naval base. Congress promptly amended the statute to preclude review. The Supreme Court then refused to give that amendment retrospective effect over pending cases, like *Hamdan*; in that case, the Court went on to find that the President's military commissions violated the Uniform Code of Military Justice, interpreted consistently with the Geneva Conventions. Political reactions to *Hamdan* were hostile, eventually resulting in the Military Commissions Act 2006; with this Act, an incensed Congress expressly stripped the federal courts of *habeas* jurisdiction over Guantánamo Bay. Finally, in *Boumediene*, the Supreme Court found this denial of *habeas* to be unconstitutional; Congress could limit *habeas* review only pursuant to the onerous requirements of the Suspension Clause,[28] which had not been met. In contrast to *Charkaoui*'s invitation to dialogue, triggering a passive-aggressive resistance by Canada's Parliament, the Guantánamo cases kicked off an ugly, open conflict between the courts and the political branches in the United States.

Congress and the President lost this inter-branch conflict only in the short term by formally complying with the Guantánamo rulings, but refusing to concede to their constitutional spirit, as discussed elsewhere by de Londras.[29] Congress and the succeeding Obama administration mainly resisted the Supreme Court by (mis)using their other constitutional powers to obstruct the rights of the Guantánamo detainees. Congress, for example, exercised its constitutional spending power to forbid President Obama from using any federal monies to transfer Guantánamo detainees to prisons within the United States or to close the Guantánamo

---

[27] See F. de Londras, 'Guantánamo Bay, the Rise of the Courts and the Revenge of Politics' in D. Jenkins, A. Henriksen and A. Jacobsen (eds.), *The 'Long Decade': How 9/11 has Changed the Law* (Oxford University Press, 2014).

[28] 'The privilege of the writ of *habeas corpus* shall not be suspended, unless when in cases of rebellion or invasion the public safety may require it', US Constitution, art. 1, s. 9.

[29] See de Londras, 'Guantánamo Bay, the Rise of the Courts and the Revenge of Politics', n. 27 above.

prisons.[30] This financial restriction not only sabotaged President Obama's personal campaign pledge to close the Guantánamo camps and his administration's plans to prosecute detainees in federal court; it also meant that wrongly-detained Guantánamo prisoners could not be released into the United States, if they could not be returned to any other country.[31] By exercising its spending power in this way, Congress effectively nullified *Boumediene* by rendering the writ of *habeas corpus* an unenforceable remedy in many cases.

The Obama administration, for its part, continued to fight Guantánamo *habeas* petitions vigorously on the merits. It also simply detained new alien terrorist suspects in other foreign locations not so clearly under the *de facto* control of the US government (like Bagram Airbase in Afghanistan). In defence against *habeas* petitions from such distant places, President Obama's lawyers relied on the *Eisentrager* rule, just as Bush's had done earlier.[32] Moreover, the new administration increasingly targeted terrorist suspects abroad using automated drone strikes – a policy neatly avoiding detention and the Guantánamo rulings altogether.

This combined executive and legislative backlash against *Rasul*, *Hamdan* and *Boumediene*, then, was not even the half-hearted attempt at dialogue that followed *Charkaoui*; it was instead an open, sometimes bitter conflict with the judiciary that damaged any future presumption that the political branches will be 'good sports' when losing litigation and work with, not against, the courts in balancing rights with security. Some cases, like *Charkaoui* and the Guantánamo decisions, can therefore 'go bad', subtly or openly, by provoking political blowback against both the courts and a constitutional rights culture that is dependent upon a political commitment to reconciling individual rights with national security.

II   Good intentions, bad results

(a)   What went wrong?

Despite being much *fêted* as civil liberties victories, the cases discussed above have all had unexpected, negative consequences for civil liberties in

---

[30] See D. M. Herszenhorn, 'Funds to close Guantánamo denied,' *New York Times*, 20 May 2009, available at www.nytimes.com/2009/05/21/us/politics/21detain.html?pagewanted=all&_r=0.

[31] See *Kiyemba* v. *Obama* (*Kiyemba III*), 605 F.3d 1046 (D.C. Cir. 2010), *cert. denied*, 131 S.Ct 1631 (2011).

[32] See *Al Maqaleh* v. *Gates*, 605 F.3d 84 (D.C. Cir. 2010).

their respective countries, in the ways already explained. This is not to say that these decisions did not advance individual rights on some level; they most certainly did. However, those advances were partial, won only with other rights trade-offs and political costs in the long term. The cases in Group I protected rights to liberty and procedural fairness for some few individuals, but only through doctrinal changes having the overall effect of weakening those same rights for the general population. Whether this was a desirable development from a standpoint of either promoting an equality principle or increasing the potential for political resistance to government counter-terrorism measures depends on one's point of view. Regardless, with hindsight it is difficult to deny that there was indeed a rights trade-off to some degree, so that the wider constitutional legacies of these decisions must now be seen as mixed. Even where courts were conservative in their doctrinal approaches, maintaining long-standing personal status and territorial distinctions that sharply defined both government security powers and categories of rights-bearers, as seen with Group II, there was significant political blowback from political branches not fully committed to a healthy dialogue with the judiciary and a wider constitutional rights culture, where national security was concerned.

Considered together, then, the cases discussed in this chapter suggest three significant, interrelated risk factors that might cause apparently rights-friendly cases eventually to 'go bad' in the national security context. These are: (1) the breach of personal status distinctions that limit the scope of certain national security powers; (2) the contextualisation of rules of procedural fairness; and (3) the judiciary's entry into a dysfunctional dialogue with the political branches. While Group I cases highlight the first two factors and Group II the third, most cases in these groups display more than one of these problems. It is perhaps not coincidental, therefore, that the two cases having the worst side-effects on rights over time, due to their actual expansion of national security powers, 'Belmarsh' and *Hamdi*, exhibit a considerable mix of all three risk factors.

(b)   Status distinctions

Why did 'Belmarsh' and *Hamdi* lead so quickly, and even counter-intuitively, to an expansion of preventive restrictions of liberty in the United Kingdom and military detention in the United States (and there even assaults upon the citizen's right to life)? First, by tampering with legal doctrines linking personal status with rights, both the UK House of

Lords and the US Supreme Court altered fundamental constitutional baselines anchoring the complex interrelationship between individual rights and government national security powers. These alterations removed established boundaries to what the government could or could not do to its own nationals. As the Supreme Court itself pointed out in *Hamdi*, categories of citizenship, permanent residency and alienage – or recognition of other conflicting loyalties to a foreign power, such as 'enemy combatancy' or membership in foreign armed forces – symbolically represented the nature of an individual's presumed relationship to a political community. This relationship, in turn, determined the extent of the individual's legal rights and privileges and, along with it, set the outer limits of government powers to restrict those rights for national security reasons. The symbolic nature of such status distinctions has legal meaning, expressing the normative proposition that civil liberties are to a great degree constructs of a polity, which an individual can belong to, join and betray.[33] Despite the opinion of the House of Lords in 'Belmarsh', which notably conflicts with the approach of the highest courts in the United States and Canada, and hinged on a particular interpretation of the ECHR at odds with common law precedent, such a notion of rights does not necessarily violate the fundamental human right to equality that, by definition, inheres to the individual regardless of political association (as the Supreme Court of Canada has suggested).[34] Weakening these distinctions, however, might very well have unpredictable results in a domestic constitutional system, where both individual rights and executive security powers have jurisprudentially evolved closely around them – which is exactly what happened with the 'Belmarsh' and *Hamdi* decisions.

Judging from the fall-out from those two cases, then, status distinctions appear to serve two important constitutional purposes (at least in the national security context); that is, they carefully allow some latitude for exceptional government powers, such as preventive detention, but create solid bulwarks beyond which they cannot go. These distinctions

---

[33] Legal doctrines of personal status and territorial distinctions for delimiting individual rights and governmental powers are not limited to the United States, United Kingdom and other common law jurisdictions, as seen, for example, in the complex jurisprudence regarding territorial jurisdiction of the European Court of Human Rights. See *Bankovic and others* v. *Belgium* [2001] ECHR 890; *Issa and others* v. *Turkey* (2004) 41 EHRR 567; and *Al Skeini and others* v. *United Kingdom* (2011) 53 EHRR 18.

[34] *Charkaoui* v. *Canada (Minister of Citizenship and Immigration)* [2007] 1 SCR 350, paras. 129–31, citing *Minister of Employment and Immigration* v. *Chiarelli* [1992] 1 SCR 711.

rest upon a categorical, common law presumption (which 'Belmarsh' rejected against precedent, but *Hamdi* and *Charkaoui* accepted) that some groups (such as aliens or those citizens belonging to foreign armed forces) are naturally more likely to be disloyal on account of their political associations and so present a greater security threat than other full members of the national community. Such a bright-line rule does not necessarily prove in fact who is or is not a security threat, as the House of Lords banally pointed out; nevertheless, it is a presumption deeply entwined within the fabric of the common law constitutional tradition, fixing critical boundaries between individual rights and national security powers. Seen from this systemic perspective, status distinctions between citizens and non-citizens are not just arbitrary, discriminatory limitations on some people's rights; like the traditionally dichotomous concepts of war and peace, they delineate how far the government may go in taking extraordinary national security measures against its domestic population. They enable a government to take swift action against a small but higher risk group having presumptively divided political loyalties (due, say, to foreign citizenship or membership in foreign armed services); at the same time, they insulate the general population from sweeping rights infringements and the ordinary legal system from exceptional processes. Loosening up status doctrines like alienage or 'enemy combatancy' (as with replacing orthodox temporal notions of war and peace with the far more nebulous concept of 'War against Terror')[35] – as 'Belmarsh' and *Hamdi* did in their own ways – necessarily meant weakening these deeply-founded constitutional bulwarks against the expansion of national security powers; without these status firewalls, such powers could easily grow to threaten rights on a much larger scale – which is exactly what happened as a result of 'Belmarsh' and *Hamdi*. In so far as the rejection of these and other status distinctions represents a wider jurisprudential shift from dichotomous legal frameworks founded on a concept of norm-versus-exception (as Mark Tushnet[36] suggests is seen in the appearance of administrative law analyses in national security cases), the unintended consequences of 'Belmarsh' and *Hamdi* demonstrate the risks that just such a change might bring.

---

[35] See Chapter 5 in this volume, M. Tushnet, 'Emergency law as administrative law'; Tushnet, 'Defending *Korematsu*?', n. 18 above.

[36] See Chapter 5 in this volume, Tushnet, 'Emergency law as administrative law'.

(c) Procedural rules

A second reason that 'Belmarsh' and *Hamdi*, in particular, went bad was that, after having enlarged the class of people subject to government national security powers, they did not ensure for them an adequate level of procedural protection before being deprived of their personal liberty. 'Belmarsh' was especially lacking in this respect; as explained, the House of Lords sent a message to the government, unintentionally or not, that the main rights problem with detention under section 23 of the ATCSA was that aliens were treated worse than citizens – *not* that they, even as aliens, were inappropriately subject to potentially indefinite detention, based on an executive suspicion of subjective risk, and pursuant to a controversial special advocate procedure that infringed upon the most basic rights to a fair hearing. In this way, the Law Lords missed the key rights issue in the case. So, after inadvertently encouraging the government to extend preventive deprivations of liberty to the whole British population, the House of Lords then failed to mandate clear, high-standard procedural rules in order to protect everyone from government misjudgement or outright abuse. As a result, citing 'Belmarsh', the British government was able to justify imposing a new control order regime upon citizens and aliens alike, simply using the same flawed special advocate procedures developed for use in national security immigration cases.

To its credit, in *Hamdi*, the US Supreme Court acknowledged the risk of permitting the military detention of citizen terrorist suspects without adequate, constitutionally mandated procedural safeguards. The Supreme Court of Canada implicitly did the same in *Charkaoui*, refusing to remove the status barrier between citizenship and alienage, and focusing on the key procedural issues in security-certificate cases; by doing so, it wholly avoided any possibility of a 'Belmarsh'-like spill-over of the security certificate regime into the regular legal system. Even so, both the US and Canadian courts still stumbled when announcing the procedural standards to be affixed to the specific detention schemes at issue; that is, both courts failed to articulate in advance any hard-edged, generally applicable procedural rules, in favour of announcing broader principles of fairness for the courts and legislature to define and implement in the future. In this way, *Hamdi* and *Charkaoui* rendered these lofty principles dependent on either circumstantially dependent, ad hoc judicial formulations or statutory implementation by political branches aggravated by court interferences; neither option offered much real security or predictability to those individuals (citizens or aliens) subject to preventive detention. *Hamdi*, in adapting the *Mathews* balancing test, again indicates the negative consequences likely to result from using ordinary administrative law doctrines in extraordinary national security cases. In any case, what 'Belmarsh', *Hamdi* and *Charkaoui* all share in common is that, whether in enlarging status categories in legal doctrine or leaving procedural standards open for later legislative definition, the highest courts of Britain, the United States and Canada carelessly overestimated the commitment of their respective national governments to civil liberties, when national security is on the line.

(d) Dysfunctional dialogue

Although 'Belmarsh' and *Hamdi*, respectively, both led to Parliament and Congress enacting legislation for control orders and military commissions, those cases were not invitations to dialogue with the political branches, as such. *Charkaoui* was – the Supreme Court of Canada suspended its judgment, giving Parliament one year to fashion a new security certificate procedure that complied with the Charter. To illustrate more proportionate alternatives than the secret, *ex parte* hearings in question, the Court offered the British special advocate system as an example, which is exactly what the Canadian government and Parliament then quickly chose to enact, with no serious consideration of better solutions. The Supreme Court's invitation to dialogue thus went awry for two reasons. First, its unnecessary reference to British special advocates (understandably) gave some policy-makers the impression that the Court had considered and constitutionally vetted that system's Charter compatibility in advance, which it had not done. This was a mistake and proves the influence that ill-considered judicial *dicta* can have over legislative drafters looking for quick, clear and easy legal answers.[37] Secondly, the Canadian Supreme Court not only assumed, but positively relied upon the good faith of the political branches in working towards a rights-optimal solution for the security certificate scheme. This did not happen; Canada's Parliament instead took the easy way out, using the special advocates *dicta* in a bid to concede no more rights than necessary to pass constitutional muster. So, while the political branches in the United Kingdom and United States took advantage of the doctrinal

---

[37] See generally, Jenkins, 'There and Back Again', n. 25 above.

innovations in 'Belmarsh' and *Hamdi* to expand their national security powers in other ways, those in Canada insincerely mimed a superficial dialogue with the Supreme Court in order to concede the fewest rights improvements possible in response to *Charkaoui*.

Thus, the political responses to 'Belmarsh', *Hamdi* and *Charkaoui* all point to a third risk factor: the judiciary's overestimation of the political branches' willingness to work constructively with, rather than against, the courts and their commitment to a constitutional rights culture, even in national security matters. At the same time, the courts have underestimated the stubborn determination of the political branches to get their way, in one manner or another. Indeed, the first two risk factors presume a political proclivity to expand national security powers over an ever larger proportion of the population, while undercutting adequate procedural protections. This tendency might result from a government's well-intended, but nonetheless myopic and rights-injurious, desire to take all feasible measures to safeguard its population. The aggressive political blowback against the Guantánamo cases, however, warns of a more worrying possibility; that is, governments might not always harbour expected commitments to a constitutional rights culture, when national security is on the line. In all of the cases seen in this chapter (but especially the Guantánamo cases), the institutional interplay between the courts and the political branches, whether or not it could be called dialogue in any meaningful sense of the word, was dysfunctional in some way. There might be many reasons for this; for example, in the United States it might be due to politicians' pursuit of political advantage over attention to constitutional principle (de Londras' 'counter-constitutional turn'),[38] while in the Westminster parliamentary model it might be symptomatic of a disciplined party system that stifles backbench dissent and favours executive policy-making, as Davis describes with reference to Australia.[39] Whatever the reasons, a stubborn security agenda politically prevailed over the rights-principles underlying the decisions considered here. Moreover, as Davis would probably agree,[40] courts ideally should not always have to 'invite' dialogue with the political branches, make up for the legislature's lack of pre-enactment

---

[38] De Londras, 'Guantánamo Bay, the Rise of the Courts and the Revenge of Politics', n. 27 above.

[39] See Chapter 6 in this volume, F. F. Davis, 'The politics of counter-terrorism judicial review: creating effective parliamentary scrutiny'.

[40] *Ibid.*

constitutional scrutiny, nor lay down iron-clad rules that anticipate the legislature or executive taking advantage of doctrinal loopholes or judicial silences; in a healthy, honourable democracy, the political branches should always make good faith efforts not only to respect a particular judicial decision, but broader constitutional rights values, thereby lessening reliance upon judicial review as a 'constitutional backstop' against rights-invasive government actions. Unfortunately, as the government reactions to all of the above cases show, this political commitment should no longer be assumed. The consequence is not only that courts have arguably shouldered a greater institutional burden in reviewing counter-terrorism measures than they should have done, had legislatures only been more rights-attentive in drafting legislation; it also means that, in the course of counter-terrorism review, any ill-considered judicial changes to long-standing legal doctrines or invitations to dialogue have become all the more unpredictable in their overall constitutional effects, when national security is at stake.

Conclusion

In the years after 9/11, the British, US and Canadian governments all suffered major legal defeats over controversial counter-terrorism measures. Those decisions – 'Belmarsh', *Hamdi*, *Charkaoui* and the Guantánamo cases – not only represented a welcome break from past patterns of judicial deference when reviewing national security powers, but bravely sought to constrain preventive detention regimes and/or guarantee some meaningful procedural protections for those subject to imprisonment. Unfortunately, however, these attempts to defend rights to personal liberty and procedural fairness backfired; over time, governments found ways around those decisions, either by taking advantage of their doctrinal weaknesses and ironically using them as justifications for *expansions* of national security powers, or resisting their implementation in other ways. So, while these judgments were at first civil liberties victories and embarrassments for the national governments affected by them, their long-term effects have been mixed due to their unintended, adverse rights consequences. These 'good cases' had somehow 'gone bad' and civil libertarians must now recognise that their constitutional legacies are now more ambivalent, and less rights-friendly, than once thought. This recognition is not merely for the sake of critical reflection on the past, but to prevent such unanticipated consequences in the future. So, how could these cases, once so promising and celebrated, have gone so wrong?

The full reasons are no doubt more complex than this chapter has been able to canvass, and so they remain subject to further, more detailed study by others. However, there are at least three risk factors to be seen in these cases: the weakening of status distinctions that guarded against the expansion of national security powers to the general population; the failure to provide clear and adequate procedural safeguards against their use in any context; and a dysfunctional institutional dialogue that presumed too much of a rights-commitment from the political branches. These risk factors, in turn, resulted from a lack of constitutional perspective and political imagination on the part of civil liberties campaigners, lawyers and judges. In regard to perspective, in all of the cases studied here, these legal actors did not look far enough beyond the specific cases before them, in order to contemplate more carefully the possible impact of their positions on the constitutional system as a whole. This blinkered, case-focused view overlooked the extent to which individual rights and government powers are complexly intertwined, so that a change in one legal doctrine can send unseen ripples (or shockwaves) throughout the rest of the legal system; overall rights protections might suffer, as a result. As for political imagination, at the time these decisions were issued, no one likely imagined the full extent of the political antipathies they would engender with the political branches. The long-term implications of this antipathy remain uncertain and so are perhaps even more troubling than the legal turns-of-events that have already occurred. What is certain, however, is that the defenders of civil liberties must take greater care when arguing or deciding future national security cases, lest they, too, turn out to do as much harm as good – because hard cases make very bad law indeed.

4

The rhetoric and reality of judicial review of counter-terrorism actions: the United States experience

JULES LOBEL

Introduction

In a series of cases between 2004 and 2008, the United States Supreme Court assertively exercised judicial review over the executive's detention and military commission policies.[1] The Court declared, in ringing rhetoric that the executive branch does not have a 'blank check' during wartime, and for the first time in American history held a wartime measure enacted by Congress to be unconstitutional.[2] These decisions led to optimism and hope that the judicial check on executive overreaching would be effective.[3]

Yet the Supreme Court's soaring rhetoric has not been matched by the reality of judicial review. The lower federal courts have uniformly rejected efforts to hold United States officials accountable for torture or other wrongdoing committed in conjunction with counter-terrorism actions.[4] The courts have refused to provide *habeas corpus* review to detainees held by the United States in Afghanistan.[5] A federal court

I would like to thank my research assistant Bret Grote for his work on this chapter and the University of Pittsburgh Law School's Document Technology Center for their invaluable assistance in the preparation of this chapter. This chapter draws on an article of mine, 'Victory Without Success: the Guantanamo Litigation, Permanent Preventive Detention and Resisting Injustice' (2013) 14 *Journal of Law in Society* 121.

[1] *Rasul* v. *Bush*, 542 US 466 (2004); *Hamdi* v. *Rumsfeld*, 542 US 507 (2004); *Hamdan* v. *Rumsfeld*, 548 US 557 (2006); *Boumediene* v. *Bush*, 553 US 723 (2008).
[2] *Hamdi* v. *Rumsfeld*, 542 US 507 (2004); *Boumediene* v. *Bush*, 553 US 723 (2008).
[3] R. Dworkin, 'Why It was a Great Victory', *New York Review of Books*, 14 August 2008 ('The Supreme Court has now declared that this shameful episode in our history must end').
[4] See e.g., *Arar* v. *Ashcroft*, 414 F.Supp.2d 250 (E.D.N.Y. 2006), *aff'd*, 532 F.3d 157 (2d Cir.), *aff'd, en banc, vacated and superseded on reh'g en banc*, 585 F.3d 559 (2d Cir. 2009); *Rasul* v. *Myers*, 555 US 1083 (2008), *aff'd on remand*, 563 F.3d 527 (D.C. Cir. 2009), *cert. denied*, 130 S. Ct 1013 (2009).
[5] *Al-Maqaleh* v. *Gates*, 605 F.3d 84 (D.C. Cir. 2010).

refused to review the constitutionality of a drone attack that executive officials were planning against a US citizen in Yemen.[6] Finally, the Courts of Appeal have developed a very narrow approach to *habeas* review at Guantánamo Bay, leading many to conclude that the main thrust of the Supreme Court's decision has been negated.[7] In the face of all these lower court decisions, the Supreme Court has remained silent, refusing to review any of these extremely deferential decisions.[8]

The tension between the Court's rhetoric and the reality of an ineffective judicial check on the executive is not unique to this context or to the United States. While these contradictions in judicial review might lead observers to suggest that the legislature could be a more effective check, the US experience is that Congress has functioned as less of a check on executive misconduct than the judiciary. This chapter will argue that the only effective check is public pressure stemming not from any branch of government, but rather from the detainees, as well as civic, activist organisations and the press that are independent of government.

I *Boumediene* and its negation

Justice Kennedy's opinion for the Supreme Court in *Boumediene* v. *Bush* held that the Guantánamo Bay detainees had a constitutional right to seek a writ of *habeas corpus* to challenge their detention.[9] The opinion rhetorically soared with ringing phrases such as '[s]ecurity subsists, too, in freedom's first principles. Chief among these are freedom from arbitrary and unlawful restraint, and the personal liberty that comes from adherence to the separation of powers'.[10] Yet, in many respects, the functional test that Justice Kennedy articulated in *Boumediene* was in tension with its lofty rhetoric.[11] While the opinion suggested that detainees held by the US military for prolonged periods of time should have some judicial mechanism to challenge their detentions, the functional test set forth by Kennedy focused on the practical considerations which might preclude any judicial review.

---

[6] *Al-Awlaqi* v. *Obama*, 727 F.Supp 1 (D.D.C. 2010).
[7] See e.g., Editorial, 'A right without a remedy', *New York Times*, 1 March 2011.
[8] *Ibid.*   [9] *Boumediene* v. *Bush*, 553 US 723 (2008).
[10] *Boumediene* v. *Bush*, 553 US 723, 797 (2008).
[11] See J. Lobel, 'Fundamental Norms, International Law, and the Extraterritorial Constitution' (2011) 36 *Yale Journal of International Law* 307, 316–18 (discussing Justice Kennedy's functional test at odds with the separation of powers rationale and rhetoric in the opinion).

Moreover, the Court left it to the lower courts to fill in the myriad of substantive and evidentiary issues that it had not addressed, and to apply the vague functional test to other situations. The District Court Circuit ('Circuit'), which oversees the Guantánamo Bay litigation, has been hostile to the detainees, with several of the judges on the Circuit publicly criticising the Supreme Court's *Boumediene* opinion for the 'mess' they made and as a 'charade'.[12]

First, the Circuit has held that the federal courts are without power to order the release of Guantánamo Bay prisoners into the United States, even where those prisoners were indisputably not enemy combatants, and where they could not be repatriated to another country, leaving no other remedy.[13] The case involved the Uighurs, members of a Muslim minority group in north-western China, whose fight had been with the Chinese government, not the Americans.[14] Although they had no connection whatsoever to Al-Qaeda or the Taliban, the Uighurs were, nonetheless, detained in Pakistan by the US military due to information provided by Pakistanis eager for reward money.[15] After the Uighurs were shipped to Guantánamo Bay, the government recognised early on that they were not enemy combatants of the United States and could not be detained as such.[16]

Most of the Uighurs were not, however, released from Guantánamo Bay, because they could not be returned to China where they would undoubtedly be jailed or persecuted by the Chinese government, and no third country would take them.[17] Finally, in a decision by the Circuit a short time after *Boumediene*, the Circuit held that the Uighurs could not be legally detained as enemy combatants.[18]

---

[12] Editorial, 'A right without a remedy', n. 7 above (quoting Hon. A. Raymond Randolph's address as part of the Joseph Story Distinguished Lecture Address at the Heritage Foundation, 'The Guantánamo Mess', delivered on 20 October 2010); *Esmail* v. *Obama*, 639 F.3d 1075, 1078 (D.C. Cir. 2011) (Silberman J concurring); S. I. Vladeck, 'The D.C. Circuit After *Boumediene*' (2011) 41 *Seton Hall Law Review* 1453.

[13] *Kiyemba* v. *Obama*, 555 F.3d 1022 (D.C. Cir. 2009), *vacated*, 130 S.Ct. 1235 (2010), *rehearing en banc denied, reinstating judgment as amended*; *Kiyemba* v. *Obama*, 605 F.3d 1022, 1046 (D.C. Cir. 2010) (*per curiam*).

[14] *Ibid.* 1023–4.   [15] *Ibid.*

[16] *Qasim* v. *Bush*, 382 F.Supp.2d 126, 127–8 (D.D.C. 2005) (noting military tribunal's holding that Uighur detainees could not be detained as enemy combatants).

[17] *Ibid.* 128.

[18] *Parhat* v. *Gates*, 532 F.2d 834, 854 (D.C. Cir. 2008). That case was decided under the mechanism that Congress had established for review that was struck down in *Boumediene*.

When the government did not seek *certiorari* in the Supreme Court, the Uighur prisoners filed *habeas* petitions in the District Court, seeking release into the United States because there was no basis for their continued detention at Guantánamo Bay and no third country to send them to where they would not be subject to persecution.[19] Moreover, religious and other humanitarian groups in the United States had agreed to sponsor and take care of the Uighurs if released into the United States.[20]

District Judge Urbina granted the Uighurs' *habeas corpus* petitions and ordered their release into the United States subject to conditions set by the court.[21] The Circuit reversed, holding that federal judges had no power to grant the relief requested absent explicit legislative authority.[22] The Circuit furthermore held that to the extent the Due Process Clause of the Fifth Amendment might bar the indefinite detention of someone whom the government had no legal basis to detain, it did not apply to non-citizens detained at Guantánamo Bay.[23] The Circuit simply ignored *Boumediene*, treating it as only applying to *habeas* jurisdiction and not substantive rights.[24]

The Supreme Court granted *certiorari* in *Kiyemba*,[25] but vacated that grant and remanded to the Circuit in light of the Obama administration's filing that the detainees had received a resettlement offer that might moot the controversy.[26] On remand, the Circuit reaffirmed its prior ruling, and this time the Supreme Court denied *certiorari*.[27]

Thus, as a practical matter, the detainees are left without any meaningful remedy and judges who find no basis for detention typically instruct the government to 'take all necessary and appropriate diplomatic steps to facilitate the prisoners' release forthwith'.[28] As one Circuit Judge

[19] *Ibid.* 852.
[20] B. Delahunt and S. Willett, 'Innocent detainees need a home', *Boston Globe*, 2 April 2009 ('The small Uighur-American community has pledged to aid the detainees with jobs and housing'); M. Barakat, 'D.C. Uighurs wait to take in Gitmo detainees', *USA Today*, 10 October 2008.
[21] *In re Guantánamo Bay Detainee Litigation*, 581 F.Supp.2d 33 (D.D.C. 2008).
[22] *Kiyemba* v. *Obama*, 555 F.3d 1022, 1027–9 (D.C. Cir. 2009).   [23] *Ibid.* 1026–7.
[24] *Ibid.* 1028.   [25] *Kiyemba* v. *Obama*, 130 S. Ct 458 (2009).
[26] *Kiyemba* v. *Obama*, 130 S. Ct 1235 (2010) (*per curiam*).
[27] *Kiyemba* v. *Obama*, 605 F.2d 1046 (D.C. Cir. 2010), *cert. denied*, 131 S. Ct 1631 (2011).
[28] See e.g., *Ahmed* v. *Obama*, 613 F.Supp.2d 51, 66 (2009); *Basardh* v. *Obama*, 612 F.Supp.2d 30, 35–6 (D.D.C. 2009). See J. Hafetz, 'Calling the Government to Account: *Habeas Corpus* After *Boumediene*' (2011) 57 *Wayne Law Review* 99, 131–5 (for an excellent discussion of the *Kiyemba* ruling). See also, Vladeck, 'The D.C. Circuit After

candidly recognised, the Circuit has reduced *habeas* review to essentially rendering 'virtual advisory opinions'.[29] Or as the *New York Times* put it, 'the appellate court has all but nullified that view of judicial power and responsibility backed by Justice Kennedy and the court majority' in *Boumediene*.[30]

As of May 2013, there are still 166 prisoners detained at Guantánamo Bay.[31] Of these, 86 have been approved for transfer or release, which means that the Department of Defense has determined that they need not be detained at Guantánamo Bay;[32] 57 of these detainees are Yemenis whose government has agreed to repatriate them.[33]

Yet, as of May 2013 these detainees have not been transferred to Yemen or the other countries where they are from for several reasons. First, in December 2009, under mounting political pressure the Obama administration imposed a blanket moratorium on transferring Guantánamo Bay detainees to Yemen.[34] Moreover, Congress has enacted legislation in the past two years, which makes it difficult for the administration to transfer a Guantánamo Bay detainee. The National Defense Authorization Act for Fiscal Year 2012 prohibits the use of Defense Department funds to transfer to or release in the United States any non-citizen held at Guantánamo Bay.[35] Congress also has imposed onerous certification requirements such as the executive certifying that the receiving state indeed meets certain national security standards.[36] And while Congress did provide that the executive could waive the transfer restrictions in particular cases, the administration had been unwilling to utilise that waiver ability. Additionally, the courts have thus far refused to allow any remedial action, with the District Courts and the Circuit effectively holding that they do not have the power under *habeas* to order the government to transfer the detainee either to

---

Boumediene', n. 12 above, 1476–85 (discussing remedies in *habeas* cases after *Boumediene*).

[29] *Esmail* v. *Obama*, 639 F.3d. 1075, 1078 (D.C. 2011) (Silberman J concurring).

[30] Editorial, 'A right without a remedy', n. 7 above.

[31] C. Savage, 'Guantánamo prison revolt driven by inmates' despair', *New York Times*, 24 April 2013.

[32] *Ibid.*

[33] The Guantánamo Docket, 'Citizens of Yemen', *New York Times*, available at http://projects.nytimes.com/guantanamo/country/yemen.

[34] B. Azmy, 'The face of indefinite detention', *New York Times*, 14 September 2012; A. Worthington, 'Does Obama Really Know or Care Who is at Guantánamo?', Truth-out.org, 10 June 2010.

[35] National Defense Authorization Act, s. 1027.   [36] *Ibid.* s. 1028.

the United States or to any other country. The upshot is that there are many detainees who should not be at Guantánamo Bay, but are nonetheless imprisoned there indefinitely.

The Circuit has also established evidentiary standards and presumptions that have made it exceedingly difficult, if not impossible, for detainees to win *habeas* claims. For example, the Circuit reversed a District Court's factual finding that the government had not demonstrated that a Yemeni citizen imprisoned at Guantánamo Bay since 2002 was an enemy fighter.[37] The Circuit Court held that the District Court had failed to accord the government's intelligence report a presumption of regularity that the report is accurate.[38] The Circuit majority reached this conclusion despite the fact that the report contained inaccuracies, was produced in a stressful and chaotic situation and by a clandestine method that was never explained, was filtered through interpreters, subject to transcription errors, and heavily redacted for national security purposes.[39] As Judge Tatel argued in a strong dissent in *Latif* v. *Obama*, 'it is hard to see what is left of the Supreme Court's command that *habeas* review be "meaningful"'.[40]

The Court of Appeals has also made clear its view that the government's evidence need not meet a particularly stringent standard. The Circuit has assumed *arguendo* that the government must meet a preponderance of the evidence standard because the Obama administration has maintained that preponderance standard was 'appropriate'.[41] A unanimous panel in *Al-Adahi* v. *Obama*, however, expressed doubt that *habeas* review 'requires the use of the preponderance standard'.[42] In a subsequent case, *Esmail* v. *Obama*, Judge Silberman wrote that he thought the preponderance standard is 'unrealistic', and candidly doubted that 'any of [his]colleagues will vote to grant a petition if he or she believes that it is *somewhat likely* that the petitioner is an Al-Qaeda adherent or active supporter'.[43] The standard Judge Silberman thought he and his colleagues were prepared to accept was the very low 'some evidence' standard.[44] As Stephen Vladeck has noted, Silberman's opinion could fairly be read as suggesting that he – and at least some of his

---

[37] *Latif* v. *Obama*, 666 F.3d 746, 748 (D.C. Cir. 2011).   [38] *Ibid.* 748–9.
[39] *Ibid.* 779.   [40] *Ibid.*
[41] *Al-Adahi* v. *Obama*, 613 F.3d 1102, 1104–5 (D.C. Cir. 2010), *cert. denied*, 131 S. Ct 1001 (2011).
[42] *Ibid.*
[43] *Esmail* v. *Obama*, 639 F.2d 1075, 1078 (D.C. 2011) (Silberman J concurring).   [44] *Ibid.*

colleagues – are in fact reviewing the government's case only for 'some evidence' rather than the 'more evidence than not' requirement of the preponderance standard.[45]

The District Court Circuit's evisceration of the *Boumediene* hope has had a profound impact on the District Courts. Since July 2010 when the Circuit began issuing its important decisions, district judges have denied ten *habeas* petitions in Guantánamo Bay cases and granted none, compared with twenty-two *habeas* petitions granted and fifteen denied in the two years before that.[46] In the nineteen *habeas* appeals the Circuit has decided, the court has never allowed a prisoner to prevail.[47] As the *New York Times* put it, the 'court has developed substantive, procedural and evidentiary rules that are unjustly one-sided in favor of the government'.[48]

Nonetheless, the Supreme Court has not decided any appeal of any Guantánamo Bay detainee in the four years since *Boumediene* was decided in 2008.[49] Most recently, it denied *certiorari* without any dissent in seven Guantánamo Bay detainee cases, including that of Mr Latif, prompting the *New York Times* to opine that 'it is devastatingly clear that the Roberts' court has no interest in ensuring meaningful [*habeas*] review for foreign prisoners'.[50]

The human consequences of the Circuit's *Latif* decision and the Supreme Court's denial of review were not long in coming. Mr Latif was cleared for release from Guantánamo Bay on three separate occasions, including 2009.[51] Yet his release was blocked, first by Obama's moratorium on transfers and then by congressional restrictions.[52] It is doubtful that officials believed that Mr Latif was a threat to the United

---

[45] Vladeck, 'The D.C. Circuit After *Boumediene*', n. 12 above, 1473.

[46] Editorial, 'Reneging on justice at Guantánamo', *New York Times*, 19 November 2011.

[47] Editorial, 'The Court retreats on *habeas*', *New York Times*, 13 June 2012.   [48] *Ibid.*

[49] *Kiyemba* v. *Obama*, 130 S. Ct 458 (2009). As previously noted, the Court did initially grant *certiorari* in *Kiyemba*, to address the question of whether a *habeas* court had the power to order a prisoner's release from Guantánamo Bay into the United States. Prior to oral argument, the government advised the Court that all of the Uighur petitioners had received offers of resettlement and that some had been resettled since the grant of *certiorari* and moved to dismiss the petition. The Court then vacated the DC Circuit's opinion and remanded to the Circuit to reconsider its ruling in light of the new facts (*Kiyemba* v. *Obama*, 130 S. Ct 458, 1235 (2009)). The Circuit reaffirmed its prior ruling and the Supreme Court denied certiorari in *Kiyemba*, 604 F.3d at 1048 (*per curiam*), *cert. denied*, 131 S. Ct 1631 (2011).

[50] Editorial, 'The Court retreats on *habeas*', n. 47 above.

[51] Editorial, 'Death at Guantánamo Bay', *New York Times*, 15 September 2012.   [52] *Ibid.*

States, although undoubtedly for political reasons the administration chose to appeal his case.[53] Mr Latif had been on a hunger strike, had attempted suicide, and after he lost his appeal he told his lawyer, 'I am a prisoner of death'.[54] On 8 September 2012, he was found dead in his cell, having committed suicide.

Most recently, a hunger strike by many Guantánamo Bay prisoners has garnered worldwide attention.[55] While the strike was apparently sparked by alleged deprivations of the Koran, the underlying reason for the strike is the hopelessness of the Guantánamo Bay detainees of ever getting released, either by judicial or executive action.

II   Refusing to extend *habeas corpus* to detainees held in Afghanistan

In addition to the District Court Circuit's very crabbed reading of *habeas* rights at Guantánamo Bay, the Circuit has refused to accord *habeas* rights to detainees confined first at Bagram Air Force Base and now at the Parwan detention facility in Afghanistan, even where the detainee was captured outside of Afghanistan and brought to Bagram for detention purposes.[56] In a unanimous panel decision joined by two of the more liberal judges on the Circuit, Edwards and Tatel, the Appeals Court reversed a District Court's ruling that the court did have *habeas* jurisdiction for non-Afghan detainees who were apprehended outside of Afghanistan far from any Afghan battlefield and brought to the theatre of war to be detained for many years at Bagram.[57] The Circuit held that since Bagram was considered a war zone, the practical considerations articulated in the *Boumediene* functional test did not allow detainees to challenge their detention in a federal court, and thus the detainees in Afghanistan were outside the scope of US judicial review.[58]

---

[53] See e.g., B. Wittes, 'Thoughts on Adnan Latif', *Lawfare Blog* (12 September 2012), available at www.lawfareblog.com/2012/09/thoughts-on-adnan-latif/. ('Almost nobody thought that Adnan Latif needed to be in custody at all ... had Congress not eventually made it virtually impossible to transfer people from Guantánamo, Latif would not have remained in custody until his presumably self inflicted death').

[54] B. Azmy, 'The face of indefinite detention', *New York Times*, 14 September 2002, available at www.nytimes.com/2012/09/14/opinion/life-and-death-at-guantanamo-bay.html?_r=0.

[55] Editorial, 'Hunger strike at Guantánamo', *New York Times*, 5 April 2013, available at www.nytimes.com/2013/04/06/opinion/hunger-strike-at-guantanamo-bay.html.

[56] *Al Maqaleh* v. *Gates*, 605 F.3d 84 (D.C. Cir. 2010).   [57] *Ibid.*   [58] *Ibid.*

The *Al Maqaleh* decision has been aptly criticised as creating a law-free zone or legal black hole at Bagram.[59]

III   Failure of judiciary to provide accountability for torture

The Circuit Courts of Appeals have uniformly refused to decide civil actions against US officials brought by aliens seeking damages for torture at Guantánamo Bay or elsewhere.[60] One particularly egregious example of the Courts of Appeals' refusal to address claims that US officials sanctioned torture is the *Maher Arar* case. Mr Arar, a Canadian citizen of Syrian descent, was changing planes at Kennedy Airport in New York when he was detained by Immigration and Naturalisation Service (INS) agents based on a tip from the Canadian police that he was a member of Al-Qaeda.[61] Questioned repeatedly by the Federal Bureau of Investigation (FBI), Mr Arar denied the allegations.[62] After two weeks of solitary confinement in Brooklyn, US officials, with the approval of then US Attorney General John Ashcroft, secretly rendered Maher Arar to Syria, where he was tortured and locked in a damp, cold underground cell, which Mr Arar subsequently described as a 'grave' cell because it measured only three feet wide, six feet long and seven feet high.[63]

After a year in detention, the Syrian government released him, concluding that Mr Arar had no connection to terrorism, and he returned home to Canada.[64] To this day, Maher Arar suffers severely from his ordeal.[65]

In 2004, Canada convened a Commission to conduct an official inquiry into the Arar affair.[66] In September 2006, the Commission issued a comprehensive report fully exonerating Maher Arar of any connection to Al-Qaeda or any terrorist group.[67] The Canadian government accepted the Commission's recommendation and officially apologised

---

[59] Editorial, 'Bagram, a legal black hole?', *Los Angeles Times*, 26 May 2010.
[60] See e.g., *Arar* v. *Ashcroft*, 414 F.Supp.2d 250 (E.D.N.Y. 2006), *aff'd*, 532 F.3d 157 (2d Cir.), *aff'd, en banc, vacated and superseded on reh'g en banc*, 585 F.3d 559 (2d Cir. 2009); *Rasul* v. *Myers*, 555 US 1083 (2008), *aff'd on remand*, 563 F.3d 527 (D.C. Cir. 2009), *cert. denied*, 130 S. Ct 1013 (2009).
[61] *Arar* v. *Ashcroft*, 414 F.Supp.2d 250, 252–3 (E.D.N.Y. 2006).   [62] *Ibid.* 253.
[63] *Ibid.*   [64] *Ibid.* 255.
[65] *Ibid.* 252–7 (the facts Maher Arar alleged in his complaint are restated in the District Court opinion in his lawsuit).
[66] Commission of Inquiry into the Activities of Canadian Officials in relation to Maher Arar, *Analysis and Recommendations* (Ottawa: Public Works, 2006), p. 59.
[67] *Ibid.*

to Mr Arar and paid him CAN$11.5 million as compensation for Canada's role in the ordeal.[68]

In January 2004, Maher Arar filed a complaint against various US officials, including former US Attorney General John Ashcroft.[69] Mr Arar sought damages and alleged that he had been sent to Syria for the purpose of being subjected to torture and detention and that the involved US officials had conspired with Syrian officials in relation to his treatment. Mr Arar and his lawyers questioned why the United States would send a man whom it suspected of being an Al-Qaeda terrorist to Syria, which the United States claimed at the time was a state sponsor of terrorism that practices torture, and not to Canada, the United States' friend and ally.[70] The only plausible explanation is that US officials must have believed that the Syrian government would detain and use coercive interrogation methods on Mr Arar to obtain information that the FBI had not been able to get, nor would Canada obtain through using normal police methods. As it turned out, Maher Arar simply did not have information to provide.

Mr Arar argued that since US officials were constitutionally forbidden from torturing him in New York, they could not intentionally subject him to torture by outsourcing it by shipping him to Syria to be tortured there.[71] Despite Maher Arar's strong claims on the merits, the District Court, a divided Second Circuit panel, and a divided *en banc* Court of Appeals' decision dismissed Mr Arar's claims.[72] Each decision found, under somewhat different reasoning, that he had no private claim for damages.

The Second Circuit's dismissal of Maher Arar's claims is not exceptional but rather the norm. Every other Circuit Court has also dismissed actions by aliens or even citizens for torture claims arising out of US officials' conduct in the 'War on Terror'. For example, the District Court Circuit has also dismissed claims of torture brought by aliens. Prior to *Boumediene*, the Circuit and District Courts in that circuit consistently held that the constitutional proscription of cruel and inhumane punishment did not reach US officials who tortured aliens

---

[68] Ian Austen, 'Canada will pay $9.75 million to man tortured in Syria', *New York Times*, 27 January 2007.

[69] The allegations in the complaint are set forth in *Arar v. Ashcroft*, 414 F.Supp.2d 250 (E.D.N.Y. 2006).

[70] I was one of Arar's lawyers.   [71] *Arar v. Ashcroft*, 414 F.Supp.2d 250 (E.D.N.Y. 2006).

[72] *Arar v. Ashcroft*, 414 F.Supp.2d 250 (E.D.N.Y. 2006), aff'd, 532 F.3d 157 (2d Cir.), aff'd, en banc, vacated and superseded on reh'g en banc, 585 F.3d 559 (2d Cir. 2009).

abroad.[73] In *Rasul* v. *Myers*, first decided by the Circuit just prior to the Supreme Court's holding in *Boumediene*, the court reiterated that rule in dismissing a damages action brought by former detainees at Guantánamo Bay against high government officials for alleged torture they suffered during their detention.[74]

The Supreme Court vacated the *Rasul* dismissal after the *Boumediene* decision, ordering the District Court Circuit to review its decision in light of *Boumediene*.[75] However, in *Kiyemba* v. *Obama*, the Circuit held that the Court's *Boumediene* decision only involved the applicability of the Suspension Clause to Guantánamo Bay and did not affect prior circuit law that stated that the Due Process Clause did not apply to aliens without property or presence within the United States.[76] When the Circuit revisited *Rasul*, it noted that 'the Court in *Boumediene* disclaimed any intention to disturb existing law governing the extraterritorial reach of any constitutional provisions, other than the Suspension Clause'.[77] While the Court is technically correct that *Boumediene* explicitly addressed only the Suspension Clause, *Boumediene*'s extended discussion of the Constitution's extra-territorial reach clearly undermined the Circuit's prior holdings that the Constitution simply did not apply to aliens tortured abroad. The Court's review of its prior extra-territorial jurisprudence in *Boumediene* made clear that 'these decisions undermine the Government's argument that, at least as applied to non-citizens, the Constitution necessarily stops where *de jure* sovereignty ends'.[78]

The District Court Circuit, however, chose not to rest its decision on the ground that the Constitution does not apply to torture of aliens abroad, holding instead that the defendants were entitled to qualified immunity, because reasonable officials would not have known that the prohibition against torture applies to Guantánamo Bay until at least after *Boumediene* was decided in 2008.[79] Indeed, the Court's dicta suggests that, even now, it is not clearly established that the constitutional

---

[73] *In Re Iraq and Afghanistan Detainee Litigation*, 479 F.Supp.2d 85 (D.D.C 2007); *Harbury* v. *Deutsch*, 233 F.3d. 596, 602–3 (D.C. Cir. 2000).

[74] *Rasul* v. *Myers*, 512 F.3d 644, 663–5 (D.C. Cir. 2008), *vacated and remanded*, 555 US 1083 (2008), *aff'd on remand*, 563 F.3d 527 (D.C. Cir. 2009), *cert. denied*, 130 S. Ct 1013 (2009).

[75] *Rasul* v. *Myers*, 555 US 1083 (2008), *aff'd on remand*, 563 F.3d 527 (D.C. Cir. 2009), *cert. denied*, 130 S. Ct 1013 (2009).

[76] *Kiyemba* v. *Obama*, 555 F.3d 1022, 1026–7 (D.C. Cir. 2009), *vacated*, 559 US 131 (2010).

[77] *Rasul* v. *Myers*, 563 F.3d 527, 529 (D.C. Cir. 2009), *cert. denied*, 130 S. Ct 1013 (2009).

[78] *Boumediene* v. *Bush*, 553 US 723, 755 (2008).

[79] *Rasul* v. *Myers*, 563 F.3d 527 (D.C. Cir. 2009).

proscription against torture applies to Guantánamo Bay or any other US military base abroad, and that US officials who engaged in torture abroad today would still be entitled to qualified immunity.[80]

The Circuit revisited the issue of whether the Constitution protects aliens abroad from torture by US officials in the context of claims brought by Iraqi citizens allegedly tortured at the Abu Ghraib prison by US officials.[81] As in *Rasul v. Myers*, the court based its decision dismissing plaintiffs' claims on qualified immunity grounds.[82] However, the Circuit reiterated the *Rasul* statement that the *Boumediene* decision was limited to the Suspension Clause and did not apply to any other constitutional provision.[83] Indeed, the court went further and noted in *dictum* that even if the *Boumediene* functional test was applicable to a claim of torture, the alleged torture took place in Iraq, at the time an 'active theater of war', and therefore the Fifth and Eighth Amendments would undoubtedly not apply under *Boumediene*.[84]

Other Circuits have similarly dismissed claims against US officials for alleged torture. The Ninth Circuit dismissed claims brought by Jose Padilla, a US citizen held as an enemy combatant, against John Yoo, the author of the infamous 'Torture Memo', on the ground that Mr Yoo was entitled to qualified immunity.[85] So too, the Fourth Circuit dismissed Mr Padilla's claims against Donald Rumsfeld, the then Secretary of Defense, and other US officials for his detention and conditions of confinement because, as in the *Arar* case, special factors counselled against implying a cause of action in a case fraught with military and national security implications.[86] Most recently, the Seventh Circuit held that two US citizens who had been working as security contractors in Iraq and were allegedly wrongfully detained for months and tortured by the military nonetheless had no claim against Mr Rumsfeld for their alleged torture because no private cause of action should be allowed given the military context of their allegations.[87]

---

[80] *Rasul*, 563 F.3d at 529 (stating that the Circuit's prior law that the Constitution does not apply to US actions against aliens abroad remains undisturbed by the Supreme Court's opinion in *Boumediene*, with the exception of the Suspension Clause, which does not apply in some circumstances).

[81] *Ali v. Rumsfeld*, 649 F.3d 762, 769 (D.C. Cir. 2011).   [82] *Ibid.* 770.   [83] *Ibid.* 771.

[84] *Ibid.* 772 (quoting *Boumediene v. Bush*, 553 US 723, 770 (2008)).

[85] *Padilla v. Yoo*, 678 F.3d 748 (9th Cir. 2012).

[86] *Lebron v. Rumsfeld*, 670 F.3d 540 (4th Cir. 2012).

[87] *Vance v. Rumsfeld*, 701 F.3d 193 (7th Cir. 2012) (*en banc*).

The Supreme Court has thus far not taken any of these cases, and is unlikely to do so in the future. Moreover, the Court in a series of recent rulings involving counter-terrorism policies, has dismissed claims without reaching the merits, by either making pleading requirements more stringent to state a claim,[88] or by dismissing on qualified immunity grounds,[89] or lack of standing to sue.[90]

Thus, despite the landmark victories that detainees won in the Supreme Court between 2004 and 2008, the judiciary's role as a check on executive misconduct in conducting counter-terrorism policies has been minimal over the past five years. The District Court Circuit has negated any meaningful judicial remedy for the Guantánamo Bay detainees; has reviewed detainees claims under an exceedingly pro-government standard; has refused to extend *Boumediene*'s grant of *habeas* jurisdiction to military bases in Afghanistan; and has not recognised the application of other closely related constitutional rights such as due process to the Guantánamo Bay detainees. Moreover, the Courts of Appeals have uniformly refused to allow any claims by aliens or citizens seeking accountability for torture committed by US officials abroad in connection with counter-terrorism policies to proceed. The Supreme Court has sat silent, refusing to hear any case involving these issues through Obama's first term in office. How does one explain this judicial retreat?

IV   Explaining the disconnect between the Supreme Court's assertive judicial review of detention decisions and the judiciary's passivity

Various scholars have offered explanations for the disconnect between the assertive judicial review represented by the Supreme Court's opinions in *Rasul*, *Hamdi*, *Hamdan* and *Boumediene* between 2004 and 2008, and the judicial passivity that has triumphed subsequently. These theories generally revolve around dichotomies between theory and practice, or process and substance, or rights versus remedies.

For example, Kim Scheppele writes in a recent article that *Boumediene* and other recent cases represent a 'new sort of [judicial] deference' based on the dichotomy between principled victories and practical losses.[91]

---

[88] *Ashcroft* v. *Iqbal*, 556 US 662 (2009).   [89] *Ashcroft* v. *al-Kidd*, 131 S.Ct 2074 (2011).
[90] *Clapper* v. *Amnesty International*, 133 S. Ct 1138 (2013).
[91] K. L. Scheppele, 'The New Judicial Deference' (2012) 92 *Boston University Law Review* 89, 93.

While the old judicial deference allowed the government to win national security or wartime cases through the judiciary's refusal to intervene, *Boumediene* represents a new deferential position where 'governments win first by losing these cases on principle and then by getting implicit permission to carry on the losing policy in concrete cases for a while longer, giving governments a victory in practice'.[92] The detainees received inspiring rhetoric while the government 'got the facts on the ground'.[93] For Scheppele, the contradiction between theory and practice is not based on practical or political resistance to the Supreme Court's decision, but is contained within the judicial opinion itself, which integrates inspiring rhetoric paired with a lack of detail and instructions as to how to implement the decision: '[t]he new judicial deference means that both sides win – with one side getting the right in theory while the other side gets the reality on the ground, each authorized by different aspects of the same judicial decision'.[94] For Scheppele, a wide gap exists 'between suspected terrorists' legal gains and their unchanged fates'.[95] Her analysis also invokes the right/remedy dichotomy, claiming that the Court boldly articulated that the detainees have important rights, but 'provided few immediate remedies'.[96]

Jenny Martinez draws attention to the Supreme Court and lower courts' focus on process as opposed to substance in the 'War on Terror' cases in an attempt to answer the question posed by her client Jose Padilla: 'Why is it that litigation concerning the alleged enemy combatants detained at Guantánamo and elsewhere has been going on for more than six years and almost nothing seems to have actually been decided?'.[97] For her, the Court's procedural focus allowed it to delay

---

[92] *Ibid.* 93.   [93] *Ibid.* 91.   [94] *Ibid.* 158.   [95] *Ibid.*

[96] *Ibid.* 91. Linda Greenhouse has noted the same gap between principle and facts on the ground in a 2009 article in which she sought to tackle what she termed the 'mystery of Guantánamo Bay', asking 'how can it be that nearly seven years after the first detainees arrived at the prison there – after numerous courtroom battles, the most significant of which resulted in defeats for the Bush Administration's position – not a single detainee has ever been released, by order of any court or any other body in a position of authority, against the wishes of the Administration? How is it, in other words, that after all this time, all this spinning of wheels and running place, nothing has happened?'. See L. Greenhouse, 'The Mystery of Guantánamo Bay' (2009) 27 *Berkeley Journal of International Law* 1, 2. Greenhouse attributes this disconnect to the interconnection of a hard-line executive position, which radicalised the Supreme Court, combined with an inherent judicial cautiousness which failed to understand that the executive would not respond to gentle nudges.

[97] J. S. Martinez, 'Process and Substance in the 'War on Terror'' (2008) 108 *Columbia Law Review* 1013.

resolution of controversial substantive claims, which may have practical advantages but comes at a significant human cost to the detainees.

Closely related to Martinez's procedural/substance dichotomy, Stephen Vladeck offers another duality to describe the Supreme Court's post 9/11 jurisprudence in terrorism cases: passive/aggressive behaviour.[98] He claims that 'by repeatedly asserting their authority only to routinely sidestep the merits, the Court has been neither passive nor active, but passive-aggressive', and argues that this approach has its distinct dangers.[99] So too, Richard Fallon has echoed Martinez's argument, noting the 'juxtaposition of the Court's assertiveness in upholding judicial jurisdiction with its reticence regarding substantive rights'.[100]

Vladeck has also articulated another related theory to help explain the disconnect between the Supreme Court's bold assertiveness in *Boumediene* and the paucity of the substantive rules it has developed to address the detainees' situation. The Court, according to Vladeck, has acted mainly to preserve the Court's role and judicial power over these detentions, and not primarily in support of the detainees' rights.[101] Separation-of-powers considerations are paramount, and not rights.[102] From this perspective, *Boumediene* achieved what the Court really wanted: to tell the executive that the Court had a role to play in this area, and the executive could not operate totally outside the reach of the judiciary. But so long as the judiciary had a role to play in the separation of powers scheme, the courts would interfere only minimally with the substantive policies that the executive had put in place at Guantánamo Bay.[103]

All of these explanations are reasonable and accurately describe the Supreme Court's detainee jurisprudence. But something deeper is at work underlying the dichotomous jurisprudence which has boldly asserted a judicial role over the detainees, yet permitted a preventive

---

[98] S. I. Vladeck, 'The Passive-Aggressive Virtues' (2011) 111 *Columbia Law Review* 122, 127 (Sidebar).

[99] *Ibid.*

[100] R. H. Fallon, Jr., 'The Supreme Court, *Habeas Corpus*, and the "War on Terror": An Essay on Law and Political Science' (2010) 110 *Columbia Law Review* 352, 391.

[101] Vladeck, 'The Passive-Aggressive Virtues', n. 98 above.

[102] *Ibid.*

[103] S. I. Vladeck, '*Boumediene*'s Quiet Theory: Access to Courts and the Separation of Powers' (2009) 84 *Notre Dame Law Review* 2107, 2111 (arguing that the injury the statute (removing *habeas* review) inflicted upon the role of the courts was at least relevant, if not central, to the constitutional analysis); see also, Greenhouse, 'The Mystery of Guantánamo Bay', n. 96 above, 8–9.

detention scheme with only minimal substantive and procedural safe-guards to be put in place at Guantánamo Bay. For the *Boumediene* contradictions reflect broader forces at work than just those involving the Guantánamo Bay detainees, but are symptomatic of the general approach of many domestic and foreign courts in this type of litigation.

Consider the Canadian Supreme Court's decisions in the case of Omar Khadr, a Canadian citizen who was captured in Afghanistan by US forces and brought to Guantánamo Bay at the age of fifteen. Mr Khadr's Canadian lawyers sought an order requiring the Canadian government to disclose the interviews conducted by Canadian officials at Guantá-namo. The Canadian government argued that Canada's Charter of Rights and Freedoms did not apply extra-territorially. A unanimous Canadian Supreme Court rejected that argument, holding that 'if Canada was participating in a process that was violative of Canada's binding obliga-tions under international law, the Charter applies to the extent of that participation'.[104]

Two years later in 2010, the Canadian Supreme Court reiterated its previous holding in the *Khadr* case and issued declaratory relief that Canada had violated the Charter in participating in Mr Khadr's deten-tion. Nonetheless, that assertive holding led to no relief for Omar Khadr, who was detained at Guantánamo Bay until the United States finally released him in 2012. For at the same time that the Canadian Court held that Canada had violated the Charter, it also reversed a lower court order requiring Canadian officials to seek Omar Khadr's repatriation to Canada because (a) the evidentiary record was incomplete; (b) of 'the limitations of the Court's institutional competence'; and (c) of the need to respect the foreign policy powers of the executive.[105]

Moreover, a subsequent case decided by the Canadian Federal Court of Appeal appeared to significantly limit the *Khadr* rulings. In *Amnesty International Canada* v. *Canada*, a unanimous Court of Appeal distin-guished the *Khadr* case in holding that the Charter did not apply during the armed conflict in Afghanistan to the detention of non-Canadians by the Canadian forces, nor to their transfer to Afghan authorities even if such transfer exposed them to a substantial risk of torture.[106] The Canadian Supreme Court refused to hear Amnesty International's

---

[104] *Canada (Justice)* v. *Khadr* 2008 SCC 28, para. 19, [2008] 2 SCR 125.
[105] *Canada (Prime Minister)* v. *Khadr* 2010 SCC 3, para. 46, [2010] 1 SCR 44, para. 46.
[106] *Amnesty International Canada* v. *Canada (Chief of the Defence Staff)* 2008 FCA 401, [2009] 4 FCR 149.

appeal.[107] The Canadian courts have thus acted in a similar fashion to the US courts, boldly asserting jurisdiction in *Khadr*, only to fail to provide meaningful relief or to extend the holding in other contexts.

Perhaps the best example of the broader contradictions contained in the US counter-terrorism litigation stems from *Brown* v. *Board of Education*. Brown was a great victory for the National Association for Advancement of Colored People (NAACP) and the rights of African Americans to be free from segregated education, and has been hailed as 'perhaps the most important judgment ever handed down by an American Supreme Court'.[108] But, as the distinguished legal historian Paul Finkleman has noted, it is ironic that fifty years after the decision, 'many scholars and some civil rights activists regard the decision as a failure'.[109] Harvard civil rights professor Charles Ogletree concludes 'that fifty years after Brown there is little left to celebrate'[110] while the great civil rights activist and professor Derrick Bell wrote that '[b]y dismissing *Plessy* without dismantling it, the Court seems to predict if not underwrite eventual failure'.[111] Or as Bell put it, the passage of years has transformed the Brown ruling 'into a magnificent mirage, the legal equivalent of that city on a hill to which all aspire without any serious thought that it will ever be attained'.[112]

Indeed, twenty years ago Gerald Rosenberg's book, *The Hollow Hope*, set off a firestorm by arguing that *Brown* had virtually no effect in ending racial discrimination or racial segregation.[113] For Rosenberg, the failure of *Brown* to have any direct or even indirect effect on segregation was symptomatic of a broader inability of courts to be effective in producing social change. Rosenberg concluded that 'US courts can almost never be

---

[107] *Ibid.*

[108] M. J. Horwitz, *The Warren Court and the Pursuit of Justice* (New York: Hill and Wang, 1998), p. 15.

[109] P. Finkleman, 'Civil Rights in Historical Context: In Defense of Brown' (2005) 118 *Harvard Law Review* 973, 974 (Book Review).

[110] C. J. Ogletree, Jr, *All Deliberate Speed: Reflections on the First Half Century of Brown v. Board of Education* (New York: W. W. Norton & Company, 2004), p. XV.

[111] D. A. Bell Jr, 'Proposed Brown Dissenting Opinion' in J. M. Balkin (ed.), *What Brown v. Board of Education Should Have Said: The Nation's Top Legal Experts Rewrite America's Landmark Civil Rights Decision* (New York University Press, 2001), pp. 185, 199.

[112] See D. Bell, *Silent Covenants: Brown v. Board of Education and the Unfilled Hopes for Racial Reform* (Oxford University Press, 2004), p. 4; see also, Bell, *Silent Covenants*, 6 ('Brown brought about transformation without real change').

[113] G. N. Rosenberg, *The Hollow Hope: Can Courts Bring About Social Change?* (2nd edn, University of Chicago Press, 2008).

effective producers of significant social reform'.[114] To him, 'courts act as "fly paper" for social reformers who succumb to the "lure of litigation"'.[115]

On the fiftieth anniversary of *Brown*, Michael J. Klarman published a massive study of the Supreme Court's role in ending racial discrimination, also minimising the effects of the decision.[116] For Klarman, the Supreme Court played a relatively minor role in changing race relations in the country.[117] The Court's constitutional interpretation generally reflects the social and political climate of the times, and racial change was coming in the 1950s irrespective of *Brown*.[118] As a legal decision, Klarman argues that *Brown* failed to accomplish much, and that its main achievement was to radicalise southern politics, resulting in white backlash and violence against civil rights activists, which ultimately rallied national opinion behind civil rights.[119]

Rosenberg and Klarman's books produced a vigorous debate about the role of *Brown* and of judicial review more generally.[120] For example, various scholars have disputed Rosenberg's view that Brown accomplished nothing and that litigation is counter-productive, correctly pointing out the indirect effects of *Brown*.[121]

Yet it is indisputable that the *Brown* decision itself produced little change in the decade that followed. The Supreme Court boldly proclaimed that segregation of schools by race was unconstitutional but provided no remedy in the decade after *Brown*. The Supreme Court intervened sparingly between 1954 and the passage of the 1964 Civil

---

[114] *Ibid.* p. 422.   [115] *Ibid.* p. 427.

[116] M. J. Klarman, *From Jim Crow to Civil Rights: the Supreme Court and the Struggle for Racial Equality* (Oxford University Press, 2004).

[117] *Ibid.*   [118] *Ibid.* pp. 5–6, 468.   [119] *Ibid.* p. 385.

[120] See e.g., Finkelman, 'Civil Rights in Historical Context', n. 109 above, 1018 ('it is impossible to imagine the civil rights revolution having succeeded so quickly in sweeping away *de jure* segregation without *Brown*'); see also, D. A. Schultz, *Leveraging the Law: Using the Courts to Achieve Social Change* (New York: Peter Lang Publishing, 1998) (evaluating Rosenberg's thesis and in part criticising it); P. H. Schuck, 'Public Law Litigation and Social Reform' (1993) 102 *Yale Law Journal* 1763 (book review) (criticising Rosenberg's thesis); S. L. Carter, 'Do Courts Matter?, Book Review: The Hollow Hope: Can Courts Bring About Social Change?' (1992) 90 *Michigan Law Review* 1216, 1221 (Rosenberg 'gives short shrift to the [*Brown*] decision's vital importance as a confidence building device for those who were fighting for reform'); B. Swedlow, 'Reason for Hope? The Spotted Owl Injunctions and Policy Change' (2009) 34 *Law and Social Inquiry* 825, 849 ('the owl litigation shows that US courts can produce significant policy change').

[121] *Ibid.*

Rights Act.[122] As of the passage of that Act in 1964, *Brown* had resulted in only 2.3 per cent of black children in the south attending schools with whites.[123] It was only after Congress and the President implemented strong measures supporting southern school desegregation, that the southern resistance to integrated schools was broken.[124]

The broader explanation for the disconnect between the Supreme Court's great pronouncements in *Boumediene* and the judiciary's failure to provide meaningful review or relief to many Guantánamo Bay detainees must be found not in specific judicial doctrine, or the Court's procedural versus substantive rulings, or even in the Court's inclination to preserve its own role as opposed to the detainees' rights. Rather, the contradictory legacy of *Boumediene* and the other detainee litigation thus far is more fundamentally the result of a deep-rooted limitation of rights-based litigation: that rights cannot be divorced from politics nor can litigation be viewed independently of the social and political context in which it is brought.

The Guantánamo Bay litigation is simply one more illustration of that broader perspective. From this perspective, the cause of the failures in the Guantánamo Bay litigation does not reside in any court announced doctrine, or the recalcitrance of the District Court Circuit. Rather, the cause lies in the consensus of the national security elites and the three branches of government that high government officials who engaged in torture and other misconduct should be shielded from judicial review of their actions and that we need a preventive detention scheme to continue to hold captured Al-Qaeda and Taliban suspects where prosecution might be difficult. That consensus has been challenged by human rights groups, but not by any grass-roots movement of the American people, who generally do not seem particularly concerned by what is happening now at Guantánamo Bay or at the other main detention centre at Parwan, Afghanistan.

---

[122] The Court issued only three full opinions in the area of school segregation in those ten years, despite the massive resistance of the south to integration. The most important of these, *Cooper* v. *Aaron*, 358 US 1 (1958) upheld the role of the Court and required southern communities to obey the decisions of the Court as part of the supreme law of the land. Rosenberg, *The Hollow Hope: Can Courts Bring About Social Change?*, n. 113 above, pp. 43–4.

[123] J. R. Dunn, 'Title VI, the Guidelines, and School Desegregation in the South' (1967) 53 *Virginia Law Review* 42, 44 n. 9.

[124] *Ibid.*

Joseph Margulies and Hope Metcalf, who were counsel in the detainee cases, have reached a similar conclusion. In an important article, they argue that legal scholars and lawyers had a flawed understanding of the role of litigation and the courts in response to the Bush administration's 'War on Terror' policies.[125] The legal academy erroneously focused 'on what Stuart Scheingold called "the myth of rights" – the belief that if we can identify, elaborate and secure judicial recognition of the legal "right", the political structures and policies will adapt their behaviour to the requirements of the law and change will follow more or less automatically'.[126] For them, the explanation for what the courts have done or failed to do in the post 9/11 context must be grounded in the political realities of our time, not in doctrinal or structural arguments.[127]

Indeed, as various scholars have noted, the confluence of a number of political factors from 2009 through 2010 underlay the failure of Obama to close Guantánamo Bay and the consolidation of a wartime preventive detention regime.[128] The Republicans in Congress and former Bush administration officials waged a concerted pushback against any attempt to close Guantánamo Bay, and more broadly to move away from the military detention model. Obama and his advisors did not vigorously contest these moves, wanting to appear strong on national security and fighting terrorism. Indeed, on certain issues such as the moratorium on transferring Yemeni detainees, the Obama administration acted even before Congress did. During this critical juncture, polls of the American people showed that support for closing Guantánamo Bay had plummeted from a majority of the population when Barack Obama was elected, to less than 40 per cent a year later.[129] While the Supreme Court's procedural, jurisdictional decisions in *Rasul* and *Boumediene* permitted the consolidation of the current system of preventive detention at Guantánamo Bay, the political context of the last four years is what fundamentally underlies its approval by the courts and the political branches.

---

[125] J. Margulies and H. Metcalf, 'Terrorizing Academia' (2011) 60 *Journal of Legal Education* 433.

[126] *Ibid*. 437.   [127] *Ibid*.

[128] See D. Frakt, 'Guantánamo Detainees: the "Other" Victims of 9/11' *JURIST Forum* (20 September 2012), available at http://jurist.org/forum/2012/09/david-frakt-guantanamo-detainees.php#. See also, D. Frakt, *Prisoners of Congress: the Constitutional and Political Clash over Detainees and the Closure of Guantánamo*, Legal Studies Research Paper Series, Working Paper No. 2012–22 (2012).

[129] See Frakt, 'Guantánamo Detainees', n. 128 above; Margulies and Metcalf, 'Terrorizing Academia', n. 125 above.

Moreover, on the question of whether former officials who authorised torture should be prosecuted criminally or even subjected to judicial review through civil damage actions, again there has been unity amongst the three branches and the national security elite. The Obama administration has vigorously defended former Bush administration officials from damages actions seeking accountability. Nor has there been any move in Congress or the administration to establish some form of alternative public accountability for the torture that occurred, such as a National Commission of Inquiry or Truth Commission. While the Senate Intelligence Committee approved an important report on the CIA's post 9/11 interrogation techniques, that report thus far has not been made public.[130] Therefore, the judiciary's abstention is part of a broader failure of accountability thus far amongst all three branches of government.

Conclusion

The recent hunger strike of over 100 detainees at Guantánamo Bay illustrates that in the aftermath of 9/11, the most effective restraint of governmental repression was often to be found by pressure put upon governmental institutions by those caught in the repressive web and by civil society organisations.[131] Since Obama's election in 2008 and his subsequent moratorium on transfers out of Guantánamo Bay, dozens of Guantánamo Bay detainees have languished in the prison without hope of ever getting out, and with no meaningful progress by the executive branch, Congress or the judiciary. Yet the enormous political pressure brought about by the prisoners' own hunger strike, resulting in numerous newspaper articles,[132] editorials,[133] statements by civic and human rights organisations,[134] as well as officials and institutions of the United

---

[130] 'Senate Panel discredits torture', *Washington Post*, 14 December 2012.

[131] See generally, D. Cole, 'Where Liberty Lies: Civil Society and Individual Rights After 9/11' (2011) 57 *Wayne Law Review* 1203 (arguing that the restraints imposed on the executive branch after 9/11, 'for the most part, were imposed not by the formal mechanisms of checks and balances, but by more informal influences, often sparked by efforts of civil society organizations that advocated, educated, organized, demonstrated and litigated for constitutional and human rights').

[132] C. Savage, 'Despair drives Guantánamo detainees to revolt', *New York Times*, 25 April 2013, as one example of many.

[133] Editorial, 'The Guantánamo stain', *New York Times*, 25 April 2013; Editorial, 'The President and the hunger strike', *New York Times*, 1 May 2013.

[134] Letter of 11 April 2013 to President Barak Obama, 'Re Concern about hunger strike and stalled efforts to close the detention center at Guantánamo', signed by twenty-five

Nations and Organization of American States,[135] has resulted in a renewed initiative by the Obama administration to resolve the situation.[136] While at the present writing it is unclear what will transpire in the future, it is clear that the hunger strike, and the resulting press and civic organisation attention, has changed the situation in a manner in which litigation and lobbying were unable to. The lesson seems to be that while judicial review and separation of powers are invaluable checks on executive overreaching, they are fundamentally dependent on public pressure, public perception and political reality to be truly effective.

prominent human rights and civic organisations, including the Center for Constitutional Rights, American Civil Liberties Union and Amnesty International, available at http://ccrjustice.org/files/2013.4.11_GTMO%20Coalition%20Letter%20to%20President %20Obama_.pdf.

[135] On 5 April 2013, in the context of the hunger strike, Navi Pillay, the UN High Commissioner for Human Rights, called on all institutions of the US government to work together to close Guantánamo. See statement at www.ohchr.org/SP/NewsEvents/Pages/DisplayNews.aspx?NewsID=13212&LangID=E.

On 1 May 2013, the Inter-American Commission on Human Rights (IACHR), the UN Working Group on Arbitrary Detention and various UN Special Rapporteurs called on the US government to end indefinite detention at Guantánamo Bay.

[136] C. Savage, 'Amid hunger strike, Obama renews push to close Cuba prison', *New York Times*, 1 May 2013; Editorial, 'The President and the Hunger Strike', n. 133 above.

PART II

Beyond counter-terrorism judicial review

5

Emergency law as administrative law

MARK TUSHNET

Introduction

Discussions on the constitutional regulation of counter-terrorism policy have often focused on issues about the relationship between constitutionalism and 'emergencies', with Carl Schmitt and Giorgio Agamben playing large roles and the idea of a suspension of legality asserted and disputed. But, as Mary Dudziak's recent work *War Time* confirms, counterterrorism policy is today better seen as dealing with a relatively permanent condition, not a transient event.[1] In this light, counter-terrorism policy could perhaps be better regulated not through a distinctive 'law of emergency powers' but rather through ordinary administrative law. As conceptualised in the United States, administrative law establishes a regime of legality that acknowledges (a) the role that expertise (here, in national security policy) plays in developing lawful regulation; (b) the interplay between the administrative bureaucracy and the 'political' branches, especially the legislature, in shaping policy; and (c) the necessary but limited role of the judiciary in ensuring that policy developed by administrative bureaucracies does not threaten fundamental 'rule of law' values. This chapter argues that many, though not all, well-established elements of modern US administrative law can satisfactorily address many, though not all, of the legality issues raised by counter-terrorism policy.[2] The term 'satisfactorily' of course conceals much. I mean that those elements provide an allocation of decision-making authority

I thank Jack Goldsmith and Adrian Vermeule for comments on a draft of this chapter.
[1] M. Dudziak, *War Time: An Idea, Its History, Its Consequences* (Oxford University Press, 2012).
[2] I emphasise that I draw upon ideas in US administrative law, lacking sufficient knowledge to assert that the same or similar features characterise administrative law in other nations. For an approach similar to mine, though somewhat more narrow, see J. Landau, '*Chevron* Meets *Youngstown*: National Security and the Administrative State' (2012) 92 *Boston University Law Review* 1917. See also, D. Franklin, 'Enemy Combatants and the Jurisdictional Fact Doctrine' (2008) 29 *Cardozo Law Review* 1001. For a relatively early treatment, see C. Sunstein, 'Administrative Law Goes to War' (2005) 118 *Harvard Law Review* 2663.

among the executive, legislatures and courts that is probably better than any other allocation realistically achievable through institutional design. That allocation might place looser constraints on the exercise of power than might be normatively desirable in the abstract. But, just as emergency power is exercised in the real world, so too must constraints on its exercise be ones that can be implemented in the real world.

I   Dimensions of War

Mary Dudziak's book reminds us that time is one of the dimensions along which we differentiate between the normal and the exceptional.[3] Other dimensions are geography and citizenship.[4] Dudziak suggests that we try to think of war as happening now, but not then (or then, but not now). We also try to think of war as happening over there, as George M. Cohan put it, but not over here, and as pitting them against us. We recognise exceptions to the exceptional, so to speak: the Civil War happened here; civil wars generally set brother against brother; fifth columnists are a 'they' who we cannot readily distinguish from 'us'. But, Dudziak argues, war is 'an enduring condition', not a passing event.[5] Temporally, individual wars extend longer than some legal formalities might indicate. They 'start' before a declaration of war, as with Roosevelt's lend-lease policy, and 'end' after the shooting stops, as with the rent control cases from the First and Second World Wars. And, they occur in close enough succession that, Dudziak suggests, we ought to think of war as the normal, and peace as the temporal exception.

If so, we also ought to think differently about the constitutional implications of war. We know that wartime can reduce our willingness to distinguish between over there and over here, and between us and them, as in the Japanese internment cases[6] and in *Schenck v. United States*, because we were at war with 'them' 'over there' we could the Supreme Court said, do things 'over here' to some of 'us' that we could not do were we not at war.[7] This way of thinking suggests that there are

---

[3] Dudziak, *War Time*, n. 1 above.
[4] I draw this point from Oren Gross as well. O. Gross, 'Chaos and Rules: Should Responses to Violent Crises Always be Constitutional?' (2003) 112 *Yale Law Journal* 1011.
[5] Dudziak, *War Time*, n. 1 above, p. 5.
[6] M. Tushnet, 'Civil Liberties in a Time of Terror: Defending *Korematsu*?: Reflections on Civil Liberties in Wartime' (2003) *Wisconsin Law Review* 273.
[7] *Schenck v. United States*, 100 US 47, 52 (1919) ('When a nation is at war, many things that might be said in time of peace are such a hindrance to its effort that their utterance will not

'fixed stars', to use Justice Jackson's term,[8] located during normal times, from which we can depart somewhat during wartime. Yet, if war is an enduring condition, the metaphor of fixed stars has to give way. Instead, we have something like a blurry ring with uncertain boundaries, as suggested by Justice Holmes' statement in *Schenck* that the boundaries of the First Amendment are determined by 'circumstances' or, more generally, by the metaphor of balancing that Justice Frankfurter derived, perhaps mistakenly, from Holmes' thought.

I want to complement this initial argument with some unoriginal observations, not about time, but about war. We have engaged in more wars than Dudziak describes because she is concerned with temporality and 'real' wars, that is, what used to be called shooting wars, in which armed adversaries confront each other, with each side risking injury and death – in which, as Dudziak puts it, 'American military personnel traveled to other nations with their military units, wearing uniforms and bearing arms'.[9] I think we might complement her thinking with two other points.

First, the category of literal shooting wars might no longer be large enough to include everything that Dudziak herself is concerned with. Without going into details here, consider three current or recent episodes:

- the US involvement in Libya (and against the Army of God), in which the Obama administration has adopted a (in my view plausible) definition of the term 'hostilities' in the War Powers Resolution (and note the title of the Resolution) to justify the President's deployment of US forces without obtaining congressional assent after sixty days;
- the use of unmanned armed aircraft ('drones') to attack 'them' without placing any of 'us' in direct danger;
- the increasing prominence of concern about waging and defending against 'cyberwar'.

I emphasise that these three items deal with something akin to 'real' wars. Policy responsibility for them, for example, is lodged in the Department of Defense (formerly, the War Department). But, the activities they describe do not fit comfortably into the image we have of a shooting war.

---

be endured so long as men fight, and that no Court could regard them as protected by any constitutional right.').

[8] *West Virginia Bd of Education* v. *Barnett*, 319 US 624, 642 (1943).

[9] Dudziak, *War Time*, n. 1 above, p. 31. Please note the geographical reference here.

Secondly, we are now involved in many metaphorical wars: on cancer, on crime, on drugs, on terror, (formerly) on poverty.[10] And, notably, arguments about government power and individual rights having the same structure as arguments about power and rights occur in connection with these metaphorical wars. In each, proponents of the war argue that the exigencies of the struggle require that we rethink previously held ideas about power and rights. That point is obvious and banal, I think, in connection with the wars on crime and terror. Consider Issacharoff and Pildes' formulation of the distinction between wartime and peacetime: it should turn on whether there are 'times of heightened risk to the physical safety' of citizens.[11] This is precisely how proponents of the war on crime characterised the situation facing the United States. Note as well that Richard Nixon's campaign for the presidency in 1968 emphasised that the Warren Court had 'gone too far in weakening the peace forces as against the criminal forces'.[12] But, it happened as well during the War on Poverty, when Congress adopted innovative programmes that stretched the previously accepted boundaries of federal power, through much more extensive conditional spending programmes with much more detailed conditions, than had been widely used earlier.

If war is a condition rather than a 'time', though, how should we think about its constitutional dimensions? Dudziak suggests that our conventional way of thinking about war must be reconsidered, because the conventional way is to say to ourselves that '[w]e can do things now – during wartime – that we didn't do then (before the war) and won't do later, after the war'. But, of course, if there is no 'now' or 'then', this is either a mistake or, more worrisome, a trap.[13]

---

[10] I first heard this thought articulated in a survey course on US intellectual history taught by Donald Fleming at Harvard University some time in the late 1960s. I later discovered that he had drawn the idea from a then recent article by someone else (as one does in survey courses), but I no longer recall the original source. A similar argument is made in J. Simon, *Governing Through Crime: How the War on Crime Transformed American Democracy and Created a Culture of Fear* (Oxford University Press, 2007).

[11] R. Pildes and S. Issacharoff, 'Between Civil Libertarianism and Executive Unilateralism: An Institutional Process Approach to Rights During Wartime' (2004) 5(1) *Theoretical Inquiries in Law* 1, quoted in Dudziak, *War Time*, n. 1 above, p. 114.

[12] Richard Nixon, Speech accepting the Republican nomination, 8 August 1968, available at www2.vcdh.virginia.edu/HIUS316/mbase/docs/nixon.html.

[13] Oren Gross refers to the worrisome dimension under the heading, 'One Can Get Used to This'. Gross, 'Chaos and Rules', n. 4 above, 1092.

II Administrative law as an alternative to 'emergency' law

An alternative way of thinking is readily available, though – ordinary administrative law.[14] The Food and Drug Administration (FDA) deals with a regular condition of our lives, that manufacturers introduce unsafe foods and medications into our economy. We rely on the FDA to police (perhaps a suggestive term in the present context) the marketplace for food and drugs. We know, of course, that whether a food or drug is unsafe is sometimes contestable, either in gross (do this medication's side-effects outweigh the benefits it offers?) or in particular (is this batch of lettuce contaminated?). Administrative law provides the legal framework for addressing these and other questions.

Begin with a standard example from administrative law. A meat inspector visits a butcher's warehouse and observes some items that in her judgement are contaminated. Without pausing to go to court, the inspector seizes the meat and closes the warehouse pending a later determination by the FDA that the meat was in fact contaminated. That determination is in turn subject to judicial review under the Administrative Procedure Act.[15] The reviewing court will (a) accept any reasonable interpretation of the underlying food and drug laws on which the agency's action rested; and (b) accept the agency's findings of fact if they are supported by substantial evidence in the record as a whole.

Turn now to counter-terrorism policy. Like the meat inspector's action, counter-terrorism actions take place before the courts get involved. Decisions are made by experts in national security and processed through a bureaucracy both before and after action is taken. For example, the experts develop criteria for determining who can be properly targeted for covert action, and (according to reports) in the United States, high-level bureaucrats and political actors retain reasonably tight control over delegated authority to find that an individual fits the criteria. There are periodic reviews of the policy and its implementation, and revisions made in light of experience. To that point, the decisions are

---

[14] Adrian Vermeule has developed this argument in detail, arguing that 'emergencies' can be understood as a category *within* administrative law, not an alternative to it. See especially, A. Vermeule, 'Our Schmittian Administrative Law' (2009) 122 *Harvard Law Review* 1095. Vermeule's analysis leads him to the conclusion that courts will have almost no role in policing agency action because they will interpret the provisions of the applicable statutes with an eye to the imperatives, as the judges see them, of national security: if they see the imperatives as strong they will adjust review to be lax, but if they think there is no strong national security threat they will engage in more vigorous review.

[15] Pub.L. 79–404, 60 Stat. 237.

quite similar to decisions made by typical administrative bureaucracies. What is lacking is some post-event evaluation by an independent judiciary, a point to which I will return.

For now, note that, under ordinary administrative law principles, reviewing courts in the United States rarely exercise their independent judgement about the propriety of administrative action – or, here, about specific actions taken pursuant to counter-terrorism policy. The so-called *Chevron* doctrine provides the analytic structure. The details of the *Chevron*[16] case are complex and irrelevant here. The *Chevron* doctrine directs the courts to proceed in three steps when they confront an agency's interpretation of some statute. First, in what is confusingly labelled 'Step Zero', the courts ask whether the legislature gave the agency the authority to interpret the statute at all. The FDA might have been given authority over food and drugs, but its interpretation of statutes dealing with court procedure have no weight beyond that rationally accorded to the agency's reasoning itself. Next, in what is conventionally labelled 'Step One', the courts ask whether Congress itself has resolved the question of interpretation, that is, whether the statute standing alone clearly requires or prohibits the agency's chosen course. If Congress has not resolved the question, the courts proceed to 'Step Two', in which they ask whether the agency's interpretation is a reasonable one. If it is, the courts are required to accept the agency's interpretation. There is one final step, drawn from administrative law generally: the courts ask, at the end, whether the agency's application of its interpretation to the facts before it was 'arbitrary or capricious' because, for example, the application rested on rationally irrelevant criteria, and whether the application was supported by substantial evidence. Here, the courts evaluate specific actions in light of the entire record, with a fair amount of deference to the agency's expert judgment about inferences to be drawn from fuzzy facts.

Through these rules the modern administrative state allocates responsibility among Congress, agencies and the courts based on our ideas about comparative institutional competence. The non-delegation, delegation and cognate 'clear statement' doctrines say that Congress, not the FDA or other administrative agencies, must make some decisions (typically, those of sufficiently large magnitude) and Congress' general authority allows it to make the more detailed ones addressed in *Chevron*'s first step. These doctrines rest on the thought that Congress is directly

---

[16] *Chevron U.S.A., Inc. v. Natural Resources Defense Council, Inc.*, 467 US 837 (1984).

politically responsible to the people. Administrative law charges agencies with making decisions that require a higher degree of technical expertise than is typically available to Congress, creating indirect political responsibility through agency attentiveness to congressional funding decisions and through the appointment of agency heads by the President. The Administrative Procedure Act authorises the courts to supervise agencies to ensure procedural regularity and minimal rationality, and the Constitution authorises them to ensure that agency actions do not violate substantive constitutional rights. Again, the underlying theory is one of comparative institutional competence.

Administrative law is shot through with analysis of and controversy over precisely how the questions of comparative institutional competence play out in particular contexts. Those fond of judges worry that agency 'mission-commitment' will lead agencies to overestimate the policy benefits of the agency's chosen course of conduct, thereby posing a risk that agencies will make choices that – to the agencies – seem to strike the right balance between benefits and costs (including costs to rights), but that seem to strike the wrong balance in the courts' eyes.[17] Those fond of agencies worry that judges' commitment to rights protections will lead them to underestimate the extent to which enforcing a supposed right will undermine the policy effectiveness of an agency's choice, thereby posing a risk that courts will make choices that strike the wrong balance between rights protection and policy effectiveness.

Suppose we thought of the Departments of Defense and Homeland Security as just another pair of administrative agencies charged with specialised tasks. Our thinking would have two components. One would deal with the courts' regulation of these agencies: like all agencies, they would receive some degree of deference from the courts for decisions, committed to them by Congress, within their areas of expertise. The judicial role in ordinary administrative law is limited. The other would deal with the political branches, offering an explanation for the limited judicial role on the ground that political constraints on agency action are likely to keep them within lawful bounds.

---

[17] For further discussion of this point, see Introduction to this volume, F. F. Davis and F. de Londras, 'Counter-terrorism judicial review: beyond dichotomies'. I simply note, but do not defend here, the obvious point that my formulation is one of balancing. Without going into detail – I doubt that the precise formulation matters. One could think of rights as trumps or as hard-edged rules and still worry about the underlying problem (which would then arise in connection with the specification of the right's content in the particular setting).

Consider some examples, beginning with ones in which national security expertise would play a role were the cases to be treated as ordinary administrative law cases. First, the use of a drone to kill Anwar al-Awlaki. The case posed two issues mixing 'law' and 'fact'. First, did al-Awlaki pose an 'imminent' threat to the United States? Here much turns on the definition of 'imminent'. The relevant 'agencies' appear to have decided that a threat is imminent when (a) the person posing the threat is engaged in ongoing efforts to plan attacks on the United States; and (b) the decision-makers lack and are probably unable to acquire precise information about when a specific attack is likely to occur.[18] For present purposes we can describe these as 'interpretations of law', which the courts would have to accept if they were reasonable. A court would almost certainly find that they are, referring to the expertise of the 'agencies' in matters of counter-terrorism policy as the predicate for the 'agency' legal interpretation.

Secondly, were alternative means of thwarting the threat such as capture and arrest rather than a physical assault reasonably available? The legal basis for using a drone rested in part on the determination that alternative methods of eliminating the threat al-Awlaki posed to the United States, such as attempted seizure by US armed forces operating in Yemen, were both less likely to succeed and more likely to threaten US lives and diplomatic relations with Yemen. This is mostly a factual question. Treating this determination as an ordinary matter of administrative law, with respect to the 'legal' component courts would defer substantially to the agencies' judgements about it, subject only to a quite weak reasonableness requirement (which, I am quite sure, was satisfied in the case). And with respect to the factual one, courts would ask whether the conclusion that capture was infeasible was arbitrary or capricious in light of the facts presented to it. It is worth noting, though, that in counter-terrorism matters the question of what 'record' might be

---

[18] The recently disclosed White Paper of the Department of Justice contains a complex definition of imminence, phrased as follows: imminence 'does not require the United States to have clear evidence that a specific attack on U.S. persons and interests will take place in the immediate future ... [Such a definition] would not allow the United States sufficient time to defend itself. The defensive options available to the United States may be reduced or eliminated if al-Qa'ida operatives disappear and cannot be found when the time of their attack approaches. Consequently, with respect to al-Qa'ida leaders who are continually planning attack, the United States is likely to have only a limited window of opportunity within which to defend Americans'. The White Paper is available at http://msnbcmedia.msn.com/i/msnbc/sections/news/020413_DOJ_White_Paper.pdf.

available to the courts is open to question because the agency might withhold information from the courts on national security grounds. Even so, I am quite sure that judicial review of 'administrative' targeting decisions would quite rarely – and possibly never – find the decisions legally unjustified.

Under ordinary administrative law, courts would play a quite limited role after the event; under counter-terrorism law they might play no role at all.[19] Yet, the incremental value of judicial participation might well be quite small, given rules of deference as to the law and the facts that courts would surely apply anyway. Seeing the al-Awlaki case in light of administrative law suggests, I think rather strongly, that the absence of judicial review would have almost no 'on the ground' consequences. We would have to rely on the political constraints on agency action to ensure compliance with fundamental law.[20] This is the conclusion we would draw were we to think about the problem as one of 'emergency' law. As noted earlier, this might not be the conclusion dictated by normative theorising in the abstract, but the outcome may be the best that is realistically achievable through the institutions we actually have to implement and constrain policy choices.

Secondly, consider the War Powers Resolution and the Libyan intervention. Administrative lawyers are familiar with the 'big deal' principle: that we (in the administrative law context, the courts) should not take general authorisation for agency action to justify exceedingly large regulatory programmes.[21] The 'big deal' principle, which I think is within the same conceptual universe as the non-delegation doctrine, counsels us that Congress rather than agencies must take a stand on 'big deals'. It might also suggest that Congress need not take a stand on smaller matters. The Obama administration's interpretation of the War Powers Resolution draws a similar 'big deal'/'smaller matters' line.

One seeming difference between ordinary administrative law and national security activities is this. Ordinary administrative law gives Congress primacy in policy-making, subject only to whatever (feeble)

---

[19] A lawsuit by al-Awlaki's father failed on standing grounds. *Al-Awlaki* v. *Obama*, 727 F.Supp 1 (D.D.C. 2010).

[20] See also Chapter 6 in this volume, F. F. Davis, 'The politics of counter-terrorism judicial review: creating effective parliamentary scrutiny'; Chapter 3 in this volume, D. Jenkins, 'When good cases go bad: unintended consequences of rights-friendly judgments'; and Chapter 8 in this volume, K. Roach, 'Public inquiries as an attempt to fill accountability gaps left by judicial and legislative review'.

[21] *FDA* v. *Brown and Williamson*, 529 US 120 (2000).

controls the theory of the unitary executive places on Congress' ability to select the personnel who get to implement congressional policy.[22] In contrast, Presidents and their more enthusiastic supporters sometimes claim fairly extensive inherent power from Article II's Take Care and, more significantly, Commander-in-Chief Clauses.[23] Again, though, administrative law provides a framework for thinking about claims of inherent presidential power.

That framework is once again the *Chevron* doctrine, which maps interestingly onto the canonical constitutional framework for dealing with claims of inherent presidential authority, Justice Jackson's three categories in the 'Steel Seizure' case.[24] Justice Stevens' opinion in *Chevron* explains its basis in expertise and political accountability:

> Judges are not experts in the field, and are not part of either political branch of the Government. Courts must, in some cases, reconcile competing political interests, but not on the basis of the judges' personal policy preferences. In contrast, an agency to which Congress has delegated policymaking responsibilities may, within the limits of that delegation, properly rely upon the incumbent administration's views of wise policy to inform its judgments. While agencies are not directly accountable to the people, the Chief Executive is, and it is entirely appropriate for this political branch of the Government to make such policy choices – resolving the competing interests which Congress itself either inadvertently did not resolve, or intentionally left to be resolved by the agency charged with the administration of the statute in light of everyday realities.[25]

Recall that Step One of *Chevron* asks whether Congress has specifically addressed the precise question at issue. If it has, the agency has no discretion and must implement the congressionally chosen policy. If Congress has not specifically addressed the precise question, Step Two

---

[22] An indication of the feebleness of the theory is S. Calabresi and C. Yoo, *The Unitary Executive: Presidential Power from Washington to Bush* (Yale University Press, 2008), which argues that Presidents have the power to fire executive appointees who refuse to carry out presidential directives with respect to congressionally-designated policies that leave discretion to agency decision-makers. *That* unitary-executive theory is weak tea.

[23] As to presidential authority to disregard statutes that affect presidential power in matters not covered by the Commander-in-Chief Clause, arguments for inherent presidential power flowing from the Take Care Clause are obviously circular. (The President has the duty to take care that all the laws, including the Constitution, be faithfully executed, but it alone cannot define the scope of presidential power.)

[24] *Youngstown Sheet & Tube Co. v. Sawyer*, 343 US 579 (1952).

[25] 467 US 837, 865–6 (1984).

asks whether the agency's policy is a reasonable one. Justice Jackson's categories are cases where Congress has specifically authorised the President's action (analogous to Step One), where Congress has neither authorised nor prohibited the action (analogous to Step Two), and where Congress has specifically prohibited the action.

According to Jackson, cases in Category Two are to be resolved by 'the imperatives of events', a notoriously opaque phrase because it fails to distinguish between a prediction about how things will in fact turn out and a standard that courts can suitably apply.[26] But, I think, the usual understanding is that the President's policy choice prevails in Category Two cases. That is true at Step Two of *Chevron* as well, subject only to the possibility that a choice neither dictated nor prohibited by Congress might somehow be unreasonable. Yet, to the extent that that *is* a possibility at *Chevron* Step Two,[27] perhaps the imperatives of events might make a presidential policy in Jackson Category Two unreasonable. If so, claims of inherent presidential power where Congress has not spoken clearly could be treated as ordinary *Chevron* Step Two questions.

Of course, all the interesting action comes in connection with Jackson's Category Three, where Congress has purported to prohibit the presidential action. In ordinary administrative law, agencies exercise authority delegated to them by Congress. Actions beyond the delegation are unlawful, and congressional prohibitions define some of the bounds of Congress' delegations. That is one side of *Chevron* Step One: if Congress has specifically said that the agency cannot do this precise thing, the agency cannot do it. Justice Jackson's formulation of Category Three is on its face a bit more tolerant of presidential action in disregard of a congressional prohibition. For Jackson, in Category Three the President's power is 'at its lowest ebb'.[28] As a matter of word meaning, 'lowest ebb' does not mean 'completely absent'. So, at least on the face of Jackson's formulation, there might be some actions a President could take even despite an express congressional prohibition, although Jackson gives us no hint of what those actions might be.

My sense of the commentary is that scholars assume that presidential actions in Category Three are simply unconstitutional – all of them. And,

---

[26] It is hard to imagine a judge saying, 'The imperatives of events lead me to conclude that the President's decision was improper'.

[27] For an argument that it is not, see M. C. Stephenson and A. Vermeule, '*Chevron* has Only One Step' (2009) 95 *Virginia Law Review* 597.

[28] *Youngstown Sheet & Tube Co.* v. *Sawyer*, 343 US 579, 637 (1952) (Jackson J concurring).

to the extent that the Supreme Court has subsequently weighed in, the Court too appears to have assumed that it follows from a determination that a presidential action falls in Category Three that the action is constitutionally impermissible. That, it seems to me, is the import of *Medellin* v. *Texas*.[29] There, the Court held, first, that various treaties establishing the International Court of Justice were not self-executing as a matter of US law; secondly, that *because* Congress had not implemented the treaties the President lacked the power to implement them on his own, that is, this was not a Category Two case; and, thirdly, for exactly the same reason – Congress' refusal to implement the treaties – Congress had prohibited the President from implementing them, thereby placing the case in Category Three. Then, with no additional analysis, that is, no discussion of whether the President still had some 'lowest ebb' power, the Court concluded that the President's action was unconstitutional.

If the President lacks inherent power in Category Three cases, the parallel to *Chevron* Step One is reasonably close: agencies cannot do what Congress has precluded them from doing, and neither can the President. To put the point another way: in the field of national security policy, constitutional doctrine arising out of the 'Steel Seizure' case converges with administrative law as articulated in *Chevron*. The possibility remains open that in a context less fraught than the death penalty, and where national security was directly implicated, the Supreme Court would find that the President has some residual power in Category Three.[30] That would create a wedge between Category Three and *Chevron*.

II   Accountability and administrative law

So far I have focused on the expertise dimension of ordinary administrative law. But, as Justice Stevens pointed out, ordinary administrative law also rests on the proposition that administrative agencies are indirectly politically accountable to the legislature that delegates authority to them and can restrict those delegations through specific statutes or expand them through general ones, and to the executive who appoints

---

[29] 522 US 491 (2008).

[30] *Medellin* might be a special case because it involved what the Supreme Court's majority clearly regarded as a distorted interpretation of international law by the International Court of Justice, provoked by hostility to the death penalty. The Court purported to be stating general principles, though, not death-penalty specific ones.

agency personnel. As a formal matter, of course, those features characterise the national security bureaucracy as well. The secrecy associated
with counter-terrorism policy brings into question accountability to the
legislature and through it accountability to the public.[31]

Administrative agencies in the United States are formally accountable
to Congress in several ways. The primary ones are legislation directing
the agency to act in specified ways or barring it from doing so; control
over the agency's budget, which can be used to signal approval and
disapproval of specific agency policies or to signal approval or disapproval of the agency's general course of conduct; and oversight hearings
in which legislators question administrators about agency policies. Without supplementation by informal mechanisms, in the United States these
formal methods can be quite weak with respect to counter-terrorism
'agencies'. The main reason is the secrecy associated with counter-
terrorism policy. Even when the broad contours of a policy are widely
known, details are tightly held, and often for good reason. That, of
course, makes it difficult for a legislator to use the accountability mechanisms. A legislator might well think that it is good to have a policy about
using drones against terrorists, and yet be concerned about the precise
conditions under which drones would be so used. The legislator might
know that the United States does indeed have such a policy – and so, for
example, might want to provide funds for some general policy – but not
know what the policy was. Accountability through budgetary decisions is
difficult under these circumstances.

In the United States some of these problems have been addressed
through a programme of disclosures to a small group of legislators who
hold specific positions on relevant committees. That group can be called
the 'Gang of Eight' or the like. If other legislators trust the 'Gang of
Eight', as they ordinarily do because of the members' leadership roles, the
'Gang of Eight' can convey assurances (though typically not specific
information) to others who might be concerned about details.[32] Reports
suggest, though, that the 'Gang of Eight' is regularly dissatisfied with the

---

[31] Without developing the analogy to administrative law, I have sketched the mechanisms of
political accountability in counter-terrorism policy in M. Tushnet, 'The Political Constitution of Emergency Powers: Some Lessons from *Hamdan*' (2007) 91 *Minnesota Law
Review* 1451 and M. Tushnet, 'The Political Constitution of Emergency Powers: Parliamentary and Separation-of-Powers Regulation' (2008) 3 *International Journal of Law in
Context* 275.

[32] And, obviously, a member who is told by one of the 'Gang of Eight' that she cannot be
given assurances about some detail can draw reasonable inferences from that statement.

quality of the information they receive. Sometimes they know, or at least strongly believe, that information has been withheld from them. They can press for additional disclosure, and make various threats about the consequences of non-disclosure, but reports suggest that dissatisfaction sometimes persists for quite a while. More important perhaps, sometimes the 'Gang of Eight' does not know what it does not know – former Vice President Donald Rumsfeld's 'unknown unknowns'. The formal mechanisms of accountability simply cannot work in such circumstances.

There may, however, be informal mechanisms that promote accountability. Jack Goldsmith has suggested several.[33] Here I focus on two: bureaucratic resistance generated by concerns about departures from professional norms, and leaks from within the counter-terrorism bureaucracy.

In the United States, counter-terrorism policy is made not in a single bureaucracy tasked with that subject. Rather, a number of agencies with other responsibilities take part in making counter-terrorism policy. Lawyers in the Department of State, in divisions of the Department of Justice other than the one focused on counter-terrorism, and in the general counsels' offices in the military branches, all have occasion to weigh in on proposed counter-terrorism policies. As legal professionals they bring a perspective different from that of counter-terrorism policy professionals. And as professionals in other bureaucracies they are socialised into bringing their departments' perspectives into the discussion. So, for example, a counter-terrorism expert might be less sensitive to some aspects of the foreign policy implications of a proposed policy than someone from the Department of State, and a non-lawyer counter-terrorism specialist might well be less sensitive to legal and constitutional constraints on policy than any lawyer would be. As counter-terrorism policy develops it is shaped by these various professional concerns. In particular, professionals not primarily associated with counter-terrorism will sometimes push back against counter-terrorism experts out of concern for compliance with the norms of their own professions. And, though the issue is quite complex, accountability to professional norms has *some* connection to public accountability.[34]

[33] J. Goldsmith, *Power and Constraint: the Accountable Presidency After 9/11* (New York: W. W. Norton, 2012).

[34] For my effort to sketch the connection between accountability to professional norms and accountability to the public, see M. Tushnet, 'Judicial Accountability in Comparative Perspective' in N. Bamforth and P. Leyland (eds.), *Accountability in the Contemporary Constitution* (Oxford University Press, 2013).

A stronger connection occurs when someone leaks information about counter-terrorism policy to the press. The press and legislators can then use that information as the basis for pursuing additional questions about the policy. As Goldsmith stresses, the makers of counter-terrorism policy do not like leaks and do what they can to suppress them. Complete suppression is impossible, though. And, I suspect that the more problematic the policy, the more likely the leak.

The accountability effects of leaks occur erratically and gradually. As journalists put it, some leaks 'have legs', others do not. Following up even the leaks with legs requires resources and persistence. Many policies will have been implemented – many drone strikes carried out – before accountability via leaks and legislative follow-up occurs.

Against these weaknesses of leaks as an accountability mechanism, Goldsmith emphasises that the mere possibility that something will be leaked constrains policy-makers. They always ask themselves 'What will happen after this is in the headlines of major newspapers?'. Of course, that is how all accountability mechanisms should work: guiding decisions as they are made, and only secondarily imposing consequences afterwards.

All bureaucracies are porous, and leaks are inevitable. They are not, however, systematic or comprehensive. People in the United States can have access to a fair amount of information about the policies guiding the use of drones. We know from leaks that the United States had a programme of secret prisons operated in some foreign nations, and we know that the present administration claims that it no longer has such a programme, but there have been strikingly few leaks about the details of the programme when it existed – and, of course, all we know about the present administration's claims is that the claims have been made and no leaks have (yet) occurred to undermine those claims.

Proponents of a vigorous judicial role in counter-terrorism law sometimes argue that it has two advantages over political accountability: (1) it is available with respect to *every* claimed constitutional violation in connection with counter-terrorism policy; and (2) it provides a timely response, exposing counter-terrorism policy to evaluation in almost real-time and sometimes even before action is taken.[35] Yet, these advantages

---

[35] For these points, see e.g., Chapter 1 in this volume, F. de Londras, 'Counter-terrorism judicial review as regulatory constitutionalism'; Chapter 13 in this volume, H. Fenwick, 'Post 9/11 UK counter-terrorism cases in the European Court of Human Rights: a "dialogic" approach to rights protection or appeasement of national authorities?'; and

may be smaller than appears. If so, courts may have fewer advantages over legislatures as institutions that generate accountability for counter-terrorism policy.

Justiciability doctrines in the United States and cognate doctrines about prerogative power elsewhere may prevent courts from considering the merits of constitutional challenges. In 2013, for example, the US Supreme Court denied standing (the right to invoke judicial authority) to plaintiffs who claimed that a federal statute dealing with covert surveillance of telephone communications unconstitutionally interfered with various constitutional rights.[36] Doctrines of prerogative power might no longer block judicial inquiry into the substance of counter-terrorism policy but still have a substantial impact on courts' ability to require that counter-terrorism agencies disclose information often essential to a challenger's ability to support his or her legal claims.

Similarly with timeliness. Begin with the proposition that accountability in the courts would be complete and entirely timely were there to be a rule that no action could be taken without prior judicial approval, as with (many) searches, which can be conducted only after the authorities obtain a warrant. The parenthetical qualification in the preceding sentence is crucial, though. I think it accurate to condense a complex body of US law into the proposition that no warrant and therefore no prior judicial approval is needed where the authorities reasonably believe that there is a pressing need to conduct a search within a timeframe that will not accommodate a pause for judicial action. Even if that timeframe is slightly wider – say, one hour – the information the authorities provide to the judicial officer will almost inevitably be quite truncated, and a great deal will depend on the judge's willingness to accept or scepticism about representations made by the authorities. I believe that most cases involving the implementation of counter-terrorism policies will have the same characteristics: urgency and quite limited information available for a judge to evaluate. Leaks might have random effects on accountability in counter-terrorism policy. So, perhaps, would a requirement of prior judicial approval for implementation of existing policies.

What of judicial approval of the policies themselves, in the abstract and outside the context of a specific instance where the policies are to be

---

Chapter 11 in this volume, G. Phillipson, 'Deference and dialogue in the real-world counter-terrorism context'.

[36] *Clapper v. Amnesty Int'l USA*, No. 11–1025 (decided 26 February 2013). See also *Al-Awlaki v. Obama*, 727 F.Supp 1 (D.D.C. 2010).

implemented? Here there are two difficulties. In the United States, doctrines about standing and doctrines barring the courts from issuing advisory opinions would almost certainly prevent the courts from determining whether policies as such were lawful. And, were these justiciability barriers somehow to be overcome, judges would have to determine lawfulness without much information, which would almost certainly lead them to rubber-stamp the policies. I believe that the increment in public accountability would be minuscule at most.

Next, consider a more standard lawsuit, rather than a one-sided process like that used to obtain search warrants. Careful analysts know better than to think that a lawsuit dealing with counter-terrorism policy filed on 15 March will be resolved the next day. Litigation of any sort takes time; litigation dealing with counter-terrorism takes a lot of time. That is particularly true because counter-terrorism agencies will typically do everything they can to slow judicial decision-making: they will resist disclosure of information, resist judicial orders purporting to compel disclosures, file interlocutory appeals, seek stays, and the like. Meanwhile, the processes of accountability through leaks and legislative oversight can proceed on their own schedule. It is clear in the United States that the mechanisms of leaks and legislative oversight have provided far more timely accountability than have judicial proceedings, even though the courts have purported to engage in at least some evaluation of counter-terrorism policy on the merits.

I must note one important qualification. Non-governmental organisations (NGOs) can use judicial proceedings as a vehicle for mounting public campaigns for accountability. Here the mechanism is not accountability by means of actions *by* the courts, but rather accountability by means of actions *in* court. The NGOs might be unable to attract substantial public attention to the issues they are concerned with in the absence of a court proceeding: mainstream media will report about court cases, even mere filings, but might not report about a press conference denouncing the way counter-terrorism policy has harmed an individual or a family.

The claim that the availability of courts aids accountability because NGOs can use cases as organising tools clearly has some merit. If one is willing to treat leaks as a mechanism for promoting accountability, one probably must treat this almost accidental characteristic of courts as another such mechanism.[37]

---

[37] Note, though, that the mechanism involves courts as institutions, not judges as resolvers of specific disputes or as articulators of general rules.

Conclusion

My conclusion is that political accountability in the domain of counter-terrorism policy is likely to reach about as high a level of accountability as we are likely to get. That level might not be high, but adding judicial review to the process is unlikely to provide a significant increment of accountability. As Vermeule puts it:

> the choice among competing 'models' for counterterrorism policy – the war model . . . and the administrative model – may not be a choice with very high stakes. If the judges and other actors who oversee . . . administrative law adjust the parameters in times of emergency, making the relevant rules . . . more deferential to the executive, then outcomes will converge. The remaining difference is only that channeling those outcomes through . . . administrative law . . . will preserve the form, although little of the content, of judicial oversight.[38]

The analogy to administrative law appears to work here as well: when courts reach Step Two in *Chevron* and when they consider whether agency action is arbitrary or capricious, the primary mechanism of accountability is through politics, with judicial review providing a quite modest increment to accountability.

Finally, some words on the security/rights trade-off, probably the most contested issue in current discussions of national security law's distinctiveness. From an administrative law perspective, this is, once again, just an ordinary question of trade-offs between policy effectiveness as determined by agencies and a combination of procedural protections dictated by Congress and substantive constitutional protections dictated by the Constitution as interpreted by the courts. When the FDA adopts a policy, we ordinarily think about it in this way: first, is the policy the agency is pursuing one that Congress has asked it to pursue? This question rests on the allocation of authority between Congress and the agency, in light of our judgement about their comparative institutional competences; it is designed to ensure that the agency is properly held indirectly politically responsible for the policy. Then we would ask whether the agency's policy is a seemingly reasonable one in light of the agency's expertise. In addressing this, we ordinarily would use a rather loose standard of reasonableness, because as outsiders and non-experts we do not have access to all the expertise lodged within the agency even if we have (as we often do not) all the information the agency had available to it. Next we

---

[38] Vermeule, 'Our Schmittian Administrative Law', n. 14 above, 1140.

would ask, is there something specific to the particular policy at hand that makes us suspect that the agency has overestimated the policy's likely benefits?[39] At this point our concerns about relative institutional competence based on expertise and political accountability for policy choices would, I think, be exhausted.

We would then turn to other issues, such as procedural regularity and constitutional rights, where our general assumption is that courts are, relatively speaking, better than agencies in determining when procedural and constitutional rights have been violated. Of course, at this point general questions about the relation between judicial constitutional interpretation and policy effectiveness – that is, about judicial review generally – arise. Suppose, for example, we were to say that the FDA must give notice to a lettuce-grower before it takes a batch of lettuce off the market, because seizures without notice are unconstitutional.[40] Providing notice undoubtedly increases the risk to public health from tainted lettuce, directly through the delay between notification and seizure and indirectly through the possibility of evasion after notification but before seizure. We typically think about this trade-off by invoking whatever account we have of the justifications for judicial review.

It seems to me that the analysis I have just gone through, focusing on an ordinary administrative agency, is what we ought to do in thinking about the security/liberty trade-off, with some minor tweaks. One tweak would be at the first question, where we almost never would question whether Congress had delegated policy-making (in gross) to the national security agencies.[41] Our usual way of thinking about the security/liberty trade-off already incorporates the second

---

[39] Here we would put to one side generic concerns about an agency's risk aversion (that is, its concern that it would unjustifiably be held accountable for policy errors based on its expert calculation of actual risks and benefits), which we would have taken into account in devising the reasonableness standard we apply to actions by the agency. We could, of course, have a graduated standard of reasonableness based on a judgement that, for agency-specific reasons, one agency is more (or less) likely to be risk averse than another. So, for example, we might think that the FDA would be less risk averse than the Department of Homeland Security because the consequences of FDA policy errors, taken as a whole, are less likely to generate substantial attacks on the FDA's approach to calculating risks and benefits, and are likely to be less severe than parallel failures by the DHS.

[40] The example is hypothetical.

[41] We might, though, sometimes ask whether Congress had delegated this specific authority to this specific agency. Perhaps, for example, we might run across situations in which the National Security Agency was doing things that Congress wanted only the Central Intelligence Agency to do.

question, and perhaps the third, when we worry about the capacity of outsiders to evaluate publicly available information dealing with national security issues and acknowledge that there is relevant information available to the decision-makers but not to the public. I suspect that the administrative law framework would get to roughly the same place we are already: quite substantial deference to the decision-makers, with some procedural techniques aimed at smoking out the possibility that something has gone wrong with the agency's internal decision-making processes.

Again, the real action is at the final stage. Do scholars treat the judicial role in national security matters implicating the Constitution as categorically different from that role in other constitutional matters? As I understand the arguments, clearly no, on the level of constitutional theory. That is, originalists about the Fourteenth Amendment are originalists about presidential power in national security, pragmatists about the Fourteenth Amendment are pragmatists about presidential power, and so on through the candidate theories. On the level of substance, though, perhaps one can find some differences, though I think they are not quite categorical enough to undermine my argument's core. From an administrative law perspective, the issue comes down to some sort of comparison – the contours of which I think are quite unclear – between the President's relative institutional competence in national security matters (involving secrecy, technical expertise about surveillance technology, and the like) and the courts' relative institutional competence in constitutional matters. Even if, as I am willing to assume, the courts' relative competence is constant across all fields, the President's might well vary, being smaller, for example, with respect to food safety than with respect to national security. But, as Vermeule suggests, these are variables, and I think that drawing categorical conclusions, such as that the administrative law perspective helps in thinking about the constitutional dimensions of food safety law but not about those of national security law, is at least premature.

To conclude: I am not arguing that existing administrative law deals with national security matters no less than it does with food safety.[42]

---

[42] For one thing, in the United States a wide swath of (and maybe all of) the relevant activities, that is, those of interest in this discussion, of the Departments of Defense and Homeland Security are exempt from the Administrative Procedure Act.

Rather, my suggestion is that administrative law provides the conceptual resources with which we could think about fitting war as a condition into our general constitutional framework. War is not a state of exception in constitutional terms. It is a rather banal domain in which administrative law could serve us as well as any version of 'emergency law' could.

The politics of counter-terrorism judicial review: creating effective parliamentary scrutiny

FERGAL F. DAVIS

Terrorism has a distorting effect on politics. After all, terrorism is designed to distort politics – it is violence being employed with the goal of bringing about a political end.[1] For example, in the aftermath of the attacks on the United States of 11 September 2001, 'instead of the rowdy, rhetorical deliberations appropriate to agnostic politics in a healthy pluralistic polity, the nation experienced a wave of patriotic fervour and political conformity in which the expression of dissenting opinions and the defence of civil liberties were equated with anti-Americanism'.[2] Similarly, following the brutal and public murder of an off-duty member of the British Army in May 2013 the immediate calls were for unity[3] – cohesion was presented as a political virtue. Problematically, such political cohesion often coincides with, or possibly feeds into, a general 'security bias' which is evident in government responses to terrorism.[4] Those responses result in a distortion of law. Liberal democratic states have employed a variety of illiberal measures – internment without trial,[5] extraordinary

The author wishes to thank George Williams and his colleagues at the Gilbert+Tobin Centre of Public Law, UNSW and Ms Lisa Burton of Monash University. All errors are entirely my own.

[1] J. Blackbourn, F. Davis and N. Taylor, 'Academic Consensus and Legislative Definitions of Terrorism: Applying Schmid and Jongman' (2013) 34(3) *Statute Law Review* 239, available at http://slr.oxfordjournals.org/content/early/2012/11/17/slr.hms041.full.pdf+html?sid=22b8e753-a7a6-4922-aa7c-90235a354a0c.

[2] R. L. Ivie, 'Rhetorical Deliberation and Democratic Politics in the Here and Now' (2002) 5 (2) *Rhetoric and Public Affairs* 277, 281.

[3] Statement by Prime Minister David Cameron, 23 May 2013, available at www.guardian.co.uk/uk/video/2013/may/23/woolwich-murder-david-cameron-video.

[4] F. de Londras and F. Davis, 'Controlling the Executive in Times of Terrorism: Competing Perspectives on Effective Oversight Mechanisms' (2010) 30(1) *Oxford Journal of Legal Studies* 19, 21.

[5] R. J. Spjut 'Internment Without Trial in Northern Ireland 1971–1975: Ministerial Policy and Practice' (1986) *Modern Law Review* 49, 712–40; G. Hogan and C. Walker, *Political Violence and the Law in Ireland* (Manchester University Press, 1989).

rendition,[6] control orders,[7] special trial procedures such as those employed at Guantánamo Bay[8] – on the basis that the threat of terrorism must be faced down. As de Londras and I have noted elsewhere, such executive reaction can be deemed rational – but for the civil libertarian it remains problematic.[9]

One of the key challenges for the counter-terrorism scholar in the field of constitutionalism is to seek to limit the potential consequences of that distorting effect. To achieve this some cast counter-terrorism measures as exceptional. Thus, adopting a Schmittian perspective, we sacrifice procedural constitutional guarantees in order to secure the substantive nature of the constitution: the constitution, after all, is not a suicide pact;[10] you are either with us, or with the terrorists.[11] But crucially, to be legitimate, any such sacrifice should be temporary: Schmitt advocated commissarial, not sovereign dictatorship.[12] Unfortunately, as is noted by Tushnet in Chapter 5, the exceptional nature of counter-terrorism powers is becoming increasingly difficult to assert.[13] The exception has become the norm.

That process has long been observable in Israel. In a country where the simple act of entering a shopping mall requires one to go through security scanning and bag searches, the risk of exceptional powers becoming routine is evident. In 1979 the Knesset adopted the Emergency Powers (Detention) Law; this Act replaced the Defense (Emergency) Regulations, which dated from the period of the British Mandate. During the debates, MK Meir Vilner proposed that administrative detention should only be possible when Israel was involved in actual war and only following a Knesset vote.[14] Vilner was concerned that in the absence of

---

[6] M. L. Satterthwaite, 'Rendered Meaningless: Extraordinary Rendition and the Rule of Law' (2007) 75(5/6) *George Washington Law Review* 1333.

[7] L. Zedner, 'Preventive Justice or Pre-punishment? The Case of Control Orders' (2007) 60(1) *Current Legal Problems* 174.

[8] F. de Londras, 'Guantanamo Bay: Towards Legality?' (2008) 71(1) *Modern Law Review* 36.

[9] De Londras and Davis, 'Controlling the Executive in Times of Terrorism', n. 4 above.

[10] R. A. Posner *Not a Suicide Pact: the Constitution in a Time of National Emergency* (Oxford University Press, 2006).

[11] Address of President George W. Bush to a Joint Session of Congress and the American People, 20 September 2001, available at http://georgewbush-whitehouse.archives.gov/news/releases/2001/09/20010920-8.html.

[12] C. Schmitt, *Die Geistesgeschichtliche Lage des heutigen Parlamentarismus* (Berlin: Duncker und Humblot, 1923), p. 22.

[13] See Chapter 5 in this volume, M. Tushnet, 'Emergency law as administrative law'.

[14] D. Sharfman, *Living Without a Constitution: Civil Rights in Israel* (New York: ME Sharpe, 1993), p. 149.

an actual declared conflict administrative detention would continue to be used as a routine counter-terrorism power. So, even if we accept the Schmittian perspective, including his belief in the temporary nature of the exception, we are entitled to ask: who will determine the end of the emergency and moderate executive excess during the state of exception? On the other hand, if we reject the state of exception thesis, we are entitled to ask: who will restrain the impact of this distorted politics and these draconian laws? Either way, the debate turns to the respective roles of the legislature, executive and judiciary – and in particular to the role of judicial review.

This chapter will begin by briefly outlining the foundations of judicial review scepticism. Obviously, it is impossible to engage in a detailed analysis of the conflict between constitutionalism and the rule of law but I will highlight three concerns, which underline my distrust of (what Keith Ewing terms) the 'juristocrats'.[15] The next section will set out Australia's Human Rights (Parliamentary Scrutiny) Act 2011 (Cth). This legislation entirely precludes the potential risks of juridification by adopting an 'exclusive parliamentary rights model'.[16] The chapter will employ the 'informal political theory'[17] method. It will critically appraise the weakness of this form of political control both in general and in the specific context of Australian politics. Finally, the chapter will return to consider the potential for dialogic review as a means of striking an effective balance between the courts and the legislature.

I   The basis of (my) judicial review scepticism

The fact of my judicial review scepticism has been set out in more detail elsewhere.[18] In short my concerns are threefold. First, I am concerned by the apparent clash between the rule of law and constitutionalism. I have

---

[15] In correspondence with the author.

[16] G. Williams and L. Burton, 'Australia's Exclusive Parliamentary Model of Rights Protection' (2013) 34(1) *Statute Law Review* 58, 59.

[17] M. Tushnet, 'Rights: An Essay in Informal Political Theory' (1989) 17 *Politics Society* 403, 404.

[18] F. Davis, 'Extra-constitutionalism, the Human Rights Act and the Labour 'Rebels': Applying Prof. Tushnet's Theories in the UK' (2006) 4 *Web Journal of Current Legal Issues*, available at http://webjcli.ncl.ac.uk/2006/issue4/davis4.html; de Londras and Davis, 'Controlling the Executive in Times of Terrorism', n. 4 above; F. Davis, 'The Human Rights Act and Juridification: Saving Democracy from Law' (2010) 30(2) *Politics* 91; F. Davis, 'Parliamentary Supremacy and the Re-invigoration of Institutional Dialogue in the UK' (2014) 67(1) *Parliamentary Affairs* 137, available at http://pa.oxfordjournals.org/content/early/2012/06/23/pa.gss034.full.pdf.

always been unconvinced by the Kelsenian notion of formal law confer-
ring legitimacy – in and of itself.[19] That formalist analysis appears
weakened by the acceptance that judges do, in fact, make law, even when
that judicial law-making is limited to the 'penumbra of uncertainty'.[20]
Once that point is conceded then the right of elected parliaments to have
the final say over any such law-making process seems apparent.[21]
Perhaps my belief in the constituent will of the people is simply a result
of early indoctrination by Bunreacht na hÉireann, the Irish Constitution,
which grandly declares: 'We, the people of Éire … Do hereby adopt,
enact, and give to ourselves this Constitution'.[22] I am strengthened in
that belief by the arguments of Waldron who concluded that 'rights-
based judicial review is inappropriate for reasonably democratic societies
whose main problem is not that their legislative institutions are dysfunctional but that their members disagree about rights'.[23] Whatever its basis,
my (informal) political and legal philosophy tends to assume that
legitimacy is dependent on a democratic mandate, either through the
actions of elected representatives of the people or through a manifestation of the constituent will of the people.[24] As a result, my initial ground
for scepticism is a broadly based suspicion of the legitimacy of an
unelected elite to make law. That suspicion is heightened in systems
where it is difficult or impossible for the democratic actors (the people
or their representatives) to overturn the decisions of the judiciary.

A further source of anxiety stems from a doubt over the capacity of the
judiciary to effectively limit the power of the executive during a state of
emergency. These concerns are based on an historicist analysis which has

---

[19] See: C. Thornhill, 'Legality, Legitimacy and the Form of Political Power: On the Construction of a False Antinomy' (2010) 3(3) *Journal of Power* 293, 295.

[20] H. L. A. Hart, *The Concept of Law* (2nd edn, Oxford University Press, 1997).

[21] J. Waldron, *The Dignity of Legislation* (Cambridge University Press, 1999). It might also
be possible to exercise that oversight function through a referendum mechanism for
directly consulting the people but that is likely to be cumbersome.

[22] Bunreacht na hÉireann, the Irish Constitution (1937) Preamble. For a thorough analysis
of the Preamble to the Irish Constitution, see M. Tushnet, 'National Identity as a
Constitutional Issue: The Case of the Preamble of the Irish Constitution of 1937' in
E. Carolan (ed.), *The Constitution of Ireland: Perspectives and Prospects* (Dublin: Blooms-
bury Professional, 2012), pp. 49–58.

[23] J. Waldron, 'The Core of the Case Against Judicial Review' (2006) 115 *Yale Law Journal*
1346, 1406.

[24] C. Thornhill, 'Legality, Legitimacy and the Form of Political Power: on the Construction
of a False Antinomy' (2010) 3(3) *Journal of Power* 293.

been set out elsewhere[25] but which has routinely demonstrated the ineffectiveness of judicial review. Critics of this viewpoint have argued that the judiciary are now steeped in a rights-based culture and as such are more attuned to rights-based arguments. Thus, the argument goes, this newly enlightened judiciary are likely to be more capable of adequately protecting human rights, even in times of emergency. Furthermore, even in 'hard cases' judges are said to be restrained by many 'institutionalized and relatively settled "steadying factors"... to assist their process of determining the scope of particular rules'.[26] However, the distorting nature of terrorism, noted in the introduction to this chapter, is likely to unsteady these steadying factors. While modern judges are, perhaps, less deferential than their counterparts during previous emergencies,[27] even proponents of judicial power acknowledge that the recent track record of the courts remains far from unimpeachable.[28] Indeed, a number of chapters in this collection highlight ongoing grounds for concern: Jenkins demonstrates the application of the law of unintended consequences to rights-based judicial review;[29] while Lobel notes that the United States 'Supreme Court's soaring rhetoric has not been matched by the reality of judicial review'.[30]

The final basis for my scepticism is that the belief in a strong form of judicial review undermines the potential of parliament. In other words parliamentarians are likely to be less willing to restrain the executive if they believe that the judiciary will act as an effective limit on executive excess.[31] In brief, politicians are self-interested actors. Particularly in the context of a fused legislature and executive, the willingness to vote

---

[25] De Londras and Davis, 'Controlling the Executive in Times of Terrorism', n. 4 above, 25–8; K. Ewing and J. C. Tham, 'The Continuing Futility of the Human Rights Act' (2008) *Public Law* 668; M. Tushnet, 'Defending *Korematsu*?: Reflections on Civil Liberties in Wartime' (2003) *Wisconsin Law Review* 273.

[26] W. Twining and D. Miers, *How to Do Things with Rules* (4th edn, London: Butterworths, 1999), p. 146.

[27] *R v. Halliday, ex parte Zadig* [1917] AC 260; *Liversidge v. Anderson* [1942] AC 206; *Korematsu v. United States*, 323 US 214 (1944).

[28] H. Fenwick and G. Phillipson, 'Covert Derogations and Judicial Deference: Redefining Liberty and Due Process Rights in Counterterrorism Law and Beyond' (2011) 56(4) *McGill Law Journal* 863.

[29] See Chapter 3 in this volume, D. Jenkins, 'When good cases go bad: unintended consequences of rights-friendly judgments'.

[30] See Chapter 4 in this volume, J. Lobel, 'The rhetoric and reality of judicial review of counter-terrorism actions: the United States experience'.

[31] De Londras and Davis, 'Controlling the Executive in Times of Terrorism', n. 4 above, 29–32.

against the government is restricted by the desire to avoid an early election. At this point it should be noted that this argument requires at least one major caveat: I have predominately made this point in relation to the United Kingdom which has a strong tradition of parliamentary dissent. Political culture is relevant, as will become apparent in the next section.

I am conscious of Gavin Phillipson's warning: political constitutionalists cannot, on the one hand, use parliamentary weakness as an opportunity for reform whilst simultaneously calling for abandonment of judicial review at the first sign of failure on the part of the courts.[32] However, my combined scepticism of judicial elitism and my belief in the potential to re-invigorate parliamentary politics attracts me to the potential of the exclusively parliamentary method of rights enforcement which has been adopted by Australia's Commonwealth Parliament. That mechanism eschews all forms of juridification and as a result, even staunch proponents of a judicially enforceable Australian Bill of Rights have acknowledged that, the Act 'offers a unique opportunity to assess the capacity of Parliament to protect human rights without court involvement'.[33]

II   Australia's parliamentary scrutiny model

Australia is said to be the only democratic nation without a national Bill of Rights, human rights Act or other general human rights law.[34] It was once argued that 'the institutional feature of "strong government" in the nature of cabinet government makes judicial intervention in the policy-making spheres of those nations unnecessary and unlikely'.[35] However, that position appears somewhat naive in light of Australia's human rights record.[36] In the counter-terrorism context Australia has been accused of 'hyper-legislating'[37] in enacting over 50 statutes in the decade since 11

---

[32] See Chapter 11 in this volume, G. Phillipson, 'Deference and dialogue in the real-world counter-terrorism Context'.

[33] G. Williams and L. Burton, 'Australia's Exclusive Parliamentary Model of Rights Protection' (2013) 34(1) *Statute Law Review* 58.

[34] *Ibid.*

[35] J. P. Giraudo, 'Judicial Review and Comparative Politics: an Explanation for the Extensiveness of American Judicial Review Offered from the Perspective of Comparative Government' (1979) 6 *Hastings Constitutional Law Quarterly* 1137, 1138.

[36] Williams and Burton, 'Australia's Exclusive Parliamentary Model of Rights Protection', n. 33 above, 63–70.

[37] K. Roach, *The 9/11 Effect: Comparative Counter-Terrorism* (Cambridge University Press, 2011), p. 309.

September 2001.[38] That legislation is not benign: sedition laws curtail the right to freedom of speech; the Australian Security and Intelligence Organisation has been granted extensive powers to detain and question; control orders enable near house arrest.[39] In response to the supposed uniqueness of its position and concerns over its human rights record there was growing pressure to adopt some form of a national Bill of Rights.[40]

Barry and Campbell refer to 'political rights review' and the 'democratic model' of rights protection.[41] In effect this is review by parliamentary committees, human rights audits, and the kind of mechanisms discussed by Jessie Blackbourn and Kent Roach in their chapters for this collection. The great advantage of this 'democratic model' is that it ought to strengthen the protection and promotion of human rights whilst avoiding the problems surrounding rights-based judicial review'.[42] Indeed, the claims made in favour of the model were straightforward:

> By giving existing bodies new powers and responsibilities, establishing new institutions such as the parliamentary committee on human rights, and adopting a national bill of rights through a democratic process, the Democratic model will improve the quality of legislation passed by Parliament, promote a stronger human rights culture within the executive branch, bring to light human rights abuses affecting minority groups, and create greater public awareness of human rights issues.[43]

In December 2011 the federal government unveiled a fresh human rights framework, which corresponds to Barry and Campbell's 'democratic model'.

Central to the government's new framework was the Human Rights (Parliamentary Scrutiny) Act 2011 (Cth), which provided for:

> a set of substantive provisions that directly incorporate international human rights norms as part of this human rights framework; and secondly, a set of enforcement mechanisms that focus on Parliament, rather than the courts, as the institution responsible for protecting human rights at the national level.[44]

---

[38] G. Williams, 'A Decade of Australian Anti-Terror Laws' (2011) *Melbourne University Law Review* 1136.

[39] *Ibid.*

[40] N. Barry and T. Campbell, 'Towards a Democratic Bill of Rights' (2011) 46(1) *Australian Journal of Political Science* 71.

[41] *Ibid.* 72.   [42] *Ibid.* 80.   [43] *Ibid.* 81.

[44] R. Dixon, 'A New (Inter)National Human Rights Experiment for Australia' (2012) 23 *Public Law Review* 75, 80.

Notably, in adopting this approach the government rejected the recommendations of the National Human Rights Consultation (NHRC). The NHRC was established in 2008 and engaged in a wide-ranging consultation. It received 35,014 written submissions and travelled the 'length and breadth of the country'.[45] In its report the NHRC supported the adoption of a dialogue model.[46] In particular, the NHRC proposed that Australia enact legislation similar to the UK Human Rights Act 1998 (UK HRA): 'that is, a law providing protection for a wide range of predominately civil and political rights through enhanced parliamentary scrutiny, judicial interpretation of legislation, and non-binding declarations of incompatibility issued by courts'.[47] Given that report, the exclusion of judicial involvement from the Parliamentary Scrutiny Act must be seen as deliberate.

'Human rights' are defined in section 3 of the Parliamentary Scrutiny Act as 'rights and freedoms recognised or declared in seven specified international human rights instruments'. Part 3 of the Parliamentary Scrutiny Act sets out the procedure for making a Statement of Compatibility (SOC). This is, in many respects, the key enforcement mechanism within the legislation. The same requirements apply to SOCs for both Bills and legislative instruments.[48] The member who introduces a Bill into either House of Parliament 'must cause a statement of compatibility to be prepared' and 'presented' to Parliament.[49] Although the Explanatory Memorandum accompanying the Parliamentary Scrutiny Act states that a SOC 'will ordinarily form part of the explanatory memorandum for the Bill'[50] there is, as a matter of fact, 'nothing to prevent a statement being introduced after debate has begun or even after the bill has been passed'.[51] Finally, Part 2 of the Act established a Parliamentary Joint

---

[45] Williams and Burton, 'Australia's Exclusive Parliamentary Model of Rights Protection', n. 33 above, 70.

[46] Brennan Committee, *National Human Rights Consultation Report* (2009), Summary, available at www.ag.gov.au/RightsAndProtections/HumanRights/TreatyBodyReporting/Documents/NHRCR-Recommendations.pdf.

[47] Williams and Burton, 'Australia's Exclusive Parliamentary Model of Rights Protection', n. 33 above, 72.

[48] Parliamentary Scrutiny Act, ss. 8 and 9.

[49] Parliamentary Scrutiny Act, s. 8(1) and (2).

[50] Explanatory Memorandum, Human Rights (Parliamentary Scrutiny) Bill 2011 (Cth), p. 4.

[51] Williams and Burton, 'Australia's Exclusive Parliamentary Model of Rights Protection', n. 33 above, 70.

Committee on Human Rights (PJCHR). The Act sets out the purpose of the PJCHR as being to:

(a) to examine Bills for Acts, and legislative instruments, that come before either House of the Parliament for compatibility with human rights, and to report to both Houses of the Parliament on that issue;
(b) to examine acts for compatibility with human rights, and to report to both Houses of the Parliament on that issue; and
(c) to inquire into any matter relating to human rights which is referred to it by the Attorney-General, and to report to both Houses of the Parliament on that matter.[52]

It would seem that the SOCs and the PJCHR are intended to act in tandem to facilitate greater human rights scrutiny of legislation: the SOC ensuring that compatibility is an issue during the parliamentary debate; the PJCHR ensuring a more in-depth post hoc examination.

Williams and Burton pour considerable cold water on the 'democratic model'.[53] While Dixon commends the incorporation of international human rights standards into domestic law,[54] Williams and Burton note that the result of this approach is that no actual rights are set out in the Act.[55] Such an approach undermines the potential educative impact of the legislation. While the Act recognises 'well over 100 rights and freedoms',[56] Williams and Burton argue that this extensiveness undermines the potential quality of rights review and public understanding.[57] A further criticism is levelled at the SOC mechanism contained within the Act.

Critics of the Act note that the legislation is silent on the quality and nature of the SOC required. Indeed, the key complaint regarding SOCs is that the legislation is underdeveloped in terms of detail.[58] However, as a parliamentary scrutiny mechanism it is unsurprising that the legislation left it for Parliament and the PJCHR to determine whether or not they are satisfied with the SOCs tabled. It is clear from the Committee's

---

[52] Parliamentary Scrutiny Act, s. 7.
[53] Williams and Burton, 'Australia's Exclusive Parliamentary Model of Rights Protection', n. 33 above.
[54] Dixon 'A New (Inter)National Human Rights Experiment for Australia', n. 44 above, 80.
[55] Williams and Burton, 'Australia's Exclusive Parliamentary Model of Rights Protection', n. 33 above, 72.
[56] D. Kinley and C. Ernst, 'Exile on Main Street: Australia's Legislative Agenda for Human Rights' (2012) 1 European Human Rights Law Review 58, 62.
[57] Williams and Burton, 'Australia's Exclusive Parliamentary Model of Rights Protection', n. 33 above, 72–3.
[58] Ibid. 75.

reports that the adequacy of SOCs is being addressed. The PJCHR is not willing to treat the SOCs as a mere box to be ticked. In the period 16 February 2013 to 19 April 2013, the PJCHR examined 34 Bills. Of these it determined that 18 required further examination and that 16 did not give rise to human rights concerns. In the same period the Committee examined 492 Legislative Instruments. Of these, the Committee sought further information on 14; 403 were deemed not to raise human rights concerns; and the remaining 74 instruments did 'not appear to raise human rights concerns but are accompanied by statements of compatibility that do not fully meet the committee's expectations'.[59] A related problem is that the sheer volume of legislation makes genuine scrutiny impossible, a problem exacerbated by the wide-ranging definition of rights contained within the Act.[60] The Committee's report for a period of just over two months runs to 373 pages. This reduces its potential utility for parliamentarians wishing to engage with the rights issues raised.

The problems identified above are not insignificant but they are potentially resolvable. The UK HRA and Ireland's European Convention of Human Rights Act 2003 both incorporate a regional treaty into domestic law. However, the UK HRA has suffered from an inability to connect the people with the rights protected – hence the ongoing discussion surrounding a UK Bill of Rights.[61] The problems identified around SOCs essentially focus on poor parliamentary process. In some respects the critique is the result of Williams and Burton's belief that parliament lacks the 'rationality and analytical capacity that judges, especially judges of appeal, can bring to questions of law and human rights'.[62] If one begins from a position of doubting the rational and analytical capacity of judges their conclusions are less immediately obvious – it becomes more

---

[59] Parliamentary Joint Committee of Human Rights, *Examination of Legislation in accordance with the Human Rights (Parliamentary Scrutiny) Act 2011: Bills introduced 18–21 March 2013; Legislative Instruments registered with the Federal Register of Legislative Instruments 16 February–19 April 2013, Sixth Report of 2013* (May 2013), pp. xi–xii, available at www.aph.gov.au/Parliamentary_Business/Committees/Senate_Committees?url=humanrights_ctte/reports/index.htm.

[60] Williams and Burton, 'Australia's Exclusive Parliamentary Model of Rights Protection', n. 33 above, 78–88.

[61] See Chapter 13 in this volume, H. Fenwick, 'Post 9/11 UK counter-terrorism cases in the European Court of Human Rights: a "dialogic" approach to rights protection or appeasement of national authorities?'.

[62] Williams and Burton, 'Australia's Exclusive Parliamentary Model of Rights Protection', n. 33 above, 92.

a case of two flawed systems, parliamentary and judicial, and the question then becomes which mechanism is likely to make fewer mistakes or which body is likely to be in a position to correct its errors more speedily.

In this respect the legislature and the courts are similar to a traditional encyclopaedia and the online resource Wikipedia. Whereas the errors contained within a published encyclopaedia will remain until the next edition, the crowd-sourced material is open to immediate editing and correction.[63] Similarly, while parliaments make mistakes, courts set precedents and as Justice Jackson famously declared in his dissent in *Korematsu*:

> once a judicial opinion rationalizes such an order to show that it conforms to the Constitution, or rather rationalizes the Constitution to show that the Constitution sanctions such an order, the Court for all time has validated ... [a] principle [that] lies about like a loaded weapon ready for the hand of any authority that bring forward a plausible claim of urgent need.[64]

As a result, if parliamentary mechanisms can be made effective I am more willing to put my faith in them. Both the legislature and the judiciary will make mistakes but only the judiciary will leave 'binding' precedent.

Despite my initial enthusiasm for the parliamentary scrutiny model there is a significant impediment to the effective scrutiny of human rights issues by the Australian Federal Parliament: political party cohesion. The Australian parliamentary framework incorporates elements of the US 'ambition countering ambition'[65] separation of powers model and elements of the United Kingdom's concept of parliamentary sovereignty. This approach has been termed the 'Washminster mutation'.[66] The premise of the Australian approach is responsible government: that is, government must be able to get its legislative programme through parliament and the people must be capable of removing the government from office at an election. Crucially, in Australia the complexity and compulsory elements of the electoral system have given rise to high levels of party discipline and cohesion.[67] The apparent levels of party cohesion have led

---

[63] D. Tapscott and A. Williams, *Wikinomics: How Mass Collaborating Changes Everything* (London: Atlantic Books, 2006).

[64] *Korematsu* v. *United States*, 323 US 244, 247 (1944).

[65] *The Federalist* No. 51, 252 (James Madison).

[66] E. Thompson, 'The 'Washminster' Mutation' (1980) 15(2) *Politics* 32.

[67] D. M. Farrell and I. McAllister, 'Australia: the Alternative Vote in a Compliant Political Culture' in M. Gallagher and P. Mitchell (eds.), *The Politics of Electoral Systems* (Oxford University Press, 2005).

Thompson to suggest that accountability in the Australian context is to the party room rather than to the floor of parliament:

> It is the fight in the party room for control of the government that is the heart of our system. It is in the party room, not on the floor of the house, that changes in leadership occur ... The cabinet is not a committee of parliament but a committee of the governing party or parties. Sharing of power exists not between the executive and its legislature but between the party and its leaders.[68]

The result of such cohesion is the absence of dissent (in public) on the floor of the house from Australian politics.

There are a number of examples of parliamentary practice, which illustrate the extent of party cohesion in Australian politics. For example:

> The Australian Labor Party (ALP) is quite open about its demand that its representatives shall be its delegates, and it enforces discipline over parliamentary members with a formal pledge. Members of the party pledge themselves to be bound by the platform and rules of the party and by the decisions of the executive and conference, not to oppose any endorsed Labor candidate at any election *and to vote according to the majority decision of the caucus*[69] *of the parliamentary party on all questions in parliament.* They face expulsion from the party if they break any aspect of the pledge. (emphasis added)[70]

Although theoretically less constrained, in practice the situation is similar for members of the Liberal Party.[71] As a result it is argued that 'Australia has gone to the extreme lengths of viewing all legislation as a vote of confidence and any legislation amended by the House of Representatives against the Government's wishes as a vote of no confidence in that Government'.[72] This enhanced concept of accountability to party has resulted in a situation whereby crossing the party floor is extremely rare.

---

[68] Thompson, 'The 'Washminster' Mutation', n. 66 above, 37.

[69] 'Caucus' is the term employed to denote a meeting of the ALP parliamentary party.

[70] D. Jaensch, *Parliament Parties and People: Australian Politics Today* (Melbourne: Longman Cheshire, 1991) cited in S. Bach, *Platypus and Parliament: the Australian Senate in Theory and Practice* (Canberra: Department of the Senate, 2003) ch. 3, available at www.aph.gov.au/About_Parliament/Senate/Research_and_Education/~/link.aspx?_id=E8EB41597AAD4ADA85E08B519F9E8FC2&_z=z.

[71] Bach, *Platypus and Parliament*, n. 70 above, ch. 3.

[72] D. Hamer, 'Senate Committees: Keeping Parliament Responsible', *Papers on Parliament* (September 1991), p. 41, available at www.aph.gov.au/About_Parliament/Senate/Research_and_Education/pops.

Sieberer has analysed the impacts of cohesion and discipline on parliamentary party groups. He notes that 'if individual MPs can reach their goals only through the party leadership, they are likely to toe the party line'.[73] In Australia political advancement is closely associated with the party room. Difference of opinion within parties is not expressed on the floor of the house but is confined to the party room and those seeking parliamentary candidacy are required to demonstrate 'strong party credentials'.[74] The dominance of the party over the individual is evident from the role of the Prime Minister in choosing their cabinet. Until recently, the ALP caucus had the power to choose ministers: an ALP Prime Minister allocated portfolios to ministers chosen by caucus.[75] Admittedly, in 2007, Prime Minister Rudd asserted his right to choose his own cabinet and Prime Minister Gillard sought to continue that practice.[76] But we must acknowledge that the context of political party cohesion is dramatically different to the United Kingdom.

In relation to the potential for the UK Parliament to uphold civil liberties and to withstand the executive I previously argued that it was possible for an MP to imagine the electoral benefits of opposing one's own party outweighing the costs.[77] I cited Shephard who had noted that, following the 2005 election, the obvious loss of public trust in Prime Minister Blair led to:

> a parliamentary backlash (fire alarm) over security policy, most notably over extraordinary rendition ... ID cards ... and the proposal to increase the number of days police would be permitted to hold terrorist suspects without charge.[78]

As a result, in the UK context my concern was not that the UK Parliament lacked the ability to withstand the executive but rather that it would be reluctant to do so:

---

[73] U. Sieberer, 'Party Unity in Parliamentary Democracies: a Comparative Analysis' (2006) 12(2) *Journal of Legislative Studies* 150, 152.

[74] D. M. Farrell and I. McAllister, 'Australia: the Alternative Vote in a Compliant Political Culture' in M. Gallagher and P. Mitchell (eds.), *The Politics of Electoral Systems* (Oxford University Press, 2005).

[75] D. McHenry, 'The Origins of Caucus Selection of Cabinet' (1955) 7(25) *Historical Studies: Australia and New Zealand* 37.

[76] See www.abc.net.au/worldtoday/content/2007/s2101239.htm.

[77] De Londras and Davis, 'Controlling the Executive in Times of Terrorism', n. 4 above, 32.

[78] M. Shephard, 'Parliamentary Scrutiny and Oversight of the British "War on Terror": From Accretion of Executive Power and Evasion of Scrutiny to Embarrassment and Concessions' (2009) 15 *Journal of Legislative Studies* 191, 204.

if a stand is not yet obviously popular, the risks associated with defying one's own party remain high. Where parliamentarians believe that another institution (namely the courts) will correct their errors and prevent Executive abuses, they have less incentive to take that risk.[79]

Thus, I argued, in the UK context if we empower parliamentarians to take rights seriously, and as an electorate if we insist that they demonstrate civil libertarian concerns, we can expect dissent. If we, the people, make it politically attractive to vote against repressive counter-terrorism measures, parliamentarians will so vote. In Australia I am less confident: 'party considerations constrain the leeway that individual MPs can exercise, not only in allowing non-party factors to influence their behaviour in Parliament, but also in how much of a personal following they can build in their constituencies'.[80] As a result, the costs of public dissent (expulsion for the party) are likely to be too high for politicians in the Australian political context.

What dissent does occur will take place within the party room – out of the public eye. An Australian politician, who in the United Kingdom might consider rebelling, will feel they have done their duty by raising concerns at caucus but then accepting the responsibility of serving the party's interests on the floor of the house – thereby stifling genuine open debate. It is difficult to see how such a hidden debate can ignite the popular imagination. As a result, parliament is unlikely to act as clarion call for the people to demonstrate their dissatisfaction with rights restricting counter-terrorism laws. This tight party cohesion undermines the potential of the 'exclusive parliamentary rights model'.[81] Thus I am forced to conclude that a role for the judiciary in 'sounding the alarm' is necessary to ensure effective restraint of executive power in counter-terrorism. This conclusion necessitates a return to the debate surrounding dialogic review.

III   Models of dialogic review

A key development in the constitutional protection of human rights over the past thirty years has been the emergence of 'new commonwealth' or

---

[79] De Londras and Davis, 'Controlling the Executive in Times of Terrorism: Competing Perspectives on Effective Oversight Mechanisms', n. 4 above, 32.

[80] D. Studlar and I. McAllister, 'Constituency Activity and Representational Roles among Australian Legislators' (1996) 58(1) *Journal of Politics* 69, 90.

[81] Williams and Burton, 'Australia's Exclusive Parliamentary Model of Rights Protection', n. 33 above, 59.

'dialogue' models of human rights protection.[82] These innovative approaches have gained popularity with legal traditions which previously had emphasised the sovereignty of parliament, such as Canada, New Zealand, the United Kingdom and some of the Australian States and territories.[83] They achieved this goal by granting the judiciary a role in defending rights without seeming to undermine the sovereignty of parliament.

The incorporation of the dialogic review model of rights protection through section 4 of the UK HRA into law was largely the result of this desire to allow judicial supervision while maintaining parliamentary sovereignty. Thus, the declaration of incompatibility restricts the courts to 'courteous requests for conversation, not pronouncements of truth from on high'.[84] In short, the Act deliberately undermines 'its own authority inviting the political back in to control the legal at just the moment when the supremacy of the legal discourse seems assured'.[85] The overall thrust for section 4 of the UK HRA was that it respected a traditional Diceyean emphasis on parliamentary supremacy while facilitating judicial oversight of rights protection. Such an approach is attractive to the judicial review sceptic since it enables the court to raise the alarm by identifying potential abuse while leaving the determination of the issue in the hands of the democratically mandated parliament.

For dialogic review to have any prospects of success in Australia it must fit within the Australian constitutional framework. The formal basis of the independence of the federal judiciary in the Australian Constitution can be located in section 71: 'The judicial power of the Commonwealth shall be vested in a Federal Supreme Court, to be called the High Court of Australia, and in such other federal courts as the Parliament creates, and in such other courts as it invests with federal jurisdiction'.[86] The Australian Constitution specifies a three-armed structure of government. That structural fact, combined with section 71, has resulted in the uncontroversial conclusion that the 'judicial power' is vested exclusively in

[82] S. Gardbaum, 'Reassessing the New Commonwealth Model of Constitutionalism' (2010) 8 I.CON 167, 193.
[83] See variously the Canadian Charter of Rights and Freedoms; New Zealand Bill of Rights; UK Human Rights Act; Charter of Human Rights and Responsibilities Act 2006 (Vic.); and Human Rights Act 2004 (ACT).
[84] C. Gearty, Can Human Rights Survive? (Cambridge University Press, 2006), p. 96.
[85] Ibid. p. 95.   [86] Commonwealth of Australia Constitution Act 1900 (Cth), Ch. III s. 71.

the courts.[87] The 1956 *Boilermakers* case expanded the scope of section 71. Here it was held that courts covered by Chapter III (namely, federal courts) may not exercise any functions other than the 'judicial power of the Commonwealth' and incidental non-judicial powers.[88] This has resulted in a rather strict interpretation of the separation of powers at the federal level.

In the rather confusing case of *Momcilovic* v. *The Queen*,[89] the High Court of Australia (HCA) indicated that 'declarations of inconsistent interpretation' under section 36 of the Charter of Human Rights and Responsibilities Act 2006 (Vic.) are not judicial in nature.[90] As a result, the power to issue such declarations cannot be exercised by a court exercising federal jurisdiction. This leads Bateman and Stellios to conclude that the 'federal separation of powers principles displace the possibility of enacting a declaration of inconsistent provision in any federal charter'.[91] That analysis is supported by Irving's view expressed prior to the HCA hearing *Momcilovic*.[92] The jurisdiction of the HCA is further limited by section 73, which restricts the court to hearing and determining 'appeals from all judgments, decrees, orders, and sentences' of federal courts, courts exercising federal jurisdiction or the Supreme Court of any State.[93] It has been argued that section 73 further restricts the HCA to appeals on 'matters'.[94] The absence of a 'matter' has been identified as a further potential problem to granting the HCA jurisdiction to issue some form of declaration of incompatibility.[95] Irving argues that if 'the declaration of incompatibility does satisfy the test of a "matter", including providing a legal remedy . . . the process ceases to be "dialogic". . . Either

[87] *Waterside Workers' Federation of Australia* v. *JW Alexander Ltd* (1918) 25 CLR 434, 442 (Griffith CJ); see R. Welsh, 'A Question of Integrity: the Role of Judges in Counterterrorism Questioning and Detention by ASIO' (2011) 22 *Public Law Review* 138, 141.
[88] *R* v. *Kirby, ex parte Boilermakers' Society of Australia* (1956) 94 CLR 254, 270.
[89] [2011] HCA 34, para. 93.
[90] W. Bateman and J. Stellios, 'Chapter III of the Constitution, Federal Jurisdiction and Dialogue Charters of Human Rights' (2012) 36(1) *Melbourne University Law Review* 1, 18.
[91] *Ibid.* 40.
[92] H. Irving, 'The Dilemmas in Dialogue: a Constitutional Analysis of the NHRC's Proposed Human Rights Act' (2010) 33(1) *University of New South Wales Law Journal* 60.
[93] Commonwealth of Australia Constitution Act 1900 (Cth), Ch. III s. 73.
[94] Irving, 'The Dilemmas in Dialogue', n. 92 above, 66.
[95] G. Lindell, 'The Statutory Protection of Rights and Parliamentary Sovereignty: Guidance from the United Kingdom?' (2006) 17 *Public Law Review* 188, 204.

the declaration fails the test for the exercise of judicial power, or it succeeds and the "dialogue" fails'.[96]

Although Williams and Burton reject the idea that *Momcilovic* has 'killed off' dialogic review at the federal level, they do so on the basis that a future HCA might 'reach a different decision if called upon to reconsider the issue at the federal level';[97] they are uncommitted advocates. Effectively, they propose strong form dialogue – they place an emphasis on the ability of Parliament to empower the courts to interpret legislation to be compatible with human rights standards.[98] The HCA appears to have upheld the interpretative power in *Momcilovic*. Importantly, the HCA did this by 'denying it any operation beyond the traditional boundaries of interpretation'[99] – that is, a more limited view of the interpretative power than that contained within section 3 of the UK HRA.

Stressing the interpretative power is problematic for a number of reasons. First, while the declarative power can be used in a manner which demands a response from the legislature, the interpretative power tends towards simple judicial monologue or juridification. All forms of dialogic models have been criticised for ultimately resulting in judicial monologue. It has been observed that over time parliaments tend to comply with the judicial statements of incompatibility;[100] the UK Parliament, for example, has complied with almost every declaration of incompatibility issued under section 4 of the UK HRA.[101] That tendency is likely to be exacerbated by a procedure which facilitates complete legislative inaction whilst enabling the judiciary to interpret laws so that they are compatible with rights. Furthermore, while declarative powers at least require a formal response, interpretative powers are not recorded in the same way: no statement of interpretation is issued by the court. That fact undermines dialogue – parliament would have to actively choose to

---

[96] Irving, 'The Dilemmas in Dialogue', n. 92 above, 72.

[97] Williams and Burton, 'Australia's Exclusive Parliamentary Model of Rights Protection', n. 33 above, 90.

[98] *Ibid.* 90.

[99] W. Bateman and J. Stellios, 'Chapter III of the Constitution, Federal Jurisdiction and Dialogue Charters of Human Rights' (2012) 36(1) *Melbourne University Law Review* 1, 16.

[100] A. Vermeule, 'The Atrophy of Constitutional Powers' (2012) 32(3) *Oxford Journal of Legal Studies* 421.

[101] Ministry of Justice, *Responding to Human Rights Judgments: Government Response to the Joint Committee on Human Rights, Fifteenth Report of Session 2009–10* (Cm 7892, 2010), available at www.justice.gov.uk/downloads/publications/moj/2010/responding-human-rights-judgements-2009-2010.pdf.

respond. In short, reliance on the interpretative power would also tend to exacerbate concerns about parliamentarians relying on the existence of the courts to correct executive excess rather than taking responsibility for such issues themselves.

Conclusion

I began from the premise that no mechanism is likely to be faultless and, indeed, a combination of the mechanisms outlined in this chapter and in the chapters by Blackbourn[102] and Roach[103] are most likely to succeed in restraining the executive. The exclusive parliamentary rights review model adopted in Australia might be effective, but the political culture in Australia militates against success. Scandinavia might provide more fertile ground for an experiment with the democratic model of rights enforcement. Sweden, for example, has an extensive, though not an exclusively parliamentary, system of pre-enactment scrutiny of proposed legislation for compatibility with human rights. Proposed legislation is scrutinised by parliamentary legislative committees, a Constitutional Committee and a Law Council comprised of current and former judges. Once enacted, legislation can also be reviewed by the courts. A court may not apply legislation if it finds it is clearly incompatible with human rights. In making this decision, the courts tend to follow the recommendations of the Law Council. This encourages parliament to follow the recommendations of the Law Council as well. Therefore the Law Council has a significant impact on the legislative process.[104] Even there, a role for the courts is envisaged.

Overall I am forced to conclude that an exclusive parliamentary model is unlikely to be robust enough, particularly in the absence of a strong culture of public parliamentary dissent. That said, a mechanism which simply empowers the judiciary to issue a declaration of incompatibility should be capable of alerting parliament to the problem and could be designed in such a way that it demands a response. Such a model is preferable to a model of judicial interpretation, which will, I believe, tend

---

[102] See Chapter 7 in this volume, J. Blackbourn, 'Independent reviewers as alternative: an empirical study from Australia and the United Kingdom'.

[103] See Chapter 8 in this volume, K. Roach, 'Public inquiries as an attempt to fill accountability gaps left by judicial and legislative review'.

[104] See further T. Bull, 'Judges Without Courts: Judicial Preview in Sweden' in T. Campbell, K. Ewing and A. Tomkins (eds.), *The Legal Protection of Human Rights* (Oxford University Press, 2011).

to judicial monologue. In the end, like many of the juristocrats, I am forced to conclude that a combination of institutional responses will be most effective. The difference between us comes down to the degree of emphasis and some theoretical underpinnings. But, ultimately, the only effective way to ensure the robust defence of human rights is to create a situation in which the people – those who retain the constituent power – demand that rights be respected.

Independent reviewers as alternative: an empirical study from Australia and the United Kingdom

JESSIE BLACKBOURN

Anti-terrorism laws, as a distinct category of legislation, possess four key features, which set them apart from the broader body of criminal law within which they sit. First, anti-terrorism laws tend to be reactive, both to terrorist attacks and to judicial decisions that find antecedent measures to be in breach of human rights norms.[1] Secondly, anti-terrorism laws are typically enacted in haste, often with little time for traditional forms of pre-enactment parliamentary scrutiny.[2] Thirdly, governments frequently rely on the insertion of a variety of post-enactment review mechanisms, in particular legislative sunset clauses, to appease parliamentary dissent and ensure the smooth passage of the Bill through parliament.[3] Fourthly, anti-terrorism laws have appeared remarkably resistant to either amendment or repeal despite post-enactment scrutiny.

As a consequence, anti-terrorism laws warrant a greater degree of post-enactment scrutiny than that which can be provided by traditional constitutionalist mechanisms. This chapter is concerned with one review mechanism that has been employed in Australia and the

---

[1] The UK Prevention of Terrorism Act 2005 replaced the indefinite detention provisions of the Anti-Terrorism, Crime and Security Act 2001 following the Law Lords judgment that they breached the European Convention on Human Rights. *A v. Secretary of State for the Home Department* [2004] UKHL 56. David Jenkins discusses the consequences of a legislative response to judicial decisions, see Chapter 3 in this volume, D. Jenkins, 'When good cases go bad: unintended consequences of rights-friendly judgments'.

[2] A. Lynch, 'Legislating with Urgency: the Enactment of the Anti-Terrorism Act (No. 1) 2005' (2006) 30 *Melbourne University Law Review* 747.

[3] J. Ip, 'Sunset Clauses and Counterterrorism Legislation' (2013) *Public Law* 74; A. Lynch, 'The Impact of Post-Enactment Review on Anti-Terrorism Laws: Four Jurisdictions Compared' (2012) 18 *Journal of Legislative Studies* 63; N. McGarrity, R. Gulati and G. Williams, 'Sunset Clauses in Australian Anti-Terror Laws' (2012) 33 *Adelaide Law Review* 320. Fergal Davis explores other, political, reasons for the suppression of parliamentary dissent during the enactment of anti-terrorism laws, see Chapter 6 in this volume, F. F. Davis, 'The politics of counter-terrorism judicial review: creating effective parliamentary scrutiny'.

United Kingdom: the independent reviewer.[4] A number of the United Kingdom's anti-terrorism laws are subject to review by the Independent Reviewer of Terrorism Legislation (Independent Reviewer).[5] In Australia this function is served by the Independent National Security Legislation Monitor (Independent Monitor).[6]

This chapter will outline the routes that Australia and the United Kingdom have taken to introduce formal offices of independent anti-terrorism review. It will then assess whether the introduction of these novel oversight mechanisms has provided meaningful and effective scrutiny of anti-terrorism laws. This will be measured against the yardstick suggested by Christopher Hood *et al.* in their work on government regulation. They identify three 'basic dimensions' necessary for meaningful and effective government oversight: first, 'one bureaucracy aims to shape the activities of another'; secondly, 'there is some degree of organizational separation between the "regulating" bureaucracy and the "regulatee"'; and thirdly, 'the "regulator" has some kind of official mandate to scrutinize the behaviour of the "regulatee" and seek to change it'.[7] The chapter argues that while both the Independent Reviewer and Independent Monitor face significant challenges to their capacity to provide meaningful and effective oversight of anti-terrorism laws, the strict regulatory structure of the Australian office of Independent Monitor mitigates these limitations to a greater extent than the non-statutory model of Independent Reviewer in the United Kingdom.

I   Path to independent anti-terrorism review

Australia and the United Kingdom have had vastly different experiences of terrorism. Australia has been described as 'fortunate' in its limited exposure to terrorism in the twentieth century.[8] An estimated twenty

---

[4] See Kent Roach on another method of non-constitutionalist post-enactment review: the independent inquiry, Chapter 8 in this volume, K. Roach, 'Public inquiries as an attempt to fill accountability gaps left by judicial and legislative review'.

[5] Anti-Terrorism, Crime and Security Act 2001, s. 28; Prevention of Terrorism Act 2005, s. 14; Terrorism Act 2006, s. 36; Terrorist Asset-Freezing etc. Act 2010, s. 31; Terrorism Prevention and Investigation Measures Act 2011, s. 20. See also https://terrorismlegislationreviewer.independent.gov.uk/about-me/.

[6] Independent National Security Legislation Monitor Act 2010 (Cth).

[7] C. Hood, O. James, G. Jones, C. Scott and T. Travers, *Regulation Inside Government: Waste-Watchers, Quality Police, and Sleazebusters* (Oxford University Press, 1999), p. 8.

[8] S. Koschade, 'Constructing a Historical Framework of Terrorism in Australia: From the Fenian Brotherhood to 21st Century Islamic Extremism' (2007) 2 *Journal of Policing,*

people have been killed in terrorist attacks on Australian soil.[9] The most notable of these attacks was the 1978 bombing of the Sydney Hilton Hotel during the Commonwealth Heads of Government Regional Meeting, in which three people died.[10] In contrast, there have been a large number of deaths from terrorist attacks in the United Kingdom. Northern Ireland was the primary locus of terrorism there in the twentieth century. More than 3,450 persons were killed.[11] A further 128 persons were killed by Northern Irish terrorists in Britain.[12] The United Kingdom has also been the target of attacks by international terrorists motivated by a variety of causes as well as by single issue terrorist groups such as animal rights activists, and domestic right-wing terrorists.[13]

These different histories of experiencing terrorism have led Australia and the United Kingdom to take different approaches to countering terrorism. Australia had no federal anti-terrorism laws prior to the terrorist attacks on the United States on 11 September 2001 ('9/11').[14] In contrast, a vast regime of anti-terrorism legislation was enacted in the United Kingdom to tackle both Northern Irish and international terrorism in the twentieth century.[15] The Northern Ireland (Emergency Provisions) Act 1973 was the first anti-terrorism law to be enacted. It was envisaged as a temporary measure[16] applicable only to Northern Ireland.[17] It was renewed annually and updated on several

---

Intelligence and Counter-Terrorism 54; N. McGarrity, 'An Example of "Worst Practice"? The Coercive Counter-Terrorism Powers of the Australian Security Intelligence Organisation' (2010) 4 *Vienna Journal on International Constitutional Law* 468; A. Lynch and N. McGarrity, *A "Watch Dog" of Australia's Counter-Terrorism Laws: the Coming of the National Security Legislation Monitor*, UNSW Law Research Paper No. 2011–26 4 (2011).

[9] C. Williams, 'No, Minister we are not free of terror', *Canberra Times*, 9 September 2006.

[10] T. Molomby, *Spies, Bombs and the Path of Bliss: Ananda Marga and the Hilton Bombing* (Sydney: Potoroo Press, 1986).

[11] D. McKittrick, S. Kelters, B. Feeney, C. Thornton and D. McVea, *Lost Lives: the Stories of the Men, Women and Children who Died as a Result of the Northern Ireland Troubles* (Edinburgh and London: Mainstream Publishing, 2007), p. 1559.

[12] *Ibid.*

[13] Lord Lloyd, *Inquiry into Legislation against Terrorism* (London: Stationery Office, 1996), pp. 2–4, 24–32.

[14] G. Williams, 'A Decade of Australian Anti-Terror Laws' (2011) 35 *Melbourne University Law Review* 1139.

[15] L. K. Donohue, *Counter-Terrorist Law and Emergency Powers in the United Kingdom 1922–2000* (Dublin: Irish Academic Press, 2007). See also J. Blackbourn. 'The Evolving Definition of Terrorism in UK Law' (2011) 3 *Behavioral Sciences of Terrorism and Political Aggression* 131.

[16] Northern Ireland (Emergency Provisions) Act 1973, s. 30(2).   [17] *Ibid.* s. 31(8).

occasions.[18] In 1974, the UK Parliament enacted a law for the whole of the United Kingdom.[19] The Prevention of Terrorism (Temporary Provisions) Act was also temporary in duration[20] and was renewed and updated a number of times.[21] These Acts were subject to a number of ad hoc reviews from 1978 to 1996,[22] as well as annual review from the mid-1980s.[23]

The annual review process was established by the UK government for one main purpose, namely, to inform Parliament on the operation of the Prevention of Terrorism (Temporary Provisions) Act 1984 prior to the annual debates on its renewal. Lord Elton, Minister of State for the Home Office, confirmed that the reviewer's report 'should be published – and published in good time before the House considered a continuation order'.[24] The annual review had two major deficiencies. First, as Clive Walker has noted, the annual review process failed to fulfil its most basic function of informing Parliament: 'publication of the reviews is quite unsatisfactory. Parliament is sometimes informed at a late stage, so that Members often fail to notice or digest scraps of information tossed their way, and there is no official publication at all to the public'.[25] This failure

---

[18] Northern Ireland (Emergency Provisions) Act 1978; Northern Ireland (Emergency Provisions) Act 1987; Northern Ireland (Emergency Provisions) Act 1991; Northern Ireland (Emergency Provisions) Act 1996; and Northern Ireland (Emergency Provisions) Act 1998.

[19] Part 1 of the Act did not apply to Northern Ireland as similar provisions were already in force in the Northern Ireland (Emergency Provisions) Act 1973. See Prevention of Terrorism (Temporary Provisions) Act 1974, s. 13(2).

[20] Prevention of Terrorism (Temporary Provisions) Act 1974, s. 12(1).

[21] Prevention of Terrorism (Temporary Provisions) Act 1976; Prevention of Terrorism (Temporary Provisions) Act 1984; Prevention of Terrorism (Temporary Provisions) Act 1989; and Prevention of Terrorism (Additional Powers) Act 1996.

[22] Lord Shackleton, *Review of the Operation of the Prevention of Terrorism (Temporary Provisions) Acts 1974 and 1976* (London: HMSO, 1978); Earl Jellicoe, *Review of the Operation of the Prevention of Terrorism (Temporary Provisions) Act 1976* (London: HMSO, 1983); Sir George Baker, *Review of the Operation of the Northern Ireland (Emergency Provisions) Act 1978* (London: HMSO, 1984); Viscount Colville of Culross, *Review of the Operation of the Prevention of Terrorism (Temporary Provisions) Act 1984* (London: HMSO, 1987); Viscount Colville of Culross, *Review of the Northern Ireland (Emergency Provisions) Acts 1978 and 1987* (London: HMSO, 1990); and J. J. Rowe, *Review of the Northern Ireland (Emergency Provisions) Act 1991* (London: HMSO, 1995); Lloyd, *Inquiry into Legislation against Terrorism*, n. 13 above.

[23] See http://terrorismlegislationreviewer.independent.gov.uk/history.

[24] HL Deb., 8 March 1984, vol. 449 col. 406.

[25] C. Walker, *The Prevention of Terrorism in British Law* (Manchester University Press, 1992), p. 37.

was further compounded by what Walker describes as 'the general lack of parliamentary interest, with the result that debates tended to be short, poorly attended and conducted late at night'.[26]

Secondly, the annual reviewers understood their function in limited terms; to report simply on the operation of the Acts, rather than assessing them against broader criteria such as reasonableness, effectiveness or necessity.[27] This practice was a continuation of the terms of reference laid out in the ad hoc reviews of the Prevention of Terrorism (Temporary Provisions) Acts and the Northern Ireland (Emergency Provisions) Acts. In each report, the reviewer was required to accept the continuing need for anti-terrorism legislation.[28] In his final report on the operation of both the Prevention of Terrorism (Temporary Provisions) Act 1989 and the Northern Ireland (Emergency Provisions) Act 1996, the annual reviewer dejectedly pointed out that it was not necessary to consider the continuing need for the legislation because it had already been repealed and replaced by a new law: 'Thereby, it seems to me, Parliament decided that there was a continuing need of a statute for the prevention of terrorism'.[29]

The United Kingdom's informal and ad hoc review mechanisms appear to have been unable to play any significant role in shaping the government's counter-terrorism policy. The same has been true in Australia. Following the enactment of new anti-terrorism laws in the aftermath of 9/11, aspects of these laws were subjected to ad hoc review on a number of occasions.[30] The reviews covered a number of anti-terrorism related insertions into the Criminal Code Act 1995 (Cth), including international terrorist activities using explosives;[31]

---

[26] *Ibid.* p. 35.

[27] Lloyd, *Inquiry into Legislation against Terrorism*, n. 13 above, p. vi.

[28] Shackleton, *Review of the Operation of the Prevention of Terrorism (Temporary Provisions) Acts 1974 and 1976*, n. 22 above, p. v; Jellicoe, *Review of the Operation of the Prevention of Terrorism (Temporary Provisions) Act 1976*, n. 22 above, p. iv; Baker, *Review of the Operation of the Northern Ireland (Emergency Provisions) Act 1978*, n. 22 above, p. 1; Colville, *Review of the Operation of the Prevention of Terrorism (Temporary Provisions) Act 1984*, n. 22 above, p. 111; Colville, *Review of the Northern Ireland (Emergency Provisions) Acts 1978 and 1987*, n. 22 above, p. 1; and Rowe, *Review of the Northern Ireland (Emergency Provisions) Act 1991*, n. 22 above, p. vii.

[29] J. Rowe, *Review of the Operation in 2000 of the Prevention of Terrorism (Temporary Provisions) Act 1989 and Northern Ireland (Emergency Provisions) Act 1996* (2002), p. 1.

[30] McGarrity, Gulati and Williams, 'Sunset Clauses in Australian Anti-Terror Laws', n. 3 above, 320, n. 88.

[31] Security Legislation Review Committee (SLRC), *Report of the Security Legislation Review Committee* (2006); Parliamentary Joint Committee on Intelligence and Security (PJCIS), *Review of Security and Counter-Terrorism Legislation* (2006).

treason;[32] sedition;[33] definitions of terrorism, the constitutional basis for anti-terrorism laws and their application;[34] acts of terrorism and preparation for terrorist acts;[35] proscription of terrorist organizations and related offences;[36] and the financing of terrorism.[37] They also examined border surveillance and customs,[38] the Australian Security Intelligence Organisation's (ASIO) questioning and detention powers,[39] and the use of the powers of arrest, detention, charging, prosecution and release of terrorist suspects under the Crimes Act 1914 (Cth).[40] The reviews were not comprehensive; some laws were not scrutinised, for example, those providing for control orders and preventative detention orders.[41]

The exclusion of some of Australia's most controversial anti-terrorism measures was not the only significant failing of these reviews. For the most part, the recommendations of the review bodies were substantially ignored by the government that commissioned them.[42] After the 2007 election, the Labor government's response demonstrated considerable selectivity in the recommendations it chose to adopt.[43] Lynch argues that

---

[32] *Ibid.*

[33] Australian Law Reform Commission, *Fighting Words: A Review of Sedition Laws in Australia* (Commonwealth of Australia, 2006).

[34] SLRC, *Report of the Security Legislation Review Committee*, n. 31 above; PJCIS, *Review of Security and Counter-Terrorism Legislation*, n. 31 above.

[35] *Ibid.*

[36] SLRC, *Report of the Security Legislation Review Committee*, n. 31 above; PJCIS, *Review of Security and Counter-Terrorism Legislation*, n. 31 above; PJCIS, *Inquiry into the Proscription of 'Terrorist Organisations' under the Australian Criminal Code* (2007).

[37] SLRC, *Report of the Security Legislation Review Committee*, n. 31 above; PJCIS, *Review of Security and Counter-Terrorism Legislation*, n. 31 above.

[38] PJCIS, *Review of Security and Counter-Terrorism Legislation*, n. 31 above.

[39] Parliamentary Joint Committee on ASIO, ASIS and DSD, *ASIO's Questioning and Detention Powers* (2005).

[40] J. Clarke, *Report of the Clarke Inquiry into the Case of Dr Mohamed Haneef* (Canberra: Commonwealth of Australia, 2008).

[41] Anti-Terrorism Act (No. 2) 2005 (Cth), Sch. 4.

[42] Lynch, 'The Impact of Post-Enactment Review on Anti-Terrorism Laws', n. 3 above, 66; Lynch and McGarrity, A 'Watch Dog' of Australia's Counter-Terrorism Laws, n. 8 above, 15. There is one exception to this; the Parliamentary Joint Committee on ASIO, ASIS and DSD review of ASIO's questioning and detention powers received a positive response from the government, which 'agreed in full with six recommendations and in part with a further six'. These recommendations were incorporated as amendments into the Australian Security Intelligence Organisation Act 1979 (Cth) by the ASIO Amendment Act 2006 (Cth). McGarrity, Gulati and Williams, 'Sunset Clauses in Australian Anti-Terror Laws', n. 3 above.

[43] Lynch, 'The Impact of Post-Enactment Review on Anti-Terrorism Laws', n. 3 above, 66; see also Lynch and McGarrity, A 'Watch Dog' of Australia's Counter-Terrorism Laws, n. 8 above, 15.

the government adopted a 'lowest common denominator' approach to implementing competing recommendations in the reviews. He cites the example of the discretion of the Attorney General 'to proscribe an organisation on the basis that it (or presumably any of its members) "praises" some terrorist incident, in cases where a person, regardless of actual or mental age, might be encouraged to engage in a terrorist act of their own'.[44] According to Lynch, the Security Legislation Review Committee recommended in its 2006 report that 'this element of the proscription regime should be repealed' or 'at the very least an amendment be made clarifying that the risk of the listener acting after the "praise" must be "substantial"'.[45] The Parliamentary Joint Committee on Intelligence and Security also recommended clarification of the risk involved, but did not recommend repeal of the 'praise' element of the proscription regime. Lynch states that 'On the back of this, the government was willing to adopt the suggested amendment of the risk level but go no further'.[46]

These reviews had only a very limited impact on Australia's anti-terrorism policy. However, one of the recommendations proposed by a number of the reviews gained sufficient political momentum to be taken up by the government, namely, the creation of an office of independent oversight to review the anti-terrorism laws.[47] In 2008, the Independent Reviewer of Terrorism Laws Bill was introduced into Parliament as a Private Member's Bill. It was defeated by the government, which launched its own oversight legislation a year later. In 2010, the Independent Monitor was formally established with the enactment of the Independent National Security Legislation Monitor Act.[48] The Independent Monitor was roughly based on the UK Independent Reviewer. The latter had been established a decade earlier by the enactment of the Terrorism Act 2000. The UK Independent Reviewer is a twenty-first century re-construction of the pre-existing annual review mechanism. The role of annual reviewer has changed significantly since 9/11, due both to the enactment of permanent, rather than temporary or emergency legislation, and significant increases in the reviewer's

---

[44] Lynch, 'The Impact of Post-Enactment Review on Anti-Terrorism Laws', n. 3 above, 66.
[45] Ibid.
[46] Ibid. See also Lynch and McGarrity, A 'Watch Dog' of Australia's Counter-Terrorism Laws, n. 8 above, 15.
[47] Lynch, 'The Impact of Post-Enactment Review on Anti-Terrorism Laws', n. 3 above, 67.
[48] Independent National Security Legislation Monitor Act 2010 (Cth), s. 5.

responsibilities. It is therefore fair to consider that the office of Independent Reviewer of Terrorism Legislation was established with the appointment of Lord Carlile in the role on 11 September 2001. The Terrorism Act 2000 required the Secretary of State to 'lay before both Houses of Parliament at least once in every 12 months a report on the working of this Act'.[49] The UK government appears to have interpreted this provision as requiring the appointment of a person to carry out an annual review of the Act. The enactment of new anti-terrorism laws in the twenty-first century has led to the expansion of the duties of the Independent Reviewer. As well as annual review of the Terrorism Act 2000, the Independent Reviewer must now also review Part 1 of the Terrorism Act 2006, the Terrorist Asset-Freezing etc. Act 2010 and the Terrorism Prevention and Investigation Measures Act 2011. The Independent Reviewer was also tasked with reviewing the now repealed Part 4 detention provisions of the Anti-Terrorism, Crime and Security Act 2001 and the control order provisions of the Prevention of Terrorism Act 2005.[50] As well as these statutory reviewing functions, 'the Independent Reviewer may on his own initiative or at the request of Ministers conduct reviews and produce reports on specific issues'.[51]

In spite of their different histories of terrorism and anti-terrorism laws, both Australia and the United Kingdom have had similar experiences of first establishing, and then supplementing, review mechanisms with formal offices of independent oversight. These new offices sit alongside those pre-existing review mechanisms. In Australia, this has been further complemented by the creation of a counter-terrorism review committee within the Council of Australian Governments (COAG), tasked with reviewing the anti-terrorism legislation enacted in Australia in the aftermath of the 2005 London bombings.[52]

Prior to the establishment of the offices of the Independent Reviewer and the Independent Monitor, there was little evidence that anti-terrorism review was meaningful or effective. This chapter will now assess whether the independent review mechanisms have achieved

---

[49] Terrorism Act 2000, s. 126.

[50] Anti-Terrorism, Crime and Security Act 2001, s. 28; Prevention of Terrorism Act 2005, s. 14; Terrorism Act 2006, s. 36; Terrorist Asset-Freezing etc. Act 2010, s. 31; and Terrorism Prevention and Investigation Measures Act 2011, s. 20.

[51] See https://terrorismlegislationreviewer.independent.gov.uk/about-me/.

[52] 'COAG to review counter-terrorism legislation', available at www.pm.gov.au/press-office/coag-review-counter-terrorism-legislation. See also www.coagctreview.gov.au/Pages/default.aspx.

greater success. It does so in terms of the three principles for effective scrutiny identified by Hood *et al.*: the official mandate of the office; independence (the distance between the reviewer and the government under review); and influence (the capability of the reviewer to shape the government's activities on anti-terrorism laws).

II   Official mandate

Australia and the United Kingdom have taken different approaches to providing an official mandate for their respective offices of Independent Monitor and Independent Reviewer. The Independent Reviewer has an informal mandate, whilst the office of Independent Monitor is strictly regulated.

Unlike the Independent Monitor, who was established and is regulated by the Independent National Security Legislation Monitor Act 2010, there is no single statutory basis for the role of Independent Reviewer in the United Kingdom. Independent review of an anti-terrorism law is mandatory only if a review provision is specifically inserted into that law. The Terrorism Act 2000, Terrorist Asset-Freezing etc. Act 2010, and Terrorism Prevention and Investigation Measures Act 2011 are all subject to review in their entirety, as was the Prevention of Terrorism Act 2005.[53] In contrast, prior to their repeal, only the Part 4 indefinite detention provisions of the Anti-Terrorism, Crime and Security Act 2001 were subject to review by the Independent Reviewer; the rest of the Act was omitted from the Independent Reviewer's remit.[54] The Independent Reviewer is only responsible for examining Part 1 of the Terrorism Act 2006,[55] and the Counter-Terrorism Act 2008 contains no provision for annual review.[56]

The Independent Reviewer must review each of these laws on an annual basis. However, there is no statutory framework governing how

---

[53] Terrorism Act 2000, s. 126; Prevention of Terrorism Act 2005, s. 14; Terrorist Asset-Freezing etc. Act 2010, s. 31; and Terrorism Prevention and Investigation Measures Act 2011, s. 20.

[54] Anti-Terrorism, Crime and Security Act 2001, s. 28. Section 122 of the Act did, however, require the Secretary of State to establish a commission to review the Act in its entirety.

[55] Terrorism Act 2006, s. 36.

[56] David Anderson has recommended the incorporation of the Anti-Terrorism, Crime and Security Act 2001 and the Counter-Terrorism Act 2008 into the remit of the Independent Reviewer. D. Anderson, *The Terrorism Acts in 2011* (London: Stationery Office, 2012), p. 135.

that review must be carried out. The reviewer has no identifiable powers to demand information from either the Home Secretary or from the security, intelligence and police services that implement the laws under review. Furthermore, the terms of reference for the Independent Reviewer date back to 1984, when the first annual review of the Prevention of Terrorism (Temporary Provisions) Acts was announced.[57] These terms suggest that the reviewer need only examine the operation of the Acts under review. The first UK Independent Reviewer, Lord Carlile, conformed to this rather narrow remit; for the most part, he provided Parliament with reports only on the practical use of the laws. In his first report on the operation of the Terrorism Act 2000, Lord Carlile outlined his approach to reviewing the United Kingdom's anti-terrorism laws: 'I have taken it as a basic tenet, not open to question as part of this reviewing process, that specific anti-terrorism legislation is necessary as an adjunct to and strengthening of the ordinary criminal law'.[58] Lord Carlile has been heavily criticised for taking this narrow approach.[59] In reference to his supportive stance on the government's proposal to increase the maximum period of pre-charge detention, one commentator even went so far as to call him an 'enthusiastic advocate for the government'.[60]

David Anderson, the current office holder, has to some extent broadened the Independent Reviewer's mandate. In his first report on the Terrorism Acts, Anderson went beyond a simple analysis of the practical use of the laws. He stated: 'Any assessment of whether they are necessary and proportionate in their operation must be conducted with an eye both to the current nature and extent of the terrorist threat in the United Kingdom, and to the range of tools available to the counter-terrorism effort'.[61] He has also assessed the Terrorism Prevention and

---

[57] See http://terrorismlegislationreviewer.independent.gov.uk/history/; Lord Carlile, *Report on the Operation in 2001 of the Terrorism Act 2000* (2002), p. 5.

[58] *Ibid.* p. 7.

[59] I. Bunglawala, 'Carlile's curious reasoning', *Guardian*, 18 December 2007; P. Lewis, 'Lord Carlile's 'credibility' as terror watchdog questioned by MP', *Guardian*, 3 February 2010; Lynch and McGarrity, *A 'Watch Dog' of Australia's Counter-Terrorism Laws*, n. 8 above, 23–5; C. O'Cinneide, 'Strapped to the Mast: the Siren Song of Dreadful Necessity, the United Kingdom Human Rights Act and the Terrorist Threat' in M. Gani and P. Matthews (eds.), *Fresh Perspectives on the 'War on Terror'* (Canberra: Australian National University Press, 2008), p. 353.

[60] Bunglawala, 'Carlile's curious reasoning', n. 59 above.

[61] D. Anderson, *Report on the Operation in 2010 of the Terrorism Act 2000 and of Part 1 of the Terrorism Act 2006* (London: Stationery Office, 2011), p. 17.

Investigations Measures Act 2011 against the test of whether the measures are 'effective' and 'fair'.[62]

The lack of a formal mandate enables the UK Independent Reviewer to construct a broad or narrow interpretation of the terms of reference. This lack of consistency highlights one of the key problems of an informal mandate: that without structured guidelines, the functioning of the office will be dependent on the person appointed. The personality, preferences and prejudices of the Independent Reviewer become central to the question of whether the office can offer meaningful and effective scrutiny of the UK anti-terrorism laws. However, it may be that it is simply not possible to eradicate the personality factor from an office of independent anti-terrorism review. In Australia, the establishment of a formal mandate in the Independent National Security Legislation Monitor Act 2010 (Cth) sought to ensure that the effectiveness of the review was not overly dependent on the personality of the Monitor; it has not entirely succeeded so far.

The Independent National Security Legislation Monitor Act 2010 (Cth) meticulously identifies and imposes strict procedures. First, the Independent Monitor's functions are tightly defined. The Monitor must review 'the operation, effectiveness and implications' of Australia's anti-terrorism and national security legislation[63] and must also consider whether that legislation 'contains appropriate safeguards for protecting the rights of individuals; remains proportionate to any threat of terrorism or threat to national security, or both; and remains necessary'.[64] These terms are substantially more expansive than those applied by Lord Carlile and even exceed the broader test used by Anderson.

Secondly, the Act grants a variety of powers to the Independent Monitor.[65] It expressly vests in the Monitor the power to access necessary information. The Act stipulates that the Independent Monitor may hold a hearing[66] and summon a person to attend.[67] The Act further provides for a witness at a hearing to be required to take an oath or affirmation.[68] More importantly, the Act states that the Independent Monitor may 'request, by written notice, a person: (a) to give the Monitor the information referred to in the notice; or (b) to produce to the Monitor the

---

[62] D. Anderson, *Terrorism Prevention and Investigation Measures in 2012* (London: Stationery Office, 2013), pp. 5–6.

[63] Independent National Security Legislation Monitor Act 2010 (Cth), s. 6(1)(a).

[64] *Ibid.* s. 6(1)(b).   [65] *Ibid.* ss. 21–5.   [66] *Ibid.* s. 21.   [67] *Ibid.* s. 22.

[68] *Ibid.* s. 23.

documents or things referred to in the notice'.[69] The Act imposes penalties for failing to produce a document or thing or for failing to provide the information requested.[70] These provisions ensure that the Independent Monitor has access to information without being dependent on the goodwill of those from whom the information is requested, as is the case in the United Kingdom. Both Lord Carlile and David Anderson have indicated that they have been granted access to all the information that they have asked to see.[71] However, there is no guarantee that this will always be the case. The Australian system ensures that the Independent Monitor will always be provided with the information demanded.

The United Kingdom's system of oversight requires the Independent Reviewer to report once every year on the operation of every Act subject to a review provision. The Independent Monitor must also report once a year.[72] However, there is broad discretion within that remit for the Monitor to choose which aspects of Australia's anti-terrorism and national security laws to examine. The current Monitor, Bret Walker, has used this to his advantage. Rather than assess all of the laws (of which there is a significant number) at a shallow level, he has targeted those aspects of the laws he considers most pressing. His first substantive review examined control orders, preventative detention orders and ASIO questioning and detention powers.[73] Neither control orders nor preventative detention orders have previously been subject to review. His next report focused in detail on the National Security Information (Criminal Proceedings) Act 2004 and on terrorist financing provisions. Walker appears to have chosen to review those aspects of Australia's anti-terrorism laws, which are some of the most contentious but least used. This approach focuses heavily on his remit to assess whether the laws 'remain necessary'. Walker is the inaugural Independent Monitor. His method of reviewing the laws could be anomalous. The next Monitor might take a different approach, which could lead to a significant decline in the level of scrutiny provided.

The Australian system of anti-terrorism review has attempted to improve on the United Kingdom's, in which personality dominates

---

[69] *Ibid.* s. 24(1).   [70] *Ibid.* s. 25(3) and (4).

[71] Anderson, *Report on the Operation in 2010 of the Terrorism Act 2000 and of Part 1 of the Terrorism Act 2006*, n. 61 above, p. 10; Carlile, *Report on the Operation in 2001 of the Terrorism Act 2000*, n. 57 above, p. 8.

[72] Independent National Security Legislation Monitor Act 2010 (Cth), s. 29(2).

[73] B. Walker, *Independent National Security Legislation Monitor Declassified Annual Report* (Canberra: Commonwealth of Australia, 2012).

process. However, it still retains elements which ensure the personal approach of the office holder has an impact on the capacity to provide meaningful and effective review. If the 'personality factor' is impossible to eliminate, then the question of who is appointed, and how, becomes critical to whether the offices of Independent Monitor and Independent Reviewer can provide meaningful and effective oversight.

III   Independence

'Independence' should be a key attribute of the offices of Independent Monitor and Independent Reviewer. The independence of the office speaks to its broader credibility and its capacity to shape the activities of the government under review. However, the offices of Independent Monitor and Independent Reviewer are not as independent as they might be.[74]

The Independent Monitor and the Independent Reviewer are both appointed by the government of the day. The Independent Monitor is appointed in accordance with the criteria used in selecting agency heads for the Australian Public Service. For the appointment of Bret Walker, the Department of the Prime Minister and Cabinet and the Attorney General's Department:

> developed an initial list of 30 possible candidates. In consultation with the former Cabinet Secretary, Senator the Hon. Joseph Ludwig, this was ultimately reduced to a short-list of seven. These candidates were invited to submit an application to the National Security Adviser. A list of those individuals interested in being considered for the position was subsequently provided to the Prime Minister.[75]

The appointment is made by the Governor General on the recommendation of the Prime Minister, who must first have consulted with the Leader of the Opposition in the House of Representatives.[76] The Monitor therefore receives some bipartisan support. In contrast, in the United Kingdom, the Independent Reviewer is simply appointed by the Home Secretary, using the criteria laid out for public appointments.[77] However,

---

[74] For a discussion on the independence of those appointed to lead independent inquiries, see Chapter 8 in this volume, K. Roach, 'Public inquiries as an attempt to fill accountability gaps left by judicial and legislative review'.

[75] Australia, FOI Request [SEC=UNCLASSIFIED] (6 December 2012).

[76] Independent National Security Legislation Monitor Act 2010 (Cth), s. 11(1) and (2).

[77] Cabinet Office, *Making and Managing Public Appointments: A Guide for Departments* (4th edn, London: Cabinet Office, 2006).

unlike most appointments, it is not regulated by the Office of the Commissioner for Public Appointments.[78]

In neither appointment process is there an open call for applications. This has been criticised by the current UK Independent Reviewer, David Anderson, who has proposed that his position should be advertised.[79] Australia and the United Kingdom have appointed a very similar type of person to the role of Independent Monitor and Independent Reviewer. Bret Walker is a Senior Counsel at the Australian Bar. David Anderson and Lord Carlile are Queen's Counsels in the United Kingdom. Whilst lawyers are undoubtedly well qualified to carry out review of anti-terrorism laws, opening up the applications process would refute any suggestion that the government was simply appointing someone who was sympathetic to their position.

Lord Carlile's approach to examining the Prevention of Terrorism Act 2005 reveals the problems which arise when a reviewer appears to be too close to the government. Lord Carlile was an avid supporter of the control order regime. Even after the Coalition government announced that it was to be replaced, he still maintained that he 'never thought there was a need to abandon the 28 days [period of pre-charge detention], just as I thought there was no need to abandon control orders'.[80] Lord Carlile's reports on control orders demonstrated this further. In each report he stated:

> As part of my function as Independent Reviewer, my task is to replicate exactly the position of the Home Secretary at the initiation of a control order. I call for and am given access to the same files as were placed before the Secretary of State when [he or she] was asked to determine whether a control order should be made.[81]

---

[78] UK, FOI Request 26205 (28 February 2013). See Commissioner for Public Appointments, *Code of Practice for Ministerial Appointments to Public Bodies* (London: Commissioner for Public Appointments, 2012).

[79] D. Anderson, 'Torture, Terrorism and Secrets', *BBC Radio 4*, 29 October 2012.

[80] Joint Committee on the Draft Detention of Terrorist Suspects (Temporary Extension) Bills, *Oral and Associated Written Evidence* (29 March 2007), Q84 (Lord Carlile).

[81] Lord Carlile, *First Report of the Independent Reviewer Pursuant to Section 14(3) of the Prevention of Terrorism Act 2005* (London: Stationery Office, 2006), p. 11; Lord Carlile, *Second Report of the Independent Reviewer Pursuant to Section 14(3) of the Prevention of Terrorism Act 2005* (London: Stationery Office, 2007), p. 12; Lord Carlile, *Third Report of the Independent Reviewer Pursuant to Section 14(3) of the Prevention of Terrorism Act 2005* (London: Stationery Office, 2008), p. 12; Lord Carlile, *Fourth Report of the Independent Reviewer Pursuant to Section 14(3) of the Prevention of Terrorism Act 2005* (London: Stationery Office, 2009), p. 12; Lord Carlile, *Fifth Report of the Independent*

In each case of the making of a control order, Lord Carlile stated that he 'would have reached the same decision as the Secretary of State'.[82] While nothing in the legislation required Lord Carlile to consider the operation of the control order regime from the position of the Home Secretary, the lack of a formal mandate enabled him to carry out his review in this way. He could have assessed whether the order was necessary, would be effective or was reasonable. Instead, he adopted a non-expansive approach to reviewing the Prevention of Terrorism Act 2005 by employing the same process used by the courts for assessing the control order regime: that of judicial review.[83] Lord Carlile therefore only assessed whether the Secretary of State's decision in making a control order was 'obviously flawed'.[84] Whilst Carlile's approach could be considered simply unimaginative, his enthusiasm for the control order powers suggests instead his sympathy for the regime and demonstrates a lack of willingness to review it in depth.

With both the Independent Reviewer and the courts utilising the same test, the control order regime was reviewed only narrowly. The Independent Reviewer operates outside of the traditional constitutional system of checks and balances; the advantage of this is that he or she may provide an additional layer of post-enactment scrutiny not already available through the courts. The unique oversight function of the office of Independent Reviewer is seriously limited if it merely replicates a pre-existing constitutional mechanism. Lord Carlile had the opportunity to review the control order regime through any method that he considered appropriate; instead, he adopted an approach that was already being used by the courts. The control order regime was therefore not being subjected to an additional layer of oversight. Instead, it received one type of scrutiny carried out by two different bodies: the courts and the Independent Reviewer. For the office of Independent Reviewer to really fulfil its

Reviewer Pursuant to Section 14(3) of the Prevention of Terrorism Act 2005 (London: Stationery Office, 2010), p. 39; Lord Carlile, Sixth Report of the Independent Reviewer Pursuant to Section 14(3) of the Prevention of Terrorism Act 2005 (London: Stationery Office, 2011), pp. 39–40.

[82] Carlile, First Report of the Independent Reviewer, n. 81 above, p. 12; Carlile, Second Report of the Independent Reviewer, n. 81 above, p. 13; Carlile, Third Report of the Independent Reviewer, n. 81 above, p. 13; Carlile, Fourth Report of the Independent Reviewer, n. 81 above, p. 13; Carlile, Fifth Report of the Independent Reviewer, n. 81 above, p. 40; Carlile, Sixth Report of the Independent Reviewer, n. 81 above, p. 40.

[83] Prevention of Terrorism Act 2005, s. 10(6).

[84] Carlile, Sixth Report of the Independent Reviewer, n. 81 above, p. 45.

function as an additional, extra-constitutional review mechanism, it would have been better if Lord Carlile had subjected the Home Secretary's decisions on control orders to a much deeper scrutiny than that already provided by the courts.

The absence of a competitive appointment process allowed the government to appoint an Independent Reviewer that appeared to be sympathetic to its position. The lack of formal regulation over the period of appointment in the United Kingdom further exacerbated the issue. The Independent Reviewer is appointed for a three-year term, which is 'renewable by mutual consent'.[85] There is no limit to the number of times the Independent Reviewer's term can be renewed. Lord Carlile's tenure as Independent Reviewer lasted for nearly nine and a half years. He could have continued longer. Lord Carlile was rarely critical of the government's counter-terrorism agenda, though he denied that he was unduly influenced by those organisations which were the subject of his reviews.[86] In contrast to the Independent Reviewer, there are strict rules about the renewal and dismissal of the Independent Monitor. The Monitor is appointed for a three-year term which may be renewed only once.[87] This shorter period is not necessarily an improvement on the United Kingdom's. Australia has a substantial volume of very complex anti-terrorism laws. Replacing the Monitor every three years might mean that comprehensive and effective scrutiny suffers from inexperience and an inability to build a substantial knowledge base. A single, non-renewable term limit of five years would ensure that the Independent Monitor has sufficient time to carry out substantive, detailed reviews, but not so much time that they become 'captured' or unduly influenced by the subject matter of those reviews.

The appointment process should, but arguably does not, ensure that the Independent Monitor and Independent Reviewer do not appear to be overly sympathetic to the government that they are subjecting to review. The location of the offices and reporting procedures further limit the capacity of the reviewers to maintain their independence.

The offices of Independent Monitor and Independent Reviewer are both housed within the department that funds and regulates their reviews. The Independent Monitor's office is located within the

---

[85] See https://terrorismlegislationreviewer.independent.gov.uk/about-me/#work_arrangements.
[86] Carlile, *Sixth Report of the Independent Reviewer*, n. 81 above, p. 5.
[87] Independent National Security Legislation Monitor Act 2010 (Cth), s. 12(1) and (2).

Department of the Prime Minister and Cabinet.[88] The Monitor's advisor is a public servant from within that same department. Similarly, the Independent Reviewer has an office at the Home Office. Furthermore, both reviewing bodies must submit their reports to the minister in charge of that department. The Independent Monitor's reports are submitted in the first instance to the Prime Minister, who must then table them in Parliament within fifteen sitting days after receipt.[89] If the annual report contains any material, which cannot be publically disclosed, the Monitor may also produce a declassified report.[90] Only the declassified report will be tabled in Parliament.[91] The Independent Reviewer's reports are submitted to the Home Secretary or, in the case of reports on the Terrorist Asset-Freezing regime, to the Treasury. The reports are then tabled in Parliament and published on the Independent Reviewer's website.[92] Unlike the legislation governing the Independent Monitor, there are no statutory guidelines on how long the process of publication should take in the United Kingdom, except that the laws provide that the Secretary of State or Treasury should lay a report before Parliament 'on receiving' it.[93] There are also no statutory guidelines on how sensitive material should be redacted in the United Kingdom.

The current UK Independent Reviewer has recognised that geographical proximity to the Home Office raises a concern as to the independence of his office. His website states:

> A room and some part-time administrative assistance is provided for the Independent Reviewer within the Home Office. The room is used on an occasional basis for meetings and for the review and storage of secret material ... However he remains based in his own office in central London, and cultivates a range of contacts without reference to the Government.[94]

Relocating the offices of Independent Monitor and Independent Reviewer outside of the department that houses, funds and regulates their reviews would enhance the independence of the office holder. The Independent Monitor and Independent Reviewer could not be entirely

---

[88] See www.dpmc.gov.au/inslm/index.cfm.
[89] Independent National Security Legislation Monitor Act 2010 (Cth), s. 29.
[90] *Ibid.* s. 29(3).   [91] *Ibid.* s. 29(5)(b).
[92] See https://terrorismlegislationreviewer.independent.gov.uk/category/reports/.
[93] Terrorism Act 2006, s. 36(5); Terrorist Asset-Freezing etc. Act 2010, s. 31(4); Terrorism Prevention and Investigation Measures Act 2011, s. 20(5).
[94] See https://terrorismlegislationreviewer.independent.gov.uk/about-me/.

separated from, respectively, the Department of the Prime Minister and Cabinet and the Home Office; provision would still need to be made within those departments for the review of sensitive material. Enabling both reviewers to report directly to Parliament rather than to the government would also help in this regard. Increasing the independence of the oversight offices would lend weight to their credibility. This would improve their capacity to shape the activities of the government's counter-terrorism agenda.

IV   Influence

To fulfil their function as offices of oversight, the Independent Monitor and Independent Reviewer must have the credibility, derived from an official mandate and a position of independence, to shape the activities of the government with regard to its counter-terrorism policy. That credibility must exist irrespective of the type of recommendations the reviewer makes, whether ones that support the government's agenda or ones that critique it. Credibility can be assessed by examining the government's response to the reviewers.

Bret Walker's first report to the Prime Minister did not make any substantive recommendations on the anti-terrorism laws.[95] The Australian government did not need to respond to it and so did not. Walker's second report was tabled in the Parliament on 14 May 2013 but has not yet received a response from the government. The government's response to it, and to future reports, will demonstrate whether the Independent Monitor has a real capacity to shape the government's agenda. However, the example from the United Kingdom does not necessarily bode well.

In the United Kingdom, the government's failure to respond meaningfully to critical reviews may be contrasted with its ready accession to reviews that support its anti-terrorism policy.[96] The majority of Lord Carlile's recommendations either proposed amending the laws to strengthen the security focus of the legislation or endorsed the legislation

---

[95] B. Walker, *Independent National Security Legislation Monitor Annual Report* (Canberra: Commonwealth of Australia, 2011).

[96] Anderson's most recent report on the Terrorism Acts was published in June 2012. It was 140 pages long. The government's response was published in March 2013. It was five pages long. Anderson, *The Terrorism Acts in 2011*, n. 56 above; Home Secretary, *The Government Response to the Annual Report on the Operation of the Terrorism Acts in 2011 by the Independent Reviewer of Terrorism Legislation* (London: Stationery Office, 2013).

in its existing form. Lord Carlile rarely recommended amending the legislation to strengthen the rights of those who came into contact with the operation of the laws.[97] This had the effect of providing the government with a very low bar to hurdle in terms of implementing recommendations. It has also had a detrimental effect on other forms of post-enactment review.

The Joint Committee on Human Rights (Joint Committee) frequently proposed radical overhaul and repeal of the UK anti-terrorism laws, in opposition to Lord Carlile's endorsement of the measures.[98] The government typically agreed with Lord Carlile's recommendations, rather than those put forward by the Joint Committee. In doing so, it pointed to Lord Carlile's reports as the authority on the subject of anti-terrorism legislation, due to his role as the Independent Reviewer. Home Secretary Charles Clarke rejected almost all of the recommendations in the Joint Committee's first report on control orders, stating: 'In the light of the report produced by Lord Carlile, the Independent Reviewer of the legislation, on the first nine months of operation of the Act, the Government did not consider that any legislative changes were necessary'.[99] Throughout the remainder of his response, Clarke continued to refer to Lord Carlile's report in order to reject the Joint Committee's various proposals.[100]

The government's prioritisation of Lord Carlile's reviews of anti-terrorism laws over that of the Joint Committee has had the effect of diminishing Parliament's (already limited) role in the post-enactment scrutiny of anti-terrorism legislation. David Anderson has envisaged a different role for himself as complementary to, rather than in conflict with, the Joint Committee.[101] He has coordinated with the Joint Committee's review of the Terrorism Prevention and Investigation Measures Act 2011 in order to combine both their strengths: Anderson's access to

---

[97] J. Blackbourn, 'Evaluating the Independent Reviewer of Terrorism Legislation' (2012) *Parliamentary Affairs* doi: 10.1093/pa/gss082.

[98] *Ibid.*

[99] Joint Committee on Human Rights, *Counter-Terrorism Policy and Human Rights: Prosecution and Pre-Charge Detention* (London: Stationery Office, 2006), p. 53.

[100] *Ibid.* pp. 54–7. See Gavin Phillipson on how the executive has also used deferential court judgments to reject recommendations made by the Joint Committee on Human Rights, Chapter 11 in this volume, G. Phillipson, 'Deference and dialogue in the real-world counter-terrorism context'.

[101] D. Anderson, *Control Orders in 2011: Final Report of the Independent Reviewer on the Prevention of Terrorism Act 2005* (London: Stationery Office, 2012), pp. 63, 83.

closed material, and the Joint Committee's broad expertise as a panel and its power to question witnesses.[102] The outcome of this more collaborative process could be a new era of cooperative anti-terrorism review, leading to enhanced scrutiny and a greater ability to shape the government's anti-terrorism agenda. However, it could have the negative effect of restraining the Joint Committee, which, though so far mostly unsuccessful at prompting the government to change the law, has substantially contributed to publicising cases in which the anti-terrorism laws have breached individual human rights.

Whilst the UK government has the ability to ignore difficult or unpopular recommendations, there is little likelihood that the Independent Reviewer will achieve any significant overhaul of the anti-terrorism laws. The same is true of the Australian government and the Independent Monitor. Whilst it is not likely that either government will ever consent to being bound by the recommendations of an oversight body, there are changes which would mitigate this problem. First, there should be a statutory requirement for the government to respond to each of the reviewer's recommendations in a way which suggests that some attention has been paid to the reports. The government should be obliged to explain why it is not pursuing a particular recommendation and should not be allowed to hide behind the excuse of 'closed material' or 'national security' to avoid answering the reviewer in public. Secondly, the government's responses to the reviewer should be tabled in Parliament; enabling a greater role for Parliament might ensure that those measures which are highly contested, but which pass into law, remain the subject of scrutiny.

Conclusion

More than a decade has passed since the 9/11 terrorist attacks on the United States. The reactive legislation that was enacted in its aftermath in Australia and the United Kingdom appears to be an enduring legacy of the continuing 'war on terror'. Many of these laws have been retained for much longer periods than that for which they were originally enacted, calling into question their characterisation as 'exceptional'. However, many of the measures within the new laws are truly exceptional to traditional criminal justice norms and processes. If these laws are no

---

[102] *Ibid.*

longer to be considered temporary additions to the criminal law, but instead a permanent part of the statute books, they must be subject to strict review and effective oversight.[103]

Independent review offers forms of scrutiny not found in traditional constitutionalist review mechanisms. There is a lot to commend in the offices of Independent Reviewer and Independent Monitor. For example, they may be given access to closed material that is not available to Parliament or the public and they can make informed decisions based on a range of sources. They have the opportunity to examine anti-terrorism laws in as broad a manner as possible, reporting not just on how the laws are used, but also on whether they are effective or even necessary. Reviewers can highlight cases of misuse of the laws, either on an individual or wider scale, and can expose longitudinal trends in counter-terrorism practice. Most importantly, they do all this in the public domain, enabling and enhancing parliamentary and public debate on anti-terrorism laws. However, this type of scrutiny is meaningless if it has *no* ability to shape the activities of the government's counter-terrorism agenda. It is essential, therefore, that offices of independent review of anti-terrorism laws are established and constructed so as to be able to inform public and parliamentary debate and to hold the government to account.

It is critical that the mandate, structure, methodology and independence of the office enable the reviewer to carry out their function in a neutral and objective manner. This is not to say that the government's anti-terrorism laws are necessarily or inherently wrong, but that the reviewer must be as credible in supporting provisions within the laws as when criticizing them. The Australian government may have achieved this balance by establishing a strictly regulated office of independent scrutiny; however, it is yet too early to tell. It is to be hoped that Bret Walker's second report has some impact in the Australian Parliament. If it does not, then it is likely that the Independent Monitor's role will become one of providing scrutiny that is consistently ignored by the government. It is also to be hoped that the current UK Independent Reviewer, David Anderson, continues to improve on Lord Carlile's poor record of scrutinising the United Kingdom's anti-terrorism laws.

---

[103] Mark Tushnet argues that administrative law should be capable of regulating anti-terrorism legislation, Chapter 5 in this volume, M. Tushnet, 'Emergency law as administrative law'.

He would be aided in this process if there were formal guidelines regulating his office and providing for a mandatory government response to each of his reviews. Whilst the UK system is solely dependent on the personal approach of the office holder, it is doubtful that any recommendations advocating radical change or repeal of anti-terrorism laws will receive government attention, irrespective of the merits of the proposal.

Postscript

In March 2014 the Australian government announced its intention to abolish the office of the Independent National Security Legislation Monitor. The Independent National Security Legislation Monitor Repeal Bill 2014 was referred to the Senate Legal and Constitutional Affairs Legislation Committee for inquiry and report. That report has yet to be published and the future of the office of the Independent Monitor is unknown. However, the comparative lessons outlined in this chapter remain relevant; the reports of the Independent Monitor will offer valuable tools when the federal Parliament examines a number of the anti-terrorism laws which are due to expire over the next two years. It will then be possible to assess the extent to which the office of the Independent Monitor managed – in practice – to provide meaningful and effective scrutiny of Australia's anti-terrorism laws.

Public inquiries as an attempt to fill accountability gaps left by judicial and legislative review

KENT ROACH

Introduction

There is a danger that evaluations of the role of courts and legislatures in reviewing counter-terrorism will replicate well-trodden and often fractious debates about the role of unelected courts in a democracy.[1] There is a particular danger that a focus on courts and legislatures will obscure the critical role played by the executive in counter-terrorism. The executive is not a monolith. It includes 'business' and 'watchdog' ends. The former include the police and security services while the latter include various commissioners, ombudspersons and other review agencies. This chapter will examine a particular form of watchdog review of the executive: ad hoc public inquiries appointed to review security activities that may make state actors complicit in torture.

Debates about the roles of legislative and judicial review of counter-terrorism activities risk distorting the complexities of reviewing the security state. Although courts have played a more important role in reviewing the state's national security activities since 11 September 2001 ('9/11')[2], they depend on litigants to establish the existence of illegal activities with public evidence. Litigants will also have to convince courts to award effective and meaningful remedies. A number of chapters in this collection illustrate the unwillingness and difficulties of courts awarding such remedies.[3]

---

[1] For some discussion see Chapter 13 in this volume, H. Fenwick, 'Post 9/11 UK counter-terrorism cases in the European Court of Human Rights: a "dialogic" approach to rights protection or appeasement of national authorities?' and Chapter 11, G. Phillipson, 'Deference and dialogue in the real-world counter-terrorism context'.

[2] For my own views on this subject see Kent Roach, 'Judicial Review of the State's Counter-Terrorism Activities' (2009) 3 *Indian J Constitutional Law* 668; Kent Roach, *The 9/11 Effect: Comparative Counter-Terrorism* (Cambridge University Press, 2011), pp. 452–9.

[3] See Chapter 1 in this volume, F. de Londras, 'Counter-terrorism judicial review as regulatory constitutionalism' and Chapter 4, J. Lobel, 'The rhetoric and reality of judicial

Legislatures, like courts, can play a role in reviewing counter-terrorism activities. Their primary role is in authorising but hopefully constraining state actions. At the same time, legislatures often find themselves unable to resist international and domestic pressures to enact broad new counter-terrorism laws. Even when they impose restraints in such laws, these restraints may not always be observed in practice. The secrecy that surrounds much counter-terrorism activities can make it difficult to hold the executive accountable for abuses. Legislative committees have the capacity to oversee counter-terrorism activities and can have access to some secret information. Such access, however, is a double-edged sword. It can prevent elected legislators from going public and being whistle-blowers about problematic and arguably illegal counter-terrorism activities.[4]

In this chapter, I will try to move beyond the traditional debate between courts and legislatures by examining public inquiries as a hybrid institution that goes beyond the traditional constitutional distinctions between the legislative, executive and judicial branches of government. My focus will be on public inquiries that have been appointed at the discretion of the government to investigate possible complicity in torture by security officials. Such inquiries are technically part of the executive. At the same time, they are often headed by sitting or retired judges in an attempt to signal that the inquiry will be independent of the government of the day. This feature of public inquiries brings them closer to courts. As will be seen, a perception that an inquiry is not independent can be fatal to its success as an effective instrument of accountability.

Even when independent, however, inquiries are not courts. They are not restricted by the case presented to them or by the need to apply pre-existing rules. Like the legislature, inquiries can create and apply their own rules and even apply them retroactively to judge past events. They

---

review of counter-terrorism actions: the United States experience'. For my own exploration of the difficulty of persuading Canadian courts to award remedies, see Kent Roach, 'The Supreme Court at the Bar of Politics: the Afghan Detainees and Omar Khadr Cases' (2010) 28 *Nat. J Constitutional Law* 115. For arguments that US courts have embraced a form of extra-legalism that frustrates the award of effective judicial remedies in the national security context, see Roach, *The 9/11 Effect*, n. 2 above, ch. 4.

[4] Legislative committees in the United States have at various times been privy to details about surveillance by the National Security Agency and targeted killing, but have generally kept the details of these activities secret until they were leaked to the press. 'Obama's claim that "every member of Congress was briefed on telephone surveillance"', *Washington Post*, 11 June 2013.

also make non-binding recommendations to the government of the day as opposed to enforcing judgments against governments. The freedom that public inquiries have to create and apply new norms to past events and not to have to implement their recommendations makes them similar to the media, law reform bodies and civil society watchdogs. In short, public inquiries are hybrid institutions that combine powers and features associated with all three branches of governments as well the fifth estate. As hybrid institutions, inquiries can illuminate the strengths and weaknesses of different types of review of counter-terrorism activities.

Both before and after 9/11, many democratic governments have appointed a number of inquiries into national security matters. Some of these inquiries have done important and valuable work while others have failed to reveal or correct wrongdoing.[5] I have suggested elsewhere that commissions of inquiry in the post 9/11 era have attempted to plug 'accountability gaps'[6] caused by the fact that watchdog review within the executive has not caught up to whole of government and often transnational cooperation in counter-terrorism. While governments have broken down walls to share information and conduct coordinated counter-terrorism, permanent executive review bodies often have their jurisdiction limited by statute to the review of specific agencies. Public inquiries can be given tailor-made remits that allow them to examine the multiple agencies that may be involved in problematic counter-terrorism. The jurisdiction of inquiries, however, is limited to domestic officials and this limits their ability to plug the accountability gap created by transnational cooperation in counter-terrorism.

The bulk of this chapter will consist of two case studies of public inquiries held in Canada and the United Kingdom into complicity in torture. The Canadian commission of inquiry chaired by Justice Dennis O'Connor was conducted between 2004 and 2006. It examined the actions of all Canadian officials in relation to Maher Arar, a Canadian citizen who was detained in the United States and subsequently rendered by US officials to Syria where he was tortured before being released. The inquiry issued a three volume report on the actions of Canadian officials

---

[5] See generally, Stuart Farson and Mark Phythian (eds.), *Commissions of Inquiry and National Security* (Santa Barbara: Praeger, 2011); Jordan Tama, *Terrorism and National Security Reform: How Commissions Can Drive Change During Crises* (Cambridge University Press, 2011).

[6] Roach, *The 9/11 Effect*, n. 2 above, ch. 8.

and another volume recommending fundamental reforms to executive review of national security activities in Canada.[7]

The British commission of inquiry was chaired by Sir Peter Gibson, a retired judge and a former Commissioner of the Intelligence Services. The Gibson inquiry was appointed by Prime Minister Cameron in the summer of July 2010 to examine whether the UK government and its intelligence services were involved in or aware of improper treatment, especially in relation to the treatment of detainees at Guantánamo Bay. Its remit was subsequently expanded by the government to include activities involving Libya. Nevertheless, the government ended its activities in 2012 in favour of police investigations into complicity in torture. Whereas the Canadian inquiry was able to deliver its public reports within two years of its appointment, the Gibson inquiry has generally been viewed as a failure. The publication of its winding up report was delayed until December 2013 because of disputes with the government about whether it could make public information about interrogations at Bagram and Guantánamo in its anodyne final report that simply raised a number of issues that the inquiry would have liked to explore.[8] Its work with respect to investigating complicity in torture has now been delegated to another part of the executive: the police. The police are less transparent than inquiries in their investigations and must apply pre-existing norms in criminal laws to past events.

A comparison of two inquiries with similar mandates but with very different outcomes will facilitate the identification of some of the conditions for success and failure of such inquiries. An examination of these conditions will also help to disaggregate some of the elements that make judicial, executive, legislative, media and civil society review of the state's counter-terrorism activities attractive and effective. It will also allow a brief comparison of public inquiries and police investigations into alleged wrongdoing in counter-terrorism. My goal will be to make the traditional

---

[7] I disclose I was a member of the inquiry's five person research advisory committee which was primarily involved in research leading to the policy report on review of national security activities.

[8] *Report of the Detainee Inquiry* (December 2013). The inquiry explained that it drew no conclusions because it had only been able to conduct a document review and that it did not wish to risk compromising ongoing police investigations or any future inquiry that might be appointed. *Ibid*. para.1.30. The timing of the government's delayed release just before Christmas holidays and on the same day as the verdict in a sensational murder case was also criticized. 'Government "risks accusation of burying bad news by publishing Gibson on same day as Woolwich verdicts"', *Daily Telegraph*, 19 December 2013.

debate between the roles of courts and legislatures more complex and to illuminate an expanded range of institutions and processes that are available to review the state's national security activities.[9]

I   Canada's Arar inquiry

Maher Arar, a Canadian citizen born in Syria, was detained in 2002 in the United States as he was returning to Canada. He was then rendered by the United States to Syria via Jordan.[10] His wife became a prominent spokesperson for him during Arar's almost year-long detention in Syria. His case received much publicity. The publicity increased when he returned to Canada in 2003 and explained that he had been tortured in Syria. Existing watchdog agencies within the executive for both the Royal Canadian Mounted Police (RCMP) and the Canadian Security Intelligence Services (CSIS) started investigations into the role of those agencies in supplying information to the United States, but soon encountered difficulties given that the information that each agency had passed on to the United States after 9/11 was classified as secret. Controversy over Arar continued because of leaks about him from government officials. Matters came to a head in early 2004 when the RCMP executed search warrants on the home and office of a journalist who was reporting the damaging (and false) leaks that alleged that Arar was involved in terrorism.[11] Shortly thereafter, the Liberal government appointed an inquiry

---

[9] Nothing in this chapter should detract from the need to strengthen permanent executive watchdog review of counter-terrorism. The Arar commission developed proposals for such reforms based on the principles that review should expand and integrate along with counter-terrorism activities and reviewers should have full access to secret information possessed by those agencies that they review. Commission of Inquiry into the Activities of Canadian Officials in relation to Maher Arar, *A New Review Mechanism for the RCMP's National Security Activities* (Ottawa: Supply and Services, 2006). The Canadian government, however, rejected these proposals and enacted new legislation that stops short of ensuring that the review agency for the RCMP has full access to secret information or allowing coordinated review of coordinated national security activities. See An Act to Amend the RCMP Act S.C. 2013 c.18. For a discussion of the role of independent reviewers as more or less permanent reviewers of counter-terrorism activities, see Chapter 7 in this volume, J. Blackbourn, 'Independent reviewers as alternative: an empirical study from Australia and the United Kingdom'.

[10] For a critical account of his unsuccessful attempts to sue US officials, see Chapter 4 in this volume, J. Lobel, 'The rhetoric and reality of judicial review of counter-terrorism actions: the United States experience'.

[11] For a full discussion of the appointment and process of the Arar inquiry see Reg Whitaker, 'Arar, the Affair and the Inquiry' (2008) 9(1) *Choices* 1.

chaired by Justice O'Connor with a mandate to report on the activities of all Canadian officials in relation to Maher Arar. Unlike the permanent review agencies that had started reviewing the matter, the ad hoc inquiry had a special jurisdiction to examine all Canadian officials involved in the Arar matter. It would eventually review the activities of the police, security services, border agencies and foreign affairs officials.

Justice O'Connor and his lead counsel had experience in conducting hard-hitting public inquiries but no prior involvement in national security matters. Under Canada's Public Inquiry Act,[12] the inquiry had power to subpoena relevant information and testimony. The inquiry and its security-cleared staff had the ability to access security information, but were subject to section 38 of the Canada Evidence Act[13] which prohibited the release of secret information without the consent of the Attorney General of Canada or a court order. Arar and his lawyers were not present when *in camera* evidence was taken, but commission counsel was allowed to cross-examine governmental witnesses and security-cleared *amicus curiae* also played a role in the *in camera* hearings.

The inquiry initially attempted to balance the competing interests of secrecy and transparency by conducting *in camera* hearings and then attempting to obtain the government's agreement to the release of redacted summaries of the evidence. This approach was abandoned after agreement could not be reached on what information taken from the Canadian Security Intelligence Service (CSIS) could be released. The Commission then held extensive *in camera* hearings that lasted from September 2004 to the end of April 2005. In total, the inquiry heard from eighty-three witnesses over the course of seventy-five days of *in camera* testimony and forty-five days of public testimony.[14] The government agreed to the release of most of the three volume factual report in 2006, but a few parts of the report were only released in 2007 following a ruling of a judge under section 38 of the Canada Evidence Act that balanced the competing interests in disclosure and continued secrecy.[15] In large part because he was not privy to the *in camera* evidence, the decision whether Mr Arar would provide testimony was deferred until the release of the public report. A fact-finder was, however, appointed to

[12] RSC 1985 c. P-1.   [13] RSC 1985 c. C-5.
[14] Commission of Inquiry into the Activities of Canadian Officials in relation to Maher Arar, *Analysis and Recommendations* (Ottawa: Public Works, 2006), p. 295.
[15] *Canada* v. *Commission of Inquiry* 2007 FC 766.

interview Mr Arar and made determinations accepted by the inquiry that Mr Arar had been tortured when detained in Syria.

The three volume public report examined the actions of CSIS, the RCMP, various customs officials and the Department of Foreign Affairs. The mandate of the inquiry to examine all Canadian officials circumvented the jurisdictional barriers that tasked separate review agencies with review of CSIS and the RCMP and provided no review bodies with respect to customs and foreign affairs officials. Increased post 9/11 emphasis on whole of government security responses will favour forms of review that are not artificially limited to review of certain agencies. Parliamentary review has the potential to examine whole of government responses, but much parliamentary review both in the question period and in committee is still divided on jurisdictional lines. This is problematic because jurisdictionally-limited review lags well behind whole of government approaches to counter-terrorism.

Although its mandate was broad in relation to Canadian involvement, the inquiry was aware that key aspects of the narrative took place in the United States and Syria. The inquiry invited both the US and Syrian governments to participate in the inquiry and to give evidence, but they both declined to do so. Justice O'Connor concluded that 'without the evidence of the American authorities',[16] he was unable to determine what exact role Canadian information played in US decisions to detain and render Arar. Although the Arar commission was able to hold Canadian officials and agencies accountable, it failed to hold the United States or Syria accountable for its more direct actions in Arar's detention and torture.

The Commission found that the RCMP had shared complete investigative files with the United States without imposing restrictions or caveats on the subsequent use of the information by US officials, but that Canadian officials had not known or participated in Arar's rendition. Canadian officials had requested the United States to place lookouts for Arar and his wife that described both of them as 'Islamic Extremist individuals suspected of being linked to the al Qaeda terrorist movement'.[17] Justice O'Connor concluded that there was 'no basis for this description' but that it had 'serious consequences for Mr Arar in light of American attitudes and practices at the time'.[18] He stated on the very first page of his report: 'I have heard evidence concerning all of the

---

[16] Commission of Inquiry, *Analysis and Recommendations*, n. 14 above, p. 14.
[17] *Ibid.* p. 13.   [18] *Ibid.*

information collected about Mr Arar in Canadian investigations, and there is nothing to indicate that Mr Arar committed an offence or that his activities constitute a threat to the security of Canada'.[19] This was seen as an exoneration of Mr Arar and to some extent it resembled a not guilty verdict at a criminal trial.

The commission concluded its report with a recommendation that the government should assess Arar's claim for compensation in light of its findings and in light of 'several very improper and unfair leaks of information'.[20] Although the inquiry was precluded under Canadian law from drawing conclusions about criminal or civil liability, it noted that Arar had endured 'mental suffering' because of the torture, leaks and inquiry process and that his reputation and employment had also suffered. The inquiry also noted the difficulties that Arar would encounter in his litigation in the United States, something that was confirmed after his civil lawsuit was thrown out by a majority of the Second Circuit in New York.[21] After the inquiry was concluded, Arar settled his CAN$37 million suit against the Canadian government for CAN$10.5 million and a formal apology from then newly elected Prime Minister Stephen Harper.[22]

The report featured a chapter entitled 'Maher Arar and the Right to be Free of Torture'. This chapter stressed that the right against torture was absolute.[23] It explained why someone might falsely confess if tortured. The chapter contained no reference to the controversial 'Suresh exception to torture' created by the Supreme Court of Canada when in early 2002, the Court stated that while the right against torture was absolute in international law, it was not prepared to say that refoulement to torture could not be justified under the Canadian Charter of Rights and Freedoms in 'exceptional circumstances'.[24] In this respect, the inquiry did not slavishly follow existing Canadian law.

The report addressed head-on leaks by 'unnamed government sources indicating that Mr Arar had admitted to having terrorist links in Syria

---

[19] *Ibid.* p. 1.   [20] *Ibid.* p. 363.

[21] The decision in *Arar* v. *Ashcroft*, 585 F.3d 599 (2d Cir. 1999) is critically discussed by Jules Lobel, Chapter 4 in this volume, 'The rhetoric and reality of judicial review of counter-terrorism actions: the United States experience'.

[22] See www.cbc.ca/news/canada/story/2007/01/26/harper-apology.html. Notably, the Conservative government settled with Arar despite the fact that the inquiry had been appointed in 2004 by a former Liberal government.

[23] Commission of Inquiry, *Analysis and Recommendations*, n. 14 above, p. 52.

[24] *Suresh* v. *Canada* [2002] 1 SCR 3.

and stating that he was not a "nice guy" or a "virgin" as would be seen when the truth came out'.[25] Justice O'Connor was clearly offended by the leaks. He stressed that the leaks 'were purposefully misleading in a way that was intended to do [Arar] harm'.[26] Subsequent police investigations into the leaks failed to identify those responsible and received much less publicity than the commission's strong criticisms of the leaks, which had the effect of holding all those privy to the leaked information as well as the media who reported the leaks collectively responsible for them. Police investigations will often be less transparent than official inquiries and limited to applying the criminal law to identified individual perpetrators.

The policy impact of the Arar commission has been mixed. Days after the release of the factual report, the government of Canada announced that it would accept the twenty-three recommendations made in the report, including those that recommended Canada make formal objection with both the United States and Syrian governments about Arar's treatment. The commission also recommended training about racial, religious and ethnic profiling and its effects on Canada's Arab and Muslim communities. The commission recommended that security officials must continue to share information, but that they should be more aware of the human rights records of other countries and that they should take various steps to eliminate 'any possible Canadian complicity in torture'.[27] Ministerial directives on information sharing have subsequently been made by the government and released through access to information requests. These directives make reference to the commission report, but they also contemplate that information can both be received and sent to other countries even if there is a risk of torture in 'exceptional circumstances'.[28] In this way, the directives follow the controversial *Suresh* exception and are in tension with the Arar commission's absolutist approach against complicity in torture.

Months after the release of its factual report, the Arar commission issued another report on policy recommendations for the review of the RCMP's national security activities. This report stressed the need for review to catch up with whole of government approaches to counterterrorism. The government has rejected most of these proposals and new legislation does not guarantee that the permanent complaints

---

[25] Commission of Inquiry, *Analysis and Recommendations*, n. 14 above, p. 61.
[26] *Ibid.* p. 263.   [27] *Ibid.* p. 345.
[28] 'CSIS ok to share information despite torture risk' (2 March 2012), available at www.cbc.ca/news/canada/story/2012/03/02/csis-torture-information-directive.html.

commission for the RCMP will have access to secret information or be able to share such information with other review bodies, as recommended by the Arar commission.[29] The government has also retreated from plans by the previous government to give parliamentarians access to secret information to review national security activities. It also refused to appoint another inquiry when controversy arose over whether Canadian forces were complicit in torture in Afghanistan. This highlights the troublesome fact that while public inquiries can be appointed and shaped to plug accountability gaps, the government retains the discretion to appoint them. In contrast, judicial and sometimes even legislative review processes can be initiated despite the government's objections.

II   United Kingdom's Detainee Inquiry

The Detainee inquiry was appointed by Prime Minister Cameron in July 2010 to examine whether the UK government was involved in or aware of improper treatment or rendition of terrorist suspects by other countries. This mandate was strikingly similar to the Arar commission's mandate in its focus on all governmental officials and its concerns about complicity in torture. The Detainee inquiry was appointed in the wake of confidential settlements with former Guantánamo detainees who were suing the United Kingdom. The government settled these cases for generous terms in part because it had lost some preliminary litigation[30] concerning the disclosure of information that the United States had shared with it.[31] The settlement of the litigation, the appointment of the Detainee inquiry and a government Green Paper[32] and subsequent law enhancing secrecy in civil litigation[33] were all part of the government's response to the judicial decisions disclosing information. The Prime Minister also announced that the inquiry would not hear public evidence from intelligence officers and that it would disclose no operational intelligence.[34] The inquiry's role in the government's pro-secrecy strategy

[29] An Act to Amend the RCMP Act S.C.2013 c. 18.
[30] *Binyam Mohamed* v. *Secretary of State* [2010] EWCA Civ 65, para. 39.
[31] 'Guantanamo Bay prisoners to get millions from British government', *Guardian*, 16 November 2010, available at www.guardian.co.uk/world/2010/nov/16/guantanamo-bay-prisoners-compensation.
[32] *Justice and Security Green Paper* (Cm 8194, October 2011).
[33] Justice and Security Act 2013.
[34] *Report of the Detainee Inquiry* (December 2013), para. 1.13.

may have adversely affected perceptions of its independence from the start. In contrast, the Arar commission was not appointed as part of a multi-pronged governmental strategy to prevent the disclosure of sensitive foreign intelligence. Indeed, the Canadian inquiry criticised the government for overclaiming secrecy and litigated against the government with some success to obtain the release of information that the government maintained should remain secret.[35]

The Detainee inquiry had much less independence from the government than the Arar commission. Its protocol agreed with the government provided that it must obtain the agreement of the Cabinet Office before making any information public, with any disputes being resolved not by the courts but by the Cabinet Secretary.[36] The government thus had a veto over what information could be released and what redactions should be applied to the information that was released. The Canadian government had a similar functional veto over what information the Arar commission could release. As discussed above, the refusal of the government to agree to the release of the summary of *in camera* hearings held with security services officials forced the Arar commission to abandon its strategy of publishing summaries of its *in camera* proceedings at regular intervals. The fact that both inquiries had to rely on government agreement to publish information underlines the difficulties of having transparent review and accountability processes in the national security context. The Arar commission, however, had an important option that the Detainee inquiry did not: namely, the possibility of taking the government to court over its refusal to agree to the release of the information. Under section 38.06 of the Canada Evidence Act,[37] a judge would then be able to decide what information should be released after balancing the competing public interests for and against disclosure. The Detainee inquiry could go no further than the Cabinet Secretary. Its protocol seemed to contemplate that the Cabinet Secretary, who in any event does not enjoy the independence of a judge, would only conduct a most limited balancing of competing interests about what could be disclosed. The criteria were that the release of information would not

---

[35] *Canada* v. *Commission of Inquiry* 2007 FC 766.
[36] Protocol, para. 17, available at http://webarchive.nationalarchives.gov.uk/20130106092456/ http://www.detaineeinquiry.org.uk/wp-content/uploads/2011/06/20110706-The-Detainee-Inquiry-and-HM-Government-Protocol.pdf.
[37] R.S.C. 1985 c. 5.

be harmful to the public interest[38] or that it was 'unnecessary or disproportionate'[39] not to release the information.

Prime Minister Cameron's transmittal letter to Sir Peter Gibson made clear that the inquiry would not examine the actions of other countries and should respect intelligence sharing relationships with other countries. It provided:

> This is an Inquiry into the actions of the UK, not any other state. It is particularly important that international intelligence sharing understandings are not undermined in the course of the Inquiry. The Inquiry can expect to take evidence from UK personnel and not the personnel of other countries ... This is a non-statutory inquiry. It will not establish legal liability, nor order financial settlement.[40]

The Arar inquiry also did not have a mandate to examine the actions of US and other foreign officials but it did have the freedom to invite them to participate. It also heard expert evidence on American and Syrian legal practices as they affected Mr Arar and its report caused significant irritation to American-Canadian security relations.

The Detainee inquiry would have faced an uphill struggle in terms of establishing its independence given the government's veto over what information it could release, but the appointment of Sir Peter Gibson as the head Commissioner was also very controversial. Gibson had been a judge since 1981 and Prime Minister Cameron stressed when appointing the inquiry that it would be 'an independent Inquiry, led by a judge' and that the inquiry will have access to all relevant Government papers,

---

[38] Protocol, Appendix A, para. 1 defined damage to the public interest broadly to include 'harm or damage to national security, economic, defence interests or international relations. This includes respecting the understandings and commitments between HMG and its security and intelligence agencies and the authorities and the agencies of any foreign government concerning the confidentiality, security and protection against disclosure outside the Inquiry of any information to which those understandings and commitments [relate]'. It also defined as harmful to the public interest the disclosure of any information that the security services had received subject to a caveat by a third party which it explained was 'the third party rule, referred to by the Courts in recent litigation as the control principle governing non-disclosure of intelligence material, or other commitments or understandings governing the release of sensitive information'. In addition, the Appendix also defined the disclosure of information covered by legal professional privilege or that 'could prejudice ongoing statutory or police investigations' as harmful to the public interest.

[39] Protocol, para. 16.

[40] Letter from Prime Minister to Sir Peter Gibson, 6 July 2010, available at www.detaineeinquiry.org.uk/wp-content/uploads/2011/06/06.07.10-Letter-from-PM-to-Sir-Peter-Gibson4.pdf.

including those held by the intelligence services.[41] These statements underline the importance that inquiries be perceived as independent from governments when reviewing counter-terrorism.

Alas, the fact that Gibson had been a judge did not guarantee that he would be perceived to be independent. Controversy immediately arose over Gibson's appointment because he had served as an Intelligence Services Commissioner (ISC) from 2006 until his appointment to head the Detainee inquiry in 2010. The ISC has statutory oversight duties with respect to covert surveillance and covert human sources used by the security services, including otherwise illegal actions outside the United Kingdom.[42] Both the parliamentary opposition and civil society groups raised concerns that Gibson may have in confidential reports already reviewed some of the matters that the inquiry would review. Clive Stafford Smith on behalf of Reprieve suggested that Gibson might even be a valuable witness before his inquiry and that applying judicial standards of bias, he should recuse himself. He elaborated:

> Do you consider that your expressed opinion in your public 2006, 2007, 2008 reports that the Security Services personnel were 'trustworthy, conscientious and dependable' reflects a bias that requires you to step aside? . . . Please could you explain how you are able to preside over an inquiry about British complicity in torture during the time period in which you were responsible for the statutory oversight of the Security and Intelligence Services? The allegation that you will have to rule on is (with apologies for putting it so frankly) that you were either asleep on your watch or were hoodwinked. Out of fairness to victims of torture, the Security Services and yourself, do you believe that you can rule fairly on such issues?[43]

Treasury solicitors responded by arguing that Gibson as ISC had not reviewed individual cases of detention or the legal issue of complicity in torture. They also argued that, because the Detainee inquiry was not a statutory inquiry, judicial tests for bias did not apply. With respect to authorizations of activities outside the United Kingdom which might otherwise be illegal, the government lawyers argued that the existence of such orders 'cannot be confirmed or denied', but that Sir Peter had considered the matter and concluded that there was no conflict. They

---

[41] Hansard, 6 July 2010.   [42] Regulation of Investigatory Powers Act 2000, s. 59.
[43] Letter from Clive Stafford Smith to Sir Peter Gibson, 19 July 2010, available at www.reprieve.org.uk/blog/2010_07_20_torture_inquiry_gibson_letter_text/.

also argued that it was 'wholly untenable' to suggest that Gibson had a closed mind because he had drawn favourable conclusions about the conduct of the security services as ISC.[44] This defence of Gibson did not work particularly well. Stafford Smith replied that the independence of the inquiry was also compromised by the fact that the government lawyers 'who will be seeking to persuade Sir Peter that all is well' were now defending him.[45] The inquiry was off to a rocky start because its independence was contested by the media and influential civil society groups. My point is not to decide whether the inquiry could have been independent, but to illustrate how its perceived independence from government was valued by all sides.

Despite the controversy over the Gibson appointment, the Detainee inquiry was perhaps not doomed from the start. In September 2010, a coalition of ten civil society groups including Amnesty International, Reprieve and Liberty outlined their expectations for an independent and thorough inquiry. They included a presumption that 'as much evidence as possible' be heard in public; that 'survivors and victims have standing as parties to the inquiry and have a right to legal representation funded by the inquiry'; and that 'an independent mechanism' be able to review the inquiry's decisions to keep information secret. In a recognition of the transnational nature of what should be reviewed, the joint NGO letter also stated that the inquiry 'must request the cooperation of agents and officials of foreign states who can provide relevant evidence, and that the government should support such requests'. The letter also argued that 'the direct participation of civil society is imperative for the proper conduct of this inquiry' because 'allowing for close NGO scrutiny will ensure that the inquiry is seen to be robust and fair'.[46] The NGOs wanted the inquiry to follow some of the practices of the Arar commission, especially with regard to participation by victims, civil society groups, attempts to involve foreign governments and decisions by an independent body about what information should be made public.

---

[44] Letter from Hugh Giles to Clive Stafford Smith, 28 July 2010, available at www.detaineeinquiry.org.uk/wp-content/uploads/2011/07/20100728-TSol-Response-to-Reprieve-RE-Torture-Inquiry-Recusal.pdf.

[45] Letter from Clive Stafford Smith to Hugh Giles, 3 August 2010, available at www.detaineeinquiry.org.uk/wp-content/uploads/2011/07/Reprieve-reply-to-TSol-2010_08_03-PUB-Giles-Letter-Gibson.pdf.

[46] Letter from AIRE Centre and others to Rt Hon. Peter Gibson, 8 September 2010, available at www.cageprisoners.com/our-work/reports/item/1187-joint-ngo-letter-to-gibson-detainee-inquiry.

A year later, many of the same civil society groups decided that they could not participate in the inquiry. They explained that 'the process currently proposed does not have the credibility or transparency' required to achieve its purposes.[47] Some lawyers representing detainees also withdrew, complaining that they would not be able to see the evidence or ask questions during *in camera* hearings.[48] Arar's lawyers had faced similar challenges of being excluded from much of that inquiry's hearings, but had been regularly briefed by inquiry counsel on the progress of the inquiry and had been able to suggest lines of questioning to commission counsel.[49] Commission counsel earned the trust of both Arar and civil society lawyers in part because they had strongly and publicly objected to governmental claims of secrecy and in part because they regularly met with them face to face. No comparable situation existed in the United Kingdom. The effective boycott of the Detainee inquiry by civil society groups and detainees damaged the inquiry greatly. It indicates how what David Cole has described as civil society constitutionalism[50] plays an important role. Cole focuses on the United States but civil society groups are arguably more important with respect to transnational counter-terrorism. Transnational NGOs have played a critical role in investigating transnational practices such as renditions and targeted killing. Their involvement in judicial and legislative review processes, as well as review processes conducted by supranational institutions, provide all those bodies with information and increased legitimacy. Inquiries are strengthened, as are courts,[51] by the participation of directly affected people and civil society.

Sir Peter Gibson tried to defend the inquiry in the wake of the civil society boycott. He argued that while the Cabinet Secretary would 'have the final word on public disclosure', this was 'not dissimilar' to what would happen 'to every statutory inquiry under the Inquiries Act 2005'.[52]

---

[47] As quoted in 'Campaigners to shun UK inquiry into detainee torture' (6 August 2011), available at www.bbc.co.uk/news/uk-14397601.

[48] *Ibid.*

[49] Such briefings were conducted even though there was some risk that commission counsel might inadvertently reveal secret information to Arar and his lawyers.

[50] David Cole, 'Where Liberty Lies: Civil Society and Individual Rights after 9/11' (2012) 57 *Wayne Law Review* 1203.

[51] Lon Fuller, *The Morality of Law* (New Haven, CT: Yale University Press, 1969).

[52] Letter from Sir Peter Gibson to the *Guardian*, 26 August 2011, available at http://webarchive.nationalarchives.gov.uk/20130106092456/www.detaineeinquiry.org.uk/wp-content/uploads/2011/09/26082011-Sir-Peter-Gibson-to-the-Guardian-ref-22-Aug-Amnesty-letter.pdf.

This was a valid point and one repeated in the Commission's final report,[53] but it discounted criticisms of the 2005 Act as impinging on the independence of public inquiries.[54] Although governments will understandably want to maintain the final word on the disclosure of sensitive and embarrassing information, there is a risk that the Inquiries Act 2005 and similar restraints on the Detainee inquiry will undermine inquiries as effective accountability mechanisms. The independence of inquiries is particularly important in national security matters where it is inevitable that the inquiry will hold *in camera* hearings and have access to some information that cannot be made public. The Arar inquiry, however, demonstrated that an inquiry with a reputation for independence and even combativeness towards the government can be credible even while holding the majority of its hearings *in camera*.

The mandate of the Detainee inquiry was also controversial. Shortly after the boycott by civil society groups, Prime Minister Cameron announced that the inquiry would examine whether British officials were complicit in torture in Libya. He expressed a desire 'to remove any stain on Britain's reputation but also to deal with these accusations of malpractice so as to enable our security services to get on with the vital work that they do'.[55] The government's tasking of the inquiry to examine a politically controversial matter, as well as its prejudgment that the inquiry would 'remove any stain on Britain's reputation', were more signs of the government's control of the inquiry. At the same time, the inquiry rejected requests by a parliamentarian to also examine questions of British involvement in US military detention beyond Guantánamo.[56] The independence of inquiries will always be bounded by their terms of reference but there is a danger when those terms are designed or altered to serve the government's interests.

The Detainee inquiry was ended by the government in January 2012 when the police announced that they were investigating allegations of MI6 involvement in the 2004 rendition to Libya and torture of two

---

[53] *Report of the Detainee Inquiry* (December 2013), para. 1.21.

[54] Justice Peter Cory who conducted inquiries in both the United Kingdom and Canada has argued that no judge should sit on any inquiry because of the lack of independence of inquiries from governments under the 2005 Act. See Bill Rolston and Phil Scaton, 'In the Full Glare of English Politics' (2005) 45 *Brit. J Crim.* 547, 562–3.

[55] 'Torture inquiry to examine UK-Libya Intelligence Links', BBC News, 5 September 2011, available at www.bbc.co.uk/news/uk-14786924.

[56] Correspondence with Andrew Tyrie MP, available at www.detaineeinquiry.org.uk/2011/07/the-inquirys-correspondence-with-andrew-tyrie-mp/.

Libyans, Sami al-Saadi and Abdul Hakim Belhaj, shortly before Prime Minister Blair announced enhanced cooperation with the Gaddafi regime on terrorism issues. The men have also commenced civil litigation against various British officials, with Saadi's suit being settled on a confidential basis for a reported £2 million. Civil lawsuits can be foreclosed by settlements in a way that inquiries cannot. The shift from an inquiry to police investigations is not promising in terms of accountability.[57] The police must apply pre-existing criminal standards for individual culpability but inquiries can create new standards and then apply them retroactively to criticise organizational conduct. Criminal liability depends on affixing specific individuals with criminal fault whereas public inquiries assess organizational fault and make recommendations about how to improve complex systems to minimise similar failings in the future.[58] Police investigations also present a danger that some may conclude that reform is not required simply because sufficient evidence to justify charges against individuals was not discovered. Inquiries, unlike courts, can create their own standards of behaviour and apply them to past events.

Conclusions

A number of conclusions can be drawn from these two case studies that are relevant to understanding the role of public inquiries in reviewing national security activities, as well as the strengths and limits of legislative, executive, judicial, media and civil society review of such activities.

(a)   Persistent transnational accountability gaps

Both the Arar and Detainee inquiries failed to provide accountability beyond their borders. From the start, it was not anticipated that the Detainee inquiry would be able to receive information about US practices at Guantánamo. Indeed, Prime Minister Cameron's mandate letter to Sir Peter Gibson provided a specific warning that the inquiry should not

---

[57] In January 2012, the police and Crown Prosecution Service announced that because of a lack of evidence of war crimes and aiding torture, it would not lay charges against other British officials. See MPS and CPS Joint Release, 12 January 2012, available at http://content.met.police.uk/News/Joint-statement-by-MPS-and-DPP/1400005902978/1257246745756.

[58] Kent Roach, 'Public Inquiries and the Processes of Accountability' in Philip Stenning (ed.), *Accountability for Criminal Justice* (Toronto: University of Toronto Press, 1995).

examine the actions of other states or interfere with international intelligence sharing relations. Consistent with its overall orientation, Canada's Arar inquiry was not so restrained at the start. It heard expert evidence about US immigration law and practices and the use of torture in Syria. It even invited both the governments of Syria and the United States to participate in the inquiry, but both states declined. The Canadian government followed the Commission's recommendation of making official protests about Arar's rendition and torture to both the United States and Syria, but little came of the protests. Maher Arar remains on US watchlists and the Syrian regime has descended into even greater brutality. Although public inquiries may be able to fill some domestic accountability gaps, they cannot fill transnational gaps. An exclusively domestic focus on accountability in any branch of government is simply inadequate given the transnational nature of terrorism and counter-terrorism.

If public inquiries cannot plug transnational accountability gaps, will courts and legislatures do any better? The courts have tried to fill the gap, with former Guantánamo detainees litigating in many countries and the European Court of Human Rights in indirect challenges to how they were treated in Guantánamo. This litigation, however, has been plagued by governmental secrecy claims and lack of US cooperation. Although the English courts were not intimidated by US threats not to continue to share intelligence,[59] the UK government reacted strongly. It settled the case with the Guantánamo detainees on confidential but generous terms. It enacted legislation to prevent the disclosure of sensitive material in civil litigation, including material about a third party's misconduct.[60] It appointed the Detainee inquiry, but retained a veto over what information the inquiry could make public. Even if domestic courts are bold in reviewing transnational counter-terrorism activities, they can only issue domestic remedies. *Habeas corpus* orders will not be effective if foreign governments refuse to produce prisoners.[61] Even with respect to domestic remedies, British and Canadian courts both stopped short of ordering their governments to make representations to the United States on behalf of Guantánamo detainees.[62]

---

[59] *Binyam Mohamed* v. *Secretary of State* [2010] EWCA Civ 65.
[60] Justice and Security Act 2013.   [61] *Secretary of State* v. *Rahmatullah* [2012] UKSC 48.
[62] *Abassi* v. *Secretary of State* [2002] EWCA 1598; *Khadr* v. *Canada* [2010] 1 SCR 44. On the difficulties of domestic litigation in filling transnational accountability gaps see Chapter 1 in this volume, de Londras, 'Counter-terrorism judicial review as regulatory constitutionalism' and Kent Roach, 'Substitute Justice? Challenges to American Counter-Terrorism Activities in Non-American Courts' (2013) 82 *Mississippi Law Journal* 907.

Transnational accountability gaps remain the most significant and troubling feature of post 9/11 counter-terrorism. Domestic courts, legislatures, executives and hybrid institutions such as public inquiries all appear unable to fill these accountability gaps. The investigative media, supranational institutions and transnational civil society groups such as Human Rights Watch and Amnesty International have all tried to fill the gap. Moreover, they have had significant success in revealing and publicizing much post 9/11 misconduct. All of these institutions, however, lack the coercive powers of their domestic counterparts.

(b) Plugging domestic accountability gaps

Although both inquiries failed to achieve transnational accountability, they were better equipped to hold multiple parts of their own government accountable. The Arar commission examined and was critical of the actions of not only the RCMP but also security, customs and foreign affairs officials who all played a role in the case. For example, it documented how information received by foreign affairs officials in Syria subsequently found its way into RCMP search warrants in Canada. If the Detainee inquiry had been allowed to continue, it would likely have examined the actions of security and foreign affairs officials and perhaps others. As counter-terrorism becomes more transnational in character, such wide-ranging jurisdiction will only become more important. Foreign affairs, customs, financial intelligence and military officials will join with the police and the intelligence services in much counter-terrorism activities. The ability to sue multiple governmental defendants can allow the judiciary to engage in whole of government review, but care needs to be taken to ensure that review by the legislature and executive watchdogs does not become mired in jurisdictional silos that are becoming less relevant given whole of government responses to counter-terrorism.

(c) Importance of independence and other quasi-judicial features

Although many critics of the courts are quick to claim that they are on the side of the people, judges are more popular than politicians or bureaucrats. Courts are popular in part because they are not perceived as having a pre-existing stake in defending the conduct of the government. The courts are not, however, the only bodies that enjoy some independence from governments. Although inquiries and other watchdogs within the executive do not enjoy formal legal guarantees of independence, they have the potential to bring some of the benefits of impartiality, thoroughness, concern with rights and revealing hidden truths that many proponents of judicial review associate with the judiciary. As the Detainee inquiry, however, reminds us, the independence of these quasi-judicial institutions is not guaranteed simply by the presence of a judge or a retired judge. The independence of the executive watchdog must be earned and exercised if such bodies are to enjoy some of the credibility of the courts.

The success of the Arar commission and the failure of the Detainee inquiry demonstrate the importance and the contingency of the independence of inquiries. Justice O'Connor came to his duties with no prior involvement in national security activities. He made clear that he would conduct a thorough review of the propriety of the government's conduct with an open mind and he and his counsel were not shy about criticizing the conduct of the Ottawa security establishment. Sir Peter Gibson's role in the Detainee inquiry was controversial precisely because of his prior involvement in overseeing the work of the security services between 2006 to 2010. The personal integrity of those conducting reviews may be a necessary but not a sufficient condition for success. The institutional positions that they have occupied are important. It is interesting to speculate what would have happened if the Canadian government had selected one of the handful of specially designated judges that review the work of CSIS to have headed the Arar inquiry.[63] Although that judge would have brought more national security expertise to the task than Justice O'Connor, and might have been even more critical of misconduct by officials, it is possible that he or she may have suffered a similar fate to Sir Peter Gibson as being perceived by many as not sufficiently independent from the security establishment.

The independence of public inquiries cannot simply be assumed by the presence of a judge or retired judge. It must be manifest to all and exercised if inquiries are to enjoy some of the same credibility as courts. In addition to the judge who headed the inquiry, commission counsel for the Arar commission played an important role in aggressively opposing

---

[63] On the role played by these judges who grant warrants, decide public interest immunity and review the use of intelligence as evidence in immigration proceedings, see Kent Roach, 'The Law Working Itself Pure? The Canadian Experience with Exceptional Courts and Guantanamo' in Fionnula Ni Aolain and Oren Gross (eds.), *Beyond Guantanamo: Exceptional Courts and Military Commissions in Comparative Perspective* (Cambridge University Press, 2014), p. 201 *et seq.*

governmental claims of secrecy and cross-examining governmental witnesses in *in camera* hearings where Mr Arar and his counsel were not present. The credibility of commissioners and their staff will be particularly important in national security inquiries which will inevitably require closed hearings.

Independence is not the only court-like attribute that can assist public inquiries. The Arar commission followed a court-like narrative of focusing on the treatment of one person. It effectively held that person not to be guilty by concluding in clear and unequivocal terms that it has seen no evidence to indicate that Mr Arar was guilty of an offence or was a threat to national security. This court-like narrative captured the imagination of the media and the interested public. The exonerating effects of the Arar commission should not be underestimated. It explains why the Conservative Canadian government quickly accepted all of the recommendations in the Commission's factual report and publicly apologised to and compensated Mr Arar. Canada's leading national newspaper named Arar as the Canadian of the year in the wake of the inquiry's report. Executive watchdog review can be more powerful if it adopts more of the trappings of the judicial process.

(d)   Dangers of simply applying pre-existing rules and the limits of police investigations

Although inquiries can benefit from having a court-like independence from government and focusing on the plight of particular individuals, they also benefit from not having to apply pre-existing rules in the same way as courts or the police. The Arar commission's failure to assign individual responsibility for leaks of damaging information about Mr Arar did not stop it from criticizing the leaks and essentially holding those with access to the secret information collectively responsible for attempting to defend themselves by leaking secret information. Its criticisms of the leaks also triggered some critical reflection in the media for their role in taking the leaks at face value. A subsequent police investigation failed to identify or charge those responsible for the leaks and had much less visibility than the Commission's strong condemnation of the leaks. Had the Detainee inquiry been able to proceed, it would have been able to devise its own standards of propriety and apply them to UK information sharing with the United States, Libya, and other countries. The abandonment of the inquiry in favour of police investigations is not a positive step for accountability. The police will often be unable to find evidence of individual fault and they will not assess organizational and governmental fault as public inquiries do. In this sense, inquiries combine judicial independence and credibility with a legislative freedom to create their own standards. The fact that inquiries only make non-binding policy recommendations also frees them from the responsibility that legislatures and executives have to implement the standards that they create. Such freedom moves inquiries closer to the media and civil society and causes many in government to be suspicious and resentful of inquiries.

(e) Inquiries and party participation and civil society constitutionalism

The Arar commission benefited from the continued participation of Mr Arar and civil society groups even when the commission was forced by governmental claims of secrecy to hold most of its hearings without them. At the same time, the Detainee inquiry was harmed by the fact that many detainees and civil society groups boycotted the inquiry because of their lack of confidence about its independence from government. Civil society support of domestic review bodies helps create legitimacy. It will also be particularly important in ensuring that domestic review mechanisms are linked with transnational ones. Transnational civil society groups such as Human Rights Watch and Amnesty International provide an important vehicle for transnational accountability.

Civil society support is also very important in dealing with issues of discrimination. A number of Arab and Muslim groups were represented in the Arar commission and the commission itself was responsive to the concerns of these groups in recommending training to avoid discriminatory profiling. The participation of those directly affected and harmed by national security activities is also important to the legitimacy of the inquiry. Although he never testified and was excluded from the *in camera* hearings, Mr Arar was an important presence in the Arar commission. Ultimately, the government was forced to apologise and compensate him because of the commission's judicial-like findings that it had found no evidence of Arar's guilt. Unfortunately, the Arar commission may be the exception that proves the rule, because the stigma of suspicion hangs over many who have been targeted in counter-terrorism investigations. Indeed, the Canadian commission's findings did not even persuade the United States to remove Arar from their watchlists.[64]

---

[64] Kent Roach, 'Uneasy Neighbors: Comparative American and Canadian Counter-Terrorism' (2012) 38 *William Mitchell L Rev.* 1701, 1729–49.

(f) Summary

Public inquiries are hybrid institutions. They can combine the impartiality and focus on party participation associated with the judiciary, with the initiative and access to secret information of the executive, and with the creativity of the legislature in creating new norms and rules to govern national security activities. The police investigations that followed the Arar commission and that eventually pre-empted the Detainee inquiry demonstrate how public inquiries can assess organizational and government fault in a more creative manner than police and courts can assess individual fault. Indeed, public inquiries can have some of the creativity usually associated with media and civil society review of counter-terrorism, albeit augmented by coercive powers of investigation.

Inquiries can play an important role in filling accountability gaps that have emerged from whole of government responses to counter-terrorism. Both the Canadian Arar and the British Detainee inquiries were given jurisdiction to examine the actions of all domestic officials. The Arar commission demonstrates how an inquiry that is perceived to be independent and even combative towards government can capture media attention and the participation of both directly affected individuals and civil society groups. Inquiries can complement processes of media and civil society constitutionalism that have played an important role in holding governments to account for many post 9/11 abuses of human rights.

Public inquiries are not, however, a panacea. Neither the Arar nor Detainee inquiries were able to hold foreign governments accountable. Canadian and British officials and agencies might be held accountable for complicity in torture, but the foreign torturers in Libya, Syria and the United States were not. The failure of the Gibson inquiry affirms the importance that inquiries must be perceived to be independent from government and that the presence of a retired or perhaps even a sitting judge cannot guarantee the independence of any public inquiries. The credibility that comes from independence and other quasi-judicial attributes of inquiries must be exercised and earned. When this is done, inquiries will also benefit, as the Arar commission did, from participation by directly affected people and civil society groups. Finally, it should not be forgotten that governments retain the discretion not to appoint public inquiries or to refuse to implement their recommendations. The Canadian government only partially implemented the recommendations of the Arar commission and subsequently refused to appoint another inquiry into suspected Canadian complicity in torture in Afghanistan.

PART III

Counter-terrorism judicial review
in the political constitution

Rebalancing the unbalanced constitution: juridification and national security in the United Kingdom

ROGER MASTERMAN

Introduction

The twentieth century history of judicial review in national security cases in the United Kingdom provides an interesting counter-perspective to the orthodox, expansionary, accounts of review of administrative discretion in that jurisdiction during the same period. While in *Ridge* v. *Baldwin*,[1] *Padfield* v. *Minister for Agriculture*[2] and *Anisminic* v. *Foreign Compensation Commission*,[3] the Appellate Committee of the House of Lords was able to reinvigorate the prerogative orders and lay the foundations of modern administrative law,[4] judicial review of decisions taken on national security grounds was, for much of the twentieth century, held in an uneasy stasis. Simultaneously haunted by precedents such as *Liversidge* v. *Anderson*[5] and hamstrung by a perceived lack of competence to challenge judgments of the elected branches supported by assertions of imminent threat, the courts found themselves powerless to effectively displace the suggestion that national security questions were tantamount to being non-justiciable.[6]

Progress towards bringing national security decisions within the supervisory jurisdiction of the courts demonstrated the common law at

---

[1] *Ridge* v. *Baldwin* [1964] AC 40.
[2] *Padfield* v. *Minister for Agriculture, Fisheries and Food* [1968] AC 997.
[3] *Anisminic* v. *Foreign Compensation Commission* [1969] 2 AC 147.
[4] For an overview see R. Stevens, *The English Judges: Their Role in the Changing Constitution* (Oxford: Hart Publishing, 2005).
[5] *Liversidge* v. *Anderson* [1942] AC 206. See also *R* v. *Halliday* [1917] AC 260.
[6] *R* v. *Secretary of State for the Home Department, ex parte Hosenball* [1977] 1 WLR 766, 778: 'There is a conflict between the interests of national security on the one hand and the freedom of the individual on the other. The balance between the two is not for a court of law. It is for the Home Secretary. He is the person entrusted by Parliament with the task'.

its incremental worst, lagging significantly behind judicial review in other spheres of executive discretion. Successes were often Pyrrhic; even in the notable *GCHQ* case (in which executive orders taken pursuant to the prerogative were found to be susceptible to review on procedural fairness grounds) Lord Diplock was able to follow his seminal restatement of the grounds of judicial review with the assertion that national security nevertheless remained:

> a matter upon which those upon whom the responsibility rests, and not the courts of justice, must have the last word. It is *par excellence* a non-justiciable question. The judicial process is totally inapt to deal with the sort of problems which it involves.[7]

The 'striking consistency'[8] of the courts' position during this period leads to the almost irresistible conclusion that national security decisions – regardless of their consequences for the rights or interests of individuals – fell unquestionably within the four corners of discretionary jurisdiction available to the executive, and therefore beyond the supervisory jurisdiction of the law courts.

In the light of broader developments in the law of judicial review, the 'mystical significance'[9] attached to the executive assertion of national security demonstrates a number of significant departures from the orthodox account of the development of the judicial function within the constitution. First, judicial review cases in which national security issues were present embraced a peculiar counter-polycentricity mindset. While judicial avoidance of intensive review of social or economic issues frequently emphasised the inability of the court to second-guess complex policy choices, national security questions were presented differently, leaving a sense that it was the simplicity (the apparent self-evidence that national security decisions are for the executive alone), rather than the complexity of the discretionary judgements made, that prompted the judicial denial of competence to intervene. Facts which melded intricate questions of public power, sensitive evidence and individual liberties

---

[7] *Council of Civil Service Unions* v. *Minister for the Civil Service* [1985] 1 AC 374, para. 412. See also *The Zamora* [1916] 2 AC 77, para. 107: 'Those who are responsible for the national security must be the sole judge of what national security requires. It would be obviously undesirable that such matters should be made the subject of evidence in a court of law or otherwise discussed in public'.

[8] A. Tomkins, 'National Security and the Role of the Court: A Changed Landscape?' (2010) 126 *Law Quarterly Review* 543.

[9] S. Brown, 'Public Interest Immunity' (1994) *Public Law* 579, 589.

were routinely distilled into a zero-sum claim. Secondly, in a constitution which has enjoyed an ambivalent relationship with separation of powers – in which the division of governmental functions is as often inferred as it is made explicit[10] – the solidity with which the courts insulated (apparently unfettered) executive competence over questions of security was remarkable. Finally, and most pertinently, for the reason that national security litigation resisted (or, at the very least, did not fully embrace) the expansionary tendencies of mainstream judicial review during the latter part of the twentieth century, one of the standard threads running through the juridification narrative – the judicially-driven nature of constitutional development – is conspicuously absent from the national security arena. The cumulative effect of these factors is that review of national security issues was seen to be either on the fringes of justiciability or on the very lowest rungs of the *Wednesbury* scale. Either way, the twentieth century history of counter-terrorism judicial review in the United Kingdom demonstrated a constitution in which courts were both powerless to counter the effects of rights-infringing decisions and unduly reliant on the fortuitous compliance of the elected branches to achieve any meaningful change.[11]

I Juridification on the Human Rights Act model

Prior to the introduction of the Human Rights Act 1998, the inability of judicial review to operate as an effective tool of scrutiny in the national security arena amounted to a significant weakness in the ability of the courts to subject government to the rule of law. This problem was compounded by the parallel inadequacy of the legislature to effectively supervise the prerogative powers (the 'dead ground' of the constitution)[12] frequently deployed in pursuance of national security objectives. It took

---

[10] M. Arden, 'Judicial Independence and Parliaments' in K. Ziegler, D. Baranger and A. W. Bradley (eds.), *Constitutionalism and the Role of Parliaments* (Oxford: Hart Publishing, 2007), p. 192.

[11] As both de Londras and Jenkins remind us, the possibility that both trends might continue has by no means been eradicated by the move towards heightened scrutiny in the counter-terrorism arena under the Human Rights Act 1998. See Chapter 1 in this volume, F. de Londras, 'Counter-terrorism judicial review as regulatory constitutionalism'; and Chapter 3, D. Jenkins, 'When good cases go bad: unintended consequences of rights-friendly judgments'.

[12] *R v. Secretary of State for the Home Department, ex parte Fire Brigades Union* [1995] 2 AC 513, para. 567.

implementation of the Human Rights Act 1998 to provide the legislative impetus to weaken, and finally break down, this rigid separation of functions and to expose national security decisions which interfered with individual rights to meaningful judicial scrutiny. The extent of this change should not be understated; in the light of the implementation of the Human Rights Act, national security justifications could (or should) no longer operate as virtually unquestionable defences to executive, or legislative, action interfering with one or more of the rights under the European Convention on Human Rights (ECHR).[13]

The reach of the Human Rights Act's provisions is potentially huge; section 3(1) directs that *all* statutory provisions be interpreted (as far as is possible to do so) in order to achieve compatibility with the Convention rights; section 6(1) requires that *all* executive decisions (other than those compelled by primary legislation or by legislation which might not be interpreted in a Convention right-compatible manner)[14] be compliant with the Convention rights. Operating in tandem, these two provisions narrowed those areas of governmental action, which could (previously in some cases without even meaningful argument) be found to fall outside the reach of judicial scrutiny. As Baroness Hale has recognised, following the implementation of the Human Rights Act, 'if a Convention right requires the court to examine and adjudicate upon matters which were previously regarded as non-justiciable, then adjudicate it must'.[15] The Human Rights Act therefore required that a higher standard of justification be applied before either legislative or executive interference with fundamental rights on national security grounds would be deemed to be necessary in a democratic society. National security might provide justification for interference with rights, but would no longer operate as an unquestionable trump.

But just as national security would no longer act to render judicial supervision meaningless, nor would the Human Rights Act subject all decisions taken in the name of the maintenance of security to judicial override. While judicial protection of ECHR rights is very clearly at the heart of the HRA scheme, the powers granted to courts do not permit the explicit invalidation of primary legislation and appreciate that

---

[13] Human Rights Act 1998, s. 1(1).   [14] *Ibid.* s. 6(2).

[15] *R (on the application of Gentle)* v. *Prime Minister* [2008] UKHL 20, para. 60. See also *International Transport Roth GmbH* v. *Secretary of State for the Home Department* [2003] QB 728, para. 27 (Simon Brown LJ): 'Judges nowadays have no alternative but to apply the Human Rights Act 1998'.

infringements of qualified rights might be permissible, so long as proportionate, in pursuance of the protection of national security objectives. In parallel, the elected branches were also to shoulder partial responsibility for the realisation of the Human Rights Act project. Far then from simply amounting to an 'unprecedented transfer of political power from the executive and legislature to the judiciary',[16] the Human Rights Act sought to realign constitutional power in a more sophisticated manner.[17] Properly construed, the juridification prompted by the Human Rights Act should be seen as a complement, rather than a challenge, to democratic government.[18] Rather than to empower the judicial branch at the explicit expense of the political, the intent behind the Human Rights Act was to encourage protection of, and sensitivity to, rights through 'institutional balance, joint responsibility and deliberative dialogue'.[19] In a departure from the classic, constitutionalised and judicially-enforced Bill of Rights model, the Human Rights Act envisaged collaboration between the branches of government in which Parliament was intended to be as active a participant in protecting rights as the independent judiciary.[20] The Act therefore serves dual constitutional aims: first (and classically) to function as a judicially-imposed stop on rights-infringing policies and to permit the higher courts to highlight rights-based inadequacies in

[16] K. D. Ewing, 'The Human Rights Act and Parliamentary Democracy' (1999) 62 *Modern Law Review* 79. See also M. Pinto-Duschinsky, *Bringing Human Rights Back Home: Making Human Rights Compatible with Parliamentary Democracy in the United Kingdom* (London: Policy Exchange, 2010), p. 9. And for an especially indignant assessment see J. Allan, 'Statutory Bills of Rights: You Read Words In, You Read Words Out, You Take Parliament's Clear Intention and You Shake It All About – Doin' the Sankey Hanky Panky' in T. Campbell, K. D. Ewing and A. Tomkins (eds.), *The Legal Protection of Human Rights: Sceptical Essays* (Oxford University Press, 2011).

[17] On which see R. Masterman, *The Separation of Powers in the Contemporary Constitution: Judicial Competence and Independence in the United Kingdom* (Cambridge University Press, 2011).

[18] *A and others* v. *Secretary of State for the Home Department* [2004] UKHL 56, [2005] 2 AC 68, para. 42: 'It is of course true that the judges in this country are not elected and are not answerable to Parliament. It is also of course true . . . that Parliament, the executive and the courts have different functions. But the function of independent judges charged to interpret and apply the law is universally regarded as a cardinal feature of the modern democratic state, a cornerstone of the rule of law itself'. And see F. Davis, 'The Human Rights Act and Juridification: Saving Democracy from Law' (2010) 30 *Politics* 91.

[19] S. Gardbaum, 'The New Commonwealth Model of Constitutionalism' (2001) 49 *American Journal of Comparative Law* 707, 710.

[20] *Rights Brought Home: The Human Rights Bill* (Cm. 3782, 1997), para. 3.6, available at www.archive.official-documents.co.uk/document/hoffice/rights/contents.htm.

primary legislation; secondly, to function as a catalyst for the development of rights-conscious policy and legislation.

In the national security arena, in which the effects of judicial supervision were historically as inconspicuous as they were ineffectual,[21] this rebalancing of constitutional supervisory powers might be seen as being unobjectionable, valuable, perhaps even to be celebrated. Given that national security decisions and policy were traditionally seen to be the sole preserve of the executive – '[t]he first duty of government is the defence of the realm'[22] – the Human Rights Act made the realisation of effective checks and balances a more tangible possibility. Yet the undoubted difficulty of the Human Rights Act was that it also brought with it the danger of breaking down the principled distinction between primary and secondary decision-maker that had traditionally supported judicial review of executive discretion. As a result, critics of juridification argued that within the enforcement of the Human Rights Act lay the potential to illegitimately stifle democratic governance through challenging the legal sovereignty of Parliament,[23] through the tendency of the elected branches to 'capitulate' to the demands of adjudicative processes[24] and through prompting the development of only policy and legislation felt to be able to withstand judicial scrutiny.[25]

Restraint of governmental power was, of course, a partial objective of the Human Rights Act, but the emergence of a so-called 'culture of compliance' under which the elected branches of government (in spite of the apparent institutional balance struck by the Human Rights Act) found themselves *subjected*, explicitly and implicitly, to judicial determinations of rights questions was also touted as a consequence of this rebalancing of constitutional power.[26] Though the likelihood of the (supposedly) sovereign UK Parliament suddenly reconceptualising itself

---

[21] On which see I. Leigh and L. Lustgarten (eds.), *In From the Cold: National Security and Parliamentary Democracy* (Oxford: Clarendon Press, 1994), ch. 12.

[22] *International Transport Roth GmbH* v. *Secretary of State for the Home Department* [2002] EWCA Civ 158, [2003] QB 728, para. 85. See also *Secretary of State for the Home Department* v. *AF (No. 3)* [2010] 2 AC 269, para. 75.

[23] Pinto-Duschinsky, *Bringing Human Rights Back Home*, n. 16 above, p. 57: '[t]he post-1998 system is unacceptable because it permits the judiciary to usurp parliamentary sovereignty in a manner that lacks democratic accountability'.

[24] Allan, 'Statutory Bills of Rights', n. 16 above, pp. 116–20.

[25] On which see J. L. Hiebert, 'Governing Like Judges?' in T. Campbell, K. D. Ewing and A. Tomkins (eds.), *The Legal Protection of Human Rights: Sceptical Essays* (Oxford University Press, 2011).

[26] D. Nicol, 'The Human Rights Act and the Politicians' (2004) 24 *Legal Studies* 451, 453.

as an 'adjunct of the courts'[27] in the aftermath of implementation of the Act seemed at best remote, this did not prevent advocates seeking to deny the ability of the courts to adjudicate over the compliance of decisions taken in the name of national security. As much is evident from the attempts of the Attorney General, in the seminal *Belmarsh* decision, to suggest that even in the light of the Human Rights Act '[i]t is for the Executive and Legislature, as a matter of political judgment, to decide what measures [are] necessary to protect public security'.[28] In response to the Attorney General's attempt to oust the supervisory jurisdiction granted by the Human Rights Act, the then Senior Law Lord, Lord Bingham, issued the following corrective:

> The Attorney General is fully entitled to insist on the proper limits of judicial authority, but he is wrong to stigmatise judicial decision making as in some way undemocratic. It is particularly inappropriate in a case such as the present in which Parliament has expressly legislated in section 6 of the 1998 Act to render unlawful any act of a public authority, including a court, incompatible with a Convention right, has required courts (in section 2) to take account of relevant Strasbourg jurisprudence, has (in section 3) required courts, so far as possible, to give effect to Convention rights and has conferred a right of appeal on derogation issues. The effect is not, of course, to override the sovereign legislative authority of the Queen in Parliament, since if primary legislation is declared to be incompatible the validity of the legislation is unaffected (section 4(6)) and the remedy lies with the appropriate minister (section 10), who is answerable to Parliament. The 1998 Act gives the courts a very specific, wholly democratic, mandate.[29]

The sentiments behind Lord Bingham's admonishment of the Attorney General were echoed elsewhere in the House of Lords' decision.[30] The consequence of the legislative direction provided by the Human Rights Act, as Lord Bingham noted in *Belmarsh*, was that judicial scrutiny of executive decisions and/or legislation taken in furtherance of national security objectives on the basis of the Convention rights enjoyed parliamentary (and therefore indirectly democratic) sanction. The fact that the Human Rights Act (a primary legislative instrument) *required* courts to exercise this counter-majoritarian function therefore provides a partial

---

[27] Ibid.
[28] *A and others* v. *Secretary of State for the Home Department* [2004] UKHL 56, [2005] 2 AC 68, para. 85.
[29] *Ibid.* para. 42.   [30] For instance *ibid.* para. 176.

rejoinder to accounts of the judicialised constitution which emphasise the empire-building tendencies of the courts under which the judges themselves have lobbied for, and developed the common law in order to obtain, a greater constitutional role.[31] By contrast with the pre-HRA emergence of a nascent common law rights jurisprudence,[32] the courts' constitutional functions under the Act come with a legislative seal of approval.

The fact that the Human Rights Act was underpinned by a manifesto commitment made by the incoming 1997 Labour administration, and subsequently enacted in primary legislation, cannot, however, fully address claims made by critics of the expanded reach of judicial power that the enforcement of standards against government 'constrains the space for any future democratic decisions on that issue'.[33] We can say that the juridification of questions of rights was a clear, albeit partial, policy objective of the enactment and implementation of the Human Rights Act; but can also state that 'political rights review'[34] is as integral to the design and operation of the Act as review undertaken by courts. Nor can the Human Rights Act's democratic heritage explain away the difficulties of its practical implementation, for, as Mark Tushnet has observed,[35] the legislative mandate underpinning the courts' role in policing ECHR compliance at the national level disguises potential difficulties in its enforcement; judicial review under the New Commonwealth model of constitutionalism[36] holds the potential to collapse into that which it seeks to eschew, namely, the polar opposites of strong form judicial review and the unchallengeable primacy of the political branches (as manifested in the formal doctrine of parliamentary sovereignty).

---

[31] M. Bevir, 'The Westminster Model, Governance and Judicial Reform' (2008) 61 *Parliamentary Affairs* 559, 569.

[32] See *R v. Lord Chancellor, ex parte Witham* [1998] QB 575.

[33] Bevir, 'The Westminster Model, Governance and Judicial Reform', n. 31 above, 565.

[34] J. L. Hiebert, 'Parliament and the Human Rights Act: Can the JCHR Help Facilitate a Culture of Rights?' (2006) 4 *International Journal of Constitutional Law* 1, 3: 'A key assumption envisaged by [the parliamentary rights] model is that rights will be protected not simply through after-the-fact evaluations by courts but by establishing opportunities and obligations for political rights review by ministers, parliamentarians and public authorities that are distinct from, and prior to, judicial review'.

[35] M. Tushnet, 'New Forms of Judicial Review and the Persistence of Rights- and Democracy-Based Worries' (2003) 38 *Wake Forest Law Review* 813.

[36] Gardbaum, *The New Commonwealth Model of Constitutionalism*, n. 19 above.

II   The continued deification of national security

In spite of the legislative prompt provided by the Human Rights Act, obstacles to the justiciability of national security issues were, however, by no means immediately eradicated following the reception of the Convention rights into domestic law. The statutory juridification of rights issues in the national security arena was, initially at least, beholden to the clear precedents regarding the perceived institutional incompetence of courts to question executive judgements taken in the interests of security.

In *Secretary of State for the Home Department* v. *Rehman*, concerning the deportation of a Pakistani national on grounds of the potential threat to national security that he posed, the House of Lords unanimously deferred to the executive assessment of the risk presented.[37] As Lord Hoffmann noted:

> In matters of national security, the cost of failure can be high. This seems to me to underline the need for the judicial arm of government to respect the decisions of ministers of the Crown on the question of whether support for terrorist activities in a foreign country constitutes a threat to national security. It is not only that the executive has access to special information and expertise in these matters. It is also that such decisions, with serious potential results for the community, require a legitimacy, which can be conferred only by entrusting them to persons responsible to the community through the democratic process. If the people are to accept the consequences of such decisions, they must be made by persons whom the people have elected and whom they can remove.[38]

Legitimacy in the field of national security decision-making, Hoffmann contends, can only result from an electoral mandate. It follows that such decisions are – regardless of content or implications – due the respect of the judiciary.

Lord Hoffmann is not the only judge to perpetuate this rigid separation of function in the HRA era. Lord Justice Laws too, in *International Transport Roth GmbH* v. *Secretary of State for the Home Department*, spoke of the paradigmatic areas of executive responsibility (security being one) within which the courts cannot 'sensibly' scrutinise the merits of decisions taken.[39]

---

[37] *Secretary of State for the Home Department* v. *Rehman* [2001] UKHL 47, [2003] 1 AC 153.

[38] *Ibid.* paras. 50–4 and 62 (Lord Hoffmann).

[39] *International Transport Roth GmbH* v. *Secretary of State for the Home Department* [2002] EWCA Civ 158, [2003] QB 728, paras. 77 and 85: 'The first duty of government is the defence of the realm'.

Both approaches reflect a territorial approach to the separation of power under which certain governmental functions are held to be so umbilically linked to the role of a particular arm of government as to exclude any legitimate review or scrutiny undertaken by another branch. The resulting 'dilution'[40] of judicial scrutiny powers in relation to such functions holds the capacity to see judicial review rendered otiose on the basis of a perceived lack of legitimacy.[41]

The continuance of this, to adopt Murray Hunt's terminology, spatial understanding of the interrelationship between the relevant powers of courts, executive and legislature in the national security arena is questionable.[42] First, it runs counter to the trend, begun in the mid-twentieth century, towards breaking down jurisdictional barriers to judicial review,[43] marking national security decisions out as being resistant to broader (judicially engineered) moves towards expanding the scope and rigour of judicial review. Secondly, through the denial of the relevance of the rights implications to the judicial assessment of the legality of national security decisions, it frustrates the purpose of the Human Rights Act, namely, to subject governmental decisions which impact on individual liberties to judicial scrutiny and supervision *regardless* of the area of policy in which the decision is taken.

III   The necessary superiority of the political

Though the Human Rights Act sought to find a middle ground between the competing primacies of law and politics, the superior democratic claims of the political branches would not be easily displaced. As has

---

[40] On which see Chapter 10 in this volume, C. Chan, 'Business as usual: deference in counter-terrorism rights review'.

[41] For the most powerful critique of deference see T. R. S. Allan, 'Human Rights and Judicial Review: A Critique of "Due Deference"' (2006) *Cambridge Law Journal* 671.

[42] M. Hunt, 'Sovereignty's Blight: Why Contemporary Public Law Needs the Concept of "Due Deference"' in N. Bamforth and P. Leyland (eds.), *Public Law in a Multi-Layered Constitution* (Oxford: Hart Publishing, 2003).

[43] *Ibid.* p. 347: 'Much of the progress of modern public law has been in rolling back what were formerly considered to be zones of immunity from judicial review, reformulating the considerations which were thought to justify total immunity and reintegrating them into substantive public law as considerations which affect the particular, contextualised application of what have increasingly become accepted as universally applicable general principles. That progress has been hard fought for, but it is constantly threatened by the failure to ground deference theory in anything other than crudely formalistic notions of the separation of powers and the supposed continued sovereignty of Parliament'.

already been alluded to, the continued influence of parliamentary sovereignty – and behind its façade the executive dominance of the legislature – perpetuates the sense that legislative decisions are (or should be) immune from challenge. While the standard common law decisions on the legal authority of Parliament (*Ellen Street Estates*[44] and *British Railways Board* v. *Pickin*[45] among them) have lost some of their allure in the light of constitutional developments,[46] the sense among many that Parliament should remain necessarily supreme, and its decisions unquestionable in the courts, remains undiminished.

Michael Howard, then Leader of the Conservative Party, for instance, responded to the *Belmarsh* decision in the following terms:

> Parliament must be supreme. Aggressive judicial activism will not only undermine the public's confidence in the impartiality of the judiciary, but it could also put our security at risk – and with it the freedoms the judges seek to defend.[47]

Similar claims resonate beyond the national security arena, underpinning criticisms of perceived overreach by the European Court of Human Rights (ECtHR)[48] and of the excessive powers allocated to the courts under the Human Rights Act. Unease over this apparent new constitutional imbalance has prompted calls to reform or repeal the Human Rights Act in order to reassert the primacy of the elected branches: David Cameron, in taking the 2011 decision to convene a Commission to examine the case for the adoption of a British Bill of Rights, argued that 'it is about time we ensured that [human rights] decisions are made in this Parliament rather than in the courts'.[49]

The picture painted is one of stark choices: between courts and Parliament, between legitimate or illegitimate decisions, between individual freedom and security. In the national security arena, this discourse is, as we have seen, underpinned by a weighty body of jurisprudence maintaining a division between questions of policy and law. At the level

---

[44] *Ellen Street Estates* v. *Minister of Health* [1934] 1 KB 590.

[45] *British Railways Board* v. *Pickin* [1974] AC 765.

[46] Not least the United Kingdom's membership of the European Union. On which see N. Barber, 'The Afterlife of Parliamentary Sovereignty' (2011) 9 *International Journal of Constitutional Law* 144.

[47] M. Howard, 'Judges must bow to the will of Parliament', *Daily Telegraph*, 10 August 2005.

[48] Pinto-Duschinsky, *Bringing Human Rights Back Home*, n. 16 above, p. 5.

[49] HC Debs, vol. 523, col. 955, 16 February 2011. And see Commission on a Bill of Rights, *A UK Bill of Rights? The Choice Before Us* (18 December 2012), available at www.justice. gov.uk/about/cbr.

of constitutional principle this approach derives further support from the political constitution's ideological preference for elected officials over courts[50] and ultimately, of course, also appeals to the Diceyan subjection of courts to the will of Parliament.[51] This binary division of powers is, to a degree, reflected in the institutional design of the Human Rights Act; parliamentary sovereignty was clearly intended to be preserved in form.[52] But to deny the valid judicial input into questions engaging both rights and national security on that basis is to discount the rather more sophisticated separation of powers envisaged by the framers of the Act.[53]

Responses of this sort to judicial decisions which are perceived to frustrate the objectives of democratically elected officials are, of course, by no means new.[54] But given the late-twentieth century rebalancing of constitutional power, culminating in the implementation of the Human Rights Act, such continued denials of judicial competence to examine legislative and executive decisions on rights grounds almost certainly tell us something about the failure of the Act to embed a culture of justifica-tion across constitutional processes and of the inability of dialogue theory to accurately capture the relative passion and dispassion of parliamen-tarians and judges.[55] The sense that Parliament be required to justify its enactments – that they be tested against (even self-imposed) standards of legality – therefore continues to sit uneasily with the constitution's traditional reverence for statutory language and the unquestionable legal authority of the legislature.[56] In the face of this tension, claims regarding the solidity of the Human Rights Act's position within the United Kingdom's new constitutional settlement should be treated with a degree of caution, but so too should those arguments which would position the elected branches as now finding themselves at the mercy of the judges.

---

[50] J. A. G. Griffith, 'The Political Constitution' (1979) 42 *Modern Law Review* 1.

[51] Cf. R. M. W. Masterman and J. E. K. Murkens, 'Skirting Supremacy and Subordination: the Constitutional Authority of the United Kingdom Supreme Court' (2013) 4 *Public Law* 800.

[52] HC Debs, vol. 306, col.772, 16 February 1998.

[53] On which see Masterman, *The Separation of Powers in the Contemporary Constitution*, n. 17 above.

[54] A. Le Sueur, 'The Judicial Review Debate: From Partnership to Friction' (1996) 31 *Government and Opposition* 8; I. Loveland, 'The War Against the Judges' (1997) 68 *Political Quarterly* 162.

[55] On which see G. Phillipson, 'The Human Rights Act, Dialogue and Constitutional Principles' in R. Masterman and I. Leigh (eds.), *The United Kingdom's Statutory Bill of Rights: Constitutional and Comparative Perspectives* (Oxford University Press, 2013).

[56] G. Marshall, *Constitutional Theory* (Oxford: Clarendon Press, 1971), p. 74.

While it has long been acknowledged that courts play a political role –
'[t]o require a supreme court to make certain kinds of political decisions
does not make those decisions any less political'[57] – the extent to which
judicial intervention is permitted, and the consequences of intervention
for the decision under scrutiny, remain issues of intense controversy. But
accurate assessment of these issues is, it is argued, hampered by base-level
denials of the role to be played by courts in the assessment of certain
areas claimed to be within the exclusive competence of the executive or
legislature. To defend an activity as being based on a 'pre-eminently
political judgement'[58] should not insulate that activity from questioning
scrutiny (within Parliament or the courts) any more than it should
automate compliance with law.

IV   Deference and relative institutional competence

Deference has in many respects become 'the classic separation of powers
device articulated in the post-Human Rights Act era'.[59] It is the method by
which the potential for HRA review to morph into something altogether
more potent, more capable (perhaps) of truly stifling democratic government, has been (for the most part) avoided.[60] That perceived institutional
superiority should impact on judicial responses to legislative initiatives
argued to infringe rights should, in a system shaped by parliamentary
sovereignty, come as no great surprise. Deference 'as submission' – that is,
the self-denial of the competence to scrutinise decisions in specific areas of
policy – is, however, incompatible with the new constitutional equilibrium which the Human Rights Act sought to cement.[61] To this extent,

---

[57] Griffith, 'The Political Constitution', n. 50 above, p. 16.
[58] *A and others* v. *Secretary of State for the Home Department* [2004] UKHL 56, [2005] 2 AC
68, para. 29.
[59] S. Tierney, 'Determining the State of Exception: What Role for Parliament and the
Courts?' (2005) 68 *Modern Law Review* 668, 670.
[60] It should be noted, however, that the House of Lords has denied the existence of a specific
methodology of deference, preferring to refer to the 'ordinary judicial task of weighing up
the competing considerations on each side and according appropriate weight to the
judgment of a person with responsibility for a given subject matter and access to special
sources of knowledge and advice' (see *Huang* v. *Secretary of State for the Home Department* [2007] UKHL 11, [2007] 2 AC 167, para. 16).
[61] See D. Dyzenhaus, 'The Politics of Deference: Judicial Review and Democracy' in
M. Taggart (ed.), *The Province of Administrative Law* (Oxford: Hart Publishing, 1997)
and for specific discussion in the HRA context, A. Kavanagh, *Constitutional Review under
the UK Human Rights Act* (Cambridge University Press, 2009), chs. 7, 8 and 9. A dedicated
account of deference in the counter-terrorism judicial review context is provided by Chan,

Lord Hoffmann, in the *ProLife Alliance* decision, was correct to highlight the inaccuracy of the apparent subjection of courts to the elected branches perpetuated by the *language* of deference.[62]

While a degree of deference is, as Lord Bingham has recognised,[63] a natural response to the uncertain territory the judges are confronted with in assessing the Convention compatibility of national security decisions, this has not (indeed should not) come at the expense of meaningful scrutiny of the rights issues raised. In *Belmarsh*, as much was recognised by Lord Rodger of Earlsferry who noted that '[d]eference does not mean abasement . . . even in matters of national security'.[64] Nor, despite the 'great weight'[65] which continues to attach to primary legislation, is deference the automated judicial response to legislative action; as Lord Bingham noted in *Lichniak*, '[t]he fact that a statute represents the settled will of the democratic assembly is not a conclusive reason for upholding it'.[66] What deference does permit, however, is the preservation of the sense that certain decisions are more appropriately determined by (elected) political actors:

> The more purely political . . . a question is, the more appropriate it will be for political resolution and the less likely it is to be an appropriate matter for judicial decision. The smaller, therefore, will be the potential role of the court. It is the function of political and not judicial bodies to resolve political questions.[67]

This concession, while perhaps a truism, importantly does not exclude the possibility, or legitimacy, of judicial review.[68]

---

with the model of deference favoured here broadly consonant with her modified 'business as usual' approach (see Chapter 10 in this volume, C. Chan, 'Business as usual: deference in counter-terrorism rights review').

[62] *R (on the application of ProLife Alliance) v. British Broadcasting Corporation* [2003] UKHL 23, [2004] 1 AC 185, para. 75.

[63] *A and others v. Secretary of State for the Home Department* [2004] UKHL 56, [2005] 2 AC 68, para. 29. See also A. Kavanagh, *Constitutional Review under the UK Human Rights Act* (Cambridge University Press, 2009), pp. 212–14.

[64] *A and others v. Secretary of State for the Home Department* [2004] UKHL 56, [2005] 2 AC 68, para. 176. See also *R (on the application of Mohamed) v. Secretary of State for Foreign and Commonwealth Affairs* [2010] EWCA Civ 65, para. 46.

[65] *R (on the application of Animal Defenders International) v. Secretary of State for Culture, Media and Sport* [2008] UKHL 15, [2008] 1 AC 1312, para. 33.

[66] *R v. Lichniak* [2002] UKHL 47, [2003] 1 AC 903, para. 14.

[67] *A and others v. Secretary of State for the Home Department* [2004] UKHL 56, [2005] 2 AC 68, para. 29.

[68] On which also see Chapter 1 in this volume, F. de Londras, 'Counter-terrorism judicial review as regulatory constitutionalism'.

However, while the abandonment of submissive deference marked by *Belmarsh* stands as a clear step towards closing the accountability loop in national security decisions this is not to suggest that the deployment of ECHR based review has been without controversy. Deference might serve to preserve respect for the policy choices of the primary decision-maker, but the balance of power apparent on the face of the Act may nonetheless present difficulties once deployed in practice.

First, the readiness of courts to 'read in' implied conditions and terms into ostensibly clear legislative provisions has, in particular, drawn criticism from the parliamentary Joint Committee on Human Rights (JCHR). In its 2008 report into *Counter Terrorism Policy and Human Rights*, the Joint Committee noted with some surprise the willingness of the Law Lords to read words into statutory provisions in order to render them compatible with the Convention rights.[69] Specifically, the JCHR considered that the use of section 3(1) in *Secretary of State for the Home Department* v. *MB* was particularly difficult to defend.[70] *MB* concerned the compatibility of the system of closed material hearings handled by special advocates in control order cases under sections 2 and 3(1)(a) of the Prevention of Terrorism Act 2005 with Article 6(1) of the ECHR. By a four-to-one majority,[71] the House of Lords held that the case should be referred back to the trial judge, relying on section 3(1) to subject the provisions to the requirements of procedural fairness inherent in Article 6(1).[72]

Given its own interpretation of the overall scheme of the Human Rights Act, the JCHR felt that the application of section 3(1) in *MB* was particularly hard to justify; the Committee argued:

> the Human Rights Act deliberately gives Parliament a central role in deciding how best to protect the rights protected in the EHCR. Striking the balance between sections 3 and 4 of the Human Rights Act is crucial to the scheme of democratic rights protection. In our view it would have been more consistent with the scheme of the Human Rights Act for the House of Lords to have given a declaration of incompatibility, requiring Parliament to think again about the balance it struck in the control order legislation between the various competing interests.[73]

---

[69] Joint Committee on Human Rights, *Counter Terrorism Policy and Human Rights* (HL 50/HC 199, 7 February 2008), para. 46.

[70] *Secretary of State for the Home Department* v. *MB* [2007] UKHL 46, [2008] 1 AC 440.

[71] *Ibid.*, Lord Hoffmann dissenting (paras. 45–55).   [72] *Ibid.* para. 72.

[73] Joint Committee on Human Rights, *Counter Terrorism Policy and Human Rights*, n. 69 above, para. 47.

Judicially assessed compatibility did not, in this instance, equate with clarity. That the precise means by which Article 6 was to be vindicated following this use of section 3 remained uncertain ultimately resulted in the issue returning to the apex court in *AF (No. 3).*[74]

By the time *AF* reached the House of Lords, the Grand Chamber of the ECtHR had handed down its decision in *A* v. *United Kingdom.*[75] The consequences of *A* for the domestic litigation were in its conclusive finding that 'national security may need to give way to the interests of a fair hearing'.[76] As Lord Scott summarised, the question for the Law Lords was did 'a judicial process the purpose of which is to impose, or to confirm the imposition of, onerous obligations on individuals on grounds and evidence of which they are not and cannot be informed constitute a fair hearing? The judgment of the Grand Chamber in *A* v. *United Kingdom* ... has made clear that, for the purpose of Strasbourg jurisprudence and article 6(1) of the Convention, it does not'.[77] The finding in *A* was that the 'requirements of a fair hearing are *never* satisfied if the decision is "based solely or to a decisive extent" on closed material'.[78] Acknowledging that the ruling might 'destroy the system of control orders', a hesitance to directly apply *A* is discernible from a number of the Law Lords' speeches.[79] Yet, in the face of a recent, authoritative and on-point decision from the Grand Chamber of the ECtHR, the Law Lords felt compelled to apply the Strasbourg ruling.

Secondly then, the nature of the appropriate response of national courts in human rights litigation may well be conditioned by factors external to the Human Rights Act itself, and to the courts' perceptions of their own institutional competence *vis-à-vis* the elected branches of government. Even though the Law Lords were conscious that the consequence of their decision might be abandonment of the control order regime, the outcome was felt to be unavoidable in the light of the state's obligations under the ECHR: '[e]ven though we are dealing with rights under a United Kingdom statute, in reality, we have no choice: *Argentoratum locutum, iudicium finitum* – Strasbourg has spoken, the case is closed'.[80]

---

[74] *Secretary of State for the Home Department* v. *AF (No. 3)* [2010] 2 AC 269.
[75] *A* v. *United Kingdom* (2009) 49 EHRR 625.
[76] *Secretary of State for the Home Department* v. *AF (No. 3)* [2010] 2 AC 269, para. 121.
[77] *Ibid.* para. 96.   [78] *Ibid.* para. 71.
[79] *Ibid.* paras. 70 and 98.   [80] *Ibid.* para. 98.

V   Engagement, refinement, dialogue?

It is of course correct to say that Parliament, the executive and courts undertake different constitutional functions,[81] and that *primary* responsibility for certain of those functions might rest with one branch of government. But to then say that, as a result, those functions should continue to be immune to scrutiny by one or more of the other branches is to suggest something quite different. The Human Rights Act has gone some way to establishing a new constitutional equilibrium.[82] HRA review does not subject the elected branches of government to the rule of the courts, but cultivates a tension between the two that is abundantly clear in the realm of state security:

> The first responsibility of government in a democratic society is owed to the public. It is to protect and safeguard the lives of its citizens. It is the duty of the court to do all that it can to respect and uphold that principle. But the court has another duty too. It is to protect and safeguard the rights of the individual.[83]

Even in the light of the developments prompted by the Human Rights Act, the role of the courts remains constitutionally secondary in at least one crucial respect; as Laws LJ has written:

> The judges are constrained ... rightly, by the fact that their role is reactive; they cannot initiate; all they can do is apply principle to what is brought before them by others. Nothing could be more distinct from the duty of political creativity owed to us by Members of Parliament.[84]

To suggest that the Human Rights Act therefore 'welcomes the courts into the policy-making process'[85] is to mislead as to the necessarily responsive role played by the domestic judiciary when asked to examine the Convention compliance of a particular policy or legislative initiative.

Having said this – looking at the recent transition from indefinite detention without trial,[86] to control orders,[87] to terrorism prevention and

---

[81] *A and others* v. *Secretary of State for the Home Department* [2004] UKHL 56, [2005] 2 AC 68, para. 42.

[82] See also J. Jowell, 'Parliamentary Sovereignty under the New Constitutional Hypothesis' (2006) *Public Law* 562, 578.

[83] *Secretary of State for the Home Department* v. *AF (No. 3)* [2010] 2 AC 269, para. 75.

[84] J. Laws, 'Law and Democracy' (1995) *Public Law* 72, 93.

[85] Bevir, 'The Westminster Model, Governance and Judicial Reform', n. 31 above, 571.

[86] Anti-Terrorism, Crime and Security Act 2001.   [87] Prevention of Terrorism Act 2005.

investigation measures[88] – it is clear that judicial decisions *have* influenced the revision and refinement of legislation in the national security field (and powers exercised under that legislation) to an extent that, pre-Human Rights Act, would have been inconceivable. Is this influence constitutionally intolerable? Those who would appeal to the Diceyan understanding of legislation immune from legal challenge, to notions of pure and (potentially) unquestionable democratic/political judgement and expertise,[89] or (increasingly) to a notion of national sovereignty,[90] would argue that it is. A rather basic counter-argument would defend this judicial refining role on pragmatic grounds, given that the initiatives responded to amount to a catalogue of 'repressive measures unprecedented in peacetime Britain',[91] that legislation in this field is occasionally hastily enacted,[92] and that – without the (limited) powers bestowed by the Human Rights Act – these powers would be all the more likely to exist in a constitutional 'vacuum in which the citizen would be kept without protection against a misuse of executive powers'.[93]

A more sophisticated thesis would suggest that the constitution has developed to the extent that claims to unquestionable or unchallengeable authority (whatever their source), and the accountability vacuums which result, are rightly regarded with scepticism.[94] The hierarchical constitution with Parliament at its pinnacle has given way to something more heterarchical, which seeks to give recognition to institutional competence and expertise without allowing either to operate as insulation from scrutiny. This is recognised structurally in the weak form of legislative review established by the Human Rights Act, and practically in the judicial processes of weighing competing considerations. Affording a degree of latitude – deference – to the range of responses available to the primary decision-maker, recognising the differing nature of the decision-making process and the reasons (and evidence) articulated in

---

[88] Terrorism Prevention and Investigation Measures Act 2012.

[89] J. Allan, 'Statutory Bills of Rights', n. 16 above, pp. 121–22.

[90] Pinto-Duschinsky, *Bringing Human Rights Back Home*, n. 16 above.

[91] Ewing, *The Bonfire of the Liberties* (Oxford University Press, 2010), p. 10.

[92] For a survey see A. Tomkins, 'Parliament, Human Rights and Counter-Terrorism' in T. Campbell, K. D. Ewing and A. Tomkins (eds.), *The Legal Protection of Human Rights: Sceptical Essays* (Oxford University Press, 2011).

[93] *R v. Secretary of State for the Home Department, ex parte Fire Brigades Union* [1995] 2 AC 513, para. 567.

[94] *International Transport Roth GmbH v. Secretary of State for the Home Department* [2002] EWCA Civ 158, [2003] QB 728, paras. 71–5.

support of a given policy decision, allow courts to acknowledge the distinct constitutional roles of the legislature and executive without either usurping them or prompting the abandonment of objective assessment of the rights implications of the impugned decision.[95]

VI   The rebalanced (juridified) constitution?

The counter-majoritarian role that the Human Rights Act envisages courts play, rather than damaging democratic governance, should be seen as supporting, or complementing, it by both subjecting the (hypothetically unlimited) legislative authority of Parliament to rights-based audit and by enabling courts to render unlawful public body decisions which disproportionately interfere with those same rights. In policing the Convention rights the courts are able to bring to bear concerns relating to liberties which the democratic or policy-making process may be ill-positioned to consider (the impact of decisions on individual liberty). That national security issues are no longer regarded as being tantamount to non-justiciable, far from amounting to a challenge to the democratic process, is a clear advance for a constitution purporting to adhere to the values of the rule of law. The Human Rights Act does not make policy-makers out of judges any more than it subjects the policy-making process to the whims of the courts. Rather it permits issues cutting across the intersection of policy, expert judgement and sensitive factual data to be analysed for compatibility with human rights norms, tempered by the acknowledgement on the part of the courts that deference preserves the primary decision-making autonomy of the elected branches. A higher standard of justification may now be required of rights-infringing decisions taken in the name of national security, but we should be careful to portray this as strengthening rather than compromising our constitutional systems of accountability.

---

[95] See generally Masterman, *The Separation of Powers in the Contemporary Constitution*, n. 17 above, ch. 5.

Business as usual: deference in counter-terrorism judicial review

CORA CHAN

A key question that courts confront when reviewing the compatibility of counter-terrorist measures with human rights norms is how intensely to scrutinise the government's claims. In determining this question, judges in the United Kingdom face two antithetical forces. On the one hand, the risks and secrecy that beset judicial decision-making in this context demand courts to accord a large degree of deference to governmental expertise and intelligence-gathering powers.[1] On the other hand, constitutional expectations in the era of the Human Rights Act 1998 (HRA) call for courts to scrutinise rights encroachments made in the name of national security intensely. The challenge for courts is to find an approach to deference that can satisfy these apparently conflicting demands.

In recent years, two distinct responses to the conundrum can be distilled from the approach of the UK judiciary.[2] The first, what I call the 'dilution approach', argues that in deciding rights cases with national security elements, judges should dilute their supervisory role over the government. The second – the 'business-as-usual approach' – contends that courts should scrutinise rights violations in national security cases just as intensely as in any other case.[3] This chapter aims to evaluate

---

[1] T. Poole, 'Courts and Conditions of Uncertainty in "Times of Crisis"' (2008) *Public Law* 234, 244–58.

[2] Judges have not been consistent in adopting either approach, embracing one at times and displaying another at other times.

[3] Cf. O. Gross and F. Ni Aolain, *Law in Times of Crisis* (Cambridge University Press, 2006). The dilution approach is similar to Gross and Ni Aolain's 'Accommodation' model in that both countenance some degree of deviation from ordinary legal norms in emergencies. The business-as-usual approach is similar to Gross and Ni Aolain's 'Business as Usual' model in that both insist that ordinary legal norms need to be followed even in exigencies. However, the approaches highlighted in this chapter focus on the deviation from/adherence to ordinary norms at the level of judicial *application* of legal norms in judicial review, while Gross and Ni Aolain's models focus on the deviation/adherence regarding the *design*

whether these existing approaches can satisfactorily quench the competing imperatives, with a view to proposing the way forward for the judiciary. It argues that courts in the United Kingdom should take into account both their institutional limitations in judging national security questions and the rules of adjudication introduced by the HRA. It contends that the dilution approach, while seeking to accommodate the former, falls foul of the latter. In contrast, the business-as-usual approach complies with the latter and has *potential* to accommodate the former.[4] Such potential consists of courts deferring, or giving weight to, the government's second-order claims of superior institutional competence when in doubt, but only if the government can establish such claims with evidence. Nonetheless, courts that support the business-as-usual approach have so far not openly adopted this alternative form of deference. By examining in detail this form of deference, this chapter seeks to reveal untapped potential in the business-as-usual approach for resolving the dilemma over the intensity of review that courts face in counter-terrorism rights adjudication.

In what follows, I will first set out the two opposing approaches to judicial deference. Next I will present the affirmative case for the business-as-usual approach. Then I will outline and rebut arguments that are commonly cited to support the dilution approach. Finally, I will propose how the business-as-usual approach can accommodate the government's superior institutional competence.

I   Two opposing approaches to judicial deference

The term 'deference' has been used loosely and widely in judgments.[5] This chapter will adopt the lowest common denominator of the various

of the legal norms. My business-as-usual approach is akin to F. de Londras' 'business as usual approach' to counter-terrorism judicial review. See F. de Londras, 'A (Tentative) Typology of Judicial Review of Counter-Terrorist Measures', paper presented at the Society of Legal Scholars Annual Conference, University of Cambridge, 2011.

[4] See Chapter 5 in this volume, M. Tushnet, 'Emergency law as administrative law'. Both Mark Tushnet and I argue that courts should treat national security cases just like any other case. Yet while for me this means that courts should continue to be activist in national security cases, for Prof. Tushnet this means that courts should continue to be deferential therein.

[5] Contrast, for example, the use of the term 'deference' in *Re E (A Child)* [2008] UKHL 66 to mean accepting the government's conclusion when the government can convince the court that it is correct, with that in *R (on the application of Louis Farrakhan)* v. *Secretary of State for the Home Department* [2002] EWCA Civ 606 to mean accepting

usages of the term, that is, the showing of respect to other branches of the government. The dilution camp and business-as-usual camp agree that courts should show respect to other branches of the government. They disagree on how such deference should be shown.

The dilution camp believes that human rights cases that involve national security issues are a special category of rights cases that call for lower standards of judicial scrutiny. According to the dilution approach, the well-established rules of adjudication for human rights cases,[6] namely, that the burden rests on the government to justify *prima facie* rights limitations;[7] that courts should only sanction rights limitations if these limitations can, at least on balance, pass the structured proportionality test;[8] that the government must prove its claims with cogent and sufficient reasons;[9] and that the scope of rights and exceptions thereto stipulated in the HRA should be respected, do not apply with full force where national security matters are concerned. Courts should defer by attenuating these judicial standards. Examples of such attenuation include:[10]

(1) at the rights definition stage: redefining, or reading in exceptions to, unqualified rights;[11]

---

the government's conclusion even when the government cannot adduce evidence to convince the court that it is correct.

[6] I argued in C. Chan, 'Proportionality and Invariable Baseline Intensity of Review' (2013) 33(1) *Legal Studies* 1, that these rules should constitute a baseline intensity of review in human rights adjudication in the United Kingdom.

[7] Recently confirmed in *Aguilar Quila* v. *Secretary of State for Home Department; Bibi* v. *Same* [2011] UKSC 45, para. 44; *AB (Jamaica)* v. *Secretary of State for Home Department* [2008] 1 WLR 1893, para. 7.

[8] *R* v. *Secretary of State for the Home Department, ex parte Daly* [2001] 2 AC 532.

[9] *Mahmood* v. *Secretary of State for the Home Department* [2001] 1 WLR 840, paras. 39–40; *Samaroo* v. *Secretary of State for the Home Department* [2001] EWCA Civ 1139, paras. 30–2; *Ghaidan* v. *Godin-Mendoza* [2004] UKHL 30, para. 19; *Naik* v. *Secretary of State for the Home Department* [2011] EWCA Civ 1546, para. 48.

[10] For a recent discussion of the ways in which US courts dilute standards of adjudication, see I. Cram, 'Failing Justice Brennan's Quest? Anticipating Terrorism Risks and the US Supreme Court' (2013) *Public Law* 30.

[11] Arguably, the UK Supreme Court in *Secretary of State for the Home Department* v. *AP* [2010] UKSC 24, effectively wrote in a new exception to Art. 5; while Lord Hoffmann in *Secretary of State for the Home Department* v. *MB; Same* v. *AF* [2007] UKHL 46, effectively wrote in an exception to Art. 6. See Chapter 13 in this volume, H. Fenwick, 'Post 9/11 UK counter-terrorism cases in the European Court of Human Rights: a "dialogic" approach to rights protection or appeasement of national authorities?'; and H. Fenwick and G. Phillipson, 'Covert Derogations and Judicial Deference: Redefining Liberty and Due Process Rights in Counterterrorism Law and Beyond' (2011) 56 *McGill Law Journal* 863.

(2) at the rights limitation stage: skipping one or more stages of the proportionality test[12] or watering down the proportionality exercise into a reasonableness or fair balance test;[13]

(3) at the rights limitation stage: asking the litigant to prove that a rights limitation is disproportionate rather than insisting that the government bears the onus of justifying a rights limitation; or sanctioning a rights limitation even if the government is unable to establish that the limitation is on balance proportionate;[14]

(4) at any stage, giving weight to the government's case on the basis of insufficient or insufficiently cogent evidence or reasons.

The notion of 'cogent reasons' in point 4 requires a little more explanation. As I have proposed elsewhere, a distinction can be drawn between first-order, substantive reasons and second-order, institutional reasons.[15] First-order reasons are those relating to the merits of the particular case in question, based on which the court makes its own determination of rights. Second-order reasons are concerns of, say, institutional capacity, which do not influence the court's own determination of rights, but which function as 'reweighting reasons'; if the court defers to the government on second-order grounds, it will be treating the government's

---

[12] See e.g., *R (on the application of Louis Farrakhan)* v. *Secretary of State for the Home Department* [2002] EWCA Civ 606.

[13] For cases in the immigration context, see *Ismet Ala* v. *Secretary of State for the Home Department*, paras. 41–4; *Mahmood* v. *Secretary of State for the Home Department* [2001] 1 WLR 840, para. 37; *Samaroo* v. *Secretary of State for the Home Department* [2001] EWCA Civ 1139, paras. 19–20, 30–3.

[14] See e.g., *R (on the application of Louis Farrakhan)* v. *Secretary of State for the Home Department* [2002] EWCA Civ 606, para. 79. Also *Secretary of State for the Home Department* v. *Rehman* [2001] UKHL 47, where the court did not require the government to show on balance that deporting the litigant was conducive to the public good. See *A* v. *Secretary of State for the Home Department* [2005] 2 AC 68, para. 154, where Lord Scott granted the government's assessment that there was a public emergency threatening the life of the nation despite having 'very great doubt'.

[15] The following explanation is adapted from C. Chan, 'Deference, Expertise and Information-Gathering Powers' (2013) 33(4) *Legal Studies* 598 and Chan, 'Proportionality and Invariable Baseline Intensity of Review', n. 6 above, 12–13. See A. Kavanagh, 'Defending Deference in Public Law and Constitutional Theory' (2010) 126 *Law Quarterly Review* 222, 230; S. Perry, 'Second-order Reasons, Uncertainty and Legal Theory' (1988–89) 62 *Southern California Law Review* 913; J. Raz, *Practical Reasons and Norms* (London: Hutchison, 1975), ch. 1. For an explanation of what 'cogent and sufficient reasons' require, see P. Daly, '*Wednesbury*'s Reason and Structure' (2011) *Public Law* 237, 251–3.

case as stronger than what the court, on its own balance of first-order reasons, regards it to be.[16]

Both first- and second-order reasons, if properly founded, can qualify as cogent reasons for supporting the government's claims.[17] Yet second-order reasons do not count as cogent reasons if they are not supported by evidence. The government establishes its case solely with first-order reasons of institutional competence when it can adduce reasons and evidence to persuade the court that it is correct on the merits of the case. It relies on second-order reasons of superior *intelligence-gathering ability* when it claims that there is useful information to support its case but it cannot disclose such information to the court. It relies on second-order claims of superior *expertise* when it claims that it has *general* expertise in deciding the *kind* of issue in question (e.g. national security matters) but is unable to persuade the court on the merits of the *particular case in question*. These second-order claims can only be validly established if the government institution can adduce evidence, such as its institutional features and past performance, to show that it indeed possesses the said general expertise or useful intelligence. If a court grants second-order claims without testing their evidential basis, it would be granting *mere assertions* or *presumptions* about the government's superior institutional competence, which may turn out to be false (the likelihood that they are false in national security matters is buttressed by the intelligence failures that have been recently exposed) and not to qualify as cogent second-order reasons.[18]

The form of deference in point 4 above precisely counsels courts to give weight to these untested assertions and presumptions. This form of deference was exhibited in *Farrakhan*[19] and *Gillan*,[20] where the courts

---

[16] Perry, 'Second-order Reasons, Uncertainty and Legal Theory', n. 15 above, 932; Kavanagh, 'Defending Deference in Public Law and Constitutional Theory', n. 15 above, 233.

[17] The following explanation is adapted from Chan, 'Proportionality and Invariable Baseline Intensity of Review', n. 6 above, 12–13.

[18] Presumptions of superior institutional competence may be based on Parliament having granted an institution powers to make certain decisions, or traditional assumptions of what realms fall within the government's exclusive competence. For challenges to presumptions about the government's superior institutional competence in making national security judgements, see e.g., D. Feldman, 'Human Rights, Terrorism and Risk: the Roles of Politicians and Judges' (2006) *Public Law* 364, 377–84.

[19] *R (on the application of Louis Farrakhan)* v. *Secretary of State for the Home Department* [2002] EWCA Civ 606, para. 78.

[20] *R (on the application of Gillan)* v. *Metropolitan Police Commissioner* [2006] 2 AC 307, paras. 62–4.

accepted without question the government's assertion that it possessed useful intelligence that could not be revealed. It was also displayed by the majority of the House of Lords in *Belmarsh*.[21] When deciding whether there was an emergency threatening the life of the nation, the majority judges granted the government's assessments in part because they presumed that the government possessed general expertise in making national security judgements. The majority did not explain why they granted the existence of such expertise notwithstanding 'widespread scepticism ... [over] intelligence assessments since the fiasco over Iraqi weapons'.[22] In these cases, the court added weight to the government's case on the basis of insufficiently cogent second-order reasons.[23]

In contrast, the business-as-usual approach insists that the normal rules of human rights adjudication apply with equal force even when national security matters are involved.[24] Courts should show respect to the decision-making capabilities of the other branches of the government, but such respect has to be earned, even in the security context.[25] As in other human rights cases, the court will only defer to the executive or legislature if these latter institutions can persuade the court that they are correct. The court shows respect by accepting the convincing arguments of these institutions.[26]

[21] *A v. Secretary of State for the Home Department* [2005] 2 AC 68, para. 154, where Lord Scott granted the government's assessment that there was a public emergency threatening the life of the nation despite having 'very great doubt'.

[22] *Ibid.* paras. 26, 29, 94, 116, 154, 166, 226.

[23] Excessive deference on the question of whether a public emergency exists is not unique to UK courts. See e.g., Gross and Ni Aolain, *Law in Times of Crisis*, n. 3 above, pp. 265–304; O. Gross and F. Ni Aolain, 'From Discretion to Scrutiny: Revisiting the Margin of Appreciation Doctrine in the Context of Article 15 of the European Convention on Human Rights' (2003) 23(3) *Human Rights Quarterly* 625; S. Marks, 'Civil Liberties at the Margin: the UK Derogation and the European Court of Human Rights' (1995) 15 *Oxford Journal of Legal Studies* 69, for accounts of the wide margin of appreciation accorded by the European Court of Human Rights in the parallel context.

[24] See e.g., *Al Rawi v. Security Service* [2011] UKSC 34; *HM Treasury v. Mohammed Jabar Ahmed* [2010] UKSC 2; *Secretary of State for the Home Department v. AF* [2009] UKHL 28; *Naik v. Secretary of State for the Home Department* [2011] EWCA Civ 1546, per Carnwath LJ.

[25] M. Hunt, 'Sovereignty's Blight: Why Public Law needs "Due Deference"' in N. Bamforth and P. Leyland (eds.), *Public Law in a Multi-Layered Constitution* (Oxford: Hart, 2003), p. 337; A Tomkins, 'National Security and the Role of the Court: A Changed Landscape?' (2010) 126 *Law Quarterly Review* 543, 567.

[26] Allan offers a sophisticated argument on why normal rules of adjudication can accommodate institutional concerns and there is no need for courts to defer on second-order grounds. T. R. S. Allan, 'Human Rights and Judicial Review: a Critique of "Due

The business-as-usual approach, *as currently practised* by courts, does not promote judicial reliance on second-order reasons, whether validly established or not. Judges adopting the approach only defer to the conclusions of the executive or legislature, insofar as these institutions can adduce persuasive first-order arguments, tailored to the circumstances of the case.[27] Nevertheless, as will be explained below, the rules of human rights adjudication do not rule out reliance on validly established second-order reasons. Such reasons therefore represent an untapped resource in the business-as-usual approach for accommodating concerns about the court's institutional limits.

There are thus two radically different approaches among the UK judiciary towards deference in counter-terrorism rights review. One advocates attenuating the usual standards of human rights adjudication in these cases, while the other advocates running business as usual. In particular, the dilution approach is ready to accept second-order claims of superior institutional competence even if these claims are not established by evidence, whereas the business-as-usual approach, *as practised*, does not advance judicial reliance on second-order reasons.

II   Case for running business as usual

The choice between the two approaches must be made within the constitutional framework of the HRA. This framework consists of the ethos and text of the European Convention on Human Rights (ECHR) and the HRA, as well as constitutional expectations regarding the rules of human rights adjudication and the role of courts. I argue that such framework mandates the business-as-usual approach, for two reasons.

First, the texts of the ECHR and HRA and constitutional expectations surrounding these instruments have already provided guidelines on how courts should strike the balance between national security and

---

Deference'" (2006) 65 *Cambridge Law Journal* 671; T. R. S. Allan, 'Judicial Deference and Judicial Review: Legal Doctrine and Legal Theory' (2011) 127 *Law Quarterly Review* 96.
[27] In addition to cases at n. 24 above, see *Abu Qatada* v. *Secretary of State for the Home Department* (Appeal no. SC/15/2005), SIAC, 12 November 2012; *W (Algeria) and BB (Algeria)* v. *Secretary of State for the Home Department* [2012] UKSC 8; *Hilal Abdul-Razzaq Ali Al-Jedda* v. *Secretary of State for the Home Department* [2012] EWCA Civ 358; *Secretary of State for the Home Department* v. *FV (Italy)* [2012] EWCA Civ 1199; *A* v. *Secretary of State for the Home Department* [2005] 2 AC 68, on the issue of whether the measure was proportionate. The conception of deference in these judgments is similar to that embraced by Allan.

human rights.[28] Setting aside or diluting these prescriptions in times of stress violates constitutional principles. Let us first examine the text of the ECHR, before examining constitutional expectations. The text contains two general prescriptions, both of which are premised on the normative significance of human rights. The first is that rights should be given procedural priority (albeit to different degrees) over competing public interests.[29] For instance, the right to freedom from torture in Article 3 is absolute. Some rights are qualified and can be limited, but only to the extent 'necessary in a democratic society' to pursue certain public interests. National security is explicitly recognised as a legitimate interest for curbing rights in Articles 8, 10 and 11. Some other rights, such as those in Articles 1, 4 and 5, are unqualified and should be upheld unless one of the stated exceptions applies. These exceptions are specific and do not contain broad exemptions like 'where necessary in the interests of national security'. The second textual prescription on how the balance between national security and rights should be struck is that the government can derogate from ECHR obligations only if threats to national security are so serious that the life of the nation is threatened; and even then derogations must only be to the extent strictly necessary (Article 15).

Admittedly these textual guidelines are extremely general and do not prescribe the degree of deference that courts should accord in implementing such guidelines. Article 15, for instance, does not stipulate the degree of deference that courts should give the government in determining whether there is a public emergency and whether a derogation is necessary.[30] Nonetheless, it is important to reiterate the basic textual prescriptions, as judges have sometimes diluted legal standards to such an extent that even the plain text has been violated. For instance, as will be illustrated below, by reading in broad exceptions to unqualified rights such as Article 5, some courts have blatantly violated the text of the HRA. Also, arguably, some courts have defied the text of Article 15 when granting the existence of a public emergency where there was apparently no, or very weak evidence, supporting such existence.[31]

---

[28] These prescriptions on when civil liberties are to be curtailed amount to what Gearty calls the first paradox of civil liberties. C. Gearty, *Civil Liberties* (Oxford University Press, 2007), p. 32.

[29] S. Greer, 'Constitutionalizing Adjudication under the European Convention on Human Rights' (2003) 23 *Oxford Journal of Legal Studies* 405.

[30] This vagueness has been manipulated by courts to accord a wide margin of appreciation to states. See nn. 21–3 above.

[31] For examples see nn. 21–3 above.

In addition, the HRA has ushered in constitutional expectations of further rules for striking the balance between national security and rights in the United Kingdom. These further rules of adjudication have been outlined in the previous section and the judiciary has unequivocally accepted that these are the rules of the game in the post-HRA era.[32] Like the express prescriptions in the HRA, these rules are also premised on the normative significance of rights and are skewed in favour of rights. For instance, the onus on the government to show that rights limitations are justified exemplifies the normative weight of rights 'where the cases for and against finding a rights violation are equally strong or it is uncertain which side is stronger'.[33] Besides, since rights are important, limitations thereon must be proportionate. Further, the HRA has ushered in a 'culture of justification'.[34] Under such culture, courts are no longer expected to take the government on blind trust and must require the government to demonstrate its claims with cogent and sufficient evidence.[35]

These prescriptions, whether introduced through the text of the ECHR or constitutional expectations, are not intended to be 'fair weather' rules and should apply with equal force even in times of stress. A number of points support this stance. First, the ethos of the ECHR is to lay down a moral order that European states should follow even when under threat.[36] This is obvious once we consider the timing of the ECHR's birth: the ECHR was introduced as a response to the egregious affronts to human dignity committed by Nazi Germany during the Second World War. The ECHR was an attempt to entrench basic values of democracy – values that are so fundamental that they attract substantial normative weight even in times of peril.[37] The HRA is an express recognition of

---

[32] See nn. 6–9 above; Chan, 'Proportionality and Invariable Baseline Intensity of Review', n. 6 above, sections 3–4.

[33] Chan, 'Proportionality and Invariable Baseline Intensity of Review', n. 6 above, 8; A. Barak, *Proportionality: Constitutional Rights and Their Limitations* (Cambridge University Press, 2012), pp. 443–6.

[34] For an exposition of what this culture requires see e.g., D. Dyzenhaus, 'Law as Justification: Etienne Mureinik's Conception of Legal Culture' (1998) 14 *South African Journal on Human Rights* 11.

[35] A similar point is made in Chapter 9 in this volume, R. Masterman, 'Rebalancing the unbalanced constitution: juridification and national security in the United Kingdom'. See Chan, 'Proportionality and Invariable Baseline Intensity of Review', n. 6 above, 7–8.

[36] Cf R. Dworkin, 'Terror and the Attack on Civil Liberties', *New York Review of Books*, 6 November 2003.

[37] See E. Bates, *The Evolution of the European Convention on Human Rights* (Oxford University Press, 2010), ch. 1 and Part 1.

these values as an indispensable part of British democracy, and can be considered a constitutional 'pre-commitment' to these values. As with all other constitutional pre-commitments, they are most important in times of emergency, when the temptation to discard them seems strongest.[38] As Koh argues, modern terrorism does not put us 'back to a state of nature in which there are no laws'.[39] The HRA and ECHR are a 'system of domestic and international laws', developed '*precisely* so that they will be consulted and obeyed, not ignored, at a time like this'.[40] Disrespecting these rules in times of crisis falls foul of the very philosophy of the Convention.

Besides, although the HRA came into force shortly after 11 September 2001 ('9/11'), still, when it was enacted, Parliament clearly envisaged that it would be used to vet counter-terrorist measures. This is not surprising given that the UK government has had much experience fighting terrorist violence in Northern Ireland. Parliamentary debates over the Human Rights Bill and counter-terrorism Bills introduced at about the same time, contain discussions on the compatibility of counter-terrorist measures with the ECHR, decisions of incompatibility handed down by Strasbourg, and the constraints that the HRA would pose on the 'War on Terror'.[41] Ironically, that Parliament enacted derogations in accordance with the ECHR, along with the passing of the HRA, demonstrated its intention, from day one, to subject counter-terrorist initiatives to the regulatory framework of the HRA.

Finally, in pronouncing the rules of adjudication under the HRA, courts have never carved out particular contexts that would be exempt from these rules. In fact, judges who adopted the dilution approach did not openly admit that they were diluting the standards of human rights adjudication in national security cases; rather, they dressed up the

---

[38] Cf. D. Cole, 'The Poverty of Posner's Pragmatism: Balancing away Liberty after 9/11' (2007) 59(6) *Stanford Law Review* 1735.

[39] H. H. Koh, 'The Spirit of the Laws' (2002) 43 *Harvard International Law Journal* 23, cited in A. Barak, 'A Judge on Judging: the Role of a Supreme Court in a Democracy' (2002) 116(16) *Harvard Law Review* 19, 151.

[40] Cf. *ibid.* Emphasis added.

[41] See e.g., On the Human Rights Bill 1998, HL Debs, vol. 582, cols. 1253–63, 3 November 1997; HL Debs, vol. 577, cols. 1737–55, 5 February 1997; HC Debs, vol. 306, cols. 768–73,16 February 1998; HC Debs, vol. 314, col. 1128, 24 June 1998; On the Prevention of Terrorism (Temporary Provisions) Act 1989 (Partial Continuance) Order 1998, HL Debs, vol. 587, cols. 201–6, 10 March 1998; HC Debs, vol. 307, cols. 1261–2, 5 March 1998; On the Criminal Justice (Terrorism and Conspiracy) Bill, HC Debs, vol. 317, col. 747, 2 September 1998.

dilution exercise in the cloak of 'relaxing the *intensity* of review', trying to create the illusion that the standards of review remain intact. This suggests that even these judges are aware that such standards should apply in counter-terrorism rights cases as well.

To summarise the first reason for supporting the business-as-usual approach: the HRA has laid down rules governing how the balance between national security and human rights should be struck. These prescriptions are designed to regulate exactly the kind of difficult balance that the government has to strike when concerns over terrorism are heightened. It would defeat the logic of the HRA and constitutional expectations to suspend or dilute these rules 'at the first sign of stress'.[42] These rules should therefore apply with equal force even when terrorism strikes.

The second reason for supporting the business-as-usual approach relates to the constitutional role of courts under the HRA. The HRA represents Parliament's endorsement of courts acting as guardians of rights. The Act is the first express parliamentary mandate for courts to review executive and legislative acts for compatibility with ECHR rights, and in cases of incompatibility, to strike down executive acts or issue declarations of incompatibility against legislative acts.[43] The judiciary is entrusted to perform a checks-and-balances function against unwarranted rights intrusions (subject to Parliament's powers to disregard a declaration of incompatibility), not least because of its independence and professionalism.[44] This constitutional role of the courts has been affirmed over and again by judges.[45]

The responsibility of courts to guard rights is not affected by the context of litigation. The fact that a human rights claim is raised in the national security context does not absolve the case from being one in

---

[42] K. D. Ewing, *Bonfire of the Liberties* (Oxford University Press, 2010), p. vii.

[43] See J. Jowell, 'Judicial Deference and Human Rights: A Question of Competence' in P. Craig and R. Rawlings (eds.), *Law and Administration in Europe: Essays in Honour of Carol Harlow* (Oxford University Press, 2003), p. 67; J. Jowell, 'Judicial Deference: Servility, Civility or Institutional Capacity?' (2003) *Public Law* 592; M. Elliott, *The Constitutional Foundations of Judicial Review* (Oxford: Hart, 2001), ch. 6.

[44] For why courts are suited to guard rights, see e.g., Feldman, 'Human Rights, Terrorism and Risk', n. 18 above.

[45] See e.g., *International Transport Roth GmbH* v. *Secretary of State for the Home Department* [2003] QB 728, para. 27; *Naik* v. *Secretary of State for the Home Department* [2011] EWCA Civ 1546, paras. 46–48, 64; *A* v. *Secretary of State for the Home Department* [2005] 2 AC 68, paras. 42–4; Chan, 'Proportionality and Invariable Baseline Intensity of Review', n. 6 above, 7.

which a potential violation of rights is at stake. Where something as important as a detainee's liberty or a terrorist suspect's right to fair trial is at risk, courts should scrutinise proposed encroachments intensely, applying the rules of adjudication that seek to recognise the value of rights. If anything, the imperative to guard against unwarranted rights intrusions might even be stronger when counter-terrorist measures are being reviewed, given that encroachments on human rights are most likely to occur in times of emergency.[46] If courts adulterate the standards of human rights adjudication in national security cases, they would abdicate their role to defend rights where such role is most needed, violating the ethos of the Convention to instigate a control mechanism over our cherished rights and liberties.[47]

III   Rebutting the case for diluting standards

In the following section, I will address three arguments that have been raised to support the dilution approach. The first is an argument from prudence and democratic legitimacy; the second is an argument about the scope of rights; and the third, an argument from institutional capacity. I will demonstrate that the first two arguments are unconvincing, and concerns expressed in the third argument, while valid, can be fully accommodated within the business-as-usual model.

(a)   The stakes are too high

The argument is that there are life-and-death consequences to national security decisions. As a matter of prudence, courts should err on the side of safety, deferring to the government whenever they are in doubt.[48] As a

---

[46] See e.g., F. de Londras, *Detention in the 'War on Terror': Can Human Rights Fight Back?* (Cambridge University Press, 2011) for an account of how panic affects counter-terrorism decision-making. See also C. Gearty, *Civil Liberties* (Oxford University Press, 2007), pp. 49–58, where Gearty analysed the results of a survey conducted in 2005 showing that the public was more willing to curtail civil liberties when security was threatened.

[47] See E. Bates, *The Evolution of the European Convention on Human Rights*, n. 37 above; J. Jowell, 'Judicial Deference: Servility, Civility or Institutional Capacity?', n. 43 above; Elliott, *The Constitutional Foundations of Judicial Review*, n. 43 above. See also Chapter 11 in this volume, G. Phillipson, 'Deference and dialogue in the real-world counter-terrorism context', who puts forward a convincing account of the crucial 'complementary' role that courts play in counter-terrorism rights review.

[48] A. Kavanagh, *Constitutional Review under the UK Human Rights Act* (Cambridge University Press, 2009), p. 213.

matter of constitutional legitimacy, these decisions, 'with serious consequences for the community, require a legitimacy which can be conferred
only by ... the democratic process'.[49] Unelected judges lack the democratic mandate to decide such questions and should therefore give the
government more leeway by attenuating legal standards.[50]

My response is, first, in calculating how much national security concerns weigh in a case, courts as guardians of rights should be careful not
to overestimate the cost of failure. Decisions to limit rights are made 'in
conditions of high uncertainty'.[51] An assessment of what the consequences of relaxing the terms of a control order against a terrorist suspect
would be turns on predictions of human behaviour, analysis of patchy
intelligence and risk assessments. Thus, in a typical counter-terrorism
rights case, the *definite* violation of human rights is pitted against the
uncertain harm to national security.[52] Many judges that rely on the high
stakes argument suffer from what Sunstein calls the 'probability neglect',
focusing on the worst-case scenario of an erroneous decision against the
government and neglecting the improbability of such a scenario arising.[53]
However, rational decision-makers ought to discount the disastrous
consequences of failure with the (im)probability of the consequences
materialising in calculating the weight of national security concerns.

In addition, as has been widely acknowledged, the executive has vested
interests in playing up risks to national security.[54] It is incumbent on
courts to not take the government's claims on trust. Finally, when we
consider the nature and timing of judicial intervention and the host of
alternative measures that the government may take to contain a national

---

[49] *Secretary of State for the Home Department* v. *Rehman* [2001] UKHL 47, per Lord
Hoffmann, para. 62.

[50] For academic discussions of these arguments, see e.g., E. A. Posner and A. Vermeule,
Terror in the Balance (Oxford University Press, 2007) and E. A. Posner and A. Vermeule,
Executive Unbound: After the Madisonian Republic (Oxford University Press, 2010).

[51] See e.g., L. Zedner, 'Securing Liberty in the Face of Terror: Reflections from Criminal
Justice' (2005) 32(4) *Journal of Law and Society* 507, 512; Poole, 'Courts and Conditions
of Uncertainty in "Times of Crisis"', n. 1 above.

[52] See e.g., Zedner, 'Securing Liberty in the Face of Terror', n. 51 above, 522; Feldman,
'Human Rights, Terrorism and Risk', n. 18 above, 372.

[53] C. R. Sunstein, *Laws of Fear: Beyond the Precautionary Principle* (Cambridge University
Press, 2005), pp. 39–49.

[54] See e.g., Feldman, 'Human Rights, Terrorism and Risk', n. 18 above, 379; F. de Londras,
Detention in the 'War on Terror': Can Human Rights Fight Back?, n. 46 above, p. 19;
Gross and Ni Aolain, *Law in Times of Crisis*, n. 3 above, pp. 103–9, 221; L. Lustgarten and
I. Leigh, *In from the Cold: National Security and Parliamentary Democracy* (Oxford
University Press, 1994), pp. 18–21, Part V.

security threat, we have reasons to believe that it is unlikely that 'the textbook scenario of a catastrophe' would be 'bound to follow if the rights of suspects are upheld'.[55] The judicial process is often lengthy, giving the government ample time to gear up alternative measures for dealing with identified suspects. Walker rightly observed that 'the detainees from Belmarsh didn't walk free from Belmarsh prison' because they were 'immediately subjected to control orders'.[56]

My second response to the high stakes argument is that, *even if* the costs of failure are high, the HRA has already stipulated a framework for accommodating these costs, and courts would violate constitutional principles if they subvert this framework and invent alternative ways of accommodating these costs. It was observed above that the HRA does cater for national security concerns. The text accommodates the *varying weight* of national security concerns in two ways. Regarding qualified rights, the varying weight of national security interests can be factored in through the proportionality device, which contains an in-built sensitivity to the weight of competing interests. When the country is under grave national security threat, such that the cost of failure is high, the weight of national security concerns becomes heavier; counter-terrorist measures that would not have been proportionate in times of peace might then be found to be proportionate.[57] Secondly, when the cost of failure becomes so high that the life of the nation is threatened, the HRA provides an 'emergency exit' for the government: derogation from rights obliga-tions.[58] As explained, these arrangements reflect the ethos of the ECHR to protect fundamental values.

The HRA has therefore prescribed rules for striking the balance between potentially serious national security consequences and the protection of rights. Courts relinquish their responsibility to protect rights if they formu-late new rules (in the form of diluting legal standards) for re-striking the balance merely because they are afraid of facing the serious consequences that might ensue had they simply followed the prescribed rules. Courts will also be *double counting* the weight of national security concerns if they

---

[55] Zedner, 'Securing Liberty in the Face of Terror', n. 51 above.

[56] C. Walker, 'Intelligence and Anti-Terrorism Legislation in the United Kingdom' (2005) 44 *Crime, Law and Social Change* 387, 407.

[57] Gross and Ni Aolain described this manipulation of the flexibility of proportionality as a form of 'interpretative accommodation' or the soft version of the 'business as usual' model. Gross and Ni Aolain, *Law in Times of Crisis*, n. 3 above, p. 89.

[58] T. R. Hickman, 'Between Human Rights and the Rule of Law: Indefinite Detention and the Derogation Model of Constitutionalism' (2005) 68(4) *Modern Law Review* 655, 658.

enforce *both* the prescribed rules *and* their own rules on dilution, for example, counting the heavy weight of national security considerations once when diluting the structured proportionality test (according to courts' own rule on dilution), and counting such weight for a second time when *applying* the diluted proportionality test to see if the rights limitation is justified (according to the HRA's prescribed rule, i.e., accommodating the weight of national security concerns within the proportionality exercise).

My third reply is targeted at the argument derived from democratic legitimacy. We must distinguish the decision as to what measures to take to protect national security from the decision as to whether these measures are compliant with human rights. The former has always been a question for the government, pre- or post-HRA. However, the HRA authorised courts to determine the latter question, subject to Parliament's ultimate power to defy the courts' determination.[59] Courts are entrusted with this task precisely because they are unelected and thus free from majoritarian pressure. In reviewing counter-terrorist measures courts are handing down a decision over the second question, not the first. In saying this I am not denying that this judicial decision may be a highly political one, in the sense that it may require a choice between competing moral values.[60] Nor am I denying that such a judicial determination may have far-reaching ramifications for society and pose constraints on the government's policy-making powers. My point is exactly that the HRA provides a mandate for the court to decide, subject to Parliament's last word, what are essentially political questions.[61] When passing the HRA, parliamentarians were fully aware of the political nature and potentially serious repercussions of judicial decisions on rights.[62] Parliament had nonetheless proceeded to enact the HRA to enhance courts' powers to constrain majoritarian decision-making. This suggests express legislative approval of a constitutional order based on new power-sharing arrangements.[63]

---

[59] See Chapter 9 in this volume, R. Masterman, 'Rebalancing the unbalanced constitution: juridification and national security in the United Kingdom'. For an influential argument against deference on democratic grounds, see J. Jowell, 'Judicial Deference and Human Rights: A Question of Competence', n. 43 above, p. 67; Jowell, 'Judicial Deference: Servility, Civility or Institutional Capacity?', n. 43 above.

[60] D. Nicol, 'Law and Politics after the Human Rights Act' (2006) *Public Law* 722, 723.

[61] *Ibid.*; cf. J. A. G. Griffith, 'The Political Constitution' (1979) 42(1) *Modern Law Review* 1.

[62] For examples, see n. 41 above.

[63] Roger Masterman argues that the HRA has 'gone some way to establishing a new constitutional equilibrium', see Chapter 9 in this volume, R. Masterman, 'Rebalancing the unbalanced constitution: juridification and national security in the United Kingdom'.

Courts should not evade making decisions on rights that may have life-and-death consequences, as their powers to do so have an entirely democratic basis.

(b) Scope of rights reduced in times of crisis

This argument may be raised to justify redefining rights or reading in new exceptions to unqualified rights when national security is endangered. The argument goes that both security and liberty are valuable goods and there is a necessary trade-off between the two.[64] Courts should try to arrive at a joint level of security and liberty that maximises the total welfare of the community. When security concerns become weighty, courts are justified in reducing the scope of individual rights by, say, redefining rights or reading in new exceptions to unqualified rights, in order to maximise total welfare.[65] As a matter of fact, courts sometimes reduce the scope of rights when security is at risk, as can be seen from judgments that sanction in times of crisis curtailments of rights that would not have been acceptable in normal times.

The main problem with this line of reasoning is that judicial decision-making is not a freewheeling ad hoc balancing act; instead, it is constrained by constitutional (or quasi-constitutional) text and settlements.[66] If the HRA has stipulated exhaustive exceptions to unqualified rights, and has expressly *not* specified exceptions grounded in national security, courts are not free to read in the latter exceptions even if they believe that allowing these exceptions would maximise welfare. Reading in new exceptions to unqualified rights like Articles 5 and 6 of the ECHR circumvents the rigorous scrutiny that derogations should pass under Article 15,[67] and is flagrant disrespect for the constitutional order that Parliament has established. If society believes that there should be new exceptions to the rights to liberty or fair trial, such

---

[64] Posner and Vermeule, *Terror in the Balance*, n. 50 above, p. 21.

[65] *Ibid.* p. 27; R. A. Posner, *Not a Suicide Pact: the Constitution in a Time of National Emergency* (Oxford University Press, 2006), p. 40.

[66] Cole, 'The Poverty of Posner's Pragmatism', n. 38 above, p. 1746.

[67] H. Fenwick and G. Phillipson, 'Covert Derogations and Judicial Deference', n. 11 above, p. 906; see also L. Lustgarten and I. Leigh, *In from the Cold*, n. 54 above, p. 359 and see Chapter 13 in this volume, H. Fenwick, 'Post 9/11 UK counter-terrorism cases in the European Court of Human Rights: a "dialogic" approach to rights protection or appeasement of national authorities?'.

changes should be effected through the signing of a new Protocol to the ECHR, not judicial creation.[68]

The *scope* and *definition* of an unqualified right should not fluctuate with the weight of countervailing considerations. Otherwise, the *raison d'être* of unqualified rights, namely, that these are rights that should not be limited, would be defeated. If a sixteen-hour curfew is considered as a deprivation of liberty during peaceful times, it should likewise be so considered when terrorism strikes. Lord Brown rightly observed in *JJ* that the 'borderline between deprivation of liberty and restriction of liberty of movement cannot vary according to the particular interests sought to be served by the restraints imposed. The siren voices urging that it must be shifted to accommodate today's need to combat terrorism (or even that it be drawn with such need in mind) must be firmly resisted. Article 5 ... is absolute'.[69] The opponent's observation that courts sometimes reduce the scope of rights when national security is imperilled may be accurate insofar as it relates to unqualified rights; yet even if it is, it only goes to show that an unjustified judicial practice exists, not that the practice is justified.

What *should* change as the level of threat to national security rises is the *degree of limitation* allowed regarding *qualified* rights. I have explained above that the HRA accommodates the varying weight of national security considerations by allowing such considerations to justify proportionate restrictions on rights. The weight of national security concerns is fed into the proportionality enquiry, resulting in the opponent's observation that courts sometimes sanction curtailments of rights in times of danger that would not have been justified in peaceful times. However, the opponent's interpretation of this phenomenon as courts diminishing the scope of rights in times of crisis, insofar as it relates to qualified rights, does not accurately reflect the conception of rights instituted by the HRA. This conception sees qualified rights as *prima facie* rights that can be restricted in certain circumstances, rather than rights whose *scope* is delimited by competing considerations.[70] According

---

[68] D. Feldman, 'Deprivation of Liberty in Anti-Terrorism Law' (2008) 67(1) *Cambridge Law Journal* 4, 8.

[69] *Secretary of State for the Home Department* v. *JJ* [2007] 3 WLR 642, para. 107.

[70] For these two conceptions of rights, see e.g., John Oberdiek, 'Specifying Rights Out of Necessity' (2008) 28(1) *OJLS* 127; Mattias Kumm, 'Who is Afraid of the Total Constitution? Constitutionalising Rights as Principles and the Constitutionalisation of Private Law' (2006) 7(4) *German Law Journal* 341; Grégoire C. N. Webber, *The Negotiable Constitution* (Cambridge University Press, 2009).

to this conception, what changes in times of danger is not the scope of qualified rights but the degree of limitation sanctioned by the proportionality machinery.

(c) Lack of institutional competence

The argument here is that national security decisions involve risk assessments and intelligence information.[71] Due to the sensitive nature of the issues, inevitably the government will not always be able to adduce all the first-order evidence required to prove its national security judgements. When the government is unable to do so, the court may lack the information and expertise to determine some, usually *factual*, national security issues. Courts may then be uncertain of the answers to *legal* questions asked under normal standards of adjudication. In these situations, courts should dilute the usual legal standards in order to accommodate the government's presumably superior institutional capacity to address the issues in question.

This argument can be illustrated with an example. Assume the court has to decide whether the government's barring of the litigant, on national security grounds, from entering the United Kingdom to address an audience violates the freedom of expression. In the normal run of human rights cases, the court would only sanction the measure if the latter passes the various stages of the proportionality enquiry, including the 'no more than necessary' test. However, in determining the legal question of whether the bar is no more than necessary, the court needs to engage in the factual enquiry of what level of threat is presented by allowing the litigant to speak in the United Kingdom. The government claims that it possesses non-discloseable intelligence that shows that the litigant is a terrorist and allowing him to speak here would jeopardise national security. The court, apparently suffering from an information gap, is unable to determine whether the bar is no more than necessary. Its only rational response is therefore to defer. It can defer by skipping the 'no more than necessary' stage of the proportionality test or watering down the test to one of reasonableness; or, if the cases for and against finding that the ban is proportionate is finely balanced, or the court does not know which side is stronger, the court can defer by giving the

---

[71] For discussions on this argument see e.g., Kavanagh, *Constitutional Review under the UK Human Rights Act*, n. 48 above, p. 212; Posner and Vermeule, *Executive Unbound*, n. 50 above; Posner and Vermeule, *Terror in the Balance*, n. 50 above, ch. 1.

government the benefit of the doubt, relaxing the burden and standard of proof that the government should meet in normal circumstances. Deference can also be in the form of granting the government's claim that the bar is no more than necessary even though the government is unable to disclose enough first-order reasons to support its claim.

I do not dispute that courts may sometimes lack the requisite expertise and intelligence information to determine national security questions. The above arguments therefore exposed a weakness in the business-as-usual approach *as practised*: due to institutional limitations, where questions of national security are involved, courts' balance of first-order reasons may be indeterminate as to the answers to legal questions asked under regular rules of human rights adjudication.[72] By insisting on judicial consideration of first-order reasons only, courts that currently subscribe to the business-as-usual attitude fail to accommodate governmental expertise and intelligence-gathering capabilities that cannot be demonstrated by first-order evidence due to the sensitivity of the matter, and risk enforcing the 'wrong rights'.[73] For example, owing to limited expertise and access to information, the courts might have been wrong in saying that no compelling ground of public security existed in *FV (Italy)*;[74] or that the Libyan government's Memorandum of Understanding was unreliable in *AS & DD (Libya)*;[75] or that releasing certain intelligence information would not compromise UK-US intelligence relations in *Binyam Mohamed*.[76] Rationality demands courts to take into account the government's superior institutional abilities when in doubt. The dilution approach attempts to accommodate these superior abilities at the cost of violating our constitutional framework. Can courts take into account the government's superior institutional abilities without compromising constitutional principles?

IV   An alternative form of deference

The way out, I suggest, is to utilise an untapped resource within the business-as-usual approach: judicial consideration of second-order

---

[72] Chan, 'Deference, Expertise and Information-Gathering Powers', n. 15 above, section 2.
[73] A. L. Young, 'In Defence of Due Deference' (2009) 72(4) *Modern Law Review* 554, 576.
[74] *Secretary of State for the Home Department* v. *FV (Italy)* [2012] EWCA Civ 1199.
[75] *AS & DD (Libya)* v. *Secretary of State for the Home Department* [2008] EWCA Civ 289.
[76] *Binyam Mohamed* v. *Secretary of State for Foreign and Commonwealth Affairs* [2010] EWCA Civ 65.

reasons. I have proposed elsewhere[77] that when the court's own balance of first-order reasons is uncertain over an issue, the court should add weight to the government's case on the basis of the latter's second-order claims of superior institutional competence, but only if the government can openly establish such claims by evidence. The amount of weight to be added depends on how strong such evidence is. In the following section, I will first outline these suggestions, and then address some potential objections.

Let us first consider how my proposal can work regarding second-order claims of superior expertise. Courts should only trust that the government possesses general expertise in a particular kind of question (e.g. national security ones) if there is evidence showing that this is the case. Courts should look at the track records, powers, resources and accountability mechanisms of the government institution to assess whether it is likely to arrive at the right answer on a certain kind of question.[78] If the government institution has repeatedly made wrong judgements in the field, then courts should not grant the government's case on the basis that it possesses general expertise in the area.

Regarding intelligence-gathering powers, courts should only trust a government institution's conclusions made based on concealed evidence, if there is evidence showing that such institution is trustworthy. Courts should consider whether the government body's sources of intelligence and assessments based on that intelligence had been credible in the past and whether the body had been honest in claiming that useful intelligence could not be disclosed.[79] If the government institution had repeatedly exaggerated risks or lied about its information, then courts should not count on it this time.

The upshot is that past intelligence failures such as the Iraq fiasco should discredit the government's second-order claims of superior expertise and intelligence-gathering powers in making national security

---

[77] This proposal was first made in, and the following discussion is adapted from Chan, 'Deference, Expertise and Information-Gathering Powers', n. 15 above, sections 3–4.

[78] Public inquiries and independent reviewers may assist courts in evaluating the credibility of intelligence bodies and government institutions acting upon the information provided by these bodies. Chapters 7 and 8 in this volume are instructive in this regard, see J. Blackbourn, 'Independent reviewers as alternative: an empirical study from Australia and the United Kingdom' and K. Roach, 'Public inquiries as an attempt to fill accountability gaps left by judicial and legislative review'.

[79] C. Walker suggested ways of vetting intelligence in 'Keeping Control of Terrorists Without Losing Control of Constitutionalism' (2007) 59 *Stanford Law Review* 1395.

judgements.[80] If the government insists on relying on such second-order claims, it must find ways of showing that the systemic problems in the intelligence machinery revealed by its negative track record have been solved or are not relevant in the case in question.

Under my proposal, the government's superior institutional competence in national security matters will have to be proved rather than, as supporters of the dilution approach advocate, merely assumed. But to the extent that it *is* proved, courts should give it due weight. This mode of deference is consistent with all the rules of adjudication under the HRA. The court need not attenuate legal tests to accommodate the government's expertise – the government still bears the onus of justifying a rights limitation, including establishing the existence of second-order reasons that support the limitation; the government is still obliged to discharge that onus with cogent and sufficient first and/or second-order reasons, and is not allowed to get by with mere assertions or presumptions about its superior institutional abilities. In fact, this mode of deference is a part of ordinary judicial reasoning. Courts need to rely on expert evidence all the time. Courts would only (rightly) attach weight to the opinion of an expert witness if the latter's expertise is established by evidence such as qualifications and past performance. If an expert had frequently committed mistakes in his field or has a bad reputation, the court would discount the weight attached to his opinion. This rational process of establishing expertise should apply without exception when the alleged expert in question is a government institution, all the more when human rights are in jeopardy and in light of the scarred track records of our security agencies.

My proposal may be objected to on the basis that courts lack the constitutional legitimacy to question government institutions' credibility to determine national security questions, especially when Parliament has empowered these institutions to make such determinations. My response is that, as has been observed above, the HRA instituted changes in judicial roles and culture. While under the pre-HRA order it might have been orthodox for courts to blindly presume, based on statutes granting government institutions powers in wholesale areas, that these institutions had expertise in particular areas, this leap of faith is no longer

---

[80] Numerous scholars have suggested that bad track records of intelligence agencies should affect whether decision-makers should trust these agencies. See e.g., Cram, 'Failing Justice Brennan's Quest?', n. 10 above, 39; J. Tham, 'Parliamentary Deliberation and the National Security Executive: the Case of Control Orders' (2010) *Public Law* 79, 88.

countenanced under the culture of justification.[81] If the government wanted courts to give extra weight to its views by virtue of expertise and intelligence-gathering abilities that are not apparent from the case, then the government must demonstrate that these abilities exist. The changes in adjudicative roles and culture themselves have democratic roots: the HRA was enacted by Parliament and its surrounding constitutional settlements were generated by judges, the government, litigants and jurists.

My suggestions may also be objected to on the ground that it is methodologically difficult for courts to probe the past performance of national security institutions given the prominence of secrecy in the security context. Space prevents a detailed reply to this objection, which I have offered elsewhere.[82] The gist of my defence is as follows.

First, this objection may be true but even if it is it does not weaken my case. All I aimed to do was to highlight what courts *should* do when reviewing the compatibility of counter-terrorist measures with human rights, according to the constitutional principles developed under the HRA. Regardless of the methodological difficulties in counter-terrorism rights review, courts must not lose sight of the fundamental nature of these cases – review of a government's attempt to encroach basic human rights – and should abide by the rules of adjudication governing these cases. It does not follow from my arguments that deference will often be warranted in these cases. If the government fails to openly justify to the court its claims using available means (owing to the alleged demands of secrecy or otherwise), then the latter should simply not defer. The implication of my arguments might well be that deference is rarely justified in counter-terrorism contexts.

Secondly, the methodological difficulty should not be overestimated. There are ways of channelling information to the courts safely, such as using *in camera* or closed material proceedings.[83] Moreover, the sensitivity of intelligence information declines with time. The information needed to establish that a government institution's past national security

---

[81] Jowell, 'Judicial Deference and Human Rights', n. 43 above, 75, 80–1; see further n. 35 above.

[82] C. Chan, 'Deference, Expertise and Information-Gathering Powers', n. 15 above, 612–19.

[83] For example, Feldman and de Londras both argued that by virtue of special schemes that enable courts to see sensitive information, courts are in a good position to evaluate national security claims. See Feldman, 'Human Rights, Terrorism and Risk', n. 18 above, 379–82; F. de Londras, 'Guantanamo Bay: Towards Legality?' (2008) 71(1) *Modern Law Review* 36, 50.

judgements had been correct should be less sensitive than that needed to show that its judgement in the present case is correct. In any case, there are reasons to believe that currently the government is hiding more information than it needs to. Experience shows that the government will open up further with pressure. We must find creative ways to 'face down the securitocracy'.[84] If courts demand more by way of justification, they might discover that the government can in fact reveal more than they had ever imagined.

Conclusion

> The fact that terrorism presents new challenges ... does not mean that the basic moral principles ... have been repealed ... We must instead ask what *different scheme* ... is appropriate to respect those principles while still effectively defending ourselves.[85]

The dilution approach must be rejected as it violates the principles of the post-HRA constitutional order. On the other hand, the business-as-usual approach as practised does not adequately account for superior governmental capabilities in defending national security. This chapter seeks to outline a 'different scheme' by exposing unexploited potential in the business-as-usual approach: courts should apply principles of human rights adjudication faithfully even when national security questions are involved, but when in doubt courts should give weight to the government's second-order claims of superior institutional capabilities insofar as such claims are validly established. I hope I have shown that it is possible to reconcile the apparent conflict between the demands of justification under the HRA and the demands of secrecy in the battle against terrorism. At any rate, I hope I have unfolded an alternative to existing judicial approaches for consideration.

---

[84] C. Walker, 'The Threat of Terrorism and the Fate of Control Orders' (2010) *Public Law* 3, 5; Poole argued that courts should 'peer through the glass darkly', questioning the government's evidential basis wherever possible, Poole, 'Courts and Conditions of Uncertainty in "Times of Crisis"', n. 1 above.

[85] Dworkin, 'Terror and the Attack on Civil Liberties', n. 36 above (emphasis added).

Deference and dialogue in the real-world counter-terrorism context

GAVIN PHILLIPSON

Introduction

> The events of September 11 are a reminder that in matters of national security the cost of failure can be high. Decisions by ministers on such questions, with serious potential results for the community, therefore require a legitimacy, which can be conferred only by entrusting them to persons responsible to the community through the democratic process.

The quotation above might sound like an argument made by a political constitutionalist arguing for the necessary primacy of democratic controls, rather than judicial review, in the counter-terrorism context. In fact, the quote comes from the well-known *dicta* of Lord Hoffmann,[1] which were repeated by a Court of Appeal judge in the *Belmarsh* case,[2] who in turn was criticised for them by Keith Ewing,[3] a leading political constitutionalist – a paradox that we will return to below.

It is not necessary to repeat in the introduction to this chapter the well-known fact that counter-terrorism measures in the United Kingdom and elsewhere have resulted in some of the worst abuses of human rights in the last ten or twenty years or more, including indefinite detention and suspicion-less stop and search. Nor is it necessary to rehearse the familiar tendency of judges to defer in this area,[4] in a way that has at times come close to giving the executive *carte blanche*.[5] What is important to note is

---

[1] *Secretary of State for the Home Department, ex parte Rehman* [2003] 1 AC 153, para. 63.
[2] *A v. Secretary of State* [2002] EWCA Civ 1502, [2004] QB 335, para. 81.
[3] K. Ewing, 'The Futility of the Human Rights Act' (2004) *Public Law* 829, 841.
[4] For these points, see the Introduction to this volume, F. F. Davis and F. de Londras, 'Counter-terrorism judicial review: beyond dichotomies'.
[5] F. de Londras, *Detention in the 'War on Terror': Can Human Rights Fight Back?* (Cambridge University Press, 2011), p. 217, having in mind the two cases exemplifying deference as submission: *Korematsu v. United States*, 323 US 214 (1944) in the United States and *Liversidge v. Anderson* [1942] AC 206 in the United Kingdom; see also D. Dyzenhaus, *The Constitution of Law: Legality in a Time of Emergency* (Cambridge

that in addition to the constitutional, precedential reasons for continuing judicial self-abnegation in this area, there is a powerful moral one. Lord Hoffman makes a point that resonates with many: where the issues really are ones of life and death, surely only our elected representatives have the legitimacy to decide what is necessary to keep us safe and how far rights must be sacrificed in that end. So the pull of democratic legitimacy may seem stronger in this stark area, where lives are at stake, than in more esoteric and technical areas of human rights law. Evidently, at least some judges advert to this very keenly. However, it also remains a well-known fact that our elected representatives are all too likely to succumb to the 'essential attractiveness of the punitive response … as an [apparently] authoritative intervention to deal with a serious, anxiety-ridden problem. Such action confers the appearance that "something is being done" here, now, swiftly and decisively',[6] something that often seems an essential palliative care to the risk-obsessed society, panicked by terrorism and by the unknowable risks of future, perhaps worse atrocities.[7] The results can be seen in the torrent of counter-terrorism legislation produced in this and other countries in the last ten to fifteen years. Thus, a strong judicial role may be seen as harder to justify in this area due to the high stakes, but as simultaneously necessary because over-broad, panic-driven legislation remains the norm – an uncomfortable contradiction for the judiciary to grapple with.

There are further such tensions. When judges do *not* defer to executive and legislative determinations as to the necessity and efficacy of even the most draconian counter-terror measures, they can provoke enormous hostility. In the United States, Senator John McCain made an extraordinary attack upon the decision of the US Supreme Court in *Boumediene* v. *Bush,* which restored to Guantánamo Bay detainees the right of *habeas corpus,* describing it as 'one of the worst decisions in the history of this country'.[8] In the United Kingdom, widespread anger at the Human Rights Act 1998 (HRA) and the European Convention on Human Rights (ECHR) has been provoked for many

University Press, 2006), p. 17. See also Chapter 9 in this volume, R. Masterman, 'Rebalancing the unbalanced constitution: juridification and national security in the United Kingdom'.

[6] D. Garland, 'The Limits of the Sovereign State: Strategies of Crime Control in Contemporary Society' (1996) 36 *British Journal of Criminology* 131.

[7] See de Londras, *Detention in the War on Terror,* n. 5 above, ch. 1.

[8] See http://elections.foxnews.com/2008/06/13/mccain-guantanamo-ruling-one-of-the-worst-decisions-inhistory.

years by the blocking on human rights grounds of the deportation of the terrorist suspect Abu Qatada by both domestic courts and Strasbourg.[9] In general, the HRA 'has been repeatedly represented as an obstacle to required counter-terrorist action';[10] Prime Minister Cameron recently pledged to do 'whatever it takes' legally to enable the United Kingdom to 'chuck [non-nationals] out of our country who threaten our country'.[11] It is now formal Conservative Party policy for the next election to pledge repeal of the HRA, and Conservative Cabinet ministers now regularly call for the hitherto 'unthinkable' policy of outright withdrawal from the ECHR itself.[12] This may place judges under further pressure to self-abnegate, fearing that unwanted muscularity may lead to the wholesale dismantling of human rights law in the United Kingdom.

Judges may respond to these kinds of pressures by restraining themselves through doctrines of deference or non-justiciability when confronted by counter-terrorism law. But they are also sometimes deliberately pushed out of the picture by the executive (often by the statutes it hurries through parliaments): this may be done quite openly, as in the case of the 'legal black hole' that is Guantánamo Bay's detention centre, or more covertly with 'preventive' schemes, such as executive detention and control orders, which retain the appearance of judicial oversight while in reality gutting the basic notions of due process that would ordinarily protect those subject to such draconian powers.[13] And then there are the academic voices, calling for continued or even increased judicial restraint in the face of the alleged expertise of the

---

[9] John Reid, when Home Secretary, referred during a House of Commons (HC) debate to 'the *Chahal* judgment, an outrageously disproportionate judgment stating that we cannot deport a terrorist suspect if there would be any threat to him if he were sent abroad' (HC Debs, vol. 460, col. 433, 24 May 2007); this view also lay behind Tony Blair's repeated calls for a 'profound rebalancing of the civil liberties debate' as quoted in M. Tempest, 'PM calls for "rebalancing" of civil liberties debate', *Guardian*, 15 May 2006.

[10] See de Londras, *Detention in the 'War on Terror'*, n. 5 above, p. 215.

[11] 'Cameron: I'd withdraw from human rights convention "to keep UK safe"', *Guardian*, 29 September 2013, available at www.theguardian.com/politics/2013/sep/29/david-cameron-human-rights-convention.

[12] See e.g., the comments of Theresa May, the current Home Secretary, in March 2013, reported as 'Tories to consider leaving European Convention on Human Rights', available at www.bbc.co.uk/news/uk-politics-21726612.

[13] D. Dyzenhaus, 'Preventive Justice and the Rule-of-Law Project' in A. Ashworth, L. Zedner and P. Tomlin (eds.), *Prevention and the Limits of the Criminal Law* (Oxford University Press, 2013), p. 91.

national security executive,[14] or for the judicial role to be confined to one
of merely labelling extraordinary powers as extra-constitutional[15] and/or
sounding a purely advisory 'alarm bell', inviting the legislature to take
action – or not – in response to the situation.[16]

Judicial adjudication on anti-terror laws then, brings together some of
the gravest threats to human rights with the strongest legislative attempts
to limit the judicial role and due process (usually contained in rushed-
through and often panic-driven legislation); strident executive calls for
judicial review to play only the most 'marginal' role;[17] the claim that only
democratic representatives can legitimately decide when stakes are
so high; and a chorus of academic voices decrying or distrusting the
judicial role as a protector of threatened rights. For all these reasons,
then, we confront the discouraging paradox that, just in the area where it
may be most needed to check the gravest threats to basic rights, judicial
review may turn out to be at its weakest and most deferential: a phenomenon that then only redoubles the calls for it to be abandoned or scaled
back, given its claimed inefficacy, even counter-productiveness. While
recent cases from *Belmarsh*[18] onwards appear to have signalled some
kind of change of approach to judicial review in the national security
context, the depth and significance of that change remains fiercely
contested.[19]

Judicial deference or restraint is thus paradoxically both one of the
ways in which judicial review may seek to accommodate itself to the

---

[14] E. A. Posner and A. Vermeule, *Terror in the Balance: Security, Liberty and the Courts*
(Oxford University Press, 2007); B. Ackerman, *Before the Next Attack: Preserving Civil
Liberties in an Age of Terrorism* (Yale University Press, 2007).

[15] M. Tushnet, 'Civil Liberties in a Time of Terror: Defending *Korematsu*?: Reflections on
Civil Liberties in Wartime' (2003) *Wisconsin Law Review* 273.

[16] See e.g., F. Davis, 'The Human Rights Act and Juridification: Saving Democracy from
Law' (2010) 30(2) *Politics* 91 and Chapter 6 in this volume, F. F. Davis, 'The politics of
counter-terrorism judicial review: creating effective parliamentary scrutiny'.

[17] Joint Cases C-402/05P and C-415/05P *Yassin Abdullah Kadi and Al Barakaat Inter-
national Foundation* v. *Council of the European Union and Commission of the European
Communities*, Opinion of Advocate General Pioares Maduro (16 January 2008) [2008]
ECR I-6351.

[18] *A and others* v. *Secretary of State for the Home Department* [2005] 2 AC 68.

[19] Cf. the works cited in n. 93 of the Introduction to this volume, F. F. Davis and F. de
Londras, 'Counter-terrorism judicial review: beyond dichotomies', with e.g. Ewing and
Tham, 'after the excitement following the *Belmarsh* case, normal service appears thus to
have been resumed': K. Ewing and J. Tham, 'The Continuing Futility of the Human
Rights Act' (2008) 4 *Public Law* 668, 692; see also A. Tomkins, 'The Rule of Law in Blair's
Britain' (2008) *University of Queensland Law Review* 1, 28–30.

so-called counter-majoritarian objection to judicial review,[20] and one of the chief sources of criticism from political constitutionalists who voice that objection. The second method of accommodation considered in this chapter arises from the fact that, under so-called 'third wave' or 'New Commonwealth model' rights instruments, such as the Canadian Charter, UK HRA and New Zealand Bill of Rights Act (NZBRA), judicial rulings that legislation violates the protected rights are open to response or disregard by the democratic branches that (at least in theory) gives the legislature the last word on the rights issue.[21] Dialogic theory, at least in some variants, thus characterises such rulings not as definitive statements of the interpretation of the right in question and its requirements, but rather as the opening of a constitutional 'conversation' about these matters, which are assumed to be open to at least some degree of reasonable contestation by the democratic branches.

In this chapter I use 'dialogue' not in the original Canadian sense as denoting openness only to legislative responses,[22] but in the broader sense whereby the judiciary, in adjudicating upon rights questions may be seen as engaged in a 'continuing colloquy with the political institutions',[23] within which I emphatically include the executive, as well as the legislative branch of government. As will become apparent, I also reject the notion that a dialogic conception of the HRA implicitly excludes or views with hostility the use of the powerful interpretive tool in section 3 of that Act,[24] on the grounds that courts should use only the non-binding declarations of incompatibility

---

[20] As discussed in the Introduction to this volume, F. F. Davis and F. de Londras, 'Counter-terrorism judicial review: beyond dichotomies'.

[21] See e.g., J. Goldsworthy, 'Judicial Review, Legislative Override and Democracy' in T. Campbell (ed.), *Protecting Human Rights Instruments and Institutions* (Oxford University Press, 2003), p. 268; P. Yap, 'Defending Dialogue' (2012) *Public Law* 527, 544; S. Gardbaum, 'The New Commonwealth Model of Constitutionalism' (2001) 49 *American Journal of Comparative Law* 707.

[22] In which dialogue is defined as occurring 'if judicial decision is open to legislature reversal, modification or avoidance' (P. Hogg and A. Bushell, 'The Charter Dialogue between Courts and Legislatures (or Perhaps the Charter of Rights isn't Such a Bad Thing After All)' 1997 (35) *Osgoode Hall Law Journal* 75, 79.

[23] A. Bickel, *The Least Dangerous Branch: the Supreme Court at the Bar of Politics* (Yale University Press, 1986), p. 240. Yap contends that this is the 'premise' of dialogic theory: P. Yap, 'Defending Dialogue' (2012) *Public Law* 527, 540.

[24] The obligation to interpret and give effect to legislation compatible with the ECHR rights 'so far as is possible'. For this critique see A. Kavanagh, *Constitutional Review under the UK Human Rights Act* (Oxford University Press, 2009), p. 409.

in section 4.[25] Rather, I regard both simply as different kinds of potentially dialogic interaction. Nor in my view does the notion of dialogue as such suggest that Parliament should regard a section 4 declaration as no more than an interesting suggestion about what the right in question might mean or require – what Tom Hickman has dubbed the 'principle proposing' model of dialogue.[26] The broad church of dialogic review can also comfortably accommodate a vision of a more muscular judicial role, under which there should be 'a presumption that legislatures will abide by court decisions and not routinely ignore them' with an exception, after proper debate, for good-faith, reasonable disagreement on matters of principle.[27]

My purpose in this chapter is not to add to the burgeoning general literature on the concepts of deference and dialogue.[28] Rather, it has three more specific aims. First, it seeks to explain why dialogic instruments like the HRA constitute a pragmatic approach to the counter-majoritarian difficulty that has particular appeal in the counter-terrorism context. Secondly, it urges a more nuanced, balanced and constructive approach to engaging with judicial deference in this area than many critics currently take. Thirdly, it argues that judicial review and parliamentary scrutiny of legislation should generally be regarded as complementary rather than dichotomous or even mutually frustrating endeavours. It then proposes a 'complementary scrutiny' model, by showing how Parliament frequently and often necessarily *relies* on the judiciary in its attempts to enhance legislative safeguards for the vulnerable (as in the control orders saga) and arguing that in such cases, the remedial use of section 3 of the HRA is fully compatible with a dialogic approach to that Act. The chapter concludes by offering some preliminary thoughts on how a 'complementary scrutiny' model might work better in practice, harmonising the notions of due deference and dialogue.

---

[25] Such a declaration, according to HRA, s. 4(2)(b) 'does not affect the validity, continuing operation or enforcement of any incompatible primary legislation'.

[26] T. Hickman, 'Constitutional Dialogue, Constitutional Theories and the HRA 1998' (2005) *Public Law* 306.

[27] S. Gardbaum, 'Reassessing the New Commonwealth Model of Constitutionalism' (2010) 8(2) *International Journal of Constitutional Law* 167, 193. Such a view is close to the author's particular view of dialogue. While presenting Gardbaum as within a 'broad church' dialogic school I acknowledge his criticism of dialogic theory and argument that his own approach is more concerned with balance than dialogue.

[28] See Yap, 'Defending Dialogue', n. 21 above.

I 'Principled objection' to judicial review and three responses

The principled objection to judicial review of legislation has been can-vassed exhaustively elsewhere.[29] The argument in a nutshell is that Bills of Rights take decisions that should properly be reached by the people, through their elected representatives, out of Parliament and into the courtroom, and thereby amount to what Waldron terms 'a denial of participatory citizenship'.[30] People disagree about rights as they do about any other political issue and the only fair and respectful way to make decisions about rights questions is through democratic deliberation. As a general, broad argument, it certainly has appeal, perhaps for three main reasons. First, Dworkin notwithstanding, many of us are more sceptical than we used to be about foundationalist philosophical conceptions of rights yielding unarguably right answers to which everyone is rationally compelled to give respectful assent. Many tend nowadays to believe in more contested and provisional truths. Secondly, it is undeniable as a matter of fact that people disagree fiercely about the proper interpret-ation of rights – there are, for example, notorious and long-standing controversies over issues such as whether hate speech, pornography or tobacco advertising should be protected by free speech clauses. In the face of such enduring, good-faith disagreement, the notion that such argu-ments should be thrashed out through the democratic process rather than having solutions judicially imposed 'from on high' has undoubted intuitive appeal. Finally, we are all aware of bad decisions of consti-tutional courts, particularly in the United States, that reveal all too clearly the dangers of judicial supremacy.[31] As one scholar has colourfully put it, '[d]ialogic theory ... represents a concession that Ronald Dworkin's Hercules ... is no more than a myth'.[32]

There are responses to the principled objection that seek to answer it in its own terms. But instead of pursuing those here, let us assume instead that we accept it has some force. This, however, does not con-clude the matter, because this objection is not the only factor relevant to a human rights lawyer or thinker. Many of us would regard it as *a* consid-eration, but not the only, or even the dominant, one in designing a

---

[29] See e.g., J. Waldron, 'The Core of the Case Against Judicial Review' (2006) 115 *Yale Law Journal* 1346.

[30] C. O'Cinneide, 'Democracy, Rights and the Constitution: New Directions in the Human Rights Act Era' (2004) 57 *Current Legal Problems* 175, 177.

[31] For example *Citizens United* v. *Federal Election Commission*, 558 US 8 (2010).

[32] Yap, 'Defending Dialogue', n. 21 above, 544.

system of constitutional rights protection. In particular, if we also believe that judges are likely (to put it modestly) to make at least some useful contribution to the protection of the basic rights of particularly vulnerable and unpopular groups, such as terrorist suspects, then we may reasonably believe that this is a factor to weigh in the balance against the counter-majoritarian objection.[33]

Attempts to respond to this line of argument are twofold. The first rejoinder seeks to persuade us that judges in fact make little or no meaningful contribution to the protection of basic rights: the 'inefficacy argument', which I consider below. The second attempts to demonstrate why, even if judicial protection may sometimes lead to better outcomes, the principled objection should nonetheless trump it. Waldron has attempted to do this by arguing that the right to participate in the determination of rights questions is 'the right of rights',[34] since such deliberations will determine the content of all other rights. The argument then is that such a right 'cannot be traded off against minimizing the violation of other rights'.[35] As Waldron has put it, '[t]here is a certain dignity in participation and an element of insult and dishonour in exclusion *that transcends issues of outcome*'.[36]

This however, seems unconvincing on a number of levels. First, in contemporary states, and particularly Western European ones, the idea that 'the people' or, more realistically, our elected representatives, can determine the content of rights *de novo* is simply unrealistic. Such states are bound into a network of international law obligations that go a long

---

[33] See A. Kavanagh, 'Participation and Judicial Review: A Reply to Jeremy Waldron' (2003) 22 *Law and Philosophy* 451; A. Kavanagh, *Constitutional Review under the UK Human Rights Act*, n. 24 above, ch. 13; J. Raz, 'Disagreement in Politics' (1998) 43 *American Journal of Jurisprudence* 43.

[34] J. Waldron, 'A Right-based Critique of Constitutional Rights' (1993) 13 *Oxford Journal of Legal Studies* 18, 20.

[35] L. Alexander, 'Is Judicial Review Democratic?' (2003) 22 *Law and Philosophy* 277, 279. See Waldron, 'A Right-based Critique of Constitutional Rights', n. 34 above, 38.

[36] *Ibid.* 39 (emphasis added). In later work, Waldron has conceded that democratic protection alone will not work in all conditions: Waldron, 'The Core of the Case Against Judicial Review', n. 29 above, 1359–1659, advancing four preconditions for his theory to apply, the third of which, a commitment by most citizens and officials 'to the idea of minority rights' (1360), might be seen as qualifying the lexical priority rule by suggesting that substantive rights must not be sacrificed to too great a degree to satisfy the participation right. However, it seems clear that the United Kingdom, for example, *is* considered by Waldron to satisfy this condition, despite the policies regarding and attitudes towards torture and deportation-to-torture discussed in the text below. Hence, Waldron's third condition does not rule out my argument.

way towards determining those questions for us; moreover, and perhaps strangely, the rights sceptics do not seem to espouse our withdrawal from all human rights treaties and international systems of protection. Thus, in practice the democratic discussion of rights is constrained at least to some degree by the state's prior international commitments and cannot attain the lofty level of principle that theoretical accounts like Waldron's assume for it.

Secondly, while the notion that the right to participate in the determination of rights questions is the 'right of rights' has a kind of philosophical neatness to it, it starts to appear implausible when we take concrete examples.[37] Let us suppose that the democratic process determines that asylum seekers whom the government suspects of involvement in terrorism may be deported to countries in which they face a real risk of being tortured; or that asylum seekers should be discouraged from coming to the United Kingdom by denying them subsistence benefits if they do not claim asylum on entry so that they might starve to death or die of exposure.[38] This denial of rights, we are told, is categorically less important than the denial of the participatory rights of citizens to determine the human rights of asylum seekers that would be entailed by judges being given the power to stop either of these things happening. Even leaving aside the fact that many of the most draconian terrorist powers in recent years have been directed at non-citizens, who have no formal participation rights at all, this argument seems unconvincing. The actual human victims of such laws and policies, as we know, struggle desperately to assert their rights to a fair hearing, *not* to be sent back to torture, *not* to be left destitute. Upholding these rights is plainly of the most pressing concern to them. In contrast, large numbers of citizens do not bother to exercise the right that Waldron insists is, in abstract, more valuable – to participate actively in such decisions, by, for example, writing to their MP, blogging about politics or engaging in public protest. Around 40 per cent of the electorate do not even bother to vote at general elections. These well-known facts irresistibly suggest that, for many people, this procedural 'right of rights' is not particularly important to them, while for the actual or threatened victims of rights violations, their substantive rights are desperately important. Waldron's argument for the lexical priority of one over the other thus begins to seem rather unreal.

---

[37] See along similar lines, Yap, 'Defending Dialogue', n. 21 above, 533.

[38] On the latter issue, see Asylum and Immigration Act 2002, s. 55, judicially considered in *Limbuela* v. *Secretary of State for the Home Department* [2005] 3 WLR 1014.

And indeed, could anyone really argue that it is more important for a given individual to be able to participate in the democratic process that determines the legal definition of torture than it is for her not to be tortured?

The notion, then, that the right to participate should be categorically prioritised over other things we care deeply about, such as the treatment meted out to acutely vulnerable people, like terrorist suspects and asylum seekers, in the end seems to fail. In turn this means that *if* we have good reason to believe that judges (because they are largely insulated from populist, media driven pressure on these points) will at least *sometimes* do a better job at protecting the most basic rights of the vulnerable than Parliament would,[39] then we may sensibly argue that preventing these extraordinarily grave rights violations justifies or outweighs a minor denial of participation rights.

II   Treating the principled objection pragmatically

I have not sought in the above to argue that the principled objection has no merit. Rather, I have tried to show why many remain unpersuaded that it constitutes a conclusive, knock-down argument against judicial review. The pragmatic conclusion then results: since both legislatures and courts *can* make mistakes on issues of rights and have different strengths and weaknesses, why not seek to devise a system that allows for the input of *both* branches; for each to have the capacity to correct the mistakes of the other – or learn from their considered judgements? Most would agree that, on occasions, one institution works better than the other: it seems hard to deny the UK Parliament has generally been better at promoting equality, employment and labour rights than the courts. But it would seem hard to deny that in recent history the courts have done rather better at protecting the rights of unpopular minorities such as terror suspects and asylum seekers than Parliament;[40] indeed, one leading comparativist's assessment of rights instruments in Canada, New Zealand and the United Kingdom leads him to conclude that in each case there is no serious argument but that fundamental rights are more effectively protected than before those instruments were

---

[39] See e.g., Kavanagh, *Constitutional Review under the UK Human Rights Act*, n. 24 above, ch. 12.

[40] See G. Phillipson, 'Deference, Discretion, and Democracy in the Human Rights Act Era' (2007) 60 *Current Legal Problems* 40.

enacted.[41] Why not, then, seek to harness *both* institutions in the cause of defending rights? Such a course avoids the purist stance of putting all one's eggs into the single, idealised basket of either the 'Herculean' judge or the ever-wisely deliberating legislature. Instead, it takes a pragmatic, mid-way position – accepting *some* of the force of the principled objection, and some of the fear of bad judicial supremacism, but counter-poising those arguments with the belief that judges and courts *do* sometimes give protection that legislatures are unlikely to provide. Such a position seems to provide at least a rough-and-ready justificatory underpinning for the so-called 'New Commonwealth model'[42] or a 'dialogic' approach to rights protection.[43]

If the above argument is broadly accepted, the question then becomes whether such a model can work and what implications it has for the role of judges. It is in considering such questions that we must grapple with the second key argument, the *inefficacy* objection: that, because of their tendency to defer excessively to the executive, particularly in the national security arena, the judges simply cannot be trusted to protect civil liberties effectively – and may even make things worse.[44] Such an argument, if true, would cast strong doubt on even my modest pragmatic proposal, and therefore must be responded to.

III Rejecting one-eyed analysis

Before it is worthy of a full response, however, the argument must be put in fair terms; but this is not always the case. Sometimes the argument against judicial review is made simply by ignoring parliamentary failures in favour of focusing on judicial shortcomings. Thus, Keith Ewing has complained that, while liberty is indeed 'ill in Britain' it is paradoxical that 'the judges who have been identified as a potential cure for the illness . . . are partly responsible for the patient's malaise in the first place'.[45] But while he acknowledges in passing that liberty is partly also 'ill' because of some

---

[41] S. Gardbaum, 'Reassessing the New Commonwealth Model of Constitutionalism', n. 27 above, 178 (Canada), 187 (New Zealand) and 198 (United Kingdom).

[42] See Gardbaum, 'The New Commonwealth Model of Constitutionalism', n. 21 above.

[43] Cf. Tushnet's slightly different justification in M. Tushnet, 'The Hartman Hotz Lecture: Dialogic Judicial Review' (2008) 61 *Arkansas Law Review* 205, 212.

[44] An argument put most energetically in Ewing, 'The Futility of the Human Rights Act', n. 3 above and Ewing and Tham, 'The Continuing Futility of the Human Rights Act', n. 19 above.

[45] Ewing, 'The Futility of the Human Rights Act', n. 3 above, 833.

very bad legislation passed by Parliament, he sees no paradox in urging *that* partial cause of the malaise as the proposed cure for it.

For another example, consider the following argument:

> In an area of such political controversy as counter-terrorism, where the judicial record is littered with judgments that have empowered executives to abuse civil liberties, the legitimate role for the courts is to highlight the need for greater parliamentary scrutiny of the executive.[46]

Suppose we modified this statement to make it more factually accurate, so that it said 'where the judicial *and parliamentary records* are littered with decisions that have empowered the executive to abuse civil liberties', it would then sound rather less persuasive to argue that the correct conclusion to draw was to rely on greater parliamentary scrutiny. (If both branches of government have failed, why simply return scrutiny to one of them?) Ignoring half the evidential picture in order to reach the desired conclusion is not a satisfactory approach. In particular, it must be accepted that where there is a persistent record of Parliament acquiescing in the rushed passage of draconian anti-terrorism legislation (but sometimes making some minor improvements to it) and of an often disappointing judicial response to it (that has sometimes ameliorated it to some degree), it is simply not satisfactory to draw from this as a conclusion that the answer is to remove judicial scrutiny and rely on a Parliament that has performed relatively poorly in the first place. As I have previously argued, whereas the response of political constitutionalists to *legislative* failure (when acknowledged) 'is to roll up their sleeves and get to work suggesting improvements, their response to *judicial* failure all too often seems to be simply to write off the judges. But since failures by the British House of Commons to protect rights do not lead Tomkins or Ewing to suggest that democratic scrutiny of legislation be abandoned or scaled back, but rather *improved*, why not adopt the same response to instances of poor judicial scrutiny?'.[47] The obvious conclusion is that, since both institutions have been at fault, both must improve. Only a one-eyed focus on the ills of the judges alone could fail to reach this conclusion.

---

[46] Davis, 'The Human Rights Act and Juridification', n. 16 above, 93.

[47] G. Phillipson, 'Review' of T. Campbell, K. D. Ewing and A. Tomkins (eds.), *The Legal Protection of Human Rights: Sceptical Essays* (Oxford University Press, 2010) (2012) *Public Law* 380, 383.

Perhaps one reason why court sceptics don't seem interested in how judges might improve is that they seem to assume that their deferential nature, particularly in the national security context, is a kind of fixed given: judges (or at least British judges) are somehow simply no good.[48] A more constructive form of engagement with excessive judicial deference, however, would be to inquire *why* it comes about – and then consider whether and how it may be changed. There are in fact a number of reasons why judges (in Australia, New Zealand and particularly the United Kingdom) may tend towards the deferential, particularly in the national security context. These might include a relatively cautious judicial culture deriving from the traditional emphasis on parliamentary sovereignty and a historically narrow judicial role; the relative newness of the HRA and NZBRA to judges used to more deferential standards of review, like *Wednesbury*; judicial awareness of the political precariousness of the HRA, subject to removal by simple majority in Parliament; the hostility of large sections of the popular press to judicial rights protection; repeated attacks on liberal judgments by senior politicians; fear of getting it wrong when the stakes are high, e.g. when quashing control orders; difficulty in second-guessing executive risk assessments; judging in ignorance of the real extent of security threats, and so on.[49] The key point is that many of these are not invariable, but *contingent* factors, subject to gradual change – a change that we have at last started to see since *Belmarsh*.[50] Legal scholarship analysing and critiquing undue judicial deference (such as the chapter by Cora Chan[51] in this volume) may play some part in achieving such change. Another route to possible change lies in efforts to reform the appointment of judges, and achieve a more diverse judiciary, and/or in good human rights training.[52] And if some change comes about, then at least some of the force of the

---

[48] For example, Ewing's summary of pro-executive court judgments makes no attempt to consider *why* courts may have decided as they did: Ewing, 'The Futility of the Human Rights Act', n. 3 above, 832–6.

[49] Aileen Kavanagh has highlighted the last three of these in *Constitutional Review under the UK Human Rights Act*, n. 24 above, pp. 211–22.

[50] See R. C. Austin, 'The New Constitutionalism, Terrorism and Torture' (2007) 60 *Current Legal Problems* 79, 117. Here, I draw on Phillipson, 'Review', n. 47 above, 384.

[51] See Chapter 10 in this volume, C. Chan, 'Business as usual: deference in counter-terrorism rights review'.

[52] On the efficacy of the latter, see C. Gearty, 'The Human Rights Act: An Academic Sceptic Changes his Mind but not His Heart' (2010) *European Human Rights Law Review* 582, 585.

'inefficacy' argument will fall away: the argument is one that should track the contemporary performance of the courts, and it should change as that performance changes.[53] In contrast, using past failures to proclaim the *inevitable* 'futility' of rights-based judicial review[54] purports to be an evidence-based argument, but if no longer fact sensitive, becomes merely ideological.

IV   Judicial review hampers parliamentary scrutiny: 'governing like judges' and the 'distraction' thesis

There is a different strand of argument that more specifically seeks to demonstrate that deferential judicial review has a negative impact on Parliament's scrutinising role. There are two different versions of it, which I will term the 'strong' and 'weak' variants. Under the weak variant, it is conceded that Bills of Rights do encourage rights-based scrutiny in legislatures – but in the wrong way. The prospect of judicial review of legislation is said to cause Parliament, and particularly parliamentary committees like the Joint Committee on Human Rights (JCHR), to engage in court-like reasoning, whereby they engage in narrow, predictive and technical scrutiny, the purpose of which is to anticipate negative court judgments and recommend changes to avoid them.[55] Thus, it is said, 'blue skies' or even independent thinking about rights, does not take place.[56] This, in essence, is Janet Hiebert's thesis that the presence of Bills of Rights leads to the democratic branches 'governing like judges'.[57] It would seem somewhat pessimistic, however, to argue that parliamentarians *cannot* change this without repealing Bills (or statutes) of Rights. Rather, bodies like the JCHR can surely remedy this fault (to the extent that it is one) themselves; and there are recent

---

[53] As, to his credit, Gearty has done: *ibid.*

[54] Ewing and Tham, 'The Continuing Futility of the Human Rights Act', n. 19.

[55] See e.g., F. Klug and H. Wildbore, 'Breaking New Ground?' (2007) *European Human Rights Law Review* 231, 243. The JCHR has indeed declared itself to be the 'parliamentary guardian' of the HRA: JCHR, *Second Report* (HL 37/HC 372, 2001–2002), para. 5.

[56] See e.g., J. Morgan, 'Amateur Operatics? The Realisation of Parliamentary Protection of Civil Liberties' in T. Campbell, K. D. Ewing and A. Tomkins (eds.), *The Legal Protection of Human Rights: Sceptical Essays* (Oxford University Press, 2010), p. 428.

[57] See J. Hiebert 'Governing Like Judges?' in T. Campbell, K. D. Ewing and A. Tomkins (eds.), *The Legal Protection of Human Rights: Sceptical Essays* (Oxford University Press, 2010), p. 64. See also J. Tham, 'Parliamentary Deliberation and the National Security Executive: The Case of Control Orders' (2010) 1 *Public Law* 79.

signs that the JCHR is doing just that.[58] For another, Hiebert's research appears to suggest that the alternative – no or very weak Bills of Rights – leads to even worse results in terms of democratic rights scrutiny (below).

The strong version of this argument is made by Tushnet[59] and, in the UK context, Davis, who has argued that the prospect of rights-based review simply distracts MPs from their proper scrutinising function.[60] 'In creating the impression that the courts can and will fulfil this crucial function', he argues 'we anaesthetize those constitutional actors who might exercise genuinely effective control namely, "the Legislature and the people acting in their constitutional capacity"'.[61] Or as he put it elsewhere: 'Parliamentarians will be less inclined to act in the defence of civil liberties if they believe that the courts will do it for them'.[62] Adam Tomkins made a similar prediction about the effect of the HRA on Parliament, arguing that the Act would make it 'more difficult [for Parliament] to make [its] scrutiny voice heard'.[63] Davis has cited Tushnet in support of his contention,[64] but it is not a normative argument; it purports at least to be an empirical one – asserting a matter of fact about the world, about why a given set of people behave in a certain way and how their behaviour would change were circumstances (such as the presence or absence of a Bill of Rights) to change. As such, to be convincing, it requires at least some kind of evidence.

As a preliminary point, it may be suggested that the argument might have force in the United States (because courts have the final word there

---

[58] See e.g., Commonwealth Human Rights Initiative, *The Parliamentary Committee as Promoter of Human Rights: The UK's Joint Committee on Human Rights* (2007), pp. 8–14 (examining the JCHR's broader work on human rights), available at www.humanrightsinitiative.org/publications/hradvocacy/parliamentary_committee_as_promoter_of_hr.pdf.

[59] M. Tushnet, 'Controlling Executive Power in the War on Terrorism' (2005) 118 *Harvard Law Review* 2673, 2680.

[60] Davis, 'The Human Rights Act and Juridification', n. 16 above, 96.

[61] F. de Londras and F. Davis, 'Controlling the Executive in Times of Terrorism: Competing Perspectives on Effective Oversight Mechanisms' (2010) 30(1) *Oxford Journal of Legal Studies* 19, 26.

[62] See also F. Davis, 'Parliamentary Supremacy and the Re-invigoration of Institutional Dialogue in the UK' (2012) *Parliamentary Affairs* 1, 5.

[63] 'Introduction: on being Sceptical about Human Rights' in T. Campbell, K. Ewing and A. Tomkins, *Sceptical Essays on Human Rights* (Oxford University Press, 2001), p. 9.

[64] Davis, 'The Human Rights Act and Juridification', n. 16 above, 96.

over constitutional rights) but less so in systems that do not give courts this kind of rights supremacy. As Gardbuam puts it:

> Where legislatures never have final responsibility for rights, and, even more, where (as often happens) courts do not take legislative considerations seriously in their own deliberations, there is an understandable tendency to leave matters of constitutionality to the judiciary and for the legislatures to spend their time on matters they do decide.[65]

Conversely, then, in countries such as the United Kingdom where legislatures retain final responsibility for rights, *and* courts are known to take their views seriously, via doctrines or practices of due deference, one would expect matters to be very different. So, Davis may be guilty simply of insufficiently sensitive constitutional borrowing: using a concept that may work in the US (or German) context of judicial supremacy, but not outside that context.

But let us assume it may apply in Britain. The argument then would boil down to this: if you were to repeal the HRA, the British Parliament *would* improve its rights-based scrutiny of legislation. It should be recognised that this is a counter-factual, for which no direct evidence can be offered. But what kind of indirect evidence might be produced? If the proposition were to be correct, then one would expect to find that, in cases in which there was (or had been) no rights-based judicial review, parliamentary scrutiny of rights was (or had been) better. One could seek to show this in at least two ways. First, one could examine the British Parliament's performance in relation to anti-terrorism legislation passed *before* the HRA, for example, the Prevention of Terrorism Act 1974 (PTA), or subsequent statutes passed before 1998. Secondly, one could scrutinise the contemporary performance of the Australian Parliament, which seeks to protect rights in the absence of a judicially enforced Bill of Rights, but now under the added impetus of a Human Rights Act that provides solely for parliamentary scrutiny in this regard[66] and thus offers 'a unique opportunity to assess the capacity of Parliament to protect human rights without court involvement'.[67] In each case one would seek to demonstrate that its performance was superior to that of the post-HRA UK Parliament.

---

[65] Gardbaum, 'Reassessing the New Commonwealth Model of Constitutionalism', n. 27 above, 173.

[66] Human Rights (Parliamentary Scrutiny) Act 2011.

[67] G. Williams and L. Burton, 'Australia's Exclusive Parliamentary Model of Rights Protection' (2013) 34(1) *Statute Law Review* 58.

As far as I am aware, however, no such evidence has been advanced. To take the Australian example first, there is substantial evidence that its performance in terms of rights-based scrutiny, both before[68] and after the recent Act, has been very disappointing and somewhat inferior to that of the British Parliament. Fergal Davis' chapter in this volume (Chapter 6) admits as much, something he attributes to the particularly strong system of party loyalty in Australian politics. As for the pre-HRA UK Parliament, I do not think that anyone seriously advances the argument that it performed better in protecting rights before the HRA than it does now. Indeed, many assert the contrary.[69] The comparison is hard to make, because Parliament did not have the benefit of the excellent work done by the Joint Committee on Human Rights before the HRA. But the conclusion seems inescapable: the 'distraction' thesis is nothing more than a counter-factual conjecture; the lack of evidence for it reveals it to be a pure ideological preference.

There is moreover an obvious counter-argument to it, to which Davis does not advert: the clear history of judicial deference in national security matters has surely given the democratic bodies 'the expectation that when crisis emerges, courts take a step back'.[70] Why then *would* MPs be distracted by the prospect of robust judicial protection of rights when the relatively poor judicial record is so well known? There is in fact a rather discouraging paradox here for political constitutionalists: the more they attack the judges for their feebly deferential judgments, the harder they find it to suggest convincingly that MPs are – unaccountably – relying on the known-to-have-failed judges to do their liberty-protecting job for them. The distraction thesis only works by postulating a mysterious state of affairs whereby judges consistently fail to protect rights, but MPs somehow fail to notice this and retain a blind faith that courts will provide such strong protection for rights that they themselves do not need to bother about the issue at all.

Moreover, the empirical work that there is in this area by Janet Hiebert and others appears to refute Davis' conjectural thesis: its findings are that unless ministers and MPs anticipate adverse consequences from

---

[68] See N. McGarrity and G. Williams, 'Counter-terrorism Laws in a Nation without a Bill of Rights: The Australian Experience' (2010) 2 *City University of Hong Kong Law Review* 45, 62–3.

[69] See D. Feldman, 'Parliamentary Scrutiny of Legislation and Human Rights' (2002) *Public Law* 323; C. Gearty, '11 September 2001, Counter-Terrorism and the Human Rights Act' (2005) 32 *Journal of Law and Society* 18.

[70] See de Londras, *Detention in the 'War on Terror'*, n. 3 above, p. 220.

judicial review of legislation, they are unlikely to take the relevant rights seriously during the legislative process. Hiebert's comparative analysis of rights scrutiny within the United Kingdom, Canada and New Zealand reaches a striking conclusion:

> [I]f rights conflict with policy objectives to which governments are strongly committed, governments are unlikely to change their position unless they anticipate serious costs from failing to abide by rights principles. Although these costs could come from political sanctions, in the sense of a strong cultural commitment to rights that would penalize governments at the ballot box, they are more likely to come from the court.[71]

Andrew Geddis' work on parliamentary scrutiny in New Zealand appears to support this conclusion, by showing how a weak Bill of Rights may be largely ignored by government. His research reveals that twenty-two Government Bills have been enacted following statutory statements by the Attorney General alerting Parliament to a risk of inconsistency with the New Zealand Bill of Rights Act; of these, eighteen were passed without amendments to address the claimed inconsistencies.[72]

All these findings, then, tend to suggest that, in Commonwealth systems, parliamentary and judicial controls often go hand in hand, complementing and reinforcing each other. Such a conclusion runs contrary to the oppositional, judiciary *versus* legislature paradigm often adopted by critics of Bills of Rights, but fits well with the pragmatic case for dialogic Bills of Rights that I advance here.

V Deferential judicial review as used *against* parliaments: the 'negative dialogue' thesis

The other sceptical line of argument examines how the executive uses deferential court judgments in seeking to frustrate more assertive parliamentary scrutiny. Again, there is a strong and weak sceptical thesis. The weak thesis points out that undue judicial deference can set up what I have previously termed a kind of 'negative' or 'suppressive' constitutional dialogue, whereby the executive attempts to use the results of overly deferential judgments to silence criticism from Parliament,

---

[71] Hiebert, 'Governing Like Judges?', n. 57 above, 64.
[72] A. Geddis, 'Inter-institutional "Rights Dialogue" under the New Zealand Bill of Rights Act' in T. Campbell, K. D. Ewing and A. Tomkins (eds.), *The Legal Protection of Human Rights: Sceptical Essays* (Oxford University Press, 2010), p. 98.

particularly the JCHR, something that certainly appeared to happen during the control orders saga.[73]

Is this an argument then that judicial decisions actually made things worse than having no judicial review at all? Not so: first, this weak thesis does not argue that overly deferential judicial review is worse than useless; it simply contends that excessive deference has worse effects than appropriate or no deference. Secondly, we must recognise that the government also did the same thing with the non-deferential, assertive decision in *AF (No. 3)*[74] (which used section 3 of the HRA to quite radically alter the meaning and effect of the legislation so as to provide greater due process rights for suspects), using it as 'proof' that the legislation itself was fully rights-compliant.[75] So both deferential and non-deferential judgments can be used against would-be reformers in Parliament. The only answer to this kind of manipulation is for parliamentarians to wise up to it. Meanwhile, a good reason for judges to get less deferential is full appreciation of the constitutional damage that overly deferential judgments can do to Parliament's role. In short, then, the answer to the 'negative dialogue' point is to abandon not judicial review, but excessive judicial deference.

In contrast, the strong sceptical thesis on this point, advanced for example by Keith Ewing, suggests that judicial review not only has some negative effects, if too deferential, but will *invariably* make things worse. Judgments will always be overly deferential and we would be better off without them altogether. But this is very hard to argue.[76] The control

---

[73] See *Annual Renewal of Control Orders Legislation 2010* (Ninth Report of Session 2009–10, HL 64, HC 395), para. 81. Tomkins has advanced this argument strongly in 'Parliament, Human Rights and Counter-Terrorism' in T. Campbell, K. D. Ewing and A. Tomkins (eds.), *The Legal Protection of Human Rights: Sceptical Essays* (Oxford University Press, 2010), pp. 34–8; see also H. Fenwick and G. Phillipson, 'Covert Derogations and Judicial Deference: Redefining Liberty and Due Process Rights in Counter-Terrorism Law and Beyond' (2011) 56(4) *McGill Law Journal* 864, 871. Fenwick has argued that this process of 'negative dialogue' then continued with the introduction of Terrorism Prevention and Investigation Measures (TPIMs) and Enhanced Terrorism Prevention and Investigation Measures (ETPIMs): H. Fenwick, 'Designing ETPIMs around ECHR Review or Normalisation of "Preventive" Non-Trial-based Executive Measures?' (2013) 76 (5) *Modern Law Review* 876.

[74] *Secretary of State for the Home Department* v. *AF (No. 3)* [2009] UKHL 28, [2010] 2 AC 269.

[75] See HL Debs, vol. 717, col. 1521, 3 March 2010.

[76] Gearty has recently said that 'only devoted antagonists would deride the HRA's effect as negative' in Gearty, 'The Human Rights Act: An Academic Sceptic Changes his Mind but not His Heart', n. 52 above, 586.

order judgments were indeed used by the government to give the legislation a misleadingly clean bill of human rights health. But without them,
we would have had the scheme as originally implemented by the Home
Secretary – a spectacularly dishonest one, which pretended that placing
people under house arrest for eighteen hours, with a host of other
draconian restrictions, amounting to a species of 'recreat[ed] internment',[77] was fully compliant with the right to liberty (under Article 5
of the ECHR), and that procedures that denied disclosure of any of the
evidence against suspects, in 'phantom' hearings, were wholly compliant
with the right to a fair trial under Article 6. What we would have had, in
other words, was a scheme that in effect derogated from the United
Kingdom's human rights obligations in the way it dealt with controlees,
without admitting it.[78] It is undeniable that the key control orders
decisions[79] improved this, even if they did not do so as much as many
would like.

In his chapter in this volume, Davis makes a final argument against
judicial review: that while both legislature and judiciary will make mistakes, only the latter leaves binding precedents, which, in Justice Jackson's famous phrase 'lie about like a loaded weapon' ready to be used by
later governments to legitimate more repressive measures.[80] But this
argument is also flawed, at least when applied in the UK context. First,
it overlooks the fact that the United Kingdom's apex court is not bound
by its own rulings – *Belmarsh*, for example, clearly broke free from a
strong precedential tradition of judicial self-abnegation in the area of
national security. Secondly, ECtHR case law, which the UK courts
broadly track, shows a fairly rapid process of development. Thus, if the
UK courts make an unfortunate ruling on a human rights matter, they
may be corrected quite quickly by a Strasbourg ruling that clarifies the
position: the application of *A* v. *United Kingdom*[81] in *AF (No. 3)* to insist
upon a minimum level of disclosure to those subject to control orders is a

---

[77] JCHR, *Twelfth Report of 2005-06*, App. 4 (Campaign Against Criminalising
Communities).

[78] See Fenwick and Phillipson, 'Covert Derogations and Judicial Deference', n. 73 above.

[79] Including *Secretary of State for the Home Department* v. *JJ* [2007] UKHL 45; *Secretary of
State for the Home Department* v. *MB and AF* [2007] UKHL 46, [2008] 1 AC 440;
Secretary of State for the Home Department v. *AF (No. 3)* [2009] UKHL 28, [2010] 2 AC
269; *Secretary of State for the Home Department* v. *AP* [2010] UKSC 24, [2010] 3 WLR 51.

[80] See Chapter 6 in this volume, F. F. Davis, 'The politics of counter-terrorism judicial
review: creating effective parliamentary scrutiny'.

[81] (2009) 49 EHRR 29.

good example. Thirdly, the concern is in any event of much less force in a dialogic polity, in which judicial mistakes can be corrected by the legislature, than in the United States, where judicial interpretations of the Constitution are supreme over the legislature. Fourthly, the idea that legislative mistakes are generally swiftly corrected is manifestly false. Bad legislation, which in the United Kingdom (and Australia) remains binding on the judges whatever its effect on human rights, can stay around on the statute book for decades.[82] Kent Roach has detailed elsewhere how successive trends in counter-terrorism legislation, each adding repressive layers of control and restriction, are typically rapidly tried in succession, with statutes often not being replaced but simply added to,[83] while the editors of this volume note in the introductory chapter that 'repealing and unpicking complex counter-terrorism measures is often problematic'.[84]

VI   A complementary scrutiny model

Briefly to summarise the argument so far, then, this chapter has argued that neither of the two 'strong' sceptical theses are sustainable; the two 'weak' theses have been conceded but argued to be remediable: essentially, judges need to become less deferential while Parliament can broaden its own rights-based scrutiny role by taking a less judge-like approach to its role, and as we have seen, there are signs in recent years that such change is beginning to come about.[85] If this is correct, then we appear to have a practical, *prima facie* case for a model that sees judicial and parliamentary scrutiny as generally complementary, rather than

---

[82] A vivid example, outside the counter-terrorism context, was Parliament's notorious failure to abolish the marital rape exemption by 1991. See *R* v. *R* [1992] 1 AC 599 for discussion.

[83] K. Roach, 'Sources and Trends in Counter-Terrorism Legislation' in B. Goold and L. Lazarus, *Security and Human Rights* (Portland, OR: Hart Publishing, 2007).

[84] See the Introduction to this volume, F. F. Davis and F. de Londras, 'Counter-terrorism judicial review: beyond dichotomies'.

[85] One former sceptic of judicial review has recently acknowledged a change of mind, stating, 'I think it is undeniable that the HRA has been deployed by the judges in a way that has done tangible social good' (Gearty, 'The Human Rights Act – an Academic Sceptic Changes his Mind but not His Heart', n. 52 above, 584). Tomkins, who has remained more of a sceptic than Gearty, and seemingly remains convinced that, as far as the top courts go, *Belmarsh* was an anomaly, not trend-setting, nevertheless acknowledges good civil liberties work done by the lower courts and specialist tribunals: A. Tomkins, 'National Security and the Role of the Court: A Changed Landscape?' (2010) 126 *Law Quarterly Review* 543. On the JCHR, see n. 58 above.

antithetical. As suggested above, such a model also appears to answer to the theoretical arguments canvassed at the beginning of this chapter.

But there is a further important point in its favour, which is simply that, in many instances of counter-terrorism law, the judiciary and legislature *must* work together in order to limit and control draconian executive policy. It's a straightforward point, but one that seems to be often overlooked by a dichotomous mindset that insists one must trust *either* the judges *or* Parliament.[86] David Feldman has observed that modern counter-terrorism laws typically grant the executive very broad powers:[87] examples proliferate, from the former power to stop and search without reasonable suspicion,[88] to the information-sharing powers under the Anti-terrorism, Crime and Security Act 2001 (ATCSA)[89] to control orders and Terrorism Prevention and Investigation Measures (TPIMs). Parliament cannot itself wholly foresee or practically oversee the use to which such discretionary powers are put in *individual* cases. It *must* therefore rely on courts to perform this vital function. But the point goes further than this: Parliament *discharges* a major part of its role of protecting civil liberties by ensuring that the courts are given robust tools to protect suspects in individual cases.[90] For example, the main efforts of both the UK and Australian Parliaments, in seeking to amend and improve the control orders legislation passed through them, were directed at enhancing the degree and effectiveness of judicial scrutiny of the imposition of particular control orders. As Tham puts it, '[T]he key issue in the Australian and British Parliaments concerned the extent of judicial involvement in the issuing of control orders'.[91] Thus, amendments passed changed the regime so that judges would have to issue control orders that overtly denied liberty,[92] and also raised the standard of proof for such orders (something of course policed by the High Court).[93] Tomkins has also recently noted these efforts, praising the role of Parliament, and particularly the JCHR, in securing 'improvements' in

---

[86] See e.g., Davis, 'The Human Rights Act and Juridification', n. 16 above, 91.

[87] D. Feldman, 'Human Rights, Terrorism and Risk: The Role of Politicians and Judges' (2006) *Public Law* 364, 383.

[88] Under Terrorism Act 2000, s. 44.   [89] ATCSA 2001, s. 17(2).

[90] Feldman, 'Human Rights, Terrorism and Risk', n. 87 above, 383.

[91] Tham, 'Parliamentary Deliberation and the National Security Executive: The Case of Control Orders', n. 57 above, 92.

[92] That is, 'derogating' control orders.

[93] Tham, 'Parliamentary Deliberation and the National Security Executive: The Case of Control Orders', n. 57 above, 94.

anti-terrorism legislation. But of what do these improvements primarily consist? The answer is: enhanced judicial safeguards.[94]

So in this important sense, Parliament and the courts really are engaged in a joint, collaborative exercise of seeking to hold the national security executive in check. And this argument may be used as a constructive one, to urge courts to engage in rigorous review on these points, in order to vindicate Parliament's trust. The sceptical-pessimist may answer that the courts will *always* disappoint, and that therefore this is precisely an example of Parliament being distracted by the chimera of effective judicial review. And this is a serious point: parliamentarians granting the executive enormously broad powers to invade individual rights are foolish if they allow themselves to be fobbed off with the prospect that judicial review will invariably provide an effective check upon the exercise of such powers. An obvious example is suspicion-less stop and search powers and *Gillan*.[95] In this case, the sheer breadth of the powers granted by Parliament to the police and the deliberate legislative choices to use expediency, rather than necessity and proportionality, as the test for triggering the powers, and to remove the usual safeguard of reasonable suspicion for their individual use, helped persuade the courts that it was not for them to cut down such a deliberately broad grant of power by reading it down. But this illustrates an important point: this instance was one (not untypical) of parliamentary failure to protect rights *followed by* judicial failure. And the judges failed partly *because* they deferred to the bad legislative choices that Parliament had already made. They did not fail simply because, as Ewing would seemingly have it, they are no good. They failed, at least in part, because Parliament had deliberately legislated to make it extremely hard for them to succeed.

To conclude this section, I have contended that the distraction thesis, at least as applied to the United Kingdom, is simply unproven as a generalised statement. However, it does serve to alert us to a more limited but important point: Parliament should *not* be distracted, when considering draconian counter-terrorism legislation, by bland government reassurances that the judges will make sure all the powers are used appropriately. Courts may well not be practically able to, may defer to

---

[94] See Tomkins, 'Parliament, Human Rights and Counter-Terrorism', n. 73 above.

[95] The reference is to former Terrorism Act 2000, 5.44 and to *R (on the application of Gillan)* v. *Commissioner of Police of the Metropolis* [2006] UKHL 12, [2006] 2 AC 307. The ECtHR took a very different approach in finding the power to violate Art. 8 ECHR: *Gillan* v. *United Kingdom* (2010) 50 EHRR 45.

the choices of the democratic branches and/or may be persuaded by risk-based security arguments, as in *Gillan* itself. Parliament should always do what it can to narrow and structure the powers it grants to the executive; it should not allow itself to be reassured that the grant of potentially arbitrary powers will be made good by intrusive judicial oversight. But the fact remains that, since Parliament cannot itself police the exercise by the executive of extraordinary powers, like control orders/TPIMs in individual cases, it must *also* both trust and empower and enable judges to do this.

VII An example of the complementary model at work using interpretation: the control order cases

Sceptics have been highly critical of the courts' exercise of their interpretive powers under section 3 of the HRA,[96] which they fear are more likely than section 4 declarations to lead to 'judicial monologue', and most likely to distract MPs from their rights-protecting role. In response I instance the control orders saga, which may be seen as a form of dialogic interaction between all three arms of government, in which very strong uses of section 3[97] were, I contend, entirely justifiable, even from a political constitutionalist perspective. The classical 'democratic' justification for judicial review of rights issues is that the judges are drawing the attention of the legislature to rights infringements that it has either neglected or caused inadvertently.[98] But in the case of control orders, the argument for the courts' intervention was even stronger: what they in effect did was to restore the effect of the legislation to that intended by Parliament when it was passed.

---

[96] See e.g., J. Allan, "Statutory Bill of Rights: You Read Words in, You Read Words Out, You Take Parliament's Clear Intention and You Shake It All About" in T. Campbell, K. D. Ewing and A. Tomkins (eds.), *The Legal Protection of Human Rights: Sceptical Essays* (Oxford University Press, 2010).

[97] I have argued elsewhere that the use of HRA, s. 3 in *AF (No. 3)* to insert a requirement that the gist of the case against the suspect must be disclosed to him, which went wholly contrary to the *prima facie* meaning of the statute, was the most significant modification of a statute made under that provision of the HRA, since it gainsaid a 'fundamental feature' of the statute in question: G. Phillipson, 'The Human Rights Act, Dialogue and Constitutional Principles' in R. Masterman and I. Leigh (eds.), *The United Kingdom's Statutory Bill of Rights: Constitutional and Comparative Perspectives* (Proceedings of the British Academy/Oxford University Press, 2013), pp. 25, 43.

[98] See R. Dixon, 'The Supreme Court of Canada, Charter Dialogue and Deference' (2009) 47 *Osgoode Hall Law Journal* 235, 258–9; Yap, 'Defending Dialogue', n. 21 above, 540–2.

Recall that Parliament was assured by the government (via section 19 HRA statements and subsequently) that the legislation was both itself compliant with the ECHR and would be exercised by the Home Secretary in a rights-compatible way. So when it emerged in cases like *JJ, MB* and *AF (No. 3)*[99] that this was emphatically not the case, it was fully legitimate for the judges to say so, loud and clear. Does the fact that the courts used section 3 rather than section 4 complicate the picture, given that they thereby modified the effect of the legislation, rather than merely 'sounding the alarm' to Parliament? I contend not. Given that Parliament passed the relevant legislation in the clear expectation that it was and would be used in a way that was fully compliant with the ECHR, the use of section 3 to achieve this end merely restored the overall meaning and effect of the legislation to that intended by Parliament, and thereby checked the government's undeclared policy of a 'covert derogation' from the ECHR.[100] As such, the judiciary's role was not counter-majoritarian but democracy-enforcing: enforcing Parliament's will that the powers it granted the executive be exercised in a rights-compliant way.

This indicates, I suggest, that any determinations of the legitimacy of judicial power in the counter-terrorism context must be sensitive to the specific factual matrix. While section 3 is the more intrusive and thus more controversial power, its use may be seen as entirely legitimate, even or especially from a political-constitutionalist perspective, when it may be seen, paradoxically, as enforcing Parliament's will.

VIII Making the complementary model work

If we have got to the stage, then, of accepting that judicial review has some practical benefits, and can be seen as often complementing, rather than challenging or impeding the role of Parliament, what can we say, finally, about the relationship between judicial deference and dialogue? One point that is often overlooked is that excessive deference negates the chance for a positive dialogue with the democratic branches of government. This kind of negation occurs when judges take restraint so far that they actually defer away the whole substance of the question they have to

---

[99] *Secretary of State for the Home Department* v. *JJ* [2007] UKHL 45; *Secretary of State for the Home Department* v. *MB and AF* [2007] UKHL 46, [2008] 1 AC 440; *Secretary of State for the Home Department* v. *AF (No. 3)* [2009] UKHL 28, [2010] 2 AC 269.

[100] On which see Fenwick and Phillipson, 'Covert Derogations and Judicial Deference', n. 73 above.

decide by finding it to be in substance (if not in form) a non-justiciable question. This was precisely the course urged by the Attorney General upon the House of Lords in the seminal *Belmarsh*[101] decision when he argued that:

> it was for Parliament and the executive to assess the threat facing the nation, so it was for those bodies and not the courts to judge the response necessary to protect the security of the public. These were matters of a political character calling for an exercise of political and not judicial judgment.[102]

While the House of Lords did not accept this argument, at least so far as it went to the necessity of the measures taken to protect the public, something like it *was* accepted in cases like *Rehman*[103] and the Court of Appeal decision in *Belmarsh*.[104] Such a course is objectionable in itself and, as discussed above, gives draconian government actions a misleading stamp of human rights compliance. But it also negates the possibility of 'an argumentative dialogue between courts, the executive, and the legislature as to the necessary and reasonable restraints on rights in order to preserve public safety in the face of the threat from terrorism'.[105] Instead of a constitutional 'conversation', we hear only the executive, with a polite murmur of agreement from the judges – and it is hard to characterise an exchange as a conversation, where one party's contribution is limited to saying in effect (however lengthily) 'I defer to your view'. Conversely, it is not often recognised that *due* deference – whether that arises simply through the inherent limitations of the judicial function,[106] or via a distinct and more comprehensive doctrine[107] – also allows for a form of 'conversation' between executive and judiciary. The latter, in affording a degree of minimal respect for the executive,

---

[101] *A and others* v. *Secretary of State for the Home Department* [2005] 2 AC 68.
[102] *Ibid.* para. 37.   [103] [2001] UKHL 47, [2003] 1 AC 153.
[104] *A* v. *Secretary of State for the Home Department* [2002] EWCA Civ 1502, [2004] QB 335.
[105] See Fenwick and Phillipson, 'Covert Derogations and Judicial Deference', n. 73 above, 916–17.
[106] As Trevor Allan would argue: 'Human Rights and Judicial Review: A Critique of "Due Deference"' (2006) *Cambridge Law Journal* 671.
[107] As the following would argue: M. Hunt, 'Sovereignty's Blight: Why Contemporary Public Law Needs the Concept of "Due Deference"' in N. Bamforth and P. Leyland (eds.), *Public Law in a Multi-Layered Constitution* (Oxford University Press, 2003); A. Kavanagh, 'Defending Deference in Public Law and Constitutional Theory' (2010) 126 *Law Quarterly Review* 222; A. Young, 'In Defence of Due Deference' (2009) 72 *Modern Law Review* 554.

and more where that is warranted,[108] 'listens' in a meaningful way to the executive's case – and listening carefully is the first step in a good conversation. Garbaum has pointed out its other virtue: it avoids the emasculation of political rights review that can come about 'where courts do not take legislative considerations [about rights] seriously in their own deliberations', which can lead to legislatures neglecting such considerations.[109] Where a court ultimately decides to disagree in whole or part with a decision of the executive or Parliament, then its judgment constitutes its considered response to the case made. The ball then goes back to the executive to decide how to respond, and whether to take matters back to the legislature – at which point, it perforce joins the 'conversation'. Thus, affording either no or excessive deference may hamper the dialogic relationship. Getting deference right facilitates it.[110]

If this argument commands broad agreement (and one area where liberal constitutionalists and court-sceptics unite is in condemning excessive judicial deference), then perhaps a further point may be conceded by critics of judicial review. Constantly stigmatising it as illegitimate[111] scarcely encourages the judges to exercise it assertively. It is well known that *due* deference has been recommended by writers such as Hunt and Kavanagh as being based at least partly on the superior democratic credentials of Parliament.[112] Seen this way, deference dials back the degree of undemocratic power wielded by courts: to pay respectful and serious attention to the views of the democratic branches on rights questions is a way of ensuring that courts do not simply ride roughshod over the views of elected representatives even when they ultimately, sometimes, disagree with them. Whether or not one agrees with this line of argument, there remains something paradoxical about those who believe that judicial review is too deferential also castigating it as

---

[108] See Chapter 10 in this volume, C. Chan, 'Business as usual: deference in counter-terrorism rights review'.

[109] Gardbaum, 'Reassessing the New Commonwealth Model of Constitutionalism', n. 27 above, 173.

[110] The response of the democratic branches is also important. See Phillipson, 'The Human Rights Act, Dialogue and Constitutional Principles', n. 99 above, 25–49.

[111] Waldron, 'The Core of the Case Against Judicial Review', n. 29 above, 1354; D. Nicol, 'Gender Reassignment and the Transformation of the Human Rights Act' (2004) 120 *Law Quarterly Review* 194.

[112] See further Hunt, 'Sovereignty's Blight', n. 107 above; Kavanagh, 'Defending Deference in Public Law and Constitutional Theory', n. 107 above; Young, 'In Defence of Due Deference', n. 107 above.

undemocratic. Thus, to return with the paradox with which we opened this chapter, when Brooke LJ in the Court of Appeal *Belmarsh* case gave a judgment that justified judicial deference in terms of the primacy of democratic decision-making,[113] instead of applauding him for abjuring the temptation of 'justocracy', Ewing scornfully comments that the judge sounded 'as if he was holding a hot potato that he wanted quickly to pass on'.[114]

It is at least possible that judges may respond to such arguments by judging too deferentially, to minimise the counter-majoritarian difficulty they are charged with creating. If their deference is then used as a further reason to castigate their role, completing the negative feedback loop, they may reasonably ask what it is that their critics would like them to do, given the role that Parliament has given them in the HRA. A more promising line of argument (noted above) urges courts to undertake review without excessive deference as a way of working collaboratively with Parliament to hold the executive in check.

Conclusion

In this chapter I have sought to sketch a brief justification for dialogue as one that takes the principled argument against judicial review pragmatically: that balances it against other considerations, such as the enhanced rights protection judicial review may at times provide for those acutely vulnerable and unpopular groups in most danger from preventive counter-terrorism measures.[115] I have also sought to show that the argument that judicial review tends only to make things worse, either by setting up negative dialogue, or distracting MPs from their proper work, cannot be sustained. The distraction thesis, for example, simply has no evidence that comes close to demonstrating that we would be better off, in rights terms, without instruments such as the HRA. But my final point is the most important: that rather than pursuing the old dichotomous argument (democratic *or* judicial protection?), sensible human rights scholars should accept, as the editors of

---

[113] In the quote appearing at the beginning of this chapter.

[114] Ewing, 'The Futility of the Human Rights Act', n. 3 above, 841.

[115] There now seems to be a fair consensus that at least some judicial rulings under the HRA have done some good: see e.g., Gearty, 'The Human Rights Act: An Academic Sceptic Changes his Mind but not His Heart', n. 52 above and A. Tomkins, 'National Security and the Role of the Court', n. 85 above.

this volume note at one point, that we do not need 'to decide definitively between one option and the other'.[116]

A more fruitful cause is surely to direct urgent attention to improving
the performance of *both* the legislative and judicial arms in protecting
rights, or perhaps we could say, continuing the improvement that both
have already shown in recent times, at least in the United Kingdom. In
many instances, both must work together (as with the grant of discretionary powers): the legislature protects the individual through inserting
judicial safeguards and the judiciary must then police those safeguards
rigorously, realising that to do otherwise is not to pay respect to the
elected branches, but simply to betray the trust of the legislature and
frustrate what should be their joint enterprise – providing a serious,
inter-locking constitutional check upon the national security executive.

---

[116] See the Introduction to this volume, F. F. Davis and F. de Londras, 'Counter-terrorism
judicial review: beyond dichotomies'.

PART IV

Internationalised counter-terrorism judicial review

Counter-terrorism law and judicial review: the challenge for the Court of Justice of the European Union

CIAN C. MURPHY

I   Union, executive power and restraint

Any discussion of European Union (EU) counter-terrorism law poses challenges. There is a challenge for the conservative observer that sees the former economic community with power akin to that of a sovereign state. For the liberal observer, the substance of much EU counter-terrorism law is so far removed from European ideals of respect for human rights and the rule of law as to be rather alarming.[1] In the present context, a book exploring judicial review of counter-terrorism action, there are also challenges. These are in some respects terminological and definitional. In their introductory chapter, Davis and de Londras set out to define 'counter-terrorism judicial review'. The terminology alone may cause distress. 'Counter-terrorist finance', for example, refers to the regulation of the financial sector for the purpose of countering terrorism. The idea of 'counter-terrorism judicial review' might then be (mis) understood as referring to the regulation of judicial review for the purpose of countering terrorism. The opposite, of course, is the case. Davis and de Londras' definition also poses challenges in respect of the current chapter. For the editors of this book our subject is 'the use of judicialised processes to challenge *state* behaviours that fall into the broad category of counter-terrorism'.[2] Whither the EU in this work? The problems that the EU poses for political theory and political science

---

[1] For an extensive critique of EU counter-terrorism law after 11 September 2001, see C. C. Murphy, *EU Counter-Terrorism Law: Pre-emption and the Rule of Law* (Oxford: Hart Publishing, 2012).

[2] See further Chapter 1 in this volume, F. de Londras, 'Counter-terrorism judicial review as regulatory constitutionalism' and Chapter 6, F. F. Davis, 'The politics of counter-terrorism judicial review: creating effective parliamentary scrutiny'.

are well known.[3] The EU is neither an international organisation nor is it a federal state. It is both a 'political system' and a 'legal system' but it does not have the capacity to exercise direct coercive force – violence – to uphold its law. Thus the EU political and legal systems do not possess a monopoly on, or even a claim on, the direct coercive force that marks the nation state as sovereign. It is this force that underpins state counter-terrorism – a force that is closely related to executive power. Thus, the very idea of EU counter-terrorism action challenges our ordinary understanding of what that action can entail.

For Davis and de Londras the problem in counter-terrorism as a field of government action is ensuring appropriate controls on those forms of executive power that the EU may not even possess.[4] The idea of executive supremacy is unacceptable and therefore it is necessary for the legislature, or the judiciary, or both, to act as a restraint. This then points to a further challenge for this chapter. Whereas (most) other contributions to this book must examine those restraints in the context of nation states' action, the particular task of this chapter is to do so in respect of the EU. Thus, before it is possible to turn to the question of restraint the subject of that restraint must be made clear. If the EU does not possess the direct coercive force central to state counter-terrorism then it may be difficult to identify what 'executive power' means in the EU. The EU certainly possesses a rule-making or legislative power, and the line between legislative and executive power is not always clear. In a nation state executive power is thought, in general, to be correlative with the power of the executive branch.[5] In the EU a simple correlation such as this is not possible. Rather, in the EU, 'there are core – political and administrative – EU institutions with far-reaching non-legislative powers'.[6] The European Commission is the obvious locus of executive power but the Council (consisting of Member State governments) also wields such power. There are also other agencies and entities with such power (for example the EU Border Agency, FRONTEX). Furthermore,

---

[3] See, for a useful introduction, S. Hix and B. Hoyland, *The Political System of the European Union* (3rd edn, Basingstoke: Palgrave Macmillan, 2011).

[4] F. Davis and F. de Londras, 'Controlling the Executive in Times of Terrorism: Competing Perspectives on Effective Oversight Mechanisms' (2010) 30(1) *Oxford Journal of Legal Studies* 19.

[5] To take an obvious example, Art. II of the US Constitution begins: 'The executive power shall be vested in a President of the United States'.

[6] D. Curtin, *Executive Power of the European Union: Law, Practices and the Living Constitution* (Cambridge University Press, 2009), p. 3.

the executive power finding expression in the EU political and legal systems may not only be that of the Union itself but also of its Member States or of other governmental organisations such as the United Nations (UN) Security Council. In this sense a study of the EU offers the opportunity to capture the 'expansiveness of executive power'[7] that now operates within and across political and legal systems. This breadth and variety of executive power in the EU finds expression in the case study chosen in this chapter: restrictive measures in counter-terrorism law.

Although the chapter may be broad in its consideration of executive power it is narrow in relation to judicial power. The chapter focuses on the Court of Justice of the European Union (CJEU) even though a comprehensive examination of judicial restraint on executive power in the EU political and legal systems would also, of necessity, take in the roles of national courts and of the European Court of Human Rights (ECtHR). The chapter will make reference to these other judiciaries, in particular the latter, but there is too little space here to give a comprehensive account of all judicial restraint in Europe. Taking all of this into account it is necessary to appropriately frame this book's question for the purpose of the present chapter. It is: what role does the CJEU play in restraining executive power in the political and legal systems of the EU when that power is being used for the purposes of counter-terrorism? A problem with this question is that in the history of the EU, the Court has found itself in the position not simply of acting as a restraint on executive power, but also acting as an ally of, perhaps even a substitute for, such power. If European lawyers speak of 'the judicial construction of Europe' then they implicitly acknowledge the role that the Court of Justice plays in ensuring that the force of law substitutes for coercive force in holding the Union together.[8] This adds a further variable to an already-complex equation: the Court's desire to secure the EU legal system in the face of challenges from above (international law) and below (national legal systems). The analysis returns to this point in the conclusion.

In the first half of this chapter the idea that the CJEU is an appropriate institution for review of counter-terrorism law is subject to challenge. The CJEU has been the subject of much praise for its judicial review of counter-terrorism law – but that praise often overlooks the Court's

---

[7] *Ibid.* p. 18.

[8] A. S. Sweet, *The Judicial Construction of Europe* (Oxford University Press, 2004).

limitations. In earlier work it was possible to speak of 'the difficult position of the European judiciary'.[9] In that work the analysis set out the problem the Court faces in striking an appropriate balance between rules of EU constitutional law on division of powers and the protection of human rights. In this chapter, the analysis takes a further look at the Court's work in light of its history and practices. A key question is whether the Court of Justice conducts review in a manner appropriate to counter-terrorism law. The substantive challenge for the Court of Justice in more recent cases has been to reconcile overlapping rules of counter-terrorism law with legal principles such as the rule of law. Thus, the second half of the chapter turns to the Court's emerging counter-terrorism jurisprudence. That jurisprudence, in particular the line of cases dealing with restrictive measures,[10] now ranks amongst the most discussed judgments in its history. After its judgment in *Kadi I*, the Court is seen as a bastion of the rule of law in the face of executive power that has a global reach. That judgment was undoubtedly a positive one for the rule of law but it left many questions without answers.[11] These questions (on intensity of review, secret evidence, and due process) have since been the subject of litigation in *Kadi II* and other cases. The choice of restrictive measures as the case study for this chapter is salient because it is in this field that the Council and the European Commission have 'operational type powers' – direct executive power.[12] It is also, perhaps as a result of those powers, the field in which the Court of Justice is developing its most rich jurisprudence on counter-terrorism law.[13] The central aim of this chapter is to challenge the complacency in much European legal debate that courts, and the Court of Justice in particular,

---

[9] C. C. Murphy, 'Fundamental Rights and Security: The Difficult Position of the European Judiciary' (2010) 16(2) *European Public Law* 289. For a further development of the argument see Murphy, *EU Counter-Terrorism Law*, n. 1 above, ch. 8.

[10] These measures were known as 'targeted asset-freezing sanctions' in my own previous work. They are a development of economic sanctions against states that target legal and natural persons and entities thought to be involved in the financing of terrorism (or other security threats such as nuclear proliferation). Treaty on the Functioning of the European Union (TFEU), Art. 215 provides for the Union to adopt 'restrictive measures' against such persons.

[11] Joined Cases C-402/05P and C-415/05P *Yassin Abdullah Kadi, Al Barakaat International Foundation* v. *Council of the European Union* [2008] ECR I-6351 ('*Kadi I*').

[12] Curtin, *Executive Power of the European Union*, n. 6 above, p. 4.

[13] The same might be said for the European Arrest Warrant (EAW) in relation to EU criminal justice cooperation. The EAW is perhaps the most ambitious example of such cooperation and it is the subject of significant litigation before the CJEU.

can be relied upon to control executive power. The chapter argues that although they are a necessary part of a system of constraint they are by no means sufficient by themselves.

II Counter-terrorism and European Courts

The Court of Justice is a newcomer to counter-terrorism law and other national security matters. Observers of other constitutional courts can hearken back to decades old cases arising out of previous national security crises that serve as exemplars, or more often cautionary tales, for lawyers today. The United States has *Korematsu*[14] and the United Kingdom has *Liversidge v. Anderson*.[15] The European Court of Human Rights' first judgment was *Lawless*: a case about preventive detention in Ireland.[16] These cases are all over a half-century old and each sought to address the appropriate scope of executive power in the face of a national security crisis. The CJEU did not enter into this debate until its judgment in *Kadi I*.[17] The Court is therefore in the invidious position of having to develop its counter-terrorism jurisprudence after 11 September 2001: 'the mother of all events'.[18]

The absence, until recently, of the CJEU from the conversation about counter-terrorism law is a consequence of its origins as the court of a common market and stands in sharp contrast to the position of that other European court, the ECtHR. In *Lawless*, the ECtHR had to consider the lawfulness of what would today be called a counter-terrorism, or perhaps counter-insurgency, measure – preventive detention. In that case the Court found no breach of the European Convention on Human Rights (ECHR) when the Irish government sought to derogate from the state's human rights obligations so as to detain the complainant without trial. The judgment marks the start of a history wherein the Court's rulings on counter-terrorism in particular and national security in general are subject to significant debate.[19]

---

[14] *Korematsu v. United States*, 323 US 214 (1944).
[15] *Liversidge v. Anderson* [1942] AC 206.   [16] *Lawless v. Ireland* (1961) 1 EHRR 15.
[17] Joined Cases C-402/05P and C-415/05P *Yassin Abdullah Kadi, Al Barakaat International Foundation v. Council of the European Union* [2008] ECR I-6351.
[18] J. Baudrillard, 'The Spirit of Terrorism', *Le Monde*, 2 November 2001.
[19] See S. Sottiaux, *Terrorism and the Limitation of Rights: The ECHR and the US Constitution* (Oxford: Hart Publishing, 2008) for an engaging comparative study also involving US constitutional law.

A certain degree of appeasement has always been apparent in ECtHR case law. In *Ireland* v. *United Kingdom*, the Court did not follow the European Commission on Human Rights in finding that the five techniques of disorientation and sensory deprivation were 'torture'. Rather, it came to the conclusion that they met the 'lesser' standard of 'inhuman or degrading treatment'.[20] Although the sense that the ECtHR engages in appeasement persists today, there have been times in the history of Europe when it was the sole refuge for those seeking justice in the face of serious abuses of power in the name of counter-terrorism.[21] In recent years, the Court has become embroiled in political dispute as to its role, in particular in its relationship with national law,[22] but it has had a largely constructive relationship with the Court of Justice to date.[23] This has seen a broad affirmation of the *Kadi* judgment in a ruling of the ECtHR on restrictive measures in *Nada* v. *Switzerland*.[24] The impact that the EU's future accession to the ECHR will have on the substantive jurisprudence of the two courts will be seen in the coming years,[25] but it may of course have a bearing on counter-terrorism law in Europe.

In seeking to understand the extent to which the ECtHR jurisprudence may find reflection in the Court of Justice's work it is important to note that the ECtHR has a different judicial function to that of the CJEU.[26] First, the ECtHR's jurisdiction is of broader geographic scope as it takes in all forty-seven members of the Council of Europe and not only the twenty-eight EU Member States. Secondly, its jurisdiction is of deeper

---

[20] *Ireland* v. *United Kingdom* (1978) 2 EHRR 25.

[21] The idea of the Court 'appeasing' the Council of Europe Member States is taken up in Chapter 13 of this volume, H. Fenwick, 'Post 9/11 UK counter-terrorism cases in the European Court of Human Rights: a "Dialogic" approach to rights protection or appeasement of national authorities?'. For an excellent case study critique of the ECtHR's work see B. Dickson, *The European Convention on Human Rights and the Conflict in Northern Ireland* (Oxford University Press, 2012).

[22] The debate on this relationship is raging at the time of writing. See e.g., E. Bates, 'British Sovereignty and the European Court of Human Rights' (2012) 128 *Law Quarterly Review* 382 and C. O'Cinneide, 'Human Rights Law in the UK: Is there Need for Fundamental Reform?' (2012) 6 *European Human Rights Law Review* 595.

[23] For a now classic analysis see S. Douglas-Scott, 'A Tale of Two Courts: Luxembourg, Strasbourg and the Growing European Human Rights Acquis' (2006) 43(3) *Common Market Law Review* 629.

[24] *Nada* v. *Switzerland* (2013) 56 EHRR 18.

[25] See C. Eckes, 'EU Accession to the ECHR: Between Autonomy and Adaptation' (2013) 76 (2) *Modern Law Review* 254.

[26] See for a general discussion S. Greer, *The European Convention on Human Rights: Achievement, Problems and Prospects* (Cambridge University Press, 2006).

material scope insofar as it examines the entirety of a state's action in a case, including operational matters, whereas the CJEU's jurisdiction is subject to a limitation that excludes operational matters.[27] Thirdly, the ECtHR has a subsidiary jurisdiction that requires a complainant to exhaust all domestic remedies before the Court will consider their application and its judgments require enforcement by the Council of Ministers.[28] This contrasts with the EU Courts that can hear direct applications for annulment and give preliminary rulings on matters that national courts refer to it. Its rulings on applications for annulment may be directly applicable in national legal systems, although litigation leading to preliminary rulings still requires resolution before national courts.[29] These differences mean that the ECtHR has a broad supervisory role, albeit one with the power to do justice in individual cases, but the CJEU has a more difficult task of creating jurisprudence for a supranational legal system without being in a position to directly address all questions of law or fact in all cases.[30]

If this difficult position cautions against optimism for the Court of Justice's role in controlling executive power, it must be recalled that none of the limitations affect its ability to act in relation to restrictive measures. It is therefore necessary to consider the practices of the Court of Justice so as to better understand its position as a distinctive forum for judicial review of counter-terrorism action. The Court's history raises some questions. The establishment of the Court as an entity to resolve disputes in relation to the common market gives rise to questions as to its expertise in the field of counter-terrorism law. The initial evidence, at least in the field of restrictive measures, is that this question of expertise is not a significant concern. Indeed, the Court has proven itself adept at adapting its jurisprudence to new fields of law such as counter-terrorism. Nevertheless, as the case study in the second half of this chapter makes

---

[27] TFEU, Art. 276 provides that the Court 'shall have no jurisdiction to review the validity or proportionality of operations carried out by the police or other law-enforcement services of a Member State or the exercise of the responsibilities incumbent upon Member States with regard to the maintenance of law and order and the safeguarding of internal Security'.

[28] See the discussion in Chapter 13 of this volume, H. Fenwick, 'Post 9/11 UK counter-terrorism cases in the European Court of Human Rights: a "Dialogic" approach to rights protection or appeasement of national authorities?'.

[29] See TFEU, Arts. 263 and 267.

[30] See C. C. Murphy and D. A. Arcarazo, 'Rethinking Freedom, Security and Justice' in D. A. Arcarazo and C. C. Murphy (eds.), *EU Security and Justice Law: After Lisbon and Stockholm* (Oxford, Hart Publishing, 2014).

clear, there remain challenges ahead that may point to limitations in the Court's institutional appropriateness, for example, in the consideration of secret evidence.

In addition to the question of expertise there is also the matter of the rather opaque operation of the Court itself. A greater degree of transparency in Court of Justice proceedings would allow the Court to serve as a discursive forum for questions about the lawfulness of a particular counter-terrorism action. The decisions of a court in judicial review of counter-terrorism measures determines what is lawful for a state, and for non-state actors, to do in the public sphere to further political goals. In such a determination, transparency and deliberation are key to both effective and legitimate decision-making. Although it is common to call for transparency and deliberation in critiques of executive action it is also an appropriate criticism of judicial practice in this case.

The first potential limitation, in terms of transparency, is the confidentiality of pleadings before the Court. All written pleadings in cases before the EU courts are confidential to the parties in the case. This stands in sharp contrast to, for example, the United States, where pleadings are not only in public, but are often the subject of re-enactment in law schools across the country.[31] These debates can serve to inform and enrich the public's understanding of a field of law where legitimacy is crucial. The opacity of Court practices, which may have been defensible when it was merely a custodian of a common market, is more problematic in a constitutional court.

The second potential limitation is the Court's practice of issuing a single judgment in a case. Although this system may provide greater certainty and clarity than one in which multiple judgments are handed down, it also requires the judiciary to agree not just on the outcome of the case, but also on the reasoning. If this proves too difficult for the Court then their judgment may be sparse in its reasoning and thus offer little guidance for future governmental action in a crucial field. Although this problem may occur in all areas of law, it is of particular significance when the executive wields as significant a power over the individual as it does in counter-terrorism law.

---

[31] Note, for example, the activities of the Georgetown University Law Centre's Supreme Court Institute, which regularly involve moots and post-argument panel discussions of litigation before the Court. See www.law.georgetown.edu/academics/centers-institutes/supreme-court-institute/.

These criticisms are about more than the balance of power between the executive and the judiciary. They concern the appropriate relationship between law and politics. If, for example, there had been a dissent in the *Kadi I* judgment, then the power of that judgment in shaping EU and UN use of restrictive measures would be diminished. Of course, if the Court had a practice of allowing dissents, and the judgment in *Kadi I* was still unanimous, the power of that judgment would be even greater. Furthermore, although the case has been the subject of debate across Europe and the world, it is only those party to the proceedings that know the arguments of the EU institutions and the Member States. This secrecy benefits parties involved in lots of litigation, as they may alter their position on the law from case to case, but it hinders public deliberation on appropriate counter-terrorism action.

In contrast to the above criticism on the grounds of lack of transparency is the Court's current practice in relation to secret evidence. The use of secret evidence, evidence made available to the court but not to the subject of the counter-terrorism measure, is one of the most contentious aspects of counter-terrorism litigation today.[32] It is not possible, at present, to use such evidence before EU courts.[33] This limitation is because of a stipulation in the Rules of Procedure of both the EU General Court and the Court of Justice that the courts may take into consideration 'only those documents which have been made available to the lawyers and agents of the parties and on which they have been given the opportunity of expressing their views'.[34] Advocate-General Sharpston suggests, in a recent Opinion, that these rules should be amended. The amendments, she claims, should 'make provision for the production of evidence that is truly confidential for consideration by that Court in a way that is compatible with its character' without causing 'unacceptable violence' to the rights of due process.[35] Thus, whereas an emphasis on

---

[32] See in general the contributions to D. Cole, F. Fabbrini and A. Vedaschi (eds.), *Secrecy, National Security and the Vindication of Constitutional Law* (Camberley: Edward Elgar Publishing, 2013).

[33] For a discussion see C. C. Murphy, 'Secret Evidence in EU Security Law: Special Advocates before the Court of Justice?' in D. Cole, F. Fabbrini and A. Vedaschi (eds.), *Secrecy, National Security and the Vindication of Constitutional Law* (Camberley: Edward Elgar Publishing, 2013).

[34] Rules of Procedure of the General Court, art. 67(3).

[35] TFEU, Arts. 253 and 254 provide that the Court of Justice, and the General Court, respectively, shall 'establish' their Rules of Procedures. However, these rules are subject to the approval of the Council.

deliberation militates in favour of more openness, the claims of the security and intelligence services require more secrecy. At present, the practices of the Court make it less than satisfactory from the perspective of either those who place security above due process concerns, or those who have the opposite priorities. The current process of reform of the Rules of Procedure raises further questions of transparency, as will be set out below.

In light of the above analysis, one might conclude that the EU courts make for a peculiar venue for arguments about the appropriate scope of executive power. The field of counter-terrorism is one that is related to the 'area of freedom, security and justice' in EU policy-making.[36] In this field, the CJEU has a record which 'has so far been ambivalent, to say the least'.[37] There were therefore little early indications that the profound judgment handed down in *Kadi I* would be forthcoming. However, as is now well known, the CJEU was to proclaim itself a champion of the rule of law in its first significant judgment on counter-terrorism law.

The *Kadi I* judgment was the subject of almost universal praise from the academy, in respect of its outcome if not always its reasoning. However, the above concerns remain. It is the problem, as Davis and de Londras put it, of institutional appropriateness. This is not a surprising concern because the Court may be, in general, struggling with the area of freedom, security and justice.[38] A brief examination of the Court's case law on restrictive measures gives some cause for optimism in relation to counter-terrorism law while pointing to further challenges that lie ahead.

III   Restrictive measures before the Court of Justice

Restrictive measures are the paradigmatic example of EU counter-terrorism law.[39] They seek to incapacitate those about whom there is suspicion of links to terrorism. The measures are therefore a pre-emptive use of executive power and pose a serious challenge to the rule of law. In

---

[36] *Ibid.*
[37] S. Douglas-Scott, 'Freedom, Security and Justice in the ECJ' in T. Campbell, K. D. Ewing and A. Tomkins (eds.), *The Legal Protection of Human Rights: Sceptical Essays* (Oxford University Press, 2011), p. 277.
[38] See in general, Arcarazo and Murphy, *EU Security and Justice Law: After Lisbon and Stockholm*, n. 30 above.
[39] See in general Murphy, *EU Counter-Terrorism Law*, n. 1 above, ch. 5.

a state, executive power is 'cleaved in two'.[40] In internal affairs, executive power is set out by national constitutional law while in external relations executive power is bound by international law and international relations. Restrictive measures, as an exercise of executive power, blur these boundaries between the internal and the external. The restrictive measures involve the designation by the UN of individuals as associated with Al-Qaeda and the implementation of those restrictive measures by the EU. As a result the lines between EU constitutional law, international law and Member State action in international relations collapse.

The various judgments in the *Kadi* litigation have been the subject of a vast literature and are not set out in detail here.[41] Mr Kadi sought to challenge the implementation in the EU of UN restrictive measures against him. He was unsuccessful in *Kadi I* before the EU General Court (then the Court of First Instance)[42] but won his appeal to the Court of Justice and has won before both the General Court and the Court of Justice in *Kadi II*.[43] The core finding of the Court of Justice judgment in *Kadi I* is well known: the EU must provide due process to those subject to restrictive measures notwithstanding the fact that the measures are the result of a UN Security Council resolution. This remains the key principle from the litigation. Several points merit rehearsal, however.

First, the distinction between the position of the General Court in *Kadi I*, where Mr Kadi lost, and the Court of Justice in the same case, where he won, turns on their characterisation of the judicial review as a review of either an external or an internal decision-making process. For the General Court, any review of the restrictive measures against EU human rights standards would amount to an indirect review of the actions of the UN Security Council against those standards. Such an

---

[40] Curtin, *Executive Power of the European Union*, n. 6 above, p. 28.

[41] For a good starting point see S. Poli and M. Tzanou, 'The *Kadi* Rulings: A Survey of the Literature' (2009) *Yearbook of European Law* 533 and the other contributions to the symposium on *Kadi* in that volume of the *Yearbook*. On restrictive measures in EU law see the canonical, if pre-*Kadi II*, C. Eckes, *EU Counter-Terrorist Policies and Fundamental Rights: The Case of Individual Sanctions* (Oxford University Press, 2009).

[42] The EU 'Court of First Instance' was renamed the 'General Court' after the Treaty of Lisbon came into effect. Thus, in *Kadi I* the court was the Court of First Instance and in *Kadi II* it was the General Court. To spare the readership of this generalist volume this idiosyncrasy of EU nomenclature, the 'General Court' is used throughout this chapter to refer to the court in both cases.

[43] Case T-85/09 *Kadi v. Commission* [2010] ECR II-5177 ('*Kadi II* (General Court)'), and Joined Cases C-584/10P, C-593/10P and C-595/10P *Commission v. Kadi* (2013, not yet published) ('*Kadi II* (ECJ)').

indirect review was not compatible with international law and was therefore not appropriate.[44] For the Court of Justice, in contrast, the matter was entirely an internal one. The internal exercise of executive power could not escape review solely because of its origin in a UN Security Council resolution. Thus, whereas the General Court found itself to be, in effect, bound to obey international law, the Court of Justice felt no such inhibition and allowed Mr Kadi's appeal.[45] In *Kadi II*, both the General Court and the Court of Justice upheld this key point from *Kadi I*.

Secondly, the judgment of the Court of Justice in *Kadi I* had its basis in EU constitutional law. The absence at that time of any judicial or quasi-judicial review, or of an independent decision-making process at European level, means that the Court's judgment did not address the more difficult questions that might arise in relation to EU administrative law if there were a decision-making process in place. However, the appeal in *Kadi II* did require the Court of Justice to address this matter. The *Kadi II* decision of the Court of Justice therefore marks a shift in the adjudication: from constitutional to administrative law. The shift is apparent as the Court moves beyond the question of whether or not to review the EU action to a consideration of how rigorous that review should be and what evidence is necessary for the review to take place. It is the subject of further discussion below.

Thirdly, all judgments except *Kadi I* in the General Court have been rather muscular. The EU courts acknowledge the national security context of the restrictive measures but give short shrift to calls for deference. The Court of Justice in *Kadi I* held that it would engage in 'review, in principle the full review' of the measures. The language of the Court of Justice was the subject of much discussion following the relisting of Mr Kadi and recommencement of his litigation. After its rebuke by the Court of Justice in *Kadi I*, the General Court took the 'in principle the full review' standard in the strictest of terms. It may be for this reason that the Court of Justice in *Kadi II* sought to ameliorate some of the stronger statements made by the General Court in that case.[46]

---

[44] Case T-315/01 *Kadi v. Council and Commission* [2005] ECR II-3649, paras. 213–26.

[45] *Kadi II* (ECJ), n. 44 above, paras. 281–8.

[46] In *Kadi II*, n. 44 above, the General Court had claimed that the failure of the European Commission to disclose evidence, which, in fact, only the UN Security Council, or UN Member States held, was in itself a breach of due process. It also held that all of the grounds given to Mr Kadi in the statement of reasons were too vague for him to rebut (paras. 173–94). The Court of Justice, on appeal, held that the European Commission could not be required to disclose evidence it did not have (paras. 137–8) and that not all

Although there has been some criticism of the *Kadi I* reasoning from within the academy that criticism has largely taken as its focus the failure of the Court to rely on international law and not the substantive outcome of the case.[47] The Court of Justice's case law considers the *Kadi* line of cases to be jurisprudence about EU constitutional and administrative law and not international law or international relations. The decision of the Court of Justice was a defiance of the UN Security Council and a challenge to the effective and legitimate exercise of power under international law. In terms of control of executive power, both that of the Union (directly) and the UN Security Council and EU Member States (indirectly), the Court of Justice proved to be willing to flex its muscles. It may be that the apparent simplicity of the central question in *Kadi I* made this possible: to review or not to review? In the absence of any due process in the UN or EU system for targeting restrictive measures it is obvious that any review at all would result in a finding of a violation of the rule of law. In respect of international relations, the decision can be cast as a sort of 'civil disobedience' against the UN Security Council's excessive interference with human rights using a mechanism that entirely failed to offer due process.[48]

IV From constitutional review to administrative review

The more difficult questions were those that arose after *Kadi I*, both for the UN and the EU, in seeking to develop systems of due process. The UN and EU put in place certain reforms in response to the judgment and it was these reforms that would bring the Court of Justice to the more complex field of administrative law. The challenge this would raise for the Court was whether it could continue its defence to the rule of law in the more complex field of administrative law or whether, like the sorcerer's apprentice, it had started something it could not finish. To assess the Court of Justice's review in the field of EU administrative law, it is

---

of the statement of reasons was too vague (para. 140). The Court of Justice still dismissed the appeals.

[47] See G. de Búrca, 'The EU, the European Court of Justice, and the International Legal Order after *Kadi*' (2009) 51(1) *Harvard International Law Journal* 1. See also K. S. Ziegler, 'Strengthening the Rule of Law, but Fragmenting International Law: The *Kadi* Decision of the ECJ from the Perspective of Human Rights' (2009) 9 *Human Rights Law Review* 288.

[48] N. Turkuler Isiksel, 'Fundamental Rights in the EU after Kadi and Al Barakaat' (2010) 16 *European Law Journal* 551.

necessary to set out briefly the response by the UN and EU to the *Kadi I* judgment. The judgment is given credit for prompting the establishment of an Office of Ombudsperson to offer a quasi-judicial review of listing decisions.[49] The Ombudsperson has seen her office evolve from its predecessor, a 'Focal Point' that was little more than an in-tray for the Sanctions Committee, to a more powerful means of review. Two principal limitations remain on that power: the Ombudsperson cannot compel UN organs or Member States to produce evidence; and her decision may be subject to override by the Sanctions Committee, the Security Council or (in effect) any one of its permanent members.[50] It was following the recommendation of this Ombudsperson that Mr Kadi saw the removal of his name first from the UN list and subsequently from the EU list.[51] This demonstrates the interplay between legal systems and political systems and represents a moderate juridification of a UN system that was previously in the realm of international relations. However, the Ombudsperson was something of a 'red herring' in the *Kadi II* litigation. At the time of Mr Kadi's relisting by the EU in 2008, the Office had not yet been established. The more significant reforms to the Office took place after the General Court handed down its judgment in *Kadi II*.[52] Too great a focus on the Office is therefore unhelpful in understanding subsequent developments in EU law.

The result of the *Kadi I* litigation in the EU was a more limited change in approach. The Council put in place a system whereby the target of restrictive measures was given an opportunity to comment on the 'narrative summary' of reasons for which they were put on the UN list before the European Commission took a final decision on whether to maintain action against the target. It was the maintenance of Mr Kadi on the EU list after such a process that was the subject of dispute in *Kadi II*. In its judgment, the Court of Justice set out general principles of law in this

---

[49] The Ombudsperson herself makes this point. See Remarks of Kimberly Prost, Ombudsperson, 1267 Al-Qaida/Taliban Sanctions Committee, delivered to the informal meeting of Legal Advisors, 25 October 2010, available at www.un.org/en/sc/ombudsperson.

[50] UN Security Council Resolution 2083 of 17 December 2012.

[51] Mr Kadi was delisted by a decision of the UN Security Council Al-Qaeda Sanctions Committee on 5 October 2012.

[52] Mr Kadi was relisted on 28 November 2008. The Office of the Ombudsperson was established by UN Security Council Resolution 1904 of 17 December 2009. The judgment in Case T-85/09 *Kadi v. Commission* [2010] ECR II-5177 was handed down on 30 September 2010 and the Office's mandate was extended by UN Security Council Resolution 1989 of 17 June 2011 and Resolution 2083 of 17 December 2012.

field and applied those principles to Mr Kadi's case. These are the subject of a brief discussion below.

However, the Court of Justice had the chance to consider these questions even before it heard *Kadi II*. The *French Republic* v. *OMPI* litigation arose as a result of a challenge to restrictive measures against the People's Mujahedin Organisation of Iran. After a decision by the Council to delist the Organisation, the French Republic sought a ruling that a Member State could not be compelled to release in court evidence or other materials that may be prejudicial to national security. Advocate-General Sharpston notes in her Opinion that the system of designation at issue in the case involves determinations at both national and EU level. She notes that in conducting its review of the listing decision the Court would also have regard to the review process at national level and adjust its process accordingly. She sought to devise a system of rules to determine if and when the EU courts would need to compel disclosure of any secret evidence to the Court.[53] The proposal sought to use, as a baseline, the British system of special advocates, one that is subject to severe criticism within its national legal system.[54] Despite the Advocate-General's efforts, the Court of Justice chose not to address the question in its judgment.[55]

The question of secret evidence was taken up once more in the case of *ZZ* v. *Secretary of State for the Home Department*.[56] The case involved a challenge to the system of secret evidence in UK immigration law. In its judgment, the Court of Justice makes clear that an individual 'must be informed, in any event, of the essence of the grounds on which a decision ... is taken'.[57] However, the Court is more circumspect in relation to the disclosure of the evidence that supports those grounds. The Court notes that disclosure of evidence may prejudice security by exposing particular persons in national security operations or by revealing the methods those operations use.[58] However, it may be difficult to apply the distinction between grounds and evidence in practice. In Mr ZZ's case the open judgment of the Special Immigration Appeals Commission (SIAC) states that he was involved in terrorist activities linked to the Armed Islamic Group network in 1995 and 1996.

---

[53] For a discussion, see Murphy, 'Secret Evidence in EU Security Law', n. 33 above.

[54] Note that notwithstanding criticism of the system, recent legislation extends it to cover all areas of civil litigation: Justice and Security Act 2013.

[55] Case C-27/09P *French Republic* v. *OMPI* [2011] ECR I-13427.

[56] Case C-300/11 *ZZ* v. *Secretary of State for the Home Department* (2013, not yet published).

[57] *Ibid.* para. 65.   [58] *Ibid.* paras. 54–68.

The judgment suggests that SIAC accepted certain evidence that Mr ZZ has brought forward to explain his activities and in particular stays in Italy and Belgium and contact with certain persons. However, SIAC did not accept all of Mr ZZ's explanations, on grounds it only made clear in the closed judgment. Herein lies the problem. It may be impossible to disclose certain grounds without revealing the supporting evidence. If one of the grounds, for example, is that Mr ZZ met with a certain person in a private place, then it may suggest that that person is a confidential informant, or that the building is under surveillance, or that Mr ZZ's communications are subject to interception. The line between grounds and evidence is a very thin – and sometimes non-existent – one. If the Court of Justice believes that due process requires disclosure of grounds then disclosure of evidence may be unavoidable.

Although the Court of Justice had at this point only given judgment in a case on the UK system of special advocates, the question of review of secret evidence in the context of restrictive measures was becoming more prominent, and the Court began to develop proposals to amend its Rules of Procedure to allow it to consider such evidence. On 21 May 2013, the UK government answered a question from Lord Pannick in the House of Lords on the subject. The UK government confirmed that such a process was underway but it declined to comment on the content of the proposals before their publication by the Court.[59] On the same day, representatives of various professional organisations in the United Kingdom and Ireland wrote to Judge Skouris, President of the Court of Justice, to call for public consultation on the proposal to change the Rules of Procedure.[60] In his reply, Judge Skouris confirmed that the Court intended 'to propose a series of amendments to the rules of procedure' but did not offer further details.[61] This ongoing secretive process of amendment of the Court of Justice's Rules of Procedure stands in stark contrast to the open debate in the United Kingdom on the Justice and Security Act 2013. That Act, of course, came about as a result of a seemingly organic spread of closed material proceedings from immigration, to counter-terrorism, to broader areas of civil law. Even if the

---

[59] See House of Lords Hansard, 21 May 2013, col. WA56.

[60] Letter to the President of the Court of Justice of the European Union, 21 May 2013, available at www.europeansanctions.com.

[61] Letter to President of the Bar Council of England and Wales, 18 June 2013, available at www.europeansanctions.com. The signatories to the first letter replied on 22 July 2013 to press the President further on the question of public consultation.

necessity of closed material procedures with secret evidence remains highly controversial, the change in the law was brought about by primary legislation that was the subject of intense public debate.

The Court's judgment in *Kadi II* was therefore the subject of much anticipation. The decision of the General Court in *Kadi II* took the logic of 'in principle, the full review' quite strictly. In contrast, the Opinion of Advocate-General Bot in *Kadi II* offers a rather different approach. The Advocate-General proposes a solution that divides the Court's exercise of judicial review in two: a review of the restrictive measures' 'external' and 'internal' lawfulness. However, as an exercise in administrative law the Opinion raises far more questions than it answers. Indeed, a review of the substance of a measure against the fundamental principles of EU law is a *sine qua non* of judicial review before the Court of Justice. It is fortunate then that the Court of Justice paid little attention to the Advocate-General's Opinion. In its judgment, the Court reiterates that the individual must be able to make his views known on the case against him.[62] In the conduct of its review the Court must determine whether there is a 'sufficiently solid factual basis' for the decision.[63] EU authorities do not have to produce all information but they must produce information and evidence sufficient to support the reasons for the decision.[64] The Court states that if there is no disclosure of information or evidence then it must base its review on the evidence of information that has been made available to it. However, the Court notes that Member States might seek cooperation from the UN to obtain further information and that the Court itself may need 'techniques' to deal with confidential information.[65] The Court then goes on to assess the grounds given for targeting Mr Kadi in the 'narrative summary of reasons'. It concludes that those reasons are either too vague to stand, or are not supported by information or evidence that could justify the targeting, in 2008, of Mr Kadi.[66] As such, the Court of Justice found in Mr Kadi's favour and dismissed the appeals.

V Judicial review and the challenge for the Court of Justice

The *Kadi II* judgment is still, at the time of writing, too fresh for its full impact to be properly understood.[67] For Mr Kadi there is vindication, on

---

[62] *Kadi II* (ECJ), n. 44 above, para. 112.   [63] *Ibid.* para. 119.   [64] *Ibid.* para. 122.
[65] *Ibid.* para. 125 *et seq.*   [66] *Ibid.* paras. 141–65.
[67] For an early reaction see A. Tzanakopoulos, '*Kadi* Showdown: Substantive Review of (UN) Sanctions by the ECJ', *EJIL: Talk!*, 19 July 2013, available at www.ejiltalk.org.

the law and on the facts, that the freezing of his assets and the travel ban imposed on him for over a decade was a violation of his rights. The removal of Mr Kadi from the UN list of individuals and entities under suspicion was a result of a recommendation of the Ombudsperson, an office whose establishment is a result of Mr Kadi's litigation before the EU Courts. Thus, the criticism that the *Kadi I* judgment was a 'pyrrhic victory of the claimant' goes too far.[68] It is, however, the case that Mr Kadi was on the EU list for as long as he was on the UN list, and that his ultimate removal from the UN and EU lists was in effect subject to the acquiescence of the UN Security Council. It is impossible to guess whether or not the Court of Justice would have found in Mr Kadi's favour if the question had not become moot, in prospective terms, before the Court's judgment in *Kadi II*.

This chapter is a deliberate exercise to challenge the general academic consensus on the CJEU and counter-terrorism after Mr Kadi's litigation. It should not be read as a criticism of the Court's judgments in *Kadi I* and *Kadi II*. Rather it aims to remove any complacency that the Court of Justice is in an ideal position to protect the rule of law or that the *Kadi* line of cases proves it to be an unerring champion of that principle. One commentary on the *Kadi* litigation suggests that in the 'EU's flawed system of governance, democracy finds solace in judicial review'.[69] There is a danger in relying on courts to uphold democracy though, however Herculean their efforts. Those who now praise the Court of Justice for its *Kadi* judgments would be much less optimistic about its institutional appropriateness if the Court had found against Mr Kadi. But one judgment does not make for an effective, or an ineffective, constitutional system.

A robust, muscular approach to judicial review must sit alongside a transparent, accountable, democratic process for devising and implementing counter-terrorism law. As other contributions to this book make clear, independent reviewers, inquiries and quasi-judicial administrative review all contribute to further the accountability of executive power in counter-terrorism.[70] However, those systems work, by and large, at the

---

[68] Douglas-Scott, 'Freedom, Security and Justice in the ECJ', n. 37 above, p. 289.

[69] T. Tridimas, 'Terrorism and the ECJ: Empowerment and Democracy in the EC Legal Order' (2009) 34 *European Law Review* 103.

[70] See Chapter 1 in this volume, F. de Londras, 'Counter-terrorism judicial review as regulatory constitutionalism', Chapter 7, J. Blackbourn, 'Independent reviewers as alternative: an empirical study from Australia and the United Kingdom', and Chapter 8,

state level and within or alongside a traditional tripartite division of state power between executive, legislative and judicial organs of government. As part of a state's system of accountability they also contribute to the discourse in the public sphere about the necessity and effectiveness of counter-terrorism action. The idea, as de Londras puts it, of regulatory constitutionalism, works in political and legal systems that are reflexive. In such an instance, the judgments of a court fit into this regulatory milieu as a form of policy-making: 'creating, conserving or changing public policies, or existing priorities among them, in areas of public policy which are subject to some sort of governmental regulation by binding rules of law'.[71] However, that policy-making itself requires open deliberation, and current Court of Justice practices, and the process for reforming those practices, are less than satisfactory in this regard.

A final observation is that all litigation runs the risk of unintended consequences and this is true too in respect of restrictive measures. The EU operates thirty-three separate systems of restrictive measures, ranging in their focus from terrorism to nuclear proliferation.[72] Some are autonomous systems of EU restrictive measures and others implement UN Security Council resolutions. In respect of the latter, the UN has begun once more to broaden the targets of its sanctions systems. This shifts the balance away from individuals and towards states and therefore returns it to the realm of international relations.[73] This may leave the Al-Qaeda list of sanctions targets as a historical aberration – an exceptional exercise of executive power following the 11 September 2001 attacks. Insofar as this power finds expression in legal systems, it falls to institutions of government, both courts and others, to deploy 'conceptual resources'[74] to hold that power to account. The *Kadi* judgments are steps in the right direction but there is no doubt that challenges remain.

K. Roach, 'Public inquiries as an attempt to fill accountability gaps left by judicial and legislative review'.

[71] H. Rasmussen, *On Law and Policy in the European Court of Justice* (Dordrecht: Martinus Nijhoff Publishers, 1986), p 4.

[72] European Commission, *Restrictive Measures in Force (Article 215 TFEU)* (5 June 2013), available at http://eeas.europa.eu/cfsp/sanctions/docs/measures_en.pdf.

[73] Tzanakopoulos, '*Kadi* Showdown: Substantive Review of (UN) Sanctions by the ECJ', n. 68 above.

[74] See Chapter 5 in this volume, M. Tushnet, 'Emergency law as administrative law'.

Post 9/11 UK counter-terrorism cases in the European Court of Human Rights: a 'dialogic' approach to rights protection or appeasement of national authorities?

HELEN FENWICK

Introduction

This chapter evaluates the developing role played by the European Court of Human Rights (ECtHR, also known as the Strasbourg Court) in a number of recent counter-terrorism cases brought against the United Kingdom: *A* v. *United Kingdom*,[1] *Gillan* v. *United Kingdom*,[2] *Othman* v. *United Kingdom*,[3] *Babar Ahmad and others* v. *United Kingdom*.[4] In light of those aspects of the Izmir, Interlaken and Brighton declarations[5] aimed at creating greater subsidiarity within the judicial process, it considers the response to arguments put by the executive to the national courts and to the ECtHR, and the resulting judgments, focusing on the developing use of the principle of subsidiarity. The interaction between Strasbourg and the United Kingdom can be viewed as a dialogue[6] in which both parties seek to find an acceptable balance between the rights of the applicants and

---

[1] (2009) 49 EHRR 29.   [2] (2010) 50 EHRR 45.   [3] (2012) 55 EHRR 1.

[4] (2013) 56 EHRR 1. These decisions are focused on, in particular, as the current tensions between the UK government and the ECtHR, especially within the counter-terrorism context, provide an example of a pertinent situation within which to examine the concept of dialogue between the national and international levels. Further, the decisions, especially that in *Othman*, have fuelled the push for 'enhanced subsidiarity' by the UK government at Brighton, as discussed below.

[5] Interlaken declaration, 19 February 2010; Izmir declaration, 27 April 2011; Brighton declaration, 20 April 2012; see further at www.coe.int/reformECHR. The declarations are discussed in some detail below.

[6] See Lord Neuberger's interview, reported on 5 March 2013 (O. Bowcott, 'Senior Judge warns over deportation of terror suspects to torture states', *Guardian*, 5 March 2013) in which he stated that the UK Supreme Court is 'not subservient' but works 'in a dialogue' with the judges in Strasbourg. See also Chapter 9 in this volume, R. Masterman, 'Rebalancing the unbalanced constitution: juridification and national security in the United Kingdom'.

countervailing considerations, rather than adopting a more absolutist approach to those rights on the Dworkinian model. It is this sense in which the term 'dialogic', already familiar to public lawyers in the *domestic* context, is being used.[7] But this chapter asks whether, especially in light of the emphasis on giving greater prominence to the principle of subsidiarity in its judgments, the ECtHR has succeeded in this and contributed to a domestic/international dialogue to protect the European Convention on Human Rights (ECHR) rights of British citizens, or whether the dialogue has at times given way to mere appeasement. Is the Court revisiting the 'true' scope of the ECHR in a more deferential spirit in this context?

I   Reform of the ECtHR via 'enhanced subsidiarity'

This is not the place to discuss the proposals for reform of the European Court of Human Rights in detail and many readers are likely to be aware of their general drift in any event.[8] Giving greater prominence to the principle of subsidiarity at Strasbourg would aid in dealing with the Court's backlog of cases and, as the follow-up to the Interlaken declaration made clear, would be in harmony with the ECHR itself and with the jurisprudence.[9] But the precise limitations that should continue to apply to that principle, which is clearly non-absolute, remain a matter of controversy. Merely reiterating that the Court's role is subsidiary to that of national authorities is of little import.

Stemming from the principle of subsidiarity, the Strasbourg system concedes a variable margin of appreciation to states,[10] one that tends to

---

[7] See e.g., T. Hickman, 'The Courts and Politics after the Human Rights Act: A Comment' (2008) *Public Law* 84.

[8] For discussion see further A. Mowbray, 'The Interlaken Declaration: The Beginning of a New Era for the European Court of Human Rights' (2010) 10(3) *Human Rights Law Review* 519; Irish Human Rights Commission, 'Reform of the European Court of Human Rights' (2 March 2011), available at www.ihrc.ie/enquiriesandlegal/europeancourtre.html; N. O'Meara, 'Reforming the European Court of Human Rights through Dialogue? Progress on Protocols 15 and 16 ECHR', UK Constitutional Law Group Blog, 31 May 2013, available at http://ukconstitutionallaw.org/tag/brighton-declaration/.

[9] 'Note by the Jurisconsult on Principle of Subsidiarity', European Court of Human Rights (8 July 2010), available at www.echr.coe.int/Documents/2010_Interlaken_Follow-up_ENG.pdf; it referred to Arts. 1 and 19 ECHR, and in particular instanced *Scordino* v. *Italy* (2006) 45 EHRR 7 (GC).

[10] See further G. Letsas, 'Two Concepts of the Margin of Appreciation' (2006) 4 *Oxford Journal of Legal Studies* 705.

be wider in relation to matters of national security.[11] The idea that a
greater emphasis on subsidiarity should form an aspect of reform of the
Court system gained purchase within the Interlaken and Izmir declarations in 2010 and 2011, which were focused on creating enhanced
subsidiarity, but not to the same extent as the Brighton one in 2012. Its
importance was stressed under the terms of the Action Plan attached to
the Interlaken declaration: 'The Conference, acknowledging the responsibility shared between the States Parties and the Court, invites the Court
to . . . take fully into account its subsidiary role in the interpretation and
application of the Convention . . . [and] invites the Court to . . . avoid
reconsidering questions of fact or national law that have been considered
and decided by national authorities, in line with its case law according to
which it is not a fourth instance court'.[12] The Interlaken follow-up
focused solely on the principle of subsidiarity, finding that the form of
subsidiarity at issue – 'complementary subsidiarity' – meant that: 'the
Court's powers of intervention are confined to those cases where the
domestic institutions are incapable of ensuring effective protection of
the rights guaranteed by the Convention'.[13] The Izmir declaration
required the Court to 'confirm in its case law that it is not a fourth-
instance court',[14] and 'to ensure that cases are dealt with in accordance
with the principle of subsidiarity'.[15]

Britain's Chairmanship of the Council of Europe[16] provided the
Conservative leadership with an opportunity to present proposals
intended to allow the current use of the margin of appreciation
doctrine to be taken much further, creating greater subsidiarity.[17]
The government's plans for reform of the Court were extensively trailed
in the run up to the Brighton Conference in April 2012. Intervening

---

[11] See the Art. 15 ECHR derogation cases such as *Brannigan and McBride* v. *United
Kingdom* (1994) 17 EHRR 539; see further T. Jones, 'The Devaluation of Human Rights
under the ECHR' (1995) *Public Law* 430.

[12] Interlaken declaration, 19 February 2010, point 9, available at www.eda.admin.ch/etc/
medialib/downloads/edazen/topics/europa/euroc.Par.0133.File.tmp/final_en.pdf.

[13] 'Note by the Jurisconsult on Principle of Subsidiarity', n. 9 above, I(a)(3).

[14] Izmir declaration, 26–27 April 2011, point 2(c), available at https://wcd.coe.int/com.
instranet.InstraServlet?command=com.instranet.CmdBlobGet&InstranetImage=2074588&
SecMode=1&DocId=1733590&Usage=2.

[15] *Ibid.* Follow-up plan, point A1.   [16] It began on 7 November 2011.

[17] According to parliamentary written answers and statements: M. Harper, HC Debs, vol
525, col. 31WS, 18 March 2011: 'We will be pressing . . . to reinforce the principle that
states rather than the [Court] have the primary responsibility for protecting Convention
rights'.

in *Scoppola v. Italy (No. 3)*,[18] the UK Attorney General Dominic Grieve said that greater acknowledgement of the margin of appreciation doctrine would result in the ECtHR intervening only when 'the decision of the national authorities is manifestly without reasonable foundation'. Prime Minister David Cameron's speech to the Parliamentary Assembly of the Council of Europe in 2012,[19] during the United Kingdom's six-month chairmanship of the Council, reiterated the theme of seeking enhanced subsidiarity as a key reform. He referenced counter-terrorism and prisoners' voting rights as examples of issues on which the Court should be very slow to intervene, once democratic debate on the issue and full scrutiny in national courts, taking the ECHR into account, had occurred. Referencing the *Qatada*[20] case as illustrating the need for reform, he said 'we have gone through all reasonable national processes ... yet we are still unable to deport [or detain] them'. The members of the assembly voted unanimously to agree that the court should be 'subsidiary' to national authorities – governments, courts and parliaments – in guaranteeing human rights.

A draft declaration for that conference was 'leaked',[21] and published in various forums, which gave even greater prominence to the principle of subsidiarity than the Brighton declaration itself did. The declaration emphasises subsidiarity:

> The Conference therefore: (a) welcomes the development by the Court in its case law of principles such as subsidiarity and the margin of appreciation, and encourages the Court to give great prominence to and apply consistently these principles in its judgments; (b) Concludes that, for reasons of transparency and accessibility, a reference to the principle of subsidiarity and the doctrine of the margin of appreciation as developed in the Court's case law should be included in the preamble to the Convention[22] [by the end of 2013].

---

[18] (2013) 56 EHRR 19.

[19] N. Watt, 'David Cameron calls for reform of ECHR', *Guardian*, 25 January 2012.

[20] *Othman v. United Kingdom* (2012) 55 EHRR 1.

[21] On 23 February 2012; the leaked draft is available at www.guardian.co.uk/law/interactive/2012/feb/28/echr-reform-uk-draft.

[22] Brighton declaration 19–20 April, point 12, available at https://wcd.coe.int/ViewDoc.jsp?Ref=BrightonDeclaration&Language=lanEnglish&Ver=original&Site=COE&BackColorInternet=C3C3C3&BackColorIntranet=EDB021&BackColorLogged=F5D383. The leaked proposals stated that the principles should be *enhanced* by their express inclusion in the Convention itself. The agreed Brighton declaration has now been realised in Protocol 15 (24 June 2013).

The leaked proposals stated that the principles should be *enhanced* by their express inclusion in the Convention itself. The declaration further 'welcomes and encourages dialogue, particularly dialogues between the Court and the highest courts of the States Parties'.[23] Point 23(b) of the leaked document on options for amending the admissibility criteria had proposed controversially that an application should be declared inadmissible if it was the same in substance as a matter that has already been determined by the national courts *unless* the Court considered that the national court had 'clearly erred in its application or interpretation of the Convention rights'. But that proposal did not make its way into the final declaration.

While the final declaration is less radical than the leaked proposals,[24] it is possible that its effect, combined with the impact of the emphasis on subsidiarity from Interlaken and Izmir, has been to persuade the Court to rein itself in, to an extent not formally required under the Brighton declaration itself. Without implying that the desire for such emphasis is uniform throughout the signatory states,[25] the three declarations read together indicate a mounting determination to emphasise subsidiarity, culminating at present in the Brighton one. Express inclusion of the principles of subsidiarity and the margin of appreciation in the Preamble, and urging the Court to give 'great prominence' to them, may appear to have a merely tokenistic or symbolic nature, but so doing sends a clear message to the Court about its role. The emphasis on subsidiarity in all

[23] *Ibid.* point 12(c).

[24] The leaked proposals are available at www.guardian.co.uk/law/interactive/2012/feb/28/echr-reform-uk-draft. Two of the most controversial were: para. 19(a): 'The conference therefore welcomes the development of the Court within its case-law of principles such as subsidiarity and the margin of appreciation doctrine . . . and encourages the Court to give great prominence to these principles in its judgements; (b) Concludes that the transparency and accessibility of the principles of the margin of appreciation and subsidiarity should be enhanced by their express inclusion in the Convention, and invites the Committee of Ministers to adopt the necessary amending instrument within one year'. Paragraph 23(b) on options for amending the admissibility criteria proposed that an application should be declared inadmissible if it was the same in substance as a matter that has already been determined by the national courts *unless* the Court considered that the national court 'clearly erred in its application or interpretation of the Convention rights or the application clearly raises a serious question concerning the application and interpretation of the Convention'.

[25] Russia, in particular, clearly has reservations about the current UK stance on subsidiarity due to its reliance on the Court; see e.g., the discussion on the relationship between Russia and the ECtHR in *Burdov* v. *Russia (No. 2)* (Application no. 33509/04), Judgment of 15 January 2009.

three declarations has arguably had an influence in the more recent cases discussed below, at times redolent of an appeasement rather than a 'dialogic' approach.

II   Interaction between the ECtHR, the UK government and the domestic courts in the Article 5 ECHR context

Two recent cases against the United Kingdom have considered, *inter alia*, the ambit that should be accorded to Article 5(1) ECHR in the counter-terrorism context. *A v. United Kingdom*[26] was the case brought against the United Kingdom by the Belmarsh detainees detained without trial under Part 4 of the Anti-Terrorism, Crime and Security Act 2001 (ATCSA), claiming compensation for their detention, while *Gillan v. United Kingdom* concerned suspicion-less stop and search under section 44 of the Terrorism Act 2000 (TA).[27] In *A v. United Kingdom*, the government sought to argue, contrary to the conclusions of the House of Lords in *A and others v. Secretary of State for the Home Department*,[28] that the derogation from Article 15 ECHR should be upheld, and in the alternative that the detention had not led to a breach of Article 5. In the derogation cases at Strasbourg, the Court has usually accorded a wide margin of appreciation to the national authorities, and has therefore upheld the derogation, normally relating to the use of executive detention, as in this instance.[29] However, the Grand Chamber relied on the Lords' judgment in finding that the domestic courts are part of the 'national authorities' to which the Court affords a wide margin of appreciation under Article 15:

> the Court considers that it would be justified in reaching a contrary conclusion only if satisfied that the national court had misinterpreted or misapplied Article 15 or the Court's jurisprudence under that Article or reached a conclusion which was manifestly unreasonable.[30]

The Court proceeded to agree with the House of Lords on both the public emergency and proportionality issues under Article 15.

As regards Article 5, the government sought to rely on a version of the argument that had been put on behalf of the Secretary of State in a

---

[26] (2009) 49 EHRR 29.   [27] Now repealed under Protection of Freedoms Act 2012, s. 59.
[28] (2004) UKHL 56.
[29] See e.g., *Brannigan and McBride v. United Kingdom* (1994) 17 EHRR 539.
[30] (2009) 49 EHRR 29, para. 174.

number of the domestic control order cases,[31] to the effect that the
purpose of a measure – to further national security – should be taken
into account in allowing it to fall outside the ambit of Article 5(1). As
Lord Hoffman put it in *JJ*, referencing that argument, Article 5 is 'so
quintessential a human right that it trumps even the interests of national
security'.[32] Therefore he found that it was essential that it should be
narrowly interpreted and confined to 'actual imprisonment or something
which is for practical purposes little different from imprisonment'[33] in
order to avoid imposing 'too great a restriction on the powers of the state
to deal with serious terrorist threats to the lives of its citizens'.[34] The
argument tends to rely, as accepted in *Austin*[35] (discussed below), on
finding that if the measure in question would satisfy the demands of
proportionality, it should fall outside the ambit of Article 5, an argument
that the Eminent Panel of Jurists[36] has suggested that a number of
governments have been seeking to use in the counter-terrorism context.
The argument comes close to transforming Article 5 into a right qualified
on the Articles 8 to 11 ECHR model, via restriction of Article 5's ambit or
via implied introduction of a new exception. In *A v. United Kingdom*, the
government relied on the latter argument in contending that the
principle of fair balance underlies the whole Convention, and that therefore sub-paragraph (f) of Article 5(1) (arguably the applicable exception,
allowing for detention pending deportation) had to be interpreted so as
to strike a balance between the interests of the individual and the
interests of the state in protecting its population from malevolent
aliens.[37] Detention, it was argued, struck that balance by advancing the
legitimate aim of the state to secure the protection of the population
without sacrificing the predominant interest of the alien to avoid being
returned to a place where he faced torture or death.[38] Rejecting that
argument, the Court found that the Article 5 exceptions are exhaustive
and to be narrowly interpreted; further 'if detention does not fit within
the confines of the [exceptions] as interpreted by the Court, it cannot be
made to fit by an appeal to the need to balance the interests of the state

---

[31] In particular, *SSHD* v. *JJ* [2007] UKHL 45.   [32] *Ibid.* para. 37.   [33] *Ibid.* para. 44.
[34] *Ibid.* para. 44.
[35] *Austin* v. *Commissioner of Police of the Metropolis* [2009] 2 WLR 372.
[36] Report of the Eminent Jurists Panel on Terrorism, Counter-Terrorism and Human
Rights, *Assessing Damage, Urging Action* (Geneva: International Commission of Jurists,
2009).
[37] (2009) 49 EHRR 29, para. 148.   [38] *Ibid.*

against those of the detainee'.[39] In other words, the purpose of the detention – to counter terrorism – was not allowed to limit the ambit of Article 5 via the introduction of a new exception.

Similar arguments were also rejected in *Gillan* v. *United Kingdom*[40] in relation to Article 5. In the domestic decision in *Gillan*, *R (on the application of Gillan)* v. *Commissioner of Police for the Metropolis*, concerning the use of the broad power under TA, section 44,[41] the Lords found that those stopped had merely been detained in the sense of being 'kept from proceeding or kept waiting',[42] and so the interference with their liberty fell outside the ambit of Article 5, failing to amount to a *deprivation* of liberty. Lord Bingham defended section 44's breadth on the basis of its purpose: it ensured 'that a constable is not deterred from stopping and searching a person whom he does suspect as a potential terrorist by the fear that he could not show reasonable grounds for his suspicion',[43] but the ECtHR found that the stop and search had all the hallmarks of a deprivation of liberty, although it did not find a breach of Article 5, rejecting the government's argument that the *purpose* of the search should allow it to fall outside the ambit of Article 5(1).[44] The Court then was again resistant to executive arguments as to the need to maintain a narrow ambit of Article 5(1) in the terrorism context, and contemplated a higher standard as to the liberty of the subject than the House of Lords had done, although significantly *without* finally deciding the case under Article 5, deciding it instead under the 'in accordance with law' aspect of Article 8(2).[45] The refusal to find the breach under the non-materially qualified Article creates leeway for states to introduce measures interfering with liberty[46] that are ECHR-compliant so long as in furthering the purposes of national security they comply with the

---

[39] *Ibid.* para. 171.   [40] (2010) 50 EHRR 45.

[41] The whole of London was covered by an authorisation until the use of the power was suspended. Ministry of Justice, 'Statistics on Race and the Criminal Justice System 2007/08' recorded a significant increase in the use of TA, s. 44 powers; available at www.justice.gov.uk/publications/statistics.htm.

[42] *R (on the application of Gillan)* v. *Commissioner of Police for the Metropolis* [2006] 2 AC 307, para. 25.

[43] (2010) 50 EHRR 45, para. 35.   [44] *Ibid.* para. 55.

[45] *Ibid.* para. 87. A breach of Art. 8 ECHR was found on that basis. TA, s. 44 was repealed under Protection of Freedoms Act 2012, s. 59.

[46] The specific replacement for TA, s. 44 in Protection of Freedoms Act 2012, s. 61, inserting s. 47A into the TA, is itself probably compliant with Art. 5 under Art. 5(1)(b); see para. 26 of *Gillan* (per Lord Bingham).

demands of proportionality, a stance which did not find favour under
Article 5(1) in either *Gillan* or *A*.

A v. *United Kingdom* and *Gillan* indicated that the ECtHR is unre-
ceptive to the conversion in effect of Article 5 into a right qualified
further than by the express exceptions on the Articles 8 to 11 model. So
far there has been reluctance to accept the argument that the ambit of
Article 5 can be narrowed by reference to the notion of creating a new
balance between the right to liberty and security interests in the
terrorist context, one that is perceived as according greater weight to
security. As indicated above, such a changed balance could be created
via the adoption of a purposive argument: that the purpose of a
restriction should take it outside that ambit so long as the demands
of proportionality are met. In neither case were those arguments
accepted domestically, since they were not put forward in *A* and were
not examined in detail in *Gillan*. But more recently, outside the
counter-terrorism context, they did receive acceptance in the House
of Lords, an acceptance that was then echoed at Strasbourg. The
decision in the House of Lords in *Austin* v. *Commissioner of Police of
the Metropolis*,[47] finding that 'kettling' peaceful protesters and bystand-
ers for seven hours did not create a deprivation of liberty, has been
heavily criticised;[48] it was expected that the ECtHR would take a
different stance. Lord Hope had considered that in making a determination as to the ambit of Article 5(1), the *purpose* of the interference
with liberty could be viewed as relevant; if so, he found that it must be
to enable a balance to be struck between what the restriction sought to
achieve and the interests of the individual.[49] Having found that purpose was relevant to the ambit given to Article 5(1), Lord Hope found
that the purpose must take account of the rights of the individual as
well as the interests of the community, and therefore any steps taken
must be resorted to in good faith, and must be proportionate to the
situation that made the measures necessary. If those requirements were
met, however, he concluded that it would be proper to find that
measures of crowd control undertaken in the interests of the community would not infringe the Article 5 rights of individual members of

---

[47] [2009] 2 WLR 372; [2009] UKHL 5.

[48] House of Lords and House of Commons Joint Committee on Human Rights, *Facilitating
Peaceful Protest, Tenth Report of Session 2010–11* (HL 111/HC 684, 25 March 2011), para.
15, available at www.parliament.uk/jchr.

[49] *Austin* v. *Commissioner of Police of the Metropolis* [2009] 2 WLR 372, para. 27.

the crowd whose freedom of movement was restricted by them if the measures were proportionate to the aim pursued.[50]

When this decision was challenged at Strasbourg in *Austin* v. *United Kingdom*,[51] the Grand Chamber took a stance towards the deprivation of liberty question which in effect followed that of the House of Lords, finding:

> the context in which action is taken is an important factor to be taken into account, since situations commonly occur in modern society where the public may be called on to endure restrictions on freedom of movement or liberty in the interests of the common good ... The Court does not consider that such commonly occurring restrictions on movement, so long as they are rendered unavoidable as a result of circumstances beyond the control of the authorities and are necessary to avert a real risk of serious injury or damage, and are kept to the minimum required for that purpose, can properly be described as 'deprivations of liberty' within the meaning of Article 5(1).[52]

Affirming that 'subsidiarity is at the very basis of the Convention, stemming as it does from a joint reading of Articles 1 and 19',[53] the Court went on to find that in accordance with the *Engel* criteria[54] (for determining when a deprivation of liberty occurs), the coercive nature of the containment within the cordon, its duration, and its effect on the applicants, in terms of physical discomfort and inability to leave, pointed towards a deprivation of liberty. However, the Court found that, relying on the context of the imposition of the 'kettle', the *purpose* of its imposition, to contain a large, volatile crowd, must be taken into account. Although the Court did not refer expressly to proportionality, it clearly adverted to that concept in finding that the measure taken appeared to be the 'least intrusive and most effective means to be applied'.[55] On that basis no deprivation of liberty was found; the Grand Chamber's judgment did not differ in essence from that of the House of Lords.

A strong joint dissenting opinion trenchantly criticised the findings of the majority as creating a new and objectionable proposition, 'implying that if it is necessary to impose a coercive and restrictive measure for a legitimate public-interest purpose, the measure does not amount to a deprivation of liberty'.[56] It was found to be objectionable since, if in the

---

[50] *Ibid.* para. 34.   [51] (2012) 55 EHRR 14.   [52] *Ibid.* para. 59.
[53] *Ibid.* para. 61.   [54] *Engel* v. *Netherlands* (1976) 1 EHRR 647.
[55] *Austin* v. *United Kingdom* (2012) 55 EHRR 14, para. 66.
[56] *Ibid.* Joint Dissenting Opinion of Judges Tulkens, Spielman and Garlicki, para. 3.

public order context liberty-depriving measures were deemed to lie
outside Article 5 if claimed to be necessary for any legitimate/
public-interest purpose, states could circumvent Article 5 for various
reasons going beyond the exceptions.[57] *Austin* in effect creates a new,
very broad, exception to Article 5, while purporting to avoid relating the
public interest argument to the issue of ambit. The Grand Chamber
reiterated, on the basis of the principle of subsidiarity, that it should only
interfere in a domestic decision as to facts on very cogent grounds. But
impliedly it went further: it applied that principle not to the findings of
fact only, but to the interpretation of Article 5(1). The House of Lords
had found that public interest considerations were relevant to ambit,
subject to a test of proportionality. The Grand Chamber, as the joint
dissenting opinion pointed out, accepted that analysis in effect (though
without overtly referring to proportionality) despite the fact that it ran
counter to the findings in *A* v. *United Kingdom* on the interpretation of
Article 5(1). Thus, the Grand Chamber came close to accepting that it
would require very compelling reasons to depart from the decision of a
superior national court that had applied the Convention, taking a particular view of its interpretation, to a set of facts, even where that court
could not point to ECHR jurisprudence bearing closely on the matter
before it. That stance would be in accordance with an expansive
approach to subsidiarity as manifested in the Interlaken and Brighton
declarations, not merely in relation to national law or fact-finding, but
also in relation to interpretation of the Convention.

Austin is obviously a public protest case in which the police had to
contain a crowd in the heat of the moment in a volatile situation; in that
sense the situation at issue differs from those in *Gillan* and in *A*.
However, no exception to Article 5 covers 'kettling', just as no exception
covers the interferences with liberty in the counter-terrorism context on
the model of control orders / Terrorism Prevention and Investigation
Measures (TPIMs) / Enhanced Terrorism Prevention and Investigation
Measures (ETPIMs)[58] (the replacements for detention under ATCSA,
Part 4), creating non-trial-based methods of curbing the liberty of those

---

[57] *Ibid.* Joint Dissenting Opinion of Judges Tulkens, Spielman and Garlicki, para. 6.
[58] TPIMs ('control orders lite') replace control orders and arise under the Terrorism
Prevention and Investigation Measures Act 2011, which also repealed the Prevention of
Terrorism Act 2005 governing control orders, which replaced ATCSA, Part 4; ETPIMs
(similar to control orders) arise under the Enhanced Terrorism Prevention and Investigation Measures Bill 2011, to be introduced in an unspecified emergency situation.

who apparently cannot be prosecuted and cannot be deported (either because they are nationals or due to the treatment they would receive in the receiving country, discussed below). It may be a small step from *Austin* to a finding that if a measure interfering with liberty appears to be necessary due to the demands of the terrorist threat, such a measure will not be found to create a deprivation of liberty if the least intrusive means needed to answer to the threat is adopted. Thus, of especial pertinence in light of reluctance in the United Kingdom to seek a derogation from Article 5 after the *A* case, *Austin* creates some leeway to allow this purposive principle to make its way into the counter-terrorism context in respect of non-paradigm interferences with liberty on the control orders model which already tend to skirt or cross the boundaries of Article 5(1) tolerance.[59]

Superficially speaking, the interaction between the UK government, domestic courts and the ECtHR could be seen to fall within a domestic dialogical model of rights protection and, on an international level, of a subsidiary model of such protection. The Strasbourg Court relied on the principle of subsidiarity to support the outcome of an interaction with the highest UK court and the UK government that resulted in creation of a restricted ambit for Article 5, based on proportionality arguments akin to those applicable under the materially qualified Articles, even in the face of the ECtHR's own recent analogous decision. But in reality the ideas of dialogue and of subsidiarity may be coming closer to veiling a capitulation to an appeasement approach, in *Austin*. There is a case for considering a new exception to Article 5, which could cover some non-paradigm interferences with liberty, but it is argued that it should be considered openly in the Council of Europe, in the context of terrorism, rather than being imported into Article 5 by stealth.

III   Interaction between the ECtHR, the UK government and the domestic courts in the Article 3 and 6 ECHR context

Post 11 September 2001 ('9/11'), prosecution has not been viewed as the main solution to the problem posed by the presence in the United Kingdom of a certain group of terrorist suspects; instead the government has sought to deport or extradite such suspects. There is also an evident

---

[59] This may be said of ETPIMs in particular. See further H. Fenwick, 'Recalibrating ECHR Rights, and the Role of the Human Rights Act Post 9/11: Reasserting International Human Rights Norms in the War on Terror?' (2010) 63 *Current Legal Problems* 153.

reluctance to seek convictions in a criminal court where the use of the material on which the suspicions against the suspects are based could endanger national security since it might reveal sources or security service techniques, or damage relations with other countries where promises have been made to keep information confidential. In instances of this nature, if the Home Secretary is genuinely pursuing the possibility of extradition or deportation,[60] which remains a realistic possibility,[61] the detention of the person in question can fall within the exception under Article 5(1)(f). Given that background, the UK government has consistently viewed itself as confronted by a dilemma in respect of persons who are suspected of being international terrorists but who cannot be removed, because there are grounds to think that they would be subject to forms of ill-treatment in the receiving country which might violate certain Convention rights, in particular Article 3, following the principle stemming from *Chahal*.[62] As a result, the government has sought to gain acceptance domestically and at Strasbourg for a balancing argument under Article 3, similar to the one discussed under Article 5, and due to legal challenges to the attempts to extradite or deport a certain group of suspects, a degree of acceptance for that argument has taken hold at Strasbourg.

(a)   Policy of deportation with assurances

The decision of the European Court of Human Rights in *Soering* v. *United Kingdom*,[63] confirmed in *Chahal* v. *United Kingdom*,[64] found that a breach of Article 3 will arise where a country deports/extradites a

---

[60] See 'The FCO's Human Rights Work in 2011, Response of the Secretary of State for Foreign and Commonwealth Affairs', *Third Report from the Foreign Affairs Committee Session 2012–13* (Cm 8506, December 2012) para. 18: 'in certain circumstances the UK will seek public and verifiable assurances from a foreign government to ensure that an individual's human rights will be respected on their removal'. See further *XX* v. *SSHD* (SC/61/2007), SIAC, 10 September 2010; *Review of Counter-Terrorism and Security Powers* (Cm 8004, January 2011), p. 35; *AS and DD* v. *SSHD, AS and DD* v. *SSHD* (SC/42 and 50/2005), SIAC, 27 April 2007. See further J. Tooze, 'Deportation with Assurances: The Approach of the UK Courts' (2010) *Public Law* 362.

[61] See *Walumba Lumba and Kadian Mighty* v. *SSHD* [2011] UKSC 12 and *Shepherd Masimba Kambadzi* v. *SSHD* [2011] UKSC 23, broadly approving the 'Hardial Singh principles', concerning the use of powers to detain someone for immigration purposes in *R* (*on the application of Hardial Singh*) v. *Governor of Durham Prison* [1983] EWHC 1 (QB).

[62] *Chahal* v. *United Kingdom* (1996) 23 EHRR 413, paras. 130–1.

[63] (1989) 11 EHRR 439, paras. 90–1.   [64] (1996) 23 EHRR 413, para. 74.

person to another country, knowing that he or she will face a substantial risk of Article 3 treatment in that other country. Post 9/11, the UK government has therefore consistently viewed itself as confronted by a dilemma in respect of persons who are suspected of being international terrorists but who cannot be extradited, or deported to their country of origin, because there are grounds to think that they would there be subject to torture or inhuman and degrading treatment, since to do so would violate Article 3 ECHR.

As a result, the UK government has been seeking for some time to achieve modification of the *Chahal* principle at Strasbourg, by arguing for the creation of a restrained ambit for Article 3 ECHR in the context of that principle. It intervened in order to argue in *Saadi*,[65] first, that the risk of torture should be balanced against the risk to the community of the terrorist suspect's continued presence in the country wishing to deport him or her,[66] meaning that the level of national security risk posed by the deportee would be allowed to influence the findings as to risk of Article 3 treatment in the receiving country. Secondly, the government argued that where there is evidence that the suspect represents a national security risk, that should affect the standard of proof he has to adduce as to the likelihood of his being tortured – he should have to prove that it is more likely than not: 'if the respondent State adduced evidence that there was a threat to national security, stronger evidence had to be adduced to prove that the applicant would be at risk of ill-treatment in the receiving country'.[67] Thus, the government appeared to be seeking to justify deporting persons at risk of Article 3 treatment abroad on the basis of implying a form of proportionality test into Article 3, allowing for narrowing of the application of the *Chahal* principle. The Court found in response[68] that the United Kingdom's first argument was incompatible with the absolute nature of Article 3, and that its second argument for balancing the risk of harm if the person is sent back against the risk of harm to the community if not was misconceived: 'they are notions that can only be assessed independently of each

---

[65] *Saadi* v. *Italy* (2009) 49 EHRR 30, paras. 117–23.

[66] *Ibid.* para. 122: 'in cases concerning the threat created by international terrorism, the approach followed by the Court in *Chahal* ... had to be altered and clarified ... the threat presented by the person to be deported must be a factor to be assessed in relation to the possibility and the nature of the potential ill-treatment ... [making] it possible ... to weigh the rights secured to the applicant by Article 3 against those secured to all other members of the community by Article 2'.

[67] *Ibid.* para. 122.   [68] *Ibid.* paras. 137–49.

other . . . Either the evidence that is adduced before the court reveals that there is substantial risk if the person is sent back or it does not'.[69]

The government's failure in *Saadi* meant that the issue that arose in the House of Lords in *RB* v. *SSHD*[70] was of especial significance to the current government since the case had the potential to determine whether deportation of a particular group of suspects, and in particular of Abu Qatada, could occur. The deportation of Qatada to Jordan, attracting a very high volume of media attention, has become politicised as something of a litmus test of the current government's competence and determination in dealing with terrorism. In the House of Lords, the argument raised in *Saadi* was not re-raised; instead the case focused on the use of diplomatic assurances to reduce the risk of Article 3 treatment, and on the real risk of treatment of Qatada in flagrant breach of Article 6 in Jordan at his retrial there. The key issue raised in the appeal was to the effect that assurances in relation to individuals cannot be relied upon where there is a pattern of human rights violations in the receiving state, coupled with a culture of impunity for the state agents in the security service, and for the persons perpetrating such violations; therefore the Special Immigration Appeals Commission's (SIAC) reliance on the diplomatic assurances that had been given against harm to Qatada in Jordan was irrational.

In two claims against Russia, the ECtHR had spoken of the need for assurances to 'ensure adequate protection against the risk of ill-treatment' contrary to Article 3.[71] Lord Phillips also noted that in *Mamatkulov* v. *Turkey*[72] the assurances against ill-treatment were treated by the Court as part of the matrix that had to be considered when deciding whether there were substantial grounds for believing in the existence of a real risk of inhuman treatment.[73] He further found that the Court had applied a similar approach in *Shamayev* v. *Georgia and Russia*,[74] and so, he pointed out, had the United Nations Committee

---

[69] *Ibid.* para. 139.
[70] *RB (Algeria)* v. *SSHD* [2009] UKHL 10; on appeal from: [2007] EWCA Civ 808, [2008] EWCA Civ 290.
[71] *Ismoilov and others* v. *Russia* [2008] ECHR 348, para. 127 and *Ryabikin* v. *Russia* (Application no. 8320/04), Judgment of 19 June 2008, para. 119.
[72] (2005) 41 EHRR 494. The Court said that it was unable to conclude that substantial grounds existed for believing that the applicants faced a real risk of treatment proscribed by Art. 3 (para. 77).
[73] *RB (Algeria)* v. *SSHD* [2009] UKHL 10, para. 112.
[74] (Application no. 36378/02), Judgment of 12 April 2005.

Against Torture in *Hanan Attia v. Sweden*.[75] The political realities in Jordan, the bilateral diplomatic relationship with the United Kingdom, and the fact that Othman (Qatada) would have a high public profile, were, he found, the most significant factors in SIAC's assessment of the Article 3 risk, which disclosed no irrationality. Lord Hope agreed, noting the UN position to the effect that in a regime systematically practising torture, the principle of *non-refoulement* must be strictly observed and diplomatic assurances should not be resorted to,[76] but viewing that position as indicating that the question of reliance would always be a matter of fact, dependent on particular circumstances relating to the individual in question; he relied on the finding in *Saadi*[77] to the effect that where evidence capable of proving that there are substantial grounds for believing that he would be exposed to ill-treatment is adduced by the applicant, it is for the government to dispel any doubts about it.[78]

As regards the Article 6 issue, SIAC had found that there was a real risk that confessions would be relied on in Othman's retrial which had been obtained by treatment that breached Article 3, but their admission would be the consequence of a judicial decision, within a system at least on its face intended to exclude evidence which was not given voluntarily.[79] So SIAC had found no total denial of the right to a fair trial, but the Court of Appeal had found that SIAC had erred in law: 'The use of evidence obtained by torture is prohibited in Convention law ... because of the connexion of the issue with Article 3, a fundamental, unconditional and non-derogable prohibition' ... 'SIAC was wrong not to recognise this crucial difference between breaches of Article 6 based on this ground and breaches of Article 6 based simply on defects in the trial process or ... composition of the court'.[80] Lord Phillips did not accept the conclusion of the Court of Appeal[81] that it required a high degree of assurance that evidence obtained by torture would not be used in the

---

[75] Communication No. 199/2002, 17 November 2003.

[76] Cited in *Sing* v. *Canada (Minister of Citizenship and Immigration)* 2007 FC 361 (UN Doc. A/59/324), para. 136.

[77] (2009) 49 EHRR 30, para. 129.   [78] *RB (Algeria)* v. *SSHD* [2009] UKHL 10, para. 114.

[79] *Mohammed Othman (Abu Qatada)* v. *Secretary of State for the Home Department* [2012] UKSIAC 15/2005_2 (12 November 2012), para. 422 (SIAC Judgment).

[80] *Othman (aka Abu Qatada)* v. *Secretary of State for the Home Department* [2013] All ER (D) 269, [2013] EWCA Civ 277, paras. 45, 49 (Court of Appeal Judgment).

[81] *Mohammed Othman (Abu Qatada)* v. *Secretary of State for the Home Department* [2012] UKSIAC 15/2005_2 (12 November 2012), para. 154. See further M. Garrod, 'Deportation of Suspected Terrorists with "Real Risk" of Torture: The House of Lords Decision in *Abu Qatada*' (2010) 73 *Modern Law Review* 631.

proceedings in Jordan before it would be lawful to deport Othman to face those proceedings. He found that the principle at issue was that the 'state must stand firm against the conduct that has produced the evidence, but that did not require a different state to retain to the detriment of national security a terrorist suspect absent a high degree of assurance that evidence obtained by torture would not be adduced in the receiving state'.[82]

The ECtHR's stance in *Othman* v. *United Kingdom*[83] echoed that of the House of Lords as far as the Article 3 issue was concerned since it considered that only in rare cases would the general situation in a country mean that no weight at all would be given to assurances. It found that its only task was to examine whether the assurances obtained in a particular case were sufficient to remove any real risk of ill-treatment.[84] The Court found that, on the evidence, the Jordanian criminal justice system lacked many of the standard, internationally recognised safeguards to prevent torture and punish its perpetrators,[85] but that the assurances under the Memoranda of Understanding (MoU) that the applicant would not be ill-treated upon return to Jordan were superior to those that the Court had previously considered in both detail and formality. They were found to have been given in good faith by the Jordanian government, at the highest levels of that government, and therefore capable of binding the state. The MoU was also found to be unique in that it had withstood the extensive examination that had been carried out by SIAC, which had had the benefit of receiving evidence adduced by both parties, including expert witnesses. The Court concluded on that basis that the applicant's return to Jordan would not expose him to a real risk of ill-treatment, meaning that no violation of Article 3 was found.[86]

In relation to Article 6, the Court found that the admission of torture-tainted evidence would be manifestly contrary, not just to the provisions of Article 6, but to the most basic international standards of fair trial.[87] Having made that finding, the remaining two issues which the Court had to consider were: (i) whether showing a real risk of the admission of torture evidence would be sufficient; and (ii) if so, whether a flagrant denial of justice (a breach so fundamental as to amount to a nullification of the very essence of the right guaranteed by Article 6) would arise in this case.[88] The Court found that on any retrial of the applicant, it would

---

[82] *RB (Algeria)* v. *SSHD* [2009] UKHL 10, para. 153.   [83] (2012) 55 EHRR 1.
[84] *Ibid.* para. 186.   [85] *Ibid.* para. 191.   [86] *Ibid.* para. 205.
[87] *Ibid.* para. 267.   [88] *Ibid.* para. 271.

undoubtedly be open to him to challenge the admissibility of statements made against him, alleged to have been obtained by torture. But the difficulties he would face in trying to do so many years after the event, and before the same court which had already rejected a claim of inadmissibility (and which routinely rejected all such claims), were very substantial indeed.[89] The Court therefore concluded that the applicant had discharged the burden that could be fairly imposed on him of establishing that the evidence that could be used against him was obtained by torture. So the Court, in agreement with the Court of Appeal, found that there was a real risk that the applicant's retrial would amount to a flagrant denial of justice, and therefore that his deportation to Jordan would create a breach of Article 6.[90]

Thus, the decision on the Article 6 question took a strict stance[91] since it meant that the prospective use of evidence obtained by torture would *automatically* constitute a flagrant denial of justice in a foreign state, regardless of other safeguards or of its importance to the outcome of the trial.[92] The decision on Article 3, like that of the House of Lords, ran contrary to the 'recurring theme in NGO advocacy that because Article 3 (ECHR/Convention Against Torture (CAT)) is absolute, the use of diplomatic assurances in the context of a risk of torture is wrong or prohibited'[93] since they are not an effective safeguard, the stance taken in the 2004 report to the UN General Assembly by the UN Special Rapporteur on Torture.[94]

---

[89] *Ibid.* para. 279.   [90] *Ibid.* paras. 280, 282.

[91] See on the Art. 6 issue *Gafgen* v. *Germany* [2011] 52 EHRR 1 and *El-Haski* v. *Belgium* (Application no. 649/08), Judgment of 25 September 2012; in *Gafgen* it was found that the risk of admission of such evidence was not viewed as *automatically* creating a flagrant denial of justice, but as raising serious issues as to the fairness of the proceedings.

[92] Note: after this decision, in *Mohammed Othman (Abu Qatada)* v. *Secretary of State for the Home Department* [2012] UKSIAC 15/2005_2 (12 November 2012), SIAC found that the Secretary of State should not have declined to revoke the deportation order, because she had not satisfied the judges that, on a retrial in Jordan, there would be no real risk that the impugned statements apparently obtained by torture would be admitted.

[93] N. Larsaeus, *The Use of Diplomatic Assurances in the Prevention of Prohibited Treatment*, Refugee Studies Centre, University of Oxford Working Paper No. 32 (October 2006), available at www.rsc.ox.ac.uk/publications/working-papers-folder_contents/RSCworkingpaper32.pdf. See also the Joint Report of Amnesty International, Human Rights Watch and the International Commission of Jurists, *Reject Rather than Regulate; Call on Council of Europe Member States not to Establish Minimum Standards for the Use of Diplomatic Assurances in Transfers to Risk of Torture and Other Ill-Treatment* (December 2005), available at www.hrw.org/legacy/backgrounder/eca/eu1205.

[94] UN Commission on Human Rights, UN Doc. A/59/324 (1 September 2004), available at www.refworld.org/docid/4267be1b4.html.

The decision not only confirmed the acceptability under Article 3 of deportation with assurances against Article 3 treatment, but it impliedly also allowed deportation with assurances against a flagrant breach of Article 6, so long as they were specific enough in relation to the potential use of torture-tainted evidence. The decision in *Othman* departed from that in *Saadi* in that an executive process – the obtaining and negotiation of unenforceable assurances – was allowed to create a departure from the absolute nature of Article 3. In that sense it is redolent of a dialogic approach in that the stance taken in the House of Lords appeared to be influential at Strasbourg. The argument that the risk posed by Qatada in the United Kingdom should influence the standard of proof he would have to adduce as to the likelihood that torture tainted evidence would be used at his trial, similar to the argument the United Kingdom put forward in *Saadi*, was rejected, a far from appeasing approach which was received with intense irritation by the UK government. But nevertheless the judgment did create a compromise between fair trial values and national security since it indicated that diplomatic assurances would be valuable in reducing that likelihood.[95]

(b) Potential maltreatment abroad and extradition

The themes explored above in relation to deportation have also arisen in relation to a long-running attempt to extradite a group of suspects,[96] including Abu Hamza, to the United States. Their challenges to extradition have been brought mainly on the basis that, if extradited from the United Kingdom to the United States and convicted there of terrorist crimes, the men would be at real risk of ill-treatment, contrary to Article 3 ECHR, as a result of the highly restrictive conditions of detention in an Administrative Maximum Facility (ADX) prison, exacerbated by the

[95] The Home Secretary has sought fresh assurances that torture-tainted evidence would not be used at trial against Qatada if deported ('Abu Qatada's legal battle to stay in Britain', *Daily Telegraph*, 13 November 2012); they were not accepted in SIAC (*Mohammed Othman (Abu Qatada) v. Secretary of State for the Home Department* [2012] UKSIAC 15/2005_2 (12 November 2012)); in *Othman (aka Abu Qatada) v. Secretary of State for the Home Department* [2013] EWCA Civ 27, the Court of Appeal accepted SIAC's decision. However, a treaty was signed between the United Kingdom and Jordan giving assurances that evidence extracted through torture would not be used against Qatada at his retrial in Jordan; he then left the United Kingdom voluntarily (see *Guardian*, 7 July 2013).

[96] Talha Ahsan, Adel Abdel Bary, Khalid Al Fawwaz and Mustafa Kamal Mustafa (Hamza), Babar Ahmad and Haroon Aswat.

imposition of 'special administrative measures', including prolonged solitary confinement and arbitrary strip-searches. The fourth applicant (Hamza) argued that a breach would arise since if convicted he would probably receive a life sentence. All the challenges failed domestically in the High Court on the basis that the measures fell far short of establishing a case under Article 3.[97] In particular, Lord Justice Scott Baker,[98] found that the decisions of the United States federal courts in *Ajaj*,[99] *Sattar*[100] and *Wilkinson* v. *Austin*[101] demonstrated that there was effective judicial oversight of 'supermax' prisons such as ADX. It was found in relation to Hamza that a life sentence would not of itself constitute a breach of Article 3, and that due to his physical condition it would be highly unlikely that he would be placed at ADX Florence.[102]

The two key questions in *Ahmad and others* v. *United Kingdom*[103] were whether the detention of three of the applicants in a 'supermax' US prison would breach Article 3, and also whether potential sentences of life imprisonment in respect of two of them would do so. The Court answered both questions in the negative. As to the first, the Court rejected the government's argument, accepted by the House of Lords in *Wellington*,[104] and already raised in *Saadi*, that if a risk of torture was not anticipated in the extra-territorial context then a relativist approach could be adopted to the possibility of inhuman or degrading treatment – one that balanced the purpose of the extradition against the nature of the anticipated treatment.[105] The Court, however, made it clear that treatment not amounting to torture that might be capable of falling within Article 3 in the member state in question, would not necessarily do so as anticipated adverse treatment in the non-member receiving state – in this instance, the United States.[106] Taking account of various procedural

---

[97] *Ahmad* v. *Government of United States* [2006] EWHC 2927 (Admin); *R (on the application of Ahsan)* v. *DPP* [2008] EWHC 666 (Admin). The House of Lords refused leave to appeal on 6 June 2007.

[98] *R (on the application of Bary)* v. *SSHD* [2009] EWHC 2068 (Admin).

[99] *Ajaj* v. *United States*, 293 Fed. Appx. 575 (10th Cir. 2008).

[100] *Sattar* v. *Gonzales* 2009 WL 606115 (D. Colo. 2009).

[101] *Wilkinson* v. *Austin*, 545 US 209 (2005).

[102] *Mustafa* v. *United States* [2008] 1357 (Admin); [2008] 1 WLR 2760.

[103] (2013) 56 EHRR 1.

[104] *R (on the application of Wellington) (FC)* v. *Secretary of State for the Home Department* [2008] UKHL 72.

[105] *Ahmad and others* v. *United Kingdom* (2013) 56 EHRR 1, paras. 172–3.

[106] *Ibid.* para. 177: 'the Convention does not purport to be a means of requiring the Contracting States to impose Convention standards on other States (*Al-Skeini and others*

safeguards, it found that there would not be a violation of Article 3 in respect of the applicants' possible detention at ADX.[107] As to the second, the Court rejected the argument that the sentences that might be imposed would be grossly disproportionate to the offences allegedly committed, given their alleged involvement in terrorist activity. The argument that imposition of life sentences in themselves would create a breach of Article 3 also failed on the basis that under the US system sufficient opportunities for review of the sentences appeared to be available.[108]

In this decision it may be said that the dialogue between the government, UK courts and the ECtHR resulted in a decisive rejection of the argument for overt adoption of a balancing approach to Article 3 in non-torture extradition cases. But, nevertheless, some aspects of it are consistent with appeasement of the national authorities at the end of this long-drawn out battle over extradition. The Court has made it clear that a form of lengthy solitary confinement coupled with 'special administrative measures' meets the requirements of Article 3. The decision as to the anticipated gross disproportionality of sentences to offences appeared to rely on the terrorist context[109] in making little effort to differentiate between the applicants; but it would appear that the positions of Babar Ahmad and Talha Ahsan could have been differentiated from those of the other suspects. It in effect sets limits to the application of Article 3 in relation to receiving states, and in so doing shows reluctance to interfere in the relationship between the United States and United Kingdom in relation to extradition. Acceptance that in principle a regime in a receiving state might not involve Article 3 treatment while adoption of the same regime in a member state might do so,[110] on the basis of the fact-sensitivity of determinations that Article 3 treatment has occurred, could be seen as a retreat from the somewhat more expansionist stance adopted towards state responsibility in relation to a non-member state's criminal justice regime taken in the *Qatada* case under Article 6.

---

v. *UK* (GC), Application no. 55721/07, Judgment 7 July 2011, para. 141) . . . treatment which might violate Article 3 [in] . . . a Contracting State might not attain the minimum level of severity which is required for there to be a violation of Article 3 in an expulsion or extradition case'.
[107] *Ibid.* para. 224.   [108] *Ibid.* paras. 243–4.
[109] *Ibid.* para. 243.   [110] *Ibid.* para. 177.

Conclusions

This chapter has covered the two main strategies that the UK government is currently pursuing in respect of suspects whom it is or is perceived to be difficult to prosecute: use of non-trial-based measures restricting their liberty, or removal from the country. In each of these strands of counter-terrorism policy operating outside the criminal justice system, the executive is clearly dominant. The UK courts have shown a degree of acceptance for a balancing approach under Articles 5 and 3 ECHR, which it is argued has then also found some purchase in the Strasbourg judgments under the guise of paying attention to the 'context'. Contextualisation thus in effect takes on to an extent the role played by the concept of proportionality in the ECHR jurisprudence on absolute and non-materially qualified rights. Some acceptance of a doctrine of enhanced subsidiarity is evident in the judgments in the sense that the findings of the domestic courts are arguably being given greater weight at Strasbourg in the context of the Izmir, Interlaken and Brighton declarations. So long as the domestic courts fully rehearse the Convention arguments, as Lord Bingham failed to do in *Gillan*, the ECtHR is showing a reluctance to depart from their findings. Strasbourg has engaged in and contributed to an ongoing domestic dialogue in the counter-terrorism context, guiding the executive towards enhanced rights' protection. But while the worst excesses of counter-terrorism policy post 9/11 have thereby been rejected (ATCSA, Part 4; TA, section 44), the checking value of the Court's intervention under the ECHR has been of relatively low impact, allowing further but less invasive executive-dominated measures to survive.

It is concluded that a Strasbourg approach that appears to accord subsidiarity and a dialogic approach an enhanced role has at times obscured its appeasement effects. The stance of the UK Conservative leadership on the Court's involvement in this context has been particularly hostile, and the political challenge posed by these cases feeds into the broader issue of the perceived appropriate role of the ECtHR in Europe.[111] With a view to its own future, and the project of rights' protection in the United Kingdom in the counter-terrorism arena, it is arguably seeking to distance itself from the image it has in the eyes of some, including the Conservative leadership – that of a quasi-constitutional, over-activist institution.

---

[111] See further Chapter 1 in this volume: F. de Londras, 'Counter-terrorism judicial review as regulatory constitutionalism'; and Chapter 11, G. Phillipson, 'Deference and dialogue in the real-world counter-terror context'.

Accountability for counter-terrorism: challenges and potential in the role of the courts

HELEN DUFFY

Introduction

'Counter-terrorism' practices since 11 September 2001 ('9/11') have involved notorious violations of some of the most sacrosanct norms of the international legal order. One consequence has been the generation of a vast group of 'victims' of counter-terrorism, and of perpetrators of crimes under national and international law. This chapter explores the role of the courts in the search for accountability and reparation *vis-à-vis* those perpetrators and victims.

It is now beyond reasonable doubt that some of the measures taken in the name of counter-terrorism, including specifically in the context of the post 9/11 putative 'War on Terror', amount to crimes under international and national law. The extraordinary rendition programme of 'enhanced interrogation' and secret detention for intelligence gathering purposes led by the CIA and widely supported in many forms by other states globally, is perhaps the most obvious example, apparently involving torture, enforced disappearance, potentially as crimes against humanity, and (for any of those detentions that were genuinely associated with an armed conflict) war crimes.[1] Egregious acts of torture in Iraq and Afghanistan have also given rise to serious and apparently well-founded allegations of war crimes.[2] Systematic prolonged arbitrary detention as seen in the Guantánamo Bay anomaly may in turn, at least arguably, amount to war crimes or to crimes against humanity.[3] The same has been alleged in respect of

---

[1] H. Duffy, *The War on Terror and the Framework of International Law* (2nd edn, Cambridge University Press, forthcoming), chs. 4 and 10.

[2] *Ibid.* chs. 6, 7B and 14.

[3] Article 7(1)(e) of the Rome Statute of the International Criminal Court ('ICC Statute') refers to the crime against humanity of 'imprisonment or other severe deprivation of physical liberty in violation of fundamental rules of international law'; see also

systematic targeted killings that have characterised the latter stages of the post 9/11 putative war with 'Al-Qaeda and associated groups',[4] but long reflected in counter-terrorism law and practice elsewhere, notably in the Russian Federation and Israel.[5] The forms of individual criminal responsibility recognised at international level, and broadly reflected in national systems, suggest a range of potential charges involving direct and indirect perpetration, such as ordering, instigation, aiding and assisting and co-perpetration against a range of the intellectual and material authors of these crimes.[6]

Section I of this chapter focuses on developments in practice, and highlights some of the many political, legal and practical challenges facing victims and their representatives arising from these practices. It will consider first the criminal law, sketching out the lack of accountability in the United States for 'War on Terror' crimes, but also the momentum towards accountability in other states. With regard to victims' right to reparation, a stark dichotomy emerges as between the treatment of victimhood in relation to victims of terrorism and of counter-terrorism. The pursuit of civil accountability litigation on the national level will be highlighted and followed by the increasing resort to international and regional human rights litigation in face of obstacles at the national level. Section II of the chapter will reflect on the impact of litigation and its contribution, alongside political solutions, to pursuing justice and accountability. It will argue

---

International Criminal Court, *Elements of Crimes* (UN Doc. PCNICC/2000/1/Add.2 (2000)), Art. 7(1)(e).

[4] On the alleged ongoing 'war' with Al-Qaeda and associates, see e.g., most recently President Obama's speech of 23 May 2013, available at www.whitehouse.gov/the-press-office/2013/05/23/remarks-president-national-defense-university. On allegations of drones as involving crimes against humanity, see e.g., 'Ferencz condemns drone attacks: "a crime against humanity" – 26 bipartisan Congress members, UN question unmanned aerial assaults', Peculiar Progressive Blog, 19 June 2012, available at http://peculiarprogressive.blogspot.co.uk/2012_06_01_archive.html.

[5] S. T. Bridge, 'Russia's New Counteracting Terrorism Law: The Legal Implications of Pursuing Terrorists Beyond the Borders of the Russian Federation' (2009) 3 *Columbia Journal of European Law* 1, in which it is argued that the law authorises targeted killings of terrorists, potentially globally, while 'dramatically expand[ing]' those defined as terrorist or extremist'. Killings of alleged terrorists in Chechnya have been common practice for many years. See also Israeli practices, for example, discussed in *Public Committee Against Torture in Israel* v. *Government of Israel* (Supreme Court of Israel, HCJ 769/02, 13 December 2006), available at http://elyon1.court.gov.il/Files_ENG/02/690/007/A34/02007690.A34.pdf.

[6] Duffy, *The War on Terror and the Framework of International Law*, n. 1 above, ch. 4.

that despite its limitations, and the enormity of the challenges posed
for victims and litigators, selective litigation can play a crucial role
in the counter-terrorism field in pursuit of a measure of recognition
and reparation for the neglected victims of counter-terrorism, as a
catalyst to broader changes in policy and law and in safeguarding the
rule of law.

I State and individual responsibility and 'counter-terrorism' measures

An enormous amount of normative and political attention, as well as
resources, have been dedicated to combating impunity in recent
decades on the basis of a shared international commitment to the
view that how states respond to violations of the past is critical, not
only to victims of the crimes but also as a deterrence for the future
and the restoration of the rule of law. A detailed body of international
criminal law, mechanisms and practice has developed around accountability for egregious wrongs. International human rights law is now
consistent across regional and international systems as regards the
absolute right to a remedy, the positive obligations of states to hold
individuals to account for egregious violations, and the impermissibility of impediments to prosecution such as amnesty, immunity or
prescription.[7] Accountability is, moreover, widely recognised as a core
indicator of respect for the 'rule of law'[8] and the international community has in turn committed itself to a 'rule of law' approach to
countering terrorism.[9]

What role then has there been for criminal accountability and for
justice for victims in counter-terrorism practice in recent years?

---

[7] See e.g., the establishment of ICC and ad hoc tribunals, and developments in relation to
international cooperation, UNGA Resolutions adopting Principles on Reparations for
Victims (Bassiouni etc.), Framework Principles for Securing the Accountability of Public
Officials for Gross or Systematic Human Rights Violations Committed in the context of
State Counter-terrorism Initiatives (A/HRC/22/52, 1 March 2013). A detailed body of
jurisprudence on accountability and impermissibility of impediments such as amnesty is
found in IHRL.

[8] The UN's rule of law website gives priority to justice and accountability as dimensions of
the rule of law, see www.unrol.org/article.aspx?article_id=3.

[9] *Uniting Against Terrorism: Recommendations for Global Counterterrorism Strategy, Report
of the UN Secretary General* (A/60/825, 2006).

*(a)   Developments and challenges in search of justice
and accountability for 'counter-terrorism'*

(i)   Role of criminal courts

In the years following 9/11 there was a flurry of legislative activity[10] across the globe aimed at expanding and facilitating the role of criminal law in addressing and preventing international terrorism. Criminal laws and principles were recast, expanded to embrace an ever-broader range of prohibited conduct, reaching further back into preparatory acts and further out to the environment that sustains or 'supports' terrorism.[11] New or altered criminal jurisdictions, procedures, rules of evidence and penalties were introduced.[12] This was accompanied by an exponential increase in terrorism prosecutions in practice in recent years.[13] Whether these developments have contributed to a rule of law approach to counter-terrorism, or incompatibility with basic principles of criminal law and an unprincipled 'law of the enemy' approach to criminal law in the context of terrorism is perhaps debatable.[14] What is clear is that the invigorated and expansive approach to criminal law in response to terrorism stands in very sharp distinction to the approach to criminal law in response to crimes committed in the name of countering terrorism.

---

[10] See e.g., Report of the Counter-Terrorism Committee, *Survey of the Implementation of Security Council Resolution 1373 (2001)* (UN Doc. S/2008/379) available at www.un.org/en/sc/ctc/docs/GIS2008.pdf.

[11] Examples include criminalisation of 'preparatory acts', 'membership' of terrorist organisations, material support for terrorism, glorification of or apology for terrorism; see Duffy, *The War on Terror and the Framework of International Law*, n. 1 above, ch. 4. In extreme cases they may involve no culpability at all; see e.g., *Holder* v. *Humanitarian Law Project*, 561 U.S. 1 (2010), 130 S. Ct. 2705. See, however, *Hamdan* v. *United States*, Court of Appeals, No. 11–1257, Judgment of 16 October 2012, where a US Court of Appeals vacated a conviction for material support as a war crime on grounds of retroactive application of criminal law.

[12] Duffy, *The War on Terror and the Framework of International Law*, n. 1 above, ch. 4.

[13] One survey cites 2,934 arrests and 2,568 convictions in the United States since 9/11: see 'Rightly or wrongly, thousands convicted of terrorism post-9/11', AP, 9 April 2011, available at www.msnbc.msn.com/id/44389156/ns/us_news-9_11_ten_years_later/t/rightly-or-wrongly-thousands-convicted-terrorism-post-/. See also Terrorist Report Card 2001–2011, available at www.lawandsecurity.org/Portals/0/documents/02_TTRCFinal-Jan142.pdf; and examples in Duffy, *The War on Terror and the Framework of International Law*, n. 1 above, ch. 4.

[14] Duffy, *The War on Terror and the Framework of International Law*, n. 1 above, chs. 4 and 7.

(ii) Developments towards criminal accountability in the United States?

Consider first the United States, the natural forum for such investigations and prosecutions. The tone was set in 2009 when President Obama famously pledged to 'look forward as opposed to looking backwards',[15] although he left open the possibility that prosecutions would proceed if there were evidence that laws had been broken.[16] Since then there have been no criminal investigations or indictments in response to the information that has come to light concerning criminality in the context of egregious allegations such as those involved in the extraordinary rendition programme.

Under the Bush administration, the CIA Inspector General referred specific incidents to the Department of Justice and federal prosecutors, reportedly including the use of death threats and torture that resulted in deaths in custody.[17] Out of 101 cases of alleged prisoner abuse, the Justice Department referred two for formal criminal investigation,[18] but decided in August 2012 that they would be closed without prosecutions, citing, *inter alia*, the insufficiency of admissible evidence.[19] This was criticised as being the completion of the 'full-scale whitewashing of the "War on Terror" crimes'.[20]

In a number of contexts, the US administration cites the *potential* role of the criminal courts, but as a defensive stance to deter other initiatives

---

[15] D. Johnston and C. Savage, 'Obama reluctant to look into Bush programs', *New York Times*, 11 January 2009, available at www.nytimes.com/2009/01/12/us/politics/12inquire. html.

[16] *Ibid.*

[17] Office of Inspector General, Central Intelligence Agency, *Special Review of Counterterrorism Detention and Interrogation Activities (September 2001 – October 2003)* (2003–7123-IG, 7 May 2004), available at www.fas.org/irp/cia/product/ig-interrog.pdf.

[18] In June 2010, the US Attorney General announced that the Justice Department would end the probe with only two cases (involving the deaths of detainees) out of 101 cases of suspected detainee abuse proceeding to formal criminal investigation: S. Ackerman, 'CIA exhales: 99 out of 101 torture cases dropped', *WIRED*, 30 June 2011, available at www. wired.com/dangerroom/2011/06/cia-exhales-99-out-of-101-torture-cases-dropped.

[19] In August 2012, the Justice Department announced it would not prosecute, noting 'the admissible evidence would not be sufficient to obtain and sustain a conviction beyond a reasonable doubt'. 'US Justice Department rules out prosecutions over CIA prison deaths', *Guardian*, 31 August 2012, available at www.guardian.co.uk/world/2012/aug/ 31/us-cia-detainee-prison-deaths.

[20] G. Greenwald, 'Obama's Justice Department grants final immunity to Bush's CIA torturers', *Guardian*, 31 August 2012, available at www.guardian.co.uk/commentisfree/2012/ aug/31/obama-justice-department-immunity-bush-cia-torturer.

to secure justice or accountability elsewhere rather than a commitment to criminal justice. In its communications to the Human Rights Committee, for example, the US government has cited provisions of its domestic law that make relevant prosecutions possible.[21] Likewise, in an effort to preclude investigation or prosecution by other states, discussed further in relation to developments in Spain and Italy below, the United States appears to have asserted its primary right – and its ability – to investigate, but stopped short of committing to exercise those rights. As noted below, they have had some degree of success in relying on their criminal law to prevent criminal justice, with a deferral having been made on this basis.[22]

There is little apparent recognition of the anti-impunity principles so long espoused by the United States in other contexts. The resulting sense of impunity is illustrated by the CIA's former head of counter-terrorism promoting his autobiography by admitting to authorising waterboarding, as well as the destruction of ninety-two videotapes of interrogation session,[23] prompting the comment 'We look forward, and not back, and we don't put our torturers on trial. We put them on book tours'.[24]

It should be acknowledged that the situation is somewhat different in the context of the genuine armed conflicts of Iraq and Afghanistan. Perhaps most promising was the commitment in the immediate aftermath of the Abu Ghraib torture scandal that 'wrongdoers will be brought to justice'.[25] At least seven investigations were conducted, reportedly with various degrees of independence, rigour and effectiveness[26] and several individuals were convicted by court-martial.[27] Notably, those

---

[21] Office of the High Commissioner for Human Rights, *Concluding Observations: United States of America 12/18/2006* (UN Doc. CCPR/C/USA/CO/3/Rev.1), available at www. unhcr.org/refworld/docid/45c30bec9.html.

[22] See Spanish and Polish processes highlighted further below in this chapter.

[23] J. Rodriguez, *Hard Measures* (New York: Threshold Editions, 2012); P. Taylor, '"Vomiting and screaming" in destroyed waterboarding tapes', interview with Jose Rodriguez, BBC Newsnight, 9 May 2012, available at www.bbc.co.uk/news/world-us-canada-17990955.

[24] C. Pierce, 'Waterboards, drones, and the drones who love them', Esquire Politics Blog, 30 April 2012, available at www.esquire.com/blogs/politics/jose-rodriguez-cia-book-8484289.

[25] Statement by President Bush following the disclosure of the Abu Ghraib torture quoted in R. Brody, 'The Road to Abu Ghraib' in K. Roth and M. Worden (eds.), *Torture* (New York: New Press, 2005), p. 150.

[26] *Ibid.* p. 151.

[27] See generally, 'Introduction: The Abu Ghraib Files', *Salon*, 14 March 2006, available at www.salon.com/2006/03/14/introduction_2/. Private First Class Lynndie England served one and a half years before being released on parole. E. Brockes, 'What happens in war

prosecuted were of a relatively low military rank, however, and in one perhaps ironic turn (when contrasted to the prosecution of terrorist suspects tortured for years then put on trial in military commissions at 'Camp Justice' Guantánamo),[28] charges against the highest ranking official were dropped as he had not been read his rights before being questioned.[29] In the context of Afghanistan, the reluctance to investigate has been criticised,[30] and those investigations that have occurred appear to have focused on isolated (albeit serious) cases where individuals were believed to have acted without authority, rather than allegations of systematic abuse.[31] Although the United States may cite domestic law in the context of the International Criminal Court (ICC)'s consideration of whether to exercise jurisdiction,[32] to the author's knowledge, few charges have been brought and no convictions secured in the United States.[33]

happens', *Guardian*, 3 January 2009, available at www.guardian.co.uk/world/2009/jan/03/abu-ghraib-lynndie-england-interview.

[28] See e.g., various American Civil Liberties Union reports or Duffy, *The War on Terror and the Framework of International Law*, n. 1 above, ch. 8, detailing denials of rights to criminal defendants. The impact of systematic torture of suspects has not precluded criminal trials in that context.

[29] Lieutenant Colonel Steven Jordan C. Flaherty, 'Abu Ghraib officer acquitted of not controlling soldiers', *JURIST*, 28 August 2011, available at http://jurist.org/thisday/2011/08/abu-ghraib-officer-acquitted-of-not-controlling-soldiers.php.

[30] For example, P. Alston, United Nations Special Rapporteur, 'UNAMA Press Conference', 15 May 2008, available at http://unama.unmissions.org/Default.aspx?tabid=12320&ctl=Details&mid=15872&Itemid=34383&language=en-US; Afghanistan Independent Human Rights Commission (AIHRC), *Torture, Transfers and Denials of Due Process: The Treatment of Conflict-related Detainees in Afghanistan* (Open Society Foundations, 27 HOOT 1390, 17 March 2012), available at www.aihrc.org.af/media/files/AIHRC%20OSF%20Detentions%20Report%20English%20Final%2017-3-2012.pdf.

[31] For example, see 'Ringleader of US Army kill team sentenced to life for murder of Afghans', *Daily Telegraph*, 11 November 2011, available at www.telegraph.co.uk/news/worldnews/northamerica/usa/8883384/Ringleader-of-US-army-kill-team-sentenced-to-life-for-murder-of-Afghans.html; 'Military prosecution faces major hurdles in massacre case', CNN News, 23 March 2012, available at http://edition.cnn.com/2012/03/23/justice/afghanistan-legal-hurdles/index.html (concerning Staff Sgt Robert Bales, charged with seventeen counts of homicide in Afghanistan for a shooting spree against civilians); 'US troops escape criminal charges for incidents that outraged Afghanistan', *Guardian*, 28 August 2012, available at www.guardian.co.uk/world/2012/aug/28/us-troops-burning-qurans-urinating-on-corpses (concerning US troops who urinated on corpses and burned Korans).

[32] On the International Criminal Court's consideration of the matter, see Office of the Prosecutor, *Report on Preliminary Examination Activities 2012* (November 2012), pp. 7–11, available at www.icc-cpi.int/NR/rdonlyres/C433C462-7C4E-4358-8A72-8D99FD00E8CD/285209/OTP2012ReportonPreliminaryExaminations22Nov2012.pdf.

[33] See e.g., the notorious case of two individuals tortured to death at Bagram, 'US Army inquiry implicates 28 soldiers in deaths of 2 Afghan detainees', *New York Times*, 15 October 2004, available at www.nytimes.com/2004/10/15/politics/15abuse.html.

(iii)   Developments outside the United States

Beyond the United States, pressure has been growing for investigation and prosecutions. In the context of the rendition programme specifically, many European states have undertaken to investigate, and developments are afoot internationally to hold to account nationals of the United States and many other states engaged in the 'spider's web' of criminality that the rendition programme represented.[34] The potential significance of some of these developments, and the practical, legal and political challenges they pose, deserve mention.

Italy: the first convictions 'in absentia'   The first convictions in this field arose in Italy, where CIA agents and some of their Italian counterparts were found guilty of aiding and abetting the kidnapping of Abu Omar from the streets of Milan.[35] The Italian prosecution is an example of tenacious investigative work,[36] but also of the challenges to effective criminal prosecutions. As the Italian court could not obtain an extradition request from its own authorities, still less the presence of the accused CIA officials,[37] nine Italian agents and twenty-six Americans, mostly CIA agents, were however tried *in absentia*.[38] Much of the evidence was deemed inadmissible on state secrecy grounds,[39] and some cases were

---

[34] D. Marty, Committee on Legal Affairs and Human Rights, *Alleged Secret Detentions in Council of Europe Member States* (AS /Jur(2006)03 rev., 22 January 2006) available at http://assembly.coe.int/main.asp?link=/committeedocs/2006/20060124_jdoc032006_e.htm.

[35] J. Hooper, 'Italian Court finds CIA agents guilty of kidnapping terrorism suspect', *Guardian*, 4 November 2009, available at www.guardian.co.uk/world/2009/nov/04/cia-guilty-rendition-abu-omar.

[36] C. Jenks and E. Jensen, 'All Human Rights are Equal, But Some are More Equal than Others: The Extraordinary Rendition of a Terror Suspect in Italy, the NATO SOFA, and Human Rights' (2010) 1 *Harvard National Security Journal* 173.

[37] The prosecutor invited the Minister of Justice to submit an extradition request but he declined.

[38] Twenty-three were convicted *in absentia*, including Robert Seldon Lady, the CIA station chief in Milan, sentenced to eight years' imprisonment. They would have to be retried if they ever were to appear in Italy. The scope of charges was also limited as the prosecutor did not originally pursue charges against Italian nationals. See further, F. Messineo, 'Extraordinary Renditions and State Obligations to Criminalize and Prosecute Torture in the Light of the Abu Omar Case in Italy' (2009) 7(5) *Journal of International Criminal Justice* 1023 and D. Marty, Committee on Legal Affairs and Human Rights, *Secret Detentions and Illegal Transfers of Detainees involving Council of Europe Member States: Second Report* (AS/Jur(2007)36, 7 June 2007), para. 316, available at http://assembly.coe.int/committeeDocs/2007/Emarty_20070608_noEmbargo.pdf. See further below for references on prosecutions set to unfold.

[39] The Constitutional Court at one point ruled that the interests of state security took precedence over any other interest, and deemed inadmissible much of the evidence on

dropped on this basis[40] or because US individuals were considered to have diplomatic immunity from prosecution.[41] Indicative of the pressures to which prosecutors have been subject in this area, the prosecutors in this case were themselves charged with violating state secrets laws through their investigation – a twist that was condemned by the Council of Europe Parliamentary Assembly as an 'intolerable impediment to the independence of justice'.[42]

A less rigid or broad-reaching approach to state secrecy may however be emerging. In 2012, the Italian Supreme Court ordered the re-trial of several high-level intelligence officials (whose cases had been thrown out by the court on state secrecy grounds),[43] and upheld existing convictions. It did so despite US arguments, via the Italian Ministry of Justice, that the acts or omissions alleged arose from official duty, and that the US personnel were protected by Status of Forces Agreements (SOFA).[44] However, judicial attempts at accountability were again partially undercut when, following the Italian court's decision to reject immunity for a

---

which the case had been built, including material seized from Italian and US intelligence operatives. See Marty, *Alleged Secret Detentions in Council of Europe Member States*, n. 34 above, para. 162; R. Donadio, 'Italian court upends trial involving CIA links', *New York Times*, 11 March 2009, available at www.nytimes.com/2009/03/12/world/europe/12italy. html; Messineo, 'Extraordinary Renditions and State Obligations to Criminalize and Prosecute Torture in the Light of the Abu Omar Case in Italy', n. 38 above, 1039–40.

[40] Amnesty International, *Italy Prevents Trial of Intelligence Agents over Abu Omar Rendition* (16 December 2010), available at www.amnesty.org/en/news-and-updates/ italy-prevents-trial-intelligence-agents-rendition-abu-omar-2010-126.

[41] Amnesty International, *Europe: Open Secret: Mounting Evidence of Europe's Complicity in Rendition and Secret Detention* (15 November 2010), pp. 18–20, available at www. amnesty.org/en/library/asset/EUR01/023/2010/en/3a3fdac5-08da-4dfc-9f94-afa8b83c6848/ eur010232010en.pdf.

[42] European Parliament Resolution of 11 September 2012 on Alleged Transportation and Illegal Detention of Prisoners in European Countries by the CIA: Follow-up of the European Parliamentary TDIP Committee Report, available at www.europarl.europa. eu/sides/getDoc.do?type=TA&reference=P7-TA-2012-0309&language=EN.

[43] US Supreme Court Judgment of 19 September 2012, as referred to in Amnesty International, 'Italy/USA: Supreme Court Orders Re-trial of Former High-Level Intelligence Officials and Upholds all Convictions in Abu Omar Kidnapping Case', Public Statement of 21 September 2012, available at www.amnesty.org/fr/library/asset/EUR30/015/2012/ en/d626ff4f-e559-4740-89c6-bad7382f5ca0/eur300152012en.pdf. Former head and deputy head and three other high-ranking officials of the Italian intelligence agency (formerly Servizio per le informazioni e la sicurezza militare or SISMI), are to be retried.

[44] The United States also challenged Italian jurisdiction on the basis, *inter alia*, that the United States had primary jurisdiction to try any criminal acts. Despite this, the convictions were upheld. See further Amnesty International, Public Statement of 21 September 2012, n. 43 above.

US air force officer, the Italian Prime Minister stepped in to issue a pardon.[45] The real practical impact of the Italian convictions was none-theless beyond doubt when the convicted former CIA station was arrested, however briefly, pursuant to the Italian cases.[46]

German overtures   Attempts to pursue accountability for other sus-pects have begun in a similar vein in Germany but had less traction. An investigation into the case of Khalid el-Masri, the German national detained at the border with Macedonia and rendered into CIA custody, got underway with the issuance of arrest warrants for CIA agents in 2007.[47] However, the German Justice Minister announced that, as the United States had made it clear that it would not cooperate, the German authorities would therefore not be pursuing a formal request for the extradition of the thirteen CIA agents allegedly involved in el-Masri's abduction.[48] Leaked cables indicate the extent of pressure from the United States not to pursue the cases, a fundamental challenge in this area, as well as German responsiveness.[49]

Ongoing Polish investigation into a secret prison   Developments in Poland are also instructive, highlighting the significance of progress and, once again, its limitations. An investigation into what is reported to be the largest CIA secret prison at Stare Kiejkuty, Poland, began in 2008,

---

[45] The pardon was handed down for a US air force officer in April 2013 with the stated intention of protecting US-Italian relations.

[46] The arrest of Robert Seldon Lady in Panama took place on 18 July 2013, and he was reportedly released due to the lack of extradition treaty and insufficient documentation from the Italian authorities; see for further details www.reuters.com/article/2013/07/19/us-usa-panama-cia-idUSBRE96I0V320130719.

[47] 'Germany issues CIA arrest orders', BBC News, 31 January 2007, available at http://news.bbc.co.uk/go/pr/fr/-/1/hi/world/europe/6316369.stm; see also Marty, *Secret Detentions and Illegal Transfers of Detainees involving Council of Europe Member States: Second Report*, n. 38 above, p. 57, available at http://assembly.coe.int/ASP/Doc/XrefDocDe-tails_E.asp?FileID=11555, on the limitations in that process including the lack of progress in identifying the German alleged to have been present on occasion.

[48] See e.g., J. Shawl, 'US rejects Germany bid for extradition of CIA agents in el-Masri rendition', *JURIST*, 22 September 2007, available at http://jurist.org/paperchase/2007/09/us-rejects-germany-bid-for-extradition.php.

[49] M. Gebauer and J. Goetz, 'The CIA's el-Masri abduction: cables show Germany caved to pressure from Washington', *De Spiegel*, 12 September 2010, available at www.spiegel.de/international/germany/the-cia-s-el-masri-abduction-cables-show-germany-caved-to-pressure-from-washington-a-733860.html; M. Slackman, 'Officials pressed Germans on kidnapping by CIA', *New York Times*, 8 December 2010, available at www.nytimes.com/2010/12/09/world/europe/09wikileaks-elmasri.html.

and rendition victims Abu Zubaydah and Abdal-Rahim al-Nashiri (both detained at Guantánamo) were granted official victim status.[50] During 2012, media reports suggested that the former head of intelligence had been charged in relation to the secret prison which, if established, would represent the first charges in relation to the secret prison system anywhere, though this remains subject to much speculation.[51]

What is apparent is the cloak of secrecy surrounding proceedings, which has rendered it difficult to know the true nature and scope of charges, to assess the real prospect for accountability in Poland, and for the applicant's representatives to meaningfully participate in the criminal process.[52] Multiple 'layers of secrecy'[53] have implications on a practical level for victims' representatives who in law have the right to access the investigative file, but in practice such access is precluded by the unchallengeable classification of the majority of it as 'top secret'. In turn, the regime of access to the part of the file that the applicant's representative is allowed to see is so narrowly construed as to be effectively meaningless: lawyers cannot take any notes from the file and are prohibited from sharing knowledge of its content with the applicant and cannot refer to it in any legal submissions and proceedings. Although formally recognising victim status, the victim has neither *de facto* access to information nor any power to use information in any legal process.[54]

The issue of suitable charging also arises, which is likely to become more present if the momentum towards accountability gains pace. Concern in the Polish context surrounds the scope of reported charges,

---

[50] The investigation is brought under art. 231 of the Polish Criminal Code. See e.g., UN Human Rights Council, *Joint Study on Secret Detention of the Special Rapporteur on Torture and Other Cruel, Inhuman or Degrading Treatment or Punishment, the Special Rapporteur on the Promotion and Protection of Human Rights and Fundamental Freedoms while Countering Terrorism, the Working Group on Arbitrary Detention and the Working Group on Enforced or Involuntary Disappearances* (A/HRC/13/42, 19 February 2010), para. 118, available at www.refworld.org/docid/4bbef04d2.html. See *Abu Zubaydah v. Poland*, INTERIGHTS, available at www.interights.org/abu-zubaydah/index.html.

[51] There has been no confirmation of the charges to the victims publicly and in February 2013 there was also media speculation that any such charges may have been dropped, so facts remain elusive: see http://wyborcza.pl/1,75478,13421165,Zarzuty_za_tajne_wiezienie_CIA_wobec_Siemiatkowskiego.html.

[52] See e.g., *Husayn (Abu Zubaydah) v. Poland* (Application no. 7511/13), communicated to the Polish Government on 9 July 2013. Human Rights Committee, *List of Issues (CCPR/C/POL/Q/6) to be Taken Up in connection with the Consideration of the Third Periodic Report of Poland* (UN Doc. CCPR/C/POL/Q/6/Add.1, 17 September 2010), available at www2.ohchr.org/english/bodies/hrc/docs/CCPR.C.POL.6.Q.Add.1_en.doc.

[53] See e.g., *Husayn (Abu Zubaydah) v. Poland* (Application no. 7511/13).   [54] *Ibid.*

described as relating to 'abuse of authority', or to corporal punishment and false imprisonment, and not to more appropriate charging of grave crimes committed under the regime of rendition, torture and enforced disappearance.[55] Meanwhile, no charges at all have been brought against the many other individuals responsible in the web of criminality associated with the crimes in question, whether Polish officials or US agents responsible for crimes of torture and illegal detention on Polish soil, to whom the Polish obligation to investigate and, where appropriate, to prosecute and punish also apply.

As in other cases, the lack of US cooperation has been recognised by international bodies and by the Polish government itself.[56] Concerns have been expressed regarding the interference by the executive with the prosecutorial function.[57]

Spanish investigation and horizontal complementarity? Another development worthy of particular note relates to two groups of Spanish investigations into mistreatment of detainees. The first are criminal investigations opened in Spain into the alleged torture and abuse of Guantánamo detainees by 'possible material and instigating perpetrators, necessary collaborators and accomplices'.[58] Letters Rogatory sent to the United States and United Kingdom inquiring whether any investigations are currently pending in the cases of four plaintiffs apparently received no response,[59] prompting the Spanish courts to decide that there was

---

[55] In March 2012, the media reported that in January 2012 the prosecutor had brought charges against the Head of the Intelligence Agency in 2002–2004, Zbigniew Siemiatkowski, for abuse of power (Criminal Code, art. 231(1)) and a violation of international law by 'unlawful detention' and 'imposition of corporal punishment' of prisoners of war.

[56] *Al Nashiri* v. *Poland* (Application no. 28761/11) 6 May 2011.

[57] The investigation has been transferred between prosecutors at critical junctures, raising doubts as to the implications for prosecutorial independence ('KRP zapowiada stanowisko po dyskusji o śledztwie ws. więzień CIA' ['The National Council of Prosecutors announces the Issue of a Statement concerning Polish Investigation of CIA Black Sites'] (9 January 2013), available at www.hfhrpol.waw.pl/cia/gw-krp-zapowiada-stanowisko-po-dyskusji-o-sledztwie-ws-wiezien-cia).

[58] Decision of Judge Garzón to open a preliminary investigation into the alleged torture and abuse of four former Guantánamo detainees (Hamed Abderrahman Ahmed, Ikassrien Lahcen, Jamiel Abdul Latif Al Banna and Omar Deghayes), Juzgado Central de Instrucción No. 5, Audiencia Nacional, Madrid (Spanish High Court), Judgment (*auto*) of 27 April 2009, Preliminary Investigations (*diligencias previas*) 150/09–N, p. 9.

[59] On 15 May 2009, Judge Garzón issued Letters Rogatory: see e.g., A. Worthington, 'Spanish Torture Investigation into Gitmo to Continue' (28 February 2011), available at www.fff.org/comment/com1102n.asp.

jurisdiction over these cases in Spain.[60] In a second case known as the 'Bush Six' case,[61] a criminal complaint was filed against six lawyers from within the US administration[62] for participating in or providing assistance to the torture and abuse of detainees.[63] In that case, the United States did respond[64] and the case was 'temporarily stayed' – transferred to the US Department of Justice 'for it to be continued, urging it to indicate at the proper time the measures finally taken by virtue of this transfer of procedure'.[65] One might well question whether, in light of US inaction, such deferral was unwarranted or, at a minimum, precipitous.[66]

As an interesting example of the 'horizontal complementarity' between national jurisdictions, the attempt by Spanish courts to engage and influence the natural forum is noteworthy, even if its likely impact remains less than obvious. In confirmation of the political challenges facing these processes, leaked cables reveal US attempts to put pressure on the Spanish chief prosecutor not to pursue charges in these cases, to

---

[60] Juzgado Central de Instrucción No. 5, Audiencia Nacional, Madrid (Spanish High Court), Judgment (*auto*) of 3 January 2012, Preliminary Investigations (*diligencias previas*), 150/2009–P, available at http://media.miamiherald.com/smedia/2012/01/13/17/35/Xfe8u. So.56.pdf.

[61] 'Spanish Investigation against the 'Bush Six', Judge Velasco, Central Tribunal of Instruction No. 6, Center for Constitutional Rights, available at http://ccrjustice.org/spain-us-torture-case. See also J. Borger and D. Fuchs, 'Spanish judge to hear torture case against six Bush officials', *Guardian*, 29 March 2009, available at www.guardian.co.uk/world/2009/mar/29/guantanamo-bay-torture-inquiry.

[62] The 'Bush Six' are Alberto Gonzales, former US Attorney General and White House Counsel; John Yoo, member of the Justice Department (author of many of the 'Torture Memos'); Douglas Feith, former Undersecretary of Defense for policy; William Haynes II, former General Counsel for the Department of Defense (chief counsel to Donald Rumsfeld); Jay Bybee, member of the Justice Department's Office of Legal Counsel (another author of the 'Torture Memos'); and David Addington, former Chief of Staff to the Vice President.

[63] Criminal Complaint Pending against Alberto Gonzales, William Haynes and John Yoo in Audiencia Nacional, Madrid Case no. 134/2009, filed 17 March 2009; Borger and Fuchs, 'Spanish judge to hear torture case against six Bush officials', n. 61 above.

[64] Response of US Department of State, 'Re: Request for Assistance from Spain in the Matter of Addington, David; Bybee, Jay; Feith, Douglas; Haynes, William; Yoo, John; and Gonzalez, Alberto; Spanish Reference Number: 0002342/2009-CAP' (1 March 2011).

[65] *Ibid.* On 21 January 2013, the Spanish Supreme Court, Division Two, notified the appellants of the dismissal of the appeal. On 22 March 2013 a petition for review was filed with the Spanish Constitutional Court. See further, 'The Spanish Investigation into US Torture', Centre for Constitutional Justice, available at http://ccrjustice.org/spain-us-torture-case.

[66] See challenge to the decision, available at http://ccrjustice.org/files/2012-09-25%20CCR%20ECCHR%20Amicus%20Brief. The judge is free to reopen the case as it was suspended not closed by Judge Velasco's decision of 13 April 2011.

which the prosecutor responded that a US investigation is 'the only way out' for the US government.[67] It remains to be seen whether such responses will contribute in any way to marginalising and influencing the US position and whether the investigation will be reopened if inactivity persists in the United States.

The countries referred to above are only part of a broader picture, though at least as yet with relatively minimal results in terms of individual accountability. In the United Kingdom, multiple enquiries have unfolded into intelligence cooperation with the United States, and have been revealing,[68] but ultimately cases have not proceeded to prosecution, with lack of evidence, including lack of US cooperation, being cited as justification.[69] Even in the notorious case concerning Baha Mousa, an enquiry concluded that the victim had been beaten and tortured to death in Iraq,[70] but accountability was scarce, with only one corporal (who pleaded guilty to the charge of inhumane treatment at the outset of the trial) being convicted and sentenced to one year in prison.[71]

---

[67] 'Garzon opens second investigation into alleged US torture of terrorism detainees', cable from US Embassy Madrid of 5 May 2009, available at http://wikileaks.org/cable/2009/05/09MADRID440.html.

[68] See Chapter 7 in this volume, J. Blackbourn, 'Independent reviewers an alternative: an empirical study from Australia and the United Kingdom' and Chapter 8, K. Roach, 'Public inquiries as an attempt to fill accountability gaps left by judicial and legislative reviews'. See further, *The Baha Mousa Public Inquiry Report* (31 December 2011), available at http://webarchive.nationalarchives.gov.uk; the ongoing Al-Sweady Public Inquiry, details available at www.alsweadyinquiry.org; the Iraq Historic Allegations Team (IHAT) investigation, details available at www.gov.uk/government/news/iraq-historic-allegations-team-starts-work. See also I. Cobain, 'UK investigations into torture and rendition: a guide', *Guardian*, 13 February 2012, available at www.guardian.co.uk/world/2012/feb/13/uk-investigations-torture-rendition-guide.

[69] See e.g., Joint Statement by the Director of Public Prosecutions and the Metropolitan Police Service, 12 January 2012, available at http://content.met.police.uk/News/Joint-statement-by-MPS-and-DPP/1400005902978/1257246741786, referring to insufficient evidence and 'not a realistic prospect of a convictions' in the Binyam Mohamed case, referring to the refusal of eye witnesses to cooperate.

[70] Nor was it found to 'amount to an entrenched culture of violence'. W. Gage, *The Baha Mousa Public Inquiry Report* (London: Stationery Office, 2011), vol. I, paras. 1, 29–30, available at www.bahamousainquiry.org.

[71] Court-martial proceedings were brought against several soldiers, though charges against four of them were dismissed and two others were found not guilty. One corporal who pleaded guilty to the charge of inhumane treatment was convicted and sentenced to one year in prison. Charges were brought for war crimes under the International Criminal Court Act (ICCA) 2001, the first time the Act has been used.

In a number of other states, such as Romania[72] and Lithuania,[73] alleged to have housed secret CIA prisons, cursory 'enquiries' reflect the pressure to respond in some way to allegations while plainly falling short of meaningful attempts towards accountability. Other investigations continue to open in other states, and whether they will catalyse judicial accountability remains uncertain.[74] As time passes, there is a danger of momentum waning, but it has thus far been maintained by persistent calls for accountability, *inter alia*, from European institutions.[75]

(iv)   Conclusion: role of criminal law and actual and potential challenges

Criminal processes serve multiple important functions: contributing to meeting the rights of victims, discharging states' obligations, providing historical narratives of wrongdoing, 'debunking the glorification of violence',[76] and serving traditional goals embraced by theories of retribution, deterrence or redress. Just as criminal trials have an 'expressive' function linked to the rule of law,[77] so too the neglect of criminal law

---

[72] For example European Parliament Temporary Committee on the Alleged Use of European Countries by the CIA for the Transport and Illegal Detention of Prisoners, *Working Document No. 9 on Certain European Countries Analysed during the Work of the Temporary Committee* (PE 382.420v03–00, 26 February 2007) p. 44, available at www.europarl.europa.eu/comparl/tempcom/tdip/working_docs/pe382420_en.pdf   (citing Romanian Senate Decision No. 29/2005).

[73] On the Lithuanian detention site, see e.g., *Abu Zubaydah* v. *Lithuania*, INTERIGHTS, available at www.interights.org/zubaydah. See report by the European Committee for the Prevention of Torture and Inhuman or Degrading Treatment or Punishment, *Report to the Lithuanian Government on the Visit to Lithuania Carried out by the European Committee for the Prevention of Torture and Inhuman or Degrading Treatment or Punishment (CPT), 14–18 June 2010* (CPT/Inf, 2011), p. 17, available at www.cpt.coe.int/documents/ltu/2011-17-inf-eng.htm. A cursory investigation was, however, closed in 2011.

[74] Investigations have opened in France and Finland for example, see Duffy, *The War on Terror and the Framework of International Law*, n. 1 above, ch. 10; for updated information see Amnesty International's 'Unlock the Truth Initiative', details of which are available at www.unlockthetruth.org.

[75] See e.g., Council of Europe Commissioner for Human Rights, *Time for Accountability in CIA Torture Cases* (11 September 2013), available at http://humanrightscomment.org/2013/09/11/time-for-accountability-in-cia-torture-cases/.

[76] M. A. Drumbl, 'The Expressive Value of Prosecuting and Punishing Terrorists: Hamdan, the Geneva Conventions, and International Criminal Law' (2007) 75 *George Washington Law Review* 1165.

[77] *Ibid.*

enforcement has an expressive function. The contrast between the rigour, and perhaps at times over-zealous exuberance, with which criminal law responses to terrorism have been embraced internationally in recent years, and the muted criminal justice response to the crimes committed in the name of counter-terrorism, is striking. The legitimacy, and hence the value, of the criminal law function can only be seriously diminished by such striking selectivity in its application.

The practice highlighted in this section shows both the momentum towards criminal accountability, and the extent of the recurrent challenges. Primary among them is the lack of political will. While this is most apparent in the United States, where there is currently no political commitment to accountability, in other states there has generally been such commitment in principle, but varying degrees of progress in practice.[78] The refusal of US cooperation,[79] and the imposition of political pressure by the United States on states not to pursue justice,[80] has been a recurrent feature of the European processes highlighted above. While this has elicited increasingly robust criticism,[81] it remains to be seen whether

---

[78] On the issues of 'concealment' and 'cover-up' by European states and the lack of political will and obstruction of investigations, see e.g., the reports by the previous Council of Europe Commissioner for Human Rights Thomas Hammarberg, available at www.coe. int/t/commissioner/WCD/annualreports_en.asp# and the two reports by Senator Dick Marty on secret detention available at http://assembly.coe.int/main.asp?link=/committee-docs/2006/20060124_jdoc032006_e.htm and http://assembly.coe.int/ASP/Doc/XrefDoc-Details_E.asp?FileID=11555.

[79] Examples include Germany, where prosecutors had expressed the intention of opening a criminal investigation in the El-Masri case, although the Ministry of Justice later announced that due to lack of cooperation from US authorities, it would not be pursuing the extradition requests. 'US rejects Germany bid for extradition of CIA agents in el-Masri rendition', n. 48 above. UK prosecutors alluded to lack of cooperation in deciding that the Mohamed case could not lead to prosecution of any individual.

[80] Thomas Hammarberg, the then Council of Europe Commissioner for Human Rights, described the 'enormous pressure from Washington . . . [and] instructions from the CIA, with the support of the White House, are not to give any facts on this. Therefore, it is not easy to investigate': T. Hammarberg, *Human Rights in Europe: No Grounds for Complacency* (Strasbourg: Council of Europe Publishing, 2010), available at www.coe.int/t/commissioner/Viewpoints/ISBN2011_en.pdf. See also references to meetings with German and Spanish prosecutors above.

[81] For example, on 9 July 2012, a unanimous resolution of the Organisation for Security and Co-Operation in Europe (OSCE) Parliamentary Assembly 'insists that the United States government cooperates with European investigations': OSCE Parliamentary Assembly Resolution at the Twenty-First Annual Session, Monaco Declaration and Resolutions, 5–9 July 2012, available at www.oscepa.org/component/content/article/2-uncategorised/1374-monaco-dec-html#first.

states will be willing to stand true to their legal obligations, and support one another in doing so, in the face of this pressure.[82]

Other challenges are, of course, more inherently linked to the clandestine nature of counter-terrorism operations, compounded by the 'cover-up' by certain arms of the state.[83] The impediment that broad-reaching approaches to state secrecy and national security poses is apparent in the Polish and Italian cases referred to above,[84] and may have been all the more defining in those preliminary investigations the findings of which never saw the light of day. The prosecution of Italian prosecutors mirrors threats to lawyers operational in this area in other states.[85]

The limited prosecutions to date mean that the extent of certain challenges for the future remains uncertain. It is unclear, for example, to what extent immunities, prescription or the application of defences that afford impunity to those responsible, which are impermissible under human rights treaties in respect of serious violations of human rights, will be invoked. Their potential relevance is foreshadowed, however, in early US executive branch memos suggesting that superior orders would constitute a defence for 'exceptional interrogations'.[86]

---

[82] States may hide behind US non-cooperation to justify their own inactivity. For example, in the Observations on the Admissibility and Merits submitted by the Government of Poland in the case of *Husayn (Abu Zubaydah) v. Poland* (Application no. 7511/13), the Polish government described obtaining information from the United States as 'very important if not key', while in its application the applicant argued that the Polish state had not taken numerous steps that did not depend on US cooperation; the Observations are available at http://s.v3.tvp.pl/repository/attachment/7/2/c/72c0ac614463f9e12e-b62823e89ef5ed1380018220980.pdf, and details of the case are available at http://hudoc.echr.coe.int/sites/eng/pages/search.aspx#{"appno":["7511/13"],"itemid":["001-123768"]}.

[83] Many of the crimes were subject to what has been described as a 'concerted cover-up' and suffer from complete lack of US cooperation. See Marty, *Secret Detentions and Illegal Transfers of Detainees involving Council of Europe Member States: Second Report*, n. 38 above, and statements by Commissioner Hammerberg, as noted above. This makes investigations challenging but not impossible.

[84] See e.g., the trial in the Abu Omar case in Italy or the Polish investigation, where broad reaching approaches to 'state secrecy' shrouded the investigation and limited charges brought.

[85] Polish lawyers report being subject to threat of prosecution, Italian investigators were prosecuted, while lawyers operating on terrorism-related cases have often been subject to myriad forms of harassment and attacks in the Russian Federation. See e.g., 'Black hole of CIA devours Poland', *Pravda.ru*, 17 June 2013, available at http://english.pravda.ru/world/europe/17-06-2013/124858-cia_secret_prisons_poland-0/; Human Rights Watch, *World Report 2012: Russia*, available at www.hrw.org/world-report-2012/world-report-2012-russia.

[86] See Working Group Report on Detainee Interrogations in the Global War on Terrorism, 'Assessment of Legal, Historical, Policy, and Operational Considerations' (4 April 2004),

Broad 'immunities' have long been granted in Afghanistan and Iraq, purporting to protect from legal action even those responsible for serious rights violations,[87] while concerns have also been expressed regarding the invocation of such immunities in relation to the rendition programme.[88] Notably, however, in the one case where they have been raised internationally to date, concerning the CIA agents convicted in Milan, claims for immunity were rejected by national courts.[89] It also remains uncertain whether prolonged investigations, such as that noted above in the Polish context, may ultimately 'prescribe' by virtue of statutes of limitations for persons under the investigation to be treated as beyond the pale of prosecution. So far as the crimes investigated are narrowly cast from the outset as common crimes, rather than crimes of torture or crimes against humanity for example, shorter periods of prescription arise.

It is perhaps wise to avoid untimely conclusions from an evolving area of practice. Undoubtedly, the lack of accountability is striking, notably in the United States, but elsewhere too results remain extremely limited. At the same time, pressure to investigate and prosecute continues to mount. What preliminary investigations and enquiries have undoubtedly done is to prise open information and contributed to building momentum towards fuller accountability. In some cases a degree of accountability, however imperfect, has begun to bear fruit with criminal investigations, and (albeit still rarely) prosecutions and arrests.[90]

---

available at www2.gwu.edu/~nsarchiv/NSAEBB/NSAEBB127/03.04.04.pdf: 'the defense of superior orders will generally be available for US Armed Forces personnel engaged in exceptional interrogations except where the conduct goes so far as to be patently unlawful'.

[87] These have been granted to foreign personnel and private contractors; see e.g., the reference to a June 2003 Order of the Coalition Provisional Authority, available at www.cnn.com/2004/LAW/06/17/mariner.contractors/. See also M. Woolf, 'Legality of Iraq occupation "flawed"', *Independent*, 5 May 2004, citing former senior UK civil servant Elizabeth Wilmshurst's criticism of the unprecedented breadth of immunities granted to US and British civilians by the occupying powers.

[88] The impact of immunity on impunity was addressed in Council of Europe Secretary-General, *Report by the Secretary-General on the Use of His Powers under Article 52 of the European Convention on Human Rights* (SG/Inf(2006)5, 28 February 2006) and *Supplementary Report by the Secretary General on the Use of His Powers under Article 52 of the European Convention on Human Rights* (SG/Inf(2006)13, 14 June 2006), para. 17.

[89] See e.g., Amnesty International, *Convictions in Abu Omar Rendition Case a Step Toward Accountability* (5 November 2009), available at www.amnesty.org/en/news-and-updates/news/convictions-abu-omar-rendition-case-step-toward-accountability-20091105.

[90] See notably the Italian experience, above.

(b)   Reparation and civil accountability litigation

(i)   Challenges to securing reparation in the domestic context

One of the most insidious aspects of the 'War on Terror' may be the
approach to 'victimisation' and reparation. The rights of victims to recognition and reparation are incontrovertibly established in international law
yet strikingly absent from international practice. As regards victims of
terrorism, while they too were long neglected in international practice,
beyond the lip service paid in public statements by UN entities, states and
others,[91] there has been a very significant shift in this respect. In various
forms, from the UN Global Counter-Terrorism Strategies[92] to the more
detailed elaborations by consecutive Special Rapporteurs on Terrorism,[93]
attention has been paid to the importance of giving effect to international
standards on reparation and the treatment of victims of crime,[94] including

---

[91] For years this was more often to justify human rights restrictive measures against
terrorism suspects than addressing the rights and the needs of victims of terrorism as
such: M. Scheinin, *Report of the Special Rapporteur on the Promotion and Protection of
Human Rights and Fundamental Freedoms while Countering Terrorism* (UN Doc. A/
HRC/10/3, 4 February 2009), available at www2.ohchr.org/english/issues/terrorism/rap-
porteur/docs/A.HRC.10.3.pdf. See also e.g., 'Ban urges world to recall terrorism's victims
in wake of Osama bin Laden's death', UN News Centre, 2 May 2011, available at www.un.
org/apps/news/story.asp?NewsID=38245#UIiQQPkiH_Q.

[92] UN General Assembly, Resolution adopted by the General Assembly on 8 September
2006: The United Nations Global Counter-Terrorism Strategy (UN Doc. A/Res/60/288)
and the revised version of 2010, UN General Assembly, With Consensus Resolution,
General Assembly Reiterates Unequivocal Condemnation of Terrorism, Reaffirms Support for 2006 UN Global Counterterrorism Strategy (UN Doc. A/64/L.69) emphasised the
victims of terrorism issue; see also UN General Assembly, Draft Resolution Referred to
the High-Level Plenary Meeting of the General Assembly by the General Assembly at its
Fifty-Ninth Meeting: 2005 World Summit Outcome (UN Doc. A/60/L.1), para. 89.

[93] See Scheinin, *Report of the Special Rapporteur on the Promotion and Protection of Human
Rights and Fundamental Freedoms while Countering Terrorism*, n. 91 above; UN General
Assembly, *Promotion and Protection of Human Rights and Fundamental Freedoms while
Countering Terrorism* (UN Doc. A/66/310), available at www.unhcr.org/refworld/pdfid/
4ea143f12.pdf; Council of Europe Guidelines, *Human Rights and the Fight against Terrorism* (Strasbourg: Council of Europe, 2005), available at www.echr.coe.int/NR/rdonlyres/
176C046F-C0E6-423C-A039-F66D90CC6031/0/LignesDirectrices_EN.pdf.

[94] These standards embrace the rights to emergency and continuing assistance, investigation, prosecution and access to justice, compensation, protection and information, as
aspects of victim's rights. UN General Assembly, Declaration of Basic Principles of Justice
for Victims of Crime and Abuse of Power (UN Doc. A/RES/40/24), available at www.un.
org/documents/ga/res/40/a40r034.htm; UN General Assembly, *Basic Principles and
Guidelines on the Right to a Remedy and Reparation for Victims of Gross Violations of
International Human Rights Law and Serious Violations of International Humanitarian*

by combating impunity.[95] The renewed focus on the rights of victims of terrorism is an important step towards a rights-focused and rule of law compatible approach to the fight against international terrorism.

However, the slew of attention, at least on paper, that has been directed to recognising the legal rights of victims of terrorism in recent years provides another point of stark contrast to the approach to victimisation in the context of counter-terrorism. Perhaps the first step towards remedy and reparation is simple recognition, yet there has been scarce willingness to recognise those subject to torture, disappearance, secret and arbitrary detention as bearers or rights and 'victims' of violations. Even where facts demonstrate mistaken identities or erroneous assessments having led to the detention or rendition of individuals, at Guantánamo or within the rendition programme for example, the picture on acknowledgement of wrongdoing and reparation remains bare.[96]

The notable exception to date may be the case of Maher Arar, the Canadian who, following a Commission of Inquiry and other steps, was publicly exonerated by his government which cleared him of any alleged Al-Qaeda links, received a government apology, compensation and a commitment by the government to implement the recommended reform to ensure non-repetition.[97] Yet this appears somewhat unique in practice to date. In several other cases, while payments, which might be seen as 'compensation' have occurred, they have not been accompanied by any sort of recognition or acknowledgement of responsibility, still less an apology.[98]

Law (UN Doc. A/RES/60/147), available at: http://daccess-dds-ny.un.org/doc/UNDOC/GEN/N05/496/42/PDF/N0549642.pdf.

[95] Accountability is a key aspect of the right to reparation, and 'from the perspective of victims' rights impunity is a key issue'. OSCE, *Countering Terrorism, Protecting Human Rights* (Warsaw: OSCE Office for Democratic Institutions and Human Rights, 2007), pp. 27–8.

[96] More detail in Duffy, *The War on Terror and the Framework of International Law*, n. 1 above, ch. 10 on rendition victims' right to reparation and its neglect.

[97] The Canadian and Syrian national was detained at JFK airport in transit on the way home from holiday, interrogated by US authorities for one week and rendered to torture in Syria. The inquiry established on 5 February 2004 ultimately found that collaboration between the Canadian police and Syrian officials had resulted in his torture. For further details on the case and the Commission of Inquiry into the Activities of Canadian Officials in relation to Maher Arar, see Chapter 8 in this volume, K. Roach, 'Public inquiries as an attempt to fill accountability gaps left by judicial and legislative reviews'.

[98] Mamdouh Habib, an Australian national, was reportedly paid an *ex gratia* award on condition that he did not bring legal action against the government, with no recognition of responsibility. P. Karvelas, 'Mamdouh Habib to drop case against Canberra', *Daily Telegraph*, 8 January 2011, available at www.dailytelegraph.com.au/archive/national-old/

The implicit categorisation of victims into a 'deserving' camp of victims of terrorism whose victimhood is recognised, and another 'undeserving' or 'suspect' camp of victims of counter-terrorism, is antithetical to a rule of law approach, and can only compound the injustice of the original wrong. Victims of violations have the right to a remedy in respect of that violation. The same provisions requiring investigation, prosecution and remedy, and the same rule of law perspective that demands satisfaction of the rights of victims of terrorism, applies to violations in the name of counter-terrorism. This should be a legal determination, not a political one, yet the extreme selectivity in the approach to victimisation is a reminder of how elusive, in the context of counter-terrorism, is the basic notion that no one is above, or beneath, the law.

In this political context, the role of the courts becomes critically important. A plethora of initiatives has therefore unfolded to try to pursue recognition or other remedy for victims through civil or human rights litigation. Consistent with the international obligation to provide remedies in domestic courts, this is where, as a general matter, legal action can most productively be pursued.[99] However, while efforts to secure damages for torture victims in national courts have been many, the results have been few, on account of a range of legal, practical and political obstacles.

In some cases, the obstacles are enshrined in legislation, as in the case of Guantánamo detainees who are, in a stunning affront to the right to a

---

mamdouh-habib-to-drop-case-against-canberra/story-e6freuzr-1225984020294. Another example is the case of Binyam Mohamed, an Ethiopian national and UK resident, arrested in Pakistan and held *incommunicado* at secret undisclosed locations for two years before being tortured in Morocco, Afghanistan and sent on to Guantánamo, where UK intelligence services are said to have provided information and facilitated interviews. The UK government has paid compensation but appears not to have accepted responsibility or to have apologised. P. Wintour, 'Guantánamo Bay detainees to be paid compensation by UK Government', *Guardian*, 16 November 2012, available at www.guardian.co. uk/world/2010/nov/16/guantanamo-bay-compensation-claim.

[99] The UN Human Rights Committee has noted that the United States is obliged to allow victims to 'follow suit for damages', as an inherent aspect of the right to a remedy. UN Human Rights Committee, *Concluding Observations on United States of America. 12/18/ 2006* (UN Doc. CCPR/C/USA/CO/3/Rev/1), para. 16, available at http://daccess-dds-ny. un.org/doc/UNDOC/GEN/G06/459/61/PDF/G0645961.pdf. 'The Committee['s] . . . concern is deepened by the so far successful invocation of State secrecy in cases where the victims of these practices have sought a remedy before the State party's courts (for example the cases of *Arar* v. *Ashcroft*, 414 F.Supp.2d 250 (E.D.N.Y. 2006) and *El-Masri* v. *Tenet*, 437 F.Supp.2d 530 (E.D. Va. 2006))'.

remedy, denied by law the right of access to US courts in respect of damages claims concerning torture or other illegal acts. Thus, those victims such as Abu Zubaydah, who continues to be detained in Guantánamo, plainly have no right to seek a remedy before US courts.[100] Where other (released) victims of extraordinary rendition have sought to bring action, these too have been thrown out by courts on various grounds. Best known perhaps is the broad-reaching approach to the state secrets doctrine, exemplified by the rejection of claims for damages brought by victims including Maher Arar,[101] Khaled el-Masri[102] and Binyam Mohamed.[103] Notably, the courts have held that the government's assertion of state secrets privilege required the court to dismiss the entire action, rather than finding a balance by, for example, withholding particular pieces of information or otherwise taking measures to accommodate national security concerns while also recognising the victims' right to a remedy.[104] Petitions seeking leave to appeal to the Supreme Court were rejected.

Other obstacles of relevance in US courts include the acceptance of official immunities from civil suit, and findings that torture and rendition are part of official duties.[105] Extra-territorial locus appears to have precluded victims of abuse in Iraq and Afghanistan from being able to secure justice through US courts.[106] While in some cases damages claims

---

[100] The author is counsel to Abu Zubaydah before the ECtHR alongside US counsel and INTERIGHTS.

[101] *Arar v. Ashcroft*, 532 F.3d 157 (2d Cir. 2008), paras. 162–3.

[102] See *El-Masri v. Tenet*, 437 F.Supp.2d 530, 532–4 (E.D. Va. 2006).

[103] *Mohamed v. Jeppesen Dataplan Inc.*, 614 F.3d 1070 (2010).

[104] *Ibid.* Cf. e.g., *A and others v. United Kingdom* (Application no. 3455/05), Judgment of 19 February 2009, for the approach of the ECtHR.

[105] In the Guantánamo-related case of *Rasul v. Myers*, 512 F.3d 644, 660 (D.C. Cir. 2008) ('*Rasul I*'), vacated *Rasul v. Myers* 129 S. Ct. 763 (2008), *aff* 9 S. Ct. 763 (20 563 F.3d 527 (D.C. Cir. 2009)) (*per curiam*), torture was held by a US court to fall within the scope of the employment of government officials who were, as a consequence, immune from civil suit. As explained by the Court of Appeal for the District of Columbia: 'the plaintiffs do not allege that the defendants acted as rogue officials or employees who implemented a policy of torture for reasons unrelated to the gathering of intelligence. Therefore, the alleged tortious conduct was incidental to the defendants' legitimate employment duties' (paras. 658–9). See also *In re Iraq and Afghanistan Detainees Litigation*, 479 F.Supp.2d 85, 91 (D.D.C. 2007), *aff.* F.Supp.2; *Ali v. Rumsfeld*, No. 07–5178 (D.C. Cir. 21 June 2011).

[106] See E. Wilson, "Damages or Nothing: The Post-*Boumediene* Constitution and Compensation for Human Rights Violations After 9/11' (2012) 41(4) *Seton Hall Law Review* 1491.

by US nationals or on US soil have at least resulted in settlements,[107] there has been no such movement for any of the individuals victimised abroad. This has been described as giving rise to a 'harsh rule' whereby 'citizens and US resident aliens get damages from someone at some level, [a]liens abroad – even though they may have suffered appalling deprivations of liberty and egregious affronts to their human dignity – get nothing'.[108]

The US position is reflected across the Atlantic in novel procedures aimed at protecting national security information in English courts, for example, by introducing 'closed material procedures' and novel rules of disclosure in civil matters.[109] The closed procedures that allow courts to consider 'sensitive' material and hear submissions about it without one of the parties seeing the material or being present, and consider handing down a closed judgment which will not be seen by one of the parties, can only have a serious detrimental impact on victims and the public's ability to secure accountability through civil courts. This is accompanied by the assertion of a broad power of the Secretary of State to terminate proceedings in the interests of national security.[110]

In the civil (as in the criminal) sphere, an obvious underlying challenge is the political pressure exerted on courts by the executive to desist from 'interference' in areas best left to executive determination. Perhaps an extreme manifestation of this lies in then Pakistani President Musharraf's condemnation of the Supreme Court for 'working at cross purposes with the executive and legislature in the fight against terrorism and extremism' by questioning the government on the practice of forced disappearances.[111] Yet elsewhere too the 'democratic credentials' of the judicial

---

[107] Al-Kidd and Iqbal settled their claims against lower-level officials, and claims against cabinet-level officials were ultimately dismissed. Wilson, 'Damages or Nothing', n. 106 above, 1502–3, 1506–7.

[108] *Ibid.* 1516.

[109] In *Al Rawi and others (Respondents) v. Security Service and others (Appellants)* [2011] UKSC 34; *Tariq v. Home Office* [2011] UKSC 35, the courts found that closed material procedures could not be authorised without legislative change. The Justice and Security Act 2013 entered into force in July 2013, expanding the categories of cases in which such procedures could be employed. See the court's critique of overuse of the procedure and the need for rigorous oversight in the first case considering such procedures: *Bank Mellat (Appellant) v. HM Treasury (Respondent) (No. 1)* [2013] UKSC 38.

[110] *R (on the application of Habib Ignaoua) v. Secretary of State for the Home Department* [2013] EWHC 2512 (Admin). The court accepted that there was such a power, but the case is subject to appeal.

[111] In 'Proclamation of Emergency' on 3 November 2007, the Pakistani President General Pervez Musharraf, criticised the Supreme Court's requests to the Interior Ministry for

role have been under fire in an attempt to encourage the judiciary to be more deferential to executive assessments.[112] Needless to say, the role of the courts can only meaningfully be realised where there are courts sufficiently independent, impartial, robust and with a capacity to discharge their functions and resist undue political influence. The political challenges sit alongside multiple practical obstacles that also arise for victims to pursue justice in the national courts in which violations arose, including fear and trauma at the prospect of return to the site of the original victimisation.[113]

(ii) Pursuing human rights litigation on the supranational level

It is the realities of the previous sections – the lack of effective investigations and prosecutions, and the obstacles that victims have encountered in pursuing justice on the national level – that underlines the importance of international oversight and the availability of remedies outside national jurisdictions. It is unsurprising, therefore, that victims of counter-terrorism are increasingly turning to supranational justice alternatives, and beginning to bring their cases to human rights supervisory mechanisms.

Due to the extensive roles played by European states in the CIA programme, the European Court of Human Rights (ECtHR) is set to play a particularly significant role in determining the extent to which European states breached their obligations in each of the ways outlined above. As noted above, a first international judgment has been handed down by the ECtHR in *El-Masri* v. *Macedonia*, condemning the state of Macedonia for its role in the rendition programme, by detaining Mr El-Masri at the behest of the United States and transferring him to the CIA, who subsequently transferred him to Afghanistan. This case is

answers on enforced disappearances; see further Human Rights Watch, *Destroying Legality: Pakistan's Crackdown on Lawyers and Judges* (December 2007), vol. 19, No. 19 (C), p. 19, available at www.hrw.org/reports/2007/pakistan1207/index.htm.

[112] For example *A and others* v. *Secretary of State for the Home Department* [2004] UKHL 56, [2005] 2 AC 68, and the English court's rebuke highlighted below. In the United States, pressure came from the higher courts critical of the frequency with which lower courts were handing down successful *habeas* review determinations. See e.g., Duffy, *The War on Terror and the Framework of International Law*, n. 1 above, ch. 8.

[113] This issue has emerged for example in *Al-Asad* v. *Djibouti*, INTERIGHTS, details available at www.interights.org/al-asad/index.html (concerning the applicant's abduction and detention in Djibouti and rendition), pending before the African Commission on Human and Peoples' Rights.

the tip of the rendition litigation iceberg, with numerous other cases having been brought to the ECtHR against Lithuania,[114] Poland,[115] Italy[116] and Romania,[117] with others in preparatory stages. Cases against the United States are now pending in the Inter-American system.[118] *Al-Asad* v. *Djibouti* is the first extraordinary rendition case opened before the African Commission on Human Rights,[119] while another case concerning Kenyan/Ugandan rendition is before the East African Court of Justice,[120] and others are unfolding on the domestic level.[121]

In some respects, these cases evade the problems on the national level, in others they reflect them and give rise to additional particular challenges and limitations. Among the myriad problems that beset international human rights litigation are the excessive delays in most systems that seriously impede the potential effectiveness of international human rights litigation generally. This is exemplified by the case concerning the killing of former Chechen leader Aslan Maskhadov and the refusal to return his corpse to his family, handed down on 6 June 2012 some eight years after the case was afforded 'priority' status by the ECtHR;[122] or the

---

[114] *Abu Zubaydah* v. *Lithuania*, INTERIGHTS, available at www.interights.org/zubaydah.

[115] *Al Nashiri* v. *Poland* (Application no. 28761/11) 6 May 2011, available at http://hudoc. echr.coe.int/sites/eng/pages/search.aspx?i=001-112302#{"itemid":["001-112302"]}; further details available at Open Society Foundations, www.opensocietyfoundations.org/ litigation/al-nashiri-v-poland; *Husayn (Abu Zubaydah)* v. *Poland* (Application no. 7511/ 13) 28 January 2013.

[116] *Nasr and Ghali* v. *Italy* (Application. No. 44883/09) 22 November 2011.

[117] *Al Nashiri* v. *Romania* (Application no. 33234/12) 1 June 2012; further details available at Open Society Foundations, www.opensocietyfoundations.org/litigation/al-nashiri-v- romania.

[118] For example, *Khaled El Masri* v. *United States* (P-419-08) Inter-American Commission on Human Rights. See further the American Civil Liberties Union involvement in *El- Masri* v. *Tenet*, 437 F.Supp.2d 530, 532–4 (E.D. Va. 2006), available at www.aclu.org/ national-security/el-masri-v-tenet.

[119] See further *Al-Asad* v. *Djibouti*, INTERIGHTS, details available at www.interights.org/ al-asad/index.html, case pending before the African Commission on Human and Peoples' Rights. Author is counsel for the applicants.

[120] The petitioners accuse the Kenyan government of violating the rule of law by sending a number of its citizens, who were accused of involvement in the July 2010 Kampala bombing, to Uganda through extraordinary rendition rather than the normal extradition process. *Omar Awadh Omar and six others (Applicants)* v. *Attorney General Republic of Kenya, Attorney General Republic of Uganda and the Secretary-General East African Community (Respondents)* (Application no. 4 of 2011), East African Court of Justice, First Instance Division.

[121] These may proceed to the sub-regional bodies or African Commission and eventually the African Court on Human and Peoples' Rights.

[122] *Maskhadova and others* v. *Russia* (Application no. 18071/05), Judgment of 6 June 2013.

African Commission decision in the 'Taba' bombings case which was not made public until a year after the Commission adopted its decision, seriously undermining its potential effect despite the fact that the applicants were on death row in Egypt at the relevant time.[123] In some cases, lack of political will to give effect to judgments once they are handed down, and a relatively weak record of implementation, further hamper effectiveness.

On the most basic level, jurisdictional limitations mean that cases can only be brought against those states over whom an international court or body has jurisdiction, seriously limiting the potential for accountability.[124] The potential scope of wrongs that may be adjudicated is also limited to the particular jurisdiction of the court or body; for example, the ability of regional courts such as the ECtHR to adjudicate claims against states responsible for 'aiding and assisting' or 'complicity' in torture where the individual was outwith the states' territory and jurisdiction is open to question.[125]

In some ways, however, where a case can be brought, the international rules and procedures favour victims. Regional and international courts do not operate a doctrine of state secrets or defer automatically to states' own assessments of the need for restrictions on rights in the interests of national security,[126] and there is no risk of cases not being considered on national grounds. They are, however, likely to continue to be put under pressure by states to shroud the cases in blanket confidentiality, which

---

[123] *INTERIGHTS and the Egyptian Initiative for Personal Rights (EIPR) (on behalf of Sabbeh and others)* v. *Egypt*, African Commission on Human and Peoples' Rights, Decision of 13 February 2012. Author is counsel for the applicants. For further details see www. interights.org/taba/index.html.

[124] The first case brought to the ECtHR by extraordinary rendition victims was found inadmissible because Bosnia was not a party to the European Convention on Human Rights (ECHR) at the time the six detainees were transferred to US custody: *Boumediene and others* v. *Bosnia* (Application nos. 38703/06, 40123/06, 43301/06, 43302/06, 2131/07 and 2141/07), Judgment of 18 November 2008.

[125] The individual has to be within the jurisdiction or the effective control of the state, through either physical control of agents or control of territory. See e.g., *Al-Skeini and others* v. *the United Kingdom* (Application no. 55721/07), Judgment of 7 July 2011; *Catan and others* v. *Russia and Moldova* (Application nos. 43370/04, 8252/05 and 18454/06), Judgment of 19 October 2012.

[126] Rather, as ECtHR jurisprudence referred to above demonstrates, they adopt a more nuanced approach to national security that seeks to respect genuine national security concerns but retaining the right to be the ultimate arbiter of the necessity and proportionality of any limitation on rights. See e.g., *Othman (Abu Qatada)* v. *United Kingdom* (Application no. 8139/09), Judgment of 17 January 2012.

will need to be resisted, while finding a way of considering particular pieces of evidence confidentially where necessary and appropriate.[127]

The evidentiary challenges facing victims in this context remain key, particularly in respect of the peripatetic, deliberately disorientating and clandestine nature of the rendition programme and its associated cover-up, but for other counter-terrorism operations too. However, the rules of human rights courts are flexible enough to accommodate these realities within a fair process, for example, through legal presumptions and shifting burdens that operate on the international level, designed to ensure that litigants can establish their case even in circumstances where the evidence lies wholly within the grasp of the respondent state.[128] Where a *prima facie* case can be made against the state, in the circumstances of these cases, the onus is likely to shift to the state to demonstrate the steps it took to protect the rights of persons subject to their jurisdiction and to investigate credible allegations of abuse, which have come to light.[129]

Particularly harsh challenges face some victims who continue to be subject to restrictive detention regimes and bans on communication with the outside world. These include Abu Zubaydah (whose ECtHR cases are referred to above), who is subject to a ban on all communication with the outside world, and who cannot therefore give direct testimony in support of his case, which has to be built largely on public source documents.[130] So far as his security-cleared American counsel can communicate with him, they cannot share that information with other counsel, or with the court, posing heightened obstacles to effective representation. Evidencing

---

[127] Judgment of the ECtHR in *Al Nashiri* v. *Poland* (Application no. 28761/11) 6 May 2011, initially afforded broad confidentiality to the case, with the ECtHR offering *propio motu* to receive information on a 'confidential basis' from the state. Confidentiality should be requested by the state and carefully evaluated by the court. However, this was lifted despite government protests as the state did not in fact share sensitive information with the court.

[128] See e.g., *Carabulea* v. *Romania* (Application no. 45661/99), Judgment of 13 July 2010.

[129] See e.g., *Saadi* v. *Italy* (Application no. 37201/06), Judgment of 28 February 2008, para. 129; *Astamirova and others* v. *Russia* (Application no. 27256/03), Judgment of 26 February 2009, paras. 70–81 (applicants had made out a *prima facie* case that their family member was abducted by servicemen. In the light of the government's failure to provide relevant documents, the burden of proof shifted to the government to disprove the applicants' allegations and 'inferences' were drawn from the government's failure).

[130] See *Abu Zubaydah* v. *Lithuania*, INTERIGHTS, n. 114 above and *Husayn (Abu Zubaydah)* v. *Poland*, n. 115 above. Al Nashiri is in the same situation, and has cases pending before Romania and Poland: *Al Nashiri* v. *Poland* (Application no. 28761/11) and *Al Nashiri* v. *Romania* (Application no. 33234/12).

the overreaching approach to national security, requests for the declassi-fication of any statement from him, even of the most basic nature, have not borne fruit.[131]

The ability of victims to secure compensation in the event that they have a successful case is also rendered vulnerable by uncertainties con-cerning the criteria for the award of damages. In the ECtHR, there is some evidence of unprincipled and certainly unclear approaches being adopted to the denial of compensation to victims of violations, on the apparent basis of their alleged association with terrorism.[132] Clearly, international litigation is no panacea and no replacement for effective national courts. But in the absence of a national remedy, be it political and/or judicial, it may provide the only avenue towards a measure of justice and accountability. The levels on which it may have a positive impact are explored further below.

II Reflections on the impact and potential of human rights litigation

Despite the challenges identified in preceding sections, in recent years, across diverse systems, there has been a burgeoning of litigation. As political solutions have proved elusive, victims have turned to the courts to give effect to their legal rights, and in turn where national courts have not provided a remedy, they have turned to international courts and bodies.

The limitations on the effectiveness of this litigation in the national security context, touched on above and well rehearsed by other contribu-tors, cannot be overlooked. Delays, politicisation, the narrow scope of judicial powers in this context, among many other factors, limit what courts can achieve. Litigation may, moreover, be counter-productive.

---

[131] *Ibid.*

[132] *McCann* v. *United Kingdom* (Application no. 19009/04), Judgment of 21 July 2009, where the alleged terrorists' rights to life had been violated but they were denied compensation. A very recent example may be the recent case of *Maskhadova and others* v. *Russia* (Application no. 18071/05), Judgment of 6 June 2013, which inexplicably denied compensation to the family despite a finding of violation of their rights in the refusal to return the body of their family member or to provide information. In accordance with Russian law they had been denied access to the body of the deceased on the basis that he was killed in the course of a terrorist operation. For further details on this case, see Request for Referral to the Grand Chamber of 8 September 2013, available at www.interights.org/maskhadov.

Judges may, for example, interpret laws exceptionally, in the exceptional circumstances of exceptional times, in a way that sets standards back for years to come. As the President of the Israeli Supreme Court J. Barak has noted:

> a mistake by the judiciary in times of war and terrorism is worse than a mistake of the legislature and the executive in times of war and terrorism. The reason is that the judiciary's mistakes will remain with the democracy when the threat of terrorism passes, and will be entrenched in the case law of the court as a magnet for the development of new and problematic laws.[133]

On another level, the existence of judicial review may run the risk of providing an underserved veneer of legitimacy to governmental conduct, without the rigorous judicial consideration. This may be seen most clearly in the cowed approach of the courts in the United States in assessing *habeas corpus* claims in recent years, which courts have been criticised for creating the impression of judicial review, thereby validating to a degree the detention regime, while failing to provide meaningful review in practice.[134] There were shadows of this concern also in the dissent in the 'control orders' case before Australian courts, for example, where concern was expressed about the limited review function afforded to the courts, which could not question the validity of the orders on human rights grounds (as their counterparts had in parallel litigation in English courts).[135] Inevitably, judges may also succumb to the political pressure that is often placed on them in the counter-terrorism or emergency contexts and add further injustice to existing violations.[136]

---

[133] A. Barak, 'The Supreme Court and the Problem of Terrorism' in *Judgments of the Israel Supreme Court: Fighting Terrorism within the Law* (2 January 2005), available at www. mfa.gov.il/MFA/Government/Law/Legal±Issues±and±Rulings/Fighting±Terrorism ±within±the±Law±2-Jan-2005.htm#barak.

[134] *Al-Adahi* v. *Obama*, 613 F.3d 1102 (D.C. Cir. 2010) and subsequent alleged refusal to engage with or challenge the facts questioning whether the role of the courts is always meaningful or may give a false sense of legitimacy to a process.

[135] In the constitutional challenge in *Thomas* v. *Mowbray* [2007] HCA 33, the courts could not question the validity of the orders on human rights grounds, as UK courts had, given the constraints of the lack of a Bill of Rights or constitutional framework enabling them to do so. On the different question before it of whether the legislation conferred a 'non-judicial power' on the court, the court upheld the law. On this note, see further e.g., the discussion of *Thomas* v. *Mowbray* in D. Dyzenhaus and R. Thwaites, 'The Judiciary in a Time of Terror' in A. Lynch, E. MacDonald and G. Williams (eds.), *Law and Liberty in the War on Terror* (Sydney: Federation Press, 2007).

[136] See further Human Rights Watch, *Destroying Legality: Pakistan's Crackdown on Lawyers and Judges*, n. 111 above, p. 19; however, courts are often criticised for engaging in security related determinations: Attorney General's submissions and Bingham LJ's retort

For victims too, litigation may in certain circumstances simply gener-ate unfulfilled expectations, or contribute to further stigmatisation and potentially revictimisation. While this can take many forms, the most obvious being the political backlash towards 'terrorist' applicants asserting their human rights, which has generated extensive coverage and debate around certain ECtHR cases in recent years (*Othman (Abu Qatada)* v. *United Kingdom*[137] is a particularly apt example). In turn, it may arise from unprincipled approaches by courts themselves in denying compensation to victims on the apparent basis of their alleged association with terrorism, as noted above. In addition, there may be slow (or no) implementation, crushingly frustrating for those bearing the ongoing consequences of injustice.

Daunted by challenges and limitations, one might be tempted to dismiss the relevance of litigation in this area. However, I would suggest a different approach. Litigation should certainly be done selectively, with a clear sense of goals, awareness of limitations and challenges, and a keen eye on whether there may be more effective alternative avenues available. The multi-layered goals of litigation should also be borne in mind in assessing the value of the role of the courts in this field. It may pursue and impact on victim-related goals (which should drive strategy as the case belongs to the victim) such as preventing or stopping wrongs, securing protection, receiving damages or other reparation, as well as broader social, legislative, policy, systemic or institutional goals, or more often a combination thereof. Likewise, the impact of the role of the courts may be felt at various stages, from before litigation begins, during the course of it or a long time after judgment is rendered, whether the outcome is positive or negative. Many of the goals strategic litigation will pursue require us to understand litigation as part of a bigger process of social, legal or other change and not in isolation; not, in other words, as providing solutions but as contributing to them. The contribution may indeed fall to be assessed through a very long time lens, particularly in assessing the effectiveness of litigation in achieving some of what we might call the broader 'rule of law' or attitude-influencing goals, identi-fied below. For some goals, the contribution of litigation may be difficult to identify and elude measurement.

---

in *A and others* v. *Secretary of State for the Home Department* [2004] UKHL 56, [2005] 2 AC 68.

[137] *Othman (Abu Qatada)* v. *United Kingdom* (Application no. 8139/09), Judgment of 17 January 2012.

Litigation may, however, provide an essential complement to political solutions, or an alternative when they fall foul of basic human rights and rule of law principles, as is so often the case in the field of national security. The remainder of the chapter will suggest and illustrate some of the ways in which I believe litigation in the field of counter-terrorism and human rights can have, and often in practice has had, a significant impact and a crucial role.

(a)   Potential levels of impact

First, on the most basic level, big-picture discussion of the politics of judicial intervention, like disillusionment with situations where courts have not fulfilled their protective mandate, should not make us lose sight of the very real effect that litigation can have on individuals' lives. It does this on many different levels. Litigation may, for example, give an individual the opportunity to challenge (and potentially to stop) torture and abuse in detention, or to seek a stay of execution pending international proceedings. A practical example of the latter from the author's practice arises in the African Commission decision to adopt precautionary measures to protect individuals on death row in the 'Taba bombings' case, pending a hearing of the merits of their case by the Commission, which the Egyptian state agreed to honour.[138] Ultimately, the Commission found they had not had a fair trial, and should be released or retried, and their sentences were suspended and a retrial is pending. In this respect, this and other types of interim, provisional or precautionary measures (such as preventing transfer to ill-treatment, for example) can provide the most concrete example of international litigation's potential to effect real-time change, unhindered by the problems of delays highlighted above.

In other ways too, the course of litigation, or indeed the mere prospect of litigation, may achieve a desired effect for victims long before judgment is ever rendered. One example of this again from my practice is the case of *Abu Zubaydah*: his capture was surrounded by exorbitant public assertions to the effect that he was (for example) the 'number three' in Al-Qaeda, yet these were dropped once litigation became a possibility, he had access to a lawyer, and it was clear that in one form or another there

---

[138] *INTERIGHTS and the Egyptian Initiative for Personal Rights (EIPR) (on behalf of Sabbeh and others) v. Egypt*, African Commission on Human and Peoples' Rights, Decision of 13 February 2012.

would be a degree of governmental accountability for assertions made.[139] In this way, we should not lose sight of how the very fact of judicial oversight is a deterrent to abuse.[140]

Simply taking a human rights violation to court may itself play a role in reframing the issue as a matter of law, not only politics, reasserting the principle of legality in the highly politicised discourse around terrorism and security. It is in the face of political pressure and public outcry, which has characterised the political debate around terrorism in many states, that the discipline of dispassionate legal and principled arguments, and judicial responses, is most needed. It is acknowledged that this is particularly challenging in the counter-terrorism context, however, given public perceptions, politics and prejudice that can arise vis-à-vis individual applicants (as opposed to more 'sympathetic victims'). In some cases, however, it enables the individual's situation to be reframed and presented as claims brought on behalf of a victim, not a suspected perpetrator,[141] and judicial determinations can carry important weight as one factor influencing public perception, and helping to question or to alter the terms of the political discussion. There has, for example, been a shift in public opinion (national and international) on Guantánamo, to which the determinations of the US Supreme Court may have been one contributor.

Critically, cases tell victims' stories, and present the human being and human suffering behind euphemisms such as 'extraordinary rendition' and 'enhanced interrogation techniques'. Judgments may in turn validate those stories and experiences, and provide a degree of recognition or vindication that is particularly important given its drastic neglect in this context, as noted above. Particular cases can give individuals a voice that is otherwise denied, bringing them back into the legal framework, and present the individual as a rights bearer and a victim, not responsible for his own mistreatment.[142] One of the essential characteristics of the War

---

[139] See e.g., *Abu Zubaydah v. Lithuania*, INTERIGHTS, n. 114 above and *Husayn (Abu Zubaydah) v. Poland*, n. 115 above.

[140] This is reflected in judicial review of detention being treated in international law as a safeguard inherent in the prohibition on torture itself. See the International Covenant on Civil and Political Rights, UN General Assembly Resolution 2200A (XXI), the full text of which is available at www.ohchr.org/en/professionalinterest/pages/ccpr.aspx.

[141] While some victims of counter-terrorism abuse are suspected terrorists, the majority, including individuals like Abu Zubaydah, detained at Guantánamo for ten years, have never been accused of any crime.

[142] See Jaime Malamud Goti, *Game Without End: State Terror and the Politics of Justice* (University of Oklahoma Press, 1996), pp. 14–17, on the importance of clarifying that

on Terror has been the attempt to put certain people beyond the reach of the law. Litigation can be a tool, as one English judge put it, not for transferring power from the executive to the judiciary, but for transferring power from the executive to the individual.[143]

Litigation may play a role in securing access to information and in prizing open facts, crucial for victims who may not themselves know the full circumstances of the violations, and for the public at large in an area shrouded by secrecy. The right to truth is increasingly accepted in international law, recently described by the ECtHR in the first extraordinary rendition case to be handed down (*El-Masri* v. *Former Yugoslav Republic of Macedonia*) as attaching to the individual and to society more broadly.[144] Litigation may have this as its goal. This has been the case, for example, in UK cases pursuing access to military files[145] or confirmation of what the government knew about operations abroad,[146] and compelling the government to share information with the public[147] or with a

victims are 'not responsible for their own disgrace'. An example of an international judgment of this type may be *El-Masri* v. *Former Yugoslav Republic of Macedonia* (Application no. 396030/09), Judgment of 13 December 2012, which addressed the extraordinary rendition of Mr El-Masri and provided recognition of wrongs, of victimisation and compensation to the individual; or *INTERIGHTS and the Egyptian Initiative for Personal Rights (EIPR) (on behalf of Sabbeh and others)* v. *Egypt*, African Commission on Human and Peoples' Rights, Decision of 13 February 2012. Author is counsel for the applicants.

143 M. Arden, 'Human Rights in the Age of Terrorism' (2005) 121 *Law Quarterly Review* 604, 623–4; T. H. Smith, 'Balancing Liberty and Security? A Legal Analysis of United Kingdom Anti-Terrorist Legislation' (2007) 13(1–2) *European Journal on Criminal Policy and Research* 73.

144 *El-Masri* v. *Former Yugoslav Republic of Macedonia* (Application no. 396030/09), Judgment of 13 December 2012.

145 J. Aston, 'Lawyers in Basra death case win access to files', *Independent*, 4 October 2007.

146 *R (on the application of Omar Awadh Omar, Habib Sulieman Njoroge and Yahya Suleiman Mbuthia)* v. *Secretary of State for Foreign and Commonwealth Affairs* [2012] EWHC 1737 (Admin). The plaintiffs were rendered from Uganda to Kenya, but the court upheld the UK government's right not to require its security services to disclose national security information.

147 *R (on the application of Binyam Mohamed)* v. *Secretary of State for Foreign and Commonwealth Affairs* [2008] EWHC 2048 (Admin) was revised with an approved judgment of 30 July 2009 by Thomas LJ and on 16 October 2009, the High Court held that seven retracted paragraphs of their initial judgment containing summaries of CIA documents relating to Binyam's 'treatment' should be made public; for further details see the analysis by Reprieve, available at www.reprieve.org.uk/publiceducation/casebriefing-binyammohamedvsforeignoffice/. On 10 February 2010, the Court of Appeal dismissed David Miliband's appeal and ordered the publication of seven paragraphs that the Foreign Secretary had sought to suppress: *R (on the application of Binyam Mohamed)* v. *Secretary of State for Foreign and Commonwealth Affairs* [2010] EWCA Civ 65.

criminal defendant.[148] Particularly noteworthy are the Freedom of Information Act (FOIA) litigation in several states,[149] including the United States, which has had a measure of success,[150] and in Romania and Poland, for example, which have revealed crucial information on how the CIA operated with close cooperation of other states, including through false flight plans and cover-up.[151] Canadian litigation where the government was compelled to produce information or evidence in relation to proceedings in another state may be another example.[152]

This unearthing of information is particularly critical in the counter-terrorism field where victims may face a wall of state secrecy, as illustrated above, and especially on issues such as rendition which as noted has been characterised by concerted or coordinated cover-up. At a minimum, litigation draws out government's positions as they engage as parties and are forced to clarify or adjust their positions in the course of litigation.[153] Through the process of hearing victims' accounts, as well as the state's, and coming to considered conclusions, cases can contribute, alongside other more obvious vehicles such as investigative journalism and civil society advocacy, to historical clarification of facts and

---

[148] In the *Binyam Mohamed* case, the UK courts required the government to provide Mohamed with information that may have been relevant to any eventual trial by military commission planned at the time by the United States.

[149] See e.g., Romanian FOIA request which elicited important information on rendition flights and the cover-up through false flight plans and other means.

[150] See e.g., *Associated Press* v. *United States Department of Defense*, 498 F.Supp.2d 707 (S.D.N.Y. 2007) and *Center for National Security Studies* v. *Department of Justice*, 331 F.3d 918 (D.C. Cir. 2003) (*cert. denied*, 540 US 1104 (2004)).

[151] See e.g., official documents disclosed by the Polish government through FOIA requests in Poland, 'Explanation of Rendition Flight Records Released by the Polish Air Navigation Services Agency', as disclosed by the Open Society Justice Initiative and Helsinki Foundation for Human Rights, available at www.therenditionproject.org.uk/pdf/PDF%20126%20[Flight%20data.%20Poland%20FOI%20-%20HFHR%20explanatory%20document].pdf.

[152] *Canada (Justice)* v. *Khadr* [2008] 2 SCR 125, 2008 SCC 28, in which the Canadian Supreme Court ruled that the government had violated Canada's Constitution and its international obligations by transmitting to US officials information resulting from Canadian officials' interviews of Omar Kadhr at the Guantánamo Bay detention centre. The Court took the unusual step of ordering Canadian officials to allow Mr Kadhr access to records of his interrogations with Canadian agents for use in preparing his defence before a Guantánamo military commission.

[153] See e.g., how the government's position shifted in the course of *Al-Skeini and others* v. *United Kingdom* (Application no. 55721/07), Judgment of 7 July 2011, a case on the applicability of the ECHR in Iraq.

responsibility, enhancing our understanding of wrongs and contributing to guarantees of non-repetition.

As a rebuke to the executive when it has failed in its role as primary protector of rights, the role of the court can be critical in reasserting the democratic credentials of the system. Some of the most renowned counter-terrorism cases emphasise the importance of a check on executive action and of judicial oversight. This was most famously seen in reminders that 'a state of war is not a blank check for the President' but it is manifest also in the willingness of courts in the United Kingdom in the *Belmarsh* case, or in Australia in the *Haneef* case,[154] to subject the executive's determination of what was necessary for and proportionate to national security to close scrutiny and firm condemnation.

Judicial deference has unsurprisingly been the order of the day, to differing degrees and effect. One may ask whether the US Supreme Court could and should have decided whether detainees have the basic right to *habeas corpus* when the matter first came before it in 2004. At what price in terms of judicial efficiency in the administration of justice – and protection of individuals – came the virtue of judicial restraint? Similar issues may arise again post-2010 where US courts conducting *habeas* reviews, once actively finding against the government, began to assume a more deferential position.[155] Courts in many other countries have been criticised for being unduly compliant with executive curtailing the judicial role.[156] While there is much scope for legitimate disagreement on the extent of due or undue judicial deference in particular cases, and whether the principles lauded are being applied so as to give them meaningful effect, there can be little doubting the importance of the principle of

---

[154] In *Haneef* v. *Minister for Immigration and Citizenship* [2007] FCA 1273 and *Minister for Immigration and Citizenship* v. *Haneef* [2007] FCAFC 203, in which the courts curbed the creeping effect of the notion of guilt by association and rejected the contention that citizenship could be denied on the basis of any broad association with terrorism.

[155] The process began with *Al-Adahi* v. *Obama*, 613 F.3d 1102 (D.C. Cir. 2010). See Chapter 4 in this volume, J. Lobel, 'The rhetoric and reality of judicial review of counter-terrorism actions: the United States experience'.

[156] See e.g., B. Galligan and E. Larking, 'The Separation of Judicial and Executive Powers in Australia: Detention Decisions', paper presented at 2008 Australasian Political Science Association Conference, University of Queensland. See Chapter 2 in this volume, J. Rytter, 'Counter-terrorism judicial review by a traditionally weak judiciary', Chapter 11, G. Phillipson, 'Deference and dialogue in the real-world counter-terrorism context', and Chapter 13, H. Fenwick, 'Post 9/11 UK counter-terrorism cases in the European Court of Human Rights: a "dialogic" approach to rights protection or appeasement of national authorities?'.

judicial oversight as a measure of accountability. It was in this vein in *A and others* that Lord Bingham rebuked the Attorney General's submissions on the limits of due judicial deference, and spoke to the importance of the role of the courts in a democracy, while raising the question of what are the proper limits on judicial authority:

> I do not in particular accept the distinction which he drew between democratic institutions and the courts ... the function of independent judges ... [is] a cardinal feature of the modern democratic state, a cornerstone of the rule of law itself. The Attorney General is fully entitled to insist on the proper limits of judicial authority, but he is wrong to stigmatize judicial decision-making as in some way undemocratic.

The case has been lauded as 'a powerful statement by the highest court in the land of what it means to live in a society where the executive is subject to the rule of law'.[157] While its operation with greater and lesser success in various cases and contexts may rightly be subject to criticism, this is a principle that cannot be undermined.

(b) Potential of human rights litigation

Despite areas where the judiciary has undoubtedly been extremely, and many would say unduly, deferential to the state, national and international courts have also been willing to subject the legitimacy, necessity or proportionality of particular measures to close scrutiny. In very many cases, regional and international courts and bodies have looked behind and questioned the 'terrorism' label as a justification for restrictions on rights, for example.[158] In other cases, they have looked beyond the purported legitimate aim of 'countering terrorism' to assess the real relationship between particular measures adopted *vis-à-vis* an individual or group and that aim, including its necessity and proportionality, thereby realigning the balance between security and human rights.[159]

---

[157] Lady Justice Arden, Clifford Chance Lecture, 27 January 2005, as quoted in M. du Plessis, 'Terrorism and National Security: The Role of the Judiciary in a Democratic Society' (2007) 4 *European Human Rights Law Review* 327.

[158] See e.g., the condemnation of the prosecution of Chilean indigenous groups as 'terrorists' in Inter-American Commission on Human Rights, *Annual Report 2010* (OEA/Ser.L/V/II. Doc. 5, rev. 1), para. 56, available at www.cidh.org/pdf%20files/IACHR-ANNUAL-REPORT-2010.pdf.

[159] The case law of the ECtHR, for example, is replete with examples of the Court questioning the legitimacy, necessity and proportionality of counter-terrorism measures: *Mamatkulov and Askarov v. Turkey* (Applications nos. 46827/99 and 46951/99),

This oversight and analysis is critical to maintaining and realigning the balanced relationship between collective security and human rights inherent in the international legal order.

In some cases, such as perhaps the *Belmarsh* judgment, changes in law and policy followed the judgments fairly directly, leading to what most would consider improved if still problematic policies (as the cases led to control orders, and further provisions that were in turn subject to challenge as discussed by others). In others, such as the *Al-Rawi* case on closed material procedures in civil proceedings in England,[160] or the Guantánamo *habeas* litigation with its famous game of legal ping-pong between the judicial and political arms, remind us that legislative changes that follow progressive litigation may of course worsen not improve the situation, depending on the decisions of the political arms. The courts can only provide the spectre of further review if those measures go beyond the legal framework.[161]

The point was emphasised at the outset that litigation is complementary to, and not an alternative to, other political arms of state or other vehicles to accountability. Litigation may, albeit unusually, seek to provoke or to support the work of other independent entities. In one UK case, victims sought to use litigation to seek to compel the government to conduct an inquiry, ultimately without success.[162] In a German case, however, the court found that the rights of parliamentarians had been violated by the government's 'sweeping invocation' of state interests as a basis to refuse to answer questions of a parliamentary inquiry.[163]

Judgment of 4 February 2005; *Belek and Ozkurt* v. *Turkey* (Application no. 1544/07), Judgment of 13 July 2013, para. 32; or the 'balancing' by the judiciary in cases concerning access to secret evidence, see e.g., *A and others* v. *United Kingdom* (Application no. 3455/05), Judgment of 19 February 2009.

[160] *Al-Rawi and others* v. *Security Services and others* [2011] UKSC 34, where the decision that the closed material procedure was unlawful absent parliamentary approval led to the adoption of a much wider closed process in the Justice and Security Act 2013.

[161] See e.g., *Al-Skeini and others* v. *United Kingdom* (Application no. 55721/07), Judgment of 7 July 2011, in which the UK government shifted its position in the course of litigation, as regards the applicability of the ECHR to individuals detained by UK officials in Iraq and allegedly tortured in detention.

[162] See e.g., 'High Court challenge over Iraqi civilian deaths', *Guardian*, 28 July 2004, available at www.guardian.co.uk/Iraq/Story/0,2763,1270930,00.html, where the families of Iraqi civilians allegedly killed by British troops challenged the UK government's refusal to order independent inquiries into the deaths.

[163] Federal Constitutional Court, Press Release no. 84/2009, 23 July 2009, available at www. bverfg.de/pressemitteilungen/bvg09-084en.html; see further discussed also in Marty, *Secret Detentions and Illegal Transfers of Detainees involving Council of Europe Member*

Unfortunately (and somewhat ironically), delays in rendering judgment limited any concrete impact on parliamentary access to the information in question, though the impact of the decision may be felt in the future.

A different example of the catalytic effect of litigation on other processes lies in the establishment and extension of the office of Ombudsperson with powers to review the Al-Qaeda Security Council sanctions lists and 'recommend' delisting.[164] While still falling far short of the right to due process that should attend listing, the creation of the Ombudsperson's office has led to the delisting of many individuals, and has stemmed in large part from cases that successfully challenged the lack of judicial oversight of Security Council listing, such as the *Kadi*, *Sayadi* and *Nada* cases.[165] Beyond cases in which litigation contributes directly to policy or legal change, it may be more difficult to tell to what extent, if at all, it may contribute to shifts in practice or approach, even in cases which do not achieve their stated aim. Such questions may arise in relation to efforts to return UK nationals from Guantánamo following 'unsuccessful' litigation seeking to oblige the state to intervene on their behalf as part of a broader range of measures seeking to bring pressure to bear.[166]

Potentially persuasive messages can also be sent through litigation, beyond the outcome of the case. These messages may relay between judicial and political arms, or inter-judicially and transnationally, as seen, for example, in the unusually robust judicial rebuke by the English Court of Appeals of the US government's refusal to allow disclosure of

---

States: Second Report, n. 38 above, note 3: 'A German Constitutional Court decision which came out on the same day as the parliamentary inquiry report, found the German government to have violated the Constitution by failing to disclose relevant information and failing to cooperate with the inquiry'.

[164] The Office of the Ombudsperson was created by Security Council Resolution 1904, adopted on 17 December 2009, and its mandate was extended by Resolution 1989, adopted on 17 June 2011; further details are available at www.un.org/en/sc/ombudsperson/. On the procedure and its positive effects, as well as limitations, which fall far short of the requirements of human rights law, see Duffy, *The War on Terror and the Framework of International Law*, n. 1 above, ch. 7B. Note other sanctions (not relevant to this study's focus on terrorism) lists have no such built-in process and less accountability.

[165] Case T-315/01 *Kadi* v. *Council of the European Union and Commission of the European Communities* [2005] ECR II-3649; *Nabil Sayadi and Partricia Vinck* v. *Belgium*, Communication No. 1472/2006 (UN Doc. CCPR/C/94/D/1472/2006, 2008); *Nada* v. *Switzerland* (Application no. 10593/08), ECtHR, Judgment of 12 September 2012.

[166] *R (Abbasi)* v. *Secretary of State for Foreign and Commonwealth Affairs* [2003] UKHRR 76.

information in the *Binyam Mohamed* case,[167] or of the Guantánamo detentions regime in the *Abbasi* case.[168] Decisions making clear that states cannot cooperate with foreign regimes that fail to meet certain human rights standards may also send important signals, and contribute to violator isolation. The course of litigation may provide a platform for the cross-fertilisation of ideas and influence from other systems, as international and comparative perspectives are brought to bear, notably through *amicus* interventions, as was the case with the unprecedented level and nature of interventions before the US Supreme Court in the *Boumediene* case, among others.[169]

The plethora of judicial practice in the counter-terrorism field in recent years has also itself significantly developed international legal standards through jurisprudence.[170] Here again, impact can be positive and negative, and jurisprudential developments in this context may in some case have served to clarify the law and in others further confuse it, but it has undoubtedly led to a more detailed body of international human rights law in relation to terrorism. Examples include issues raised on the scope of *non-refoulement* obligations, including, for example, in *Othman* v. *United Kingdom*, the clarification of the duty not to transfer a person due to a 'flagrant denial of justice' and the limits on reliance on diplomatic assurances. The 'Taba' bombings case referred to above[171] made clear the incompatibility of terrorism trials by state security courts with the African Charter, and that the safeguards against torture in the counter-terrorism context were undoubtedly part of African human

---

[167] The Appeal Court in the *Binyam Mohamed* case, n. 147 above, stated that 'we did not consider that a democracy governed by the rule of law would expect a court in another democracy to suppress a summary of the evidence contained in reports by its own officials or officials of another State where the evidence was relevant to allegations of torture and cruel, inhuman or degrading treatment, politically embarrassing though it might be'.

[168] *R (Abbasi)* v. *Secretary of State for Foreign and Commonwealth Affairs* [2003] UKHRR 76, where the English Court of Appeal criticised the system of Guantánamo detentions in unusually strident terms. See also e.g., the indirect call from UK courts to the ECtHR to clarify the law on extra-territoriality in the *Al-Skeini* case, n. 161 above.

[169] *Amicus* interventions have appeared from such diverse quarters as the British House of Lords and Israeli military lawyers. Such interventions are growing in international practice.

[170] On how judicial decisions affect legal standards, see Duffy, *The War on Terror and the Framework of International Law*, n. 1 above, ch. 1.

[171] *INTERIGHTS and the Egyptian Initiative for Personal Rights (EIPR) (on behalf of Sabbeh and others)* v. *Egypt*, African Commission on Human and Peoples' Rights, Decision of 13 February 2012.

rights standards. Some cases may have exposed areas of the law that may not be clear or that may, in the view of the court at least, be ripe for elaboration through reform or practice.[172] Many others have simply reinforced established principles that have increasingly been cast in doubt, as, for example, in the *Saadi* v. *Italy* judgment, which found that there was no room for balancing the obligations in respect of torture with those concerning national security.[173] Holding ground on rights that are well established but have been rendered vulnerable in the course of the War on Terror, is itself an important contribution to preserving the legal framework from the erosion of legal standards.[174]

Conclusion

Recent practice illustrates the multiplicity of overlapping challenges to securing justice for victims of crimes committed in the name of 'counter-terrorism', whether in the form of remedy or reparation for victims or criminal accountability of those responsible. Yet there is reason to hold out hope. The crimes in question will not prescribe and recent history's examples of prosecutions many years after the fact pay testament to the persistence that can accompany demands for justice.[175] While justice should be done at home, the supranational criminal proceedings provide both a catalyst and an alternative to pursue accountability where the offending state does not assume the responsibility. The existing convictions, ongoing proceedings and new investigations that continue to emerge despite pressures and obstacles indicate a momentum that will not readily be thwarted. The fact that those responsible for the rendition programme are vulnerable to arrest if they travel outside the United

---

[172] The scope of complicity in torture, and the obligations of third states not to receive information obtained through torture, may be one area; cf. inadmissibility of torture evidence where the law is more established; the issue was raised in *Rangzieb Ahmed and Habib Ahmed* v. *R* [2011] EWCA Crim 184 in the Court of Appeal (Criminal Division).

[173] This works both ways and can also weaken or confuse the framework of rights protection, as is suggested may have been the outcome of the *Al-Skeini* case, n. 161 above, for example.

[174] Standards may change in part through changes in customary law, or less directly through judicial interpretations of treaty obligations; see Duffy, *The War on Terror and the Framework of International Law*, n. 1 above, ch. 1.

[175] For example, current prosecutions for crimes in Argentina, Guatemala and Cambodia in the 1970s and 1980s. The pursuit of justice elsewhere for many of these crimes was a catalyst to justice at home.

States, resulting in what has been described as the creation of 'their own legal black hole', shows that these measures have an effect.[176]

The denial to date of recognition and reparation for victims of egregious violations in the name of counter-terrorism, and the emerging perception of deserving and undeserving categories of victims, is antithetical to basic notions of equality before the law and human rights. In this context, criminal courts, civil courts and international human rights courts and bodies have complementary, and particularly critical, roles to play in addressing this anomaly and providing a measure of truth and justice for victims. While a discussion on the advantages of political over judicial solutions may be important to avoid unnecessary, ineffective or detrimental litigation, it must be recalled that generally it is due to the lack of a political solution that the role of courts is triggered. For those disenfranchised or even demonised groups of 'victims' with little or no political clout, the reality is that recourse to the courts may represent the only hope (however bright or slight) of catalysing political solutions. Litigation is not the only tool, and in many circumstances not the most appropriate one, to address the many challenges posed by counter-terrorism practices. If ever the need for a complement to, and a check on, the exercise of political power was clear, however, it must surely be in the context of the notorious political failures and brutality of counter-terrorism practice post 9/11. In this context, the role of the courts, in the protection, recognition and reparation of the rights of the individual, and in reasserting the basic rule of law principles on which the democratic system depends, may be more important than ever.

---

[176] J. Meyer, 'The Bush Six', *New Yorker*, 13 April 2009, available at www.newyorker.com/talk/2009/04/13/090413ta_talk_mayer. This impact has been seen with the 2013 arrest of the former CIA station chief in Panama, see for further details www.reuters.com/article/2013/07/19/us-usa-panama-cia-idUSBRE96I0V320130719.

INDEX